strawberries and claret

melon and moscato

white truffles and nebbiolo

Want to pick wine for

D1387836

bouillabaisse and fino

radicchio and barbera

Wondering what to eat with a special bottle?

Let *The Wine Dine Dictionary* be your guide. Arranged A–Z by food and then A–Z by wine, this unique handbook will help you make more informed, more creative and more delicious choices about what to eat and drink. As one of the country's most popular and influential wine journalists, as well as an expert in the psychology of smell and taste, Victoria Moore doesn't just explain what goes with what, but why and how the combination works. Written with her trademark authority, warmth and wit, this is a book to consult and to savour.

preserved lemon and assyrtiko

salmon and white burgundy

asparagus and sauvignon blanc

paella and rioja rosado

crayfish mayo and chardonnay

THE
WINE DINE
DICTIONARY

THE WINE DINE DICTIONARY

GOOD FOOD AND GOOD WINE:

An A to Z of suggestions

for happy eating and drinking

Victoria Moore

GRANTA

Granta Publications, 12 Addison Avenue, London, W11 4QR

First published in Great Britain by Granta Books, 2017

A CIP catalogue record is available from the British Library

1 3 5 7 9 10 8 6 4 2

Hardback ISBN 978 1 78378 209 3
Ebook ISBN 978 1 78378 211 6

www.grantabooks.com

Text designed by www.salu.io

Typeset in Caslon by M Rules

Printed and bound in Italy by L.E.G.O. Spa

CONTENTS

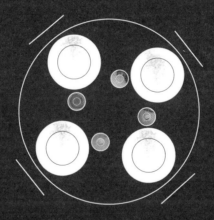

I
INTRODUCTION

This is a book about the pleasures of eating, and drinking wine. I hope that is obvious from the title.

I love to eat and I love to drink and I love to do both together. Ever since beginning to buy wine and cook my own dinner, I have thought about the flavours in the glass and the flavours on the plate as being part of the same experience. I mean that in the same way that sun (or rain) is part of your day on the beach, or that you might feel happier choosing different clothes to go to a football match than you would put on for dinner in a restaurant.

I very much hope that it will be taken in the right spirit. That is, as a book crammed with ideas for what is good to eat with what wine (and vice versa), not just from me but also from winemakers, sommeliers and cooks from all over the world. These are offered in the same way that a food writer might point out that basil and peach are quite magical together. They are guidelines, not rules; suggestions, not shouldn'ts and shoulds.

Anyone who has ever brushed their teeth and then drunk a glass of orange juice knows that what you eat changes your perception of what you drink, and part of the aim of this book is to remind readers that this also applies to wine and food, and to offer tools and rules of thumb to help prevent a glass of wine (or dinner) being wrecked by a similar experience.

I am a tiny bit alarmed by how much *The Wine Dine Dictionary* has grown from the shortish guide of its original conception, and how greedily opinionated that means I must be. But then, I guess, I have been writing it in my head for ever, and it has taken a full year of weekends, very early mornings and long evenings to set it down on paper.

My favourite parts of the book are not my own. They are the contributions from all the winemakers who have been kind enough to take the time to talk or write about what they most enjoy eating with their own wines. These have not always been straightforward to collect – I have had to harry and hassle, and in some cases stalk winemakers at tastings and in their own wineries. But they have been worth the hunt because they are so evocative, and say so much about the personalities of the winemakers and the places they live. You will find quite a few vitriolic recommendations for eating vineyard pests, from rabbits to wild boars; instructions (thanks to Adam Mason of Mulderbosch in South Africa) for making a smoker from an old metal dustbin and using it to cook shoulder of pork to eat with potato flour rolls, coleslaw and sriracha sauce; and envy-inducing tales from the New Zealand crew of freshly caught fish served up at baches in the Marlborough Sounds. There are also, of course, recipes that you can cook in a normal kitchen after a visit to the supermarket or a trip to the allotment.

I hope it is as pleasing for you to read and use as it has been for me to put together. If this book inspires happy, convivial lunches and dinners and new gastronomic experiences, then it will have done its job.

Victoria Moore
April 2017

II
TASTE,
FLAVOUR
AND THE BRAIN

What is flavour?

I could start here with a dictionary definition. It would be the obvious way; but it would lead us astray. Oh, go on then, let's have a go. I've still got a fat copy of the *Collins English Dictionary* on the shelf from university days. Here's how it begins:

> **flavour** *n*. **1.** Taste perceived in food or liquid in the mouth.

So far, so simple, yes? That's just about what you'd have expected. But before we get too complacent, let's just check on what we mean by taste.

> **taste** *n*. **1.** The sense by which the qualities and flavour of a substance are distinguished by the taste buds.

The taste buds. To take this conversation forward, we need to look at what exactly the taste buds can do. Beware of language here, though – it is an unreliable narrator. The words, and the definitions that have massed and settled around them, came before science had taught us to be more precise about how our senses of taste and smell really work.

The sense of taste

Much of what we think we taste, we actually smell. If you've never tried it, the jelly bean test is a good demonstration of this: shut your eyes so that you can't see what colour you're taking, pick a jelly bean from a bag of sweets, pinch your nose closed with your fingers, pop the jelly bean in your mouth and chew. You will find that you can't tell what colour – what flavour of jelly bean – it is until you release your nose and breathe. Breathing creates an internal airflow that wafts scent molecules to your olfactory receptors, giving you the information you need to identify lime, bubble gum, orange or whatever. Without the input of our sense of smell, all we notice of the jelly bean is a mixture of sugar and acidity.

So what can taste do? We have about 10,000 taste buds, located on our tongue, palate, pharynx and larynx, which are activated when they encounter food dissolved in saliva. In common with most other vertebrates, humans can detect a relatively small number of qualities through the taste buds.

It used to be thought that the taste buds were capable of detecting just four basic tastes: salt, sweet, sour and bitter. In the Western world these are all very familiar flavour-enhancers and can be represented by the white flakes of sea salt we sprinkle over our plates of food; the sugar we add to tea, or to a bowl of strawberries; vinegar shaken over fish and chips, or lemon squeezed over tuna carpaccio; and the bitterness of dark chocolate or quinine in tonic water.

In 1908, the Tokyo chemist Kikunae Ikeda identified a fifth, umami ('savouriness' in Japanese), in seaweed dashi, and proposed that the molecule responsible for it was glutamate. Umami is best described as the deep, savoury quality that makes food taste intense and moreish. It is found in high quantities in soy sauce, tomatoes (it's especially noticeable in oven-dried tomatoes), mushrooms, beef, yeast and yeast extracts (such as Marmite), Parmesan, fish sauce and shellfish.

The debate over whether umami really was a true fifth taste went on for decades, but after glutamate receptors were identified in the mouth, it was widely accepted as ranking equally with the basic four. The question now is – how many more are there?

Fat is considered by most experts to be the sixth basic taste. Initially it was thought that we could only recognize fat by its creamy texture and its odour (which is actually very unattractive, however much we might crave foods with a high fat content). But researchers showed that rats with no sense of smell still showed a preference for liquids containing fatty acids and, also, receptors for fatty acids have now been located in the mouth.

If you have ever undergone an operation, you might have been warned by the anaesthetist to expect a metallic taste in the mouth just as you go under. This is also sometimes experienced by pregnant women and by chemotherapy patients (supertasters seem particularly susceptible). Metallic – in normal life it's the taste you find if you lick blood from a cut – is also in contention for recognition as another basic taste, as are a dozen or more other qualities.

One of the ways we can corroborate that the tastes found in the foods we eat are recognized in a distinct way is that they have been shown by fMRI scans to activate different parts of the primary gustatory cortex in the brain. The evolutionary argument is that these basic tastes developed and survived because they helped to guide us towards the right foods.

Our early response to at least some of the basic tastes appears to be innate, rather than learnt. Studies have shown that babies respond favourably to sweet sensations, but reject bitter liquids, screwing up their faces in disgust. So, the theory goes, a taste for sweetness steers us towards the calorie-heavy carbohydrates we need for fuel. Salt draws us to replace lost minerals. Umami may be a protein signal. We have different bitter receptors specialized to detect many types of bitterness and these are thought to warn us away from hazardous plants, such as unripe fruit and poisonous roots and berries. A liking for bitterness usually develops later, by which time we have learnt which plants may do us harm.

It's clear, then, that while the last two decades of scientific research have demonstrated that our sense of taste is much more sophisticated than originally thought, when we talk colloquially about 'the taste' of food or drink, we're actually talking about much more than that. If you ask me what a wine 'tastes' like, or to describe its flavour, and I mention only its acidity, sweetness, bitterness, saltiness and any metallic qualities (they do exist: I find an iron tang in wines made from the grape fer servadou, for instance), you might feel a bit short-changed. The assumption is that flavour encompasses more than the information given to us by our sense of taste.

The sense of smell

Occasionally I stick my nose in a glass of wine, inhale and am surprised to find a freeze-frame image dropping down in front of my inner eye. It's rarely a neat picture, more like the sort of Instagram your phone would take if you were hanging on to it while fumbling for something in your bag – a half-obscured view across a field towards some mountains; the wooden legs of a picnic table buried in deep grass, with a bowl of strawberries and red wine just in shot; the edge of someone's face and a track up to a winery behind them. But I can usually place the picture straight away, and, as I do so, I'm also able to identify the wine because I know that smell and picture come from the same place.

What's happening here demonstrates two of the quite extraordinary powers of our olfactory system. Our sense of smell does not just have the ability to differentiate accurately between the many hundreds of thousands of different odours it encounters each year – from foods to perfumes, people, environments and, in my case, bottles of wine. Our mind is also able to take the scent of that individual wine and file it away, linking it to other memory traces that are retrieved the next time the brain encounters the same, very particular, smell.

Smell often feels like a luxury, in the sense that if you are anosmic (have lost the ability to smell) it is possible to navigate modern life much more easily than if you had lost one of your other senses. Indeed, if you are not someone who pays particular attention to smell, the disability might even go undetected. Perhaps because of this, olfaction is much neglected and underappreciated. In fact, our olfactory system is a remarkable thing, second only to our highly complex visual system in its number of sensory receptor cells. Until recently, scientific literature reckoned that humans could differentiate between about 10,000 different odours. Now it is claimed that this is a gargantuan underestimate and that we can discriminate between more than 1 trillion different smells, making the nose arguably more discerning than the eyes (thought to be able to detect 2.3–7.5million different colour shades) or the ears (we can hear around 340,000 different tones). It's all the more remarkable when you consider that this is possible from a set of only around 350 different smell receptors.

In order for us to perceive an odour, a tiny molecule of a substance must float through the air to make contact and bind with our olfactory receptors, which are located in the nasal cavity, behind the nose. There are two routes to the olfactory receptors: through the nostrils (orthonasal), which is how we process smoke, perfume, and other environmental odours, such as the smell of food as it's cooking on the stove, or the aroma of coffee on the street; and in through the 'back entrance' (retronasal) via our mouth and throat, which is how we smell (or taste, as we inaccurately call it) food as we eat. The retronasal route is only activated when you breathe out through the nose, which is why the jelly bean test described earlier is so effective, and why we can't taste food properly when we have a cold.

An interesting thing is that the two different routes to our olfactory receptors do not appear to give the same results. A good example of this is the stinky cheese paradox. As lovers of pongy cheese will be aware, the pungent smell of a ripe piece of Epoisses is often quite unpleasant and yet the cheese is delicious to eat – it appears to smell different, or we have a different response to it, when it is sampled through the orthonasal rather than the retronasal route. This is the reason why, returning from Paris once with a bag of very strong cheese, I was careful to pop it in the luggage rack of the adjacent Eurostar carriage. With coffee, the effect is reversed: the smell of freshly ground coffee always seems better when you sniff it in the air than when you have it in your mouth. Studies using fMRI scans have confirmed the orthonasal/retronasal effect, showing that, aside from the brain activity caused by the action of chewing, or the sensation of texture and so on, the two routes can result in different patterns of brain activity for the same smells.

Once they reach the nasal cavity, the volatile odorant molecules bind to one or more of the 350 or so types of receptor, creating a pattern of activity that could be likened to playing chords on a piano in the sense that a relatively small number of keys (receptors) can produce a high number of different sounds (spatial patterns). These patterns then move through the brain as smell images.

Our sense of smell is phenomenally sensitive, capable of detecting odours at tiny concentrations, although different molecules have different perception thresholds. For instance, we can smell the compound 2-isobutyl-3-methoxypyrazine (which is found in bell peppers and also in sauvignon blanc) at low concentrations (of 0.01nM for the scientists among you), whereas other molecules are invisible to our brains and noses until they are more abundant in the air. A peculiarity of this sense is that our response to some smells varies according to their concentration. For instance, indole, which is found in jasmine and used in perfumes, is perceived as being pleasantly floral at low concentrations but at higher concentrations as revoltingly faecal.

The scientist, and subject of the popular book *The Emperor of Scent*, Luca Turin finds the human ability to detect the most subtle of smells from the other side of a room so remarkably fast-acting and powerful that he contends it cannot be accounted for by the traditional – and accepted establishment – explanation of how smell works. He has devoted years of his life to attempting to prove an alternative theory of smell, contending that rather than being a chemical sense, smell works because our nose is fitted with a biological spectroscope so what we actually smell are molecular vibrations – 'a totally insane idea, and I still have to convince my colleagues that might be so, but I'm working on it'.

It's the ability of smells to unlock vivid emotional memories that so often stops us in our tracks. Of all the senses, smell appears to have the most potent ability to transport us through space and time. Sufferers of post-traumatic stress disorder sometimes talk about the problems smell can cause as a violent emotional trigger of events they would prefer to forget. More positively, I think we all have experiences of catching a skein of scent that sends us tumbling through a wormhole into our past; studies have shown that, compared to sight and sound, smell is particularly likely to trigger autobiographical memories from our early childhood.

It has been suggested that the close links of the olfactory bulb to two areas of the brain involved in memory and emotion – the amygdala and the hippocampus – could be one reason for this close association between emotional memories and smell.

Another contributing factor might be the mind's ability to differentiate between such a large number of smells. As anyone who has ever thought themselves back into a place and time in an effort to recall a lost piece of information knows, memories can be triggered in many ways – by stories, places, certain noises, songs, and all kinds of visual cues, such as a spider chart or the face of the person speaking – as well as by smells. But memories are not firm and immutable, they are susceptible to interference. When a memory trace is retrieved and revisited, it can easily be corrupted as the mind knits to it new associations. Perhaps our ability to encode so many different smells as unique memory traces means that they are subject to less interference, and is one of the factors that makes a rare rediscovery seem so joltingly fresh.

Flavour and the somatic senses

I've talked about the impact of smell and taste on flavour, but when we describe food and drink we refer to other qualities too. The somatosensory system – which covers not just touch, but also temperature and pain – has a huge role to play.

The feel of a food or wine – whether it's slimy or rough, full-bodied or insubstantial – has a big impact on the way we perceive it. I don't like snails because I'm not keen on the chewiness. A friend can't abide oysters – 'Like eating snot,' as he says, and my apologies if that sentiment stays with you and spoils your appreciation of this bivalve for good. It's not just the immediate sensation of softness, slime or ruggedness on our tongue and against the roof of our mouth that we notice, and which contributes to the way we feel about food, but also how hard our jaw has to work, what muscles have to get involved, because mastication, too, is part of the eating and drinking experience.

One particularly important sensation when it comes to wine (as well as tea and plain chocolate) is the drying, puckering effect caused by tannin. Is this a taste? Or a feel? Some astringent phenols do activate the bitter receptors in the mouth, which is why the sensations of bitterness and astringency are so closely associated. But whether the detection of astringency and tannins is the responsibility of our taste or our somatosensory system has been a matter of some debate. A study published in 2014 suggests the latter. It explored astringency perception in humans by comparing the effects of anaesthetizing the chorda tympani taste nerve, and also the trigeminal nerve (which conveys somatosensory information), and showed that only when both were blocked was there a loss of astringency perception on the tongue, demonstrating that we don't depend on our taste system alone to feel tannin.

I haven't yet mentioned chilli – a very vigorous contributor to the flavour of any dish that contains it. The perception of chilli is also mediated by the somatosensory system. We feel its burn as pain, which is picked up by the nociceptors (pain receptors) and conveyed via the trigeminal nerve to the brain. Aspects of garlic (its heat) and cinnamon (its jagged texture) are sensed in a similar way, and these condiments and spices would taste like a shadow of themselves if we ignored this somatosensory input.

So, it seems fairly clear that it's wrong to talk only about taste when we talk about taste. At least three of the senses play a vital role in flavour:

> Flavour = taste + smell + somatic senses (temperature, touch and pain)

Flavour and the other senses

Is it possible to go further? Can we say that the other senses are involved in flavour perception as well? The impact of hearing and vision on the perception of flavour is less direct but it certainly can't be ignored. When we taste a wine or eat a bowl of cereal (especially those cereals that snap, crackle and pop), our brain doesn't simply rely on the input from our mouth and nose, it grabs any information that comes in to help build up a picture.

For instance, if I were to deepen the shade of a rosé wine by adding a few drops of red food colouring, the chances are that it would taste 'more pink' to you – that is, more of red fruits and berries – because your brain would be primed to look for and be receptive towards those flavours.

Charles Spence is an Oxford psychologist who has done a lot of work in this area. His book *The Perfect Meal: The Multisensory Science of Food and Dining*, co-authored by Betina Piqueras-Fiszman, is a good read for anyone interested in learning more about the way all of our senses feed into what we feed ourselves.

Spence looks, among other things, at the way that our perception of flavour is affected by what we can see and hear. For instance, he has found that strawberry mousse will taste 10 per cent sweeter if eaten out of a white rather than a black container and that if there is yellow in our sight line then the small amount of lemon we squeeze on our smoked salmon will taste more noticeable (another way of expressing this is: if you're running short on lemons, put a vase of yellow flowers or a yellow dish on the table to make them go further). Spence's experiments also show that listening to sounds of the sea make the marine flavours in seafood seem more intense and that listening to low-pitched music boosts the bitter component of anything you are eating.

One of his most famous experiments is known as The Sonic Chip. For this one, Spence had volunteers eat crisps while wearing headphones that played the sound of their own crunchy munching back to them. Unbeknown to the subjects, he manipulated the crunching sound to see if the noise they heard affected the way the participants appreciated the crisps. He found that a crisp that emits (or appears to emit) a louder, higher-pitched sound is rated as being more crispy and more fresh by the person eating it than one with a quieter, lower-pitched sound.

The territory of Spence's research, where the data input from one sense impacts on the processing of another, is known as cross-modal perception, and it makes a very good case for arguing that all the senses are involved in flavour.

Flavour = taste + smell + somatic senses + vision + hearing

Never mind taste. We really need a new verb to describe the act of trying food and drink – to flave, perhaps?

The language of wine

Jacques Polge is the French perfumer who for nearly four decades was the nose for Chanel. A literary man, who studied poetry before being tempted into the fragrance industry, he was charming and interesting when I interviewed him one wet spring morning in Provence, shortly after watching pink May roses being picked near Grasse. We compared a few professional notes – for instance, both of us find our sense of smell most acute in the morning and prefer to do important practical work then – but there was something Polge felt quite pained about and needed to get out. It was this: he didn't like the way that wine critics talk about wine.

'When perfumers talk about a perfume, its pine notes, or its Damascus rose, or ylang-ylang, they're talking about things that are actually there. When you describe the smell of a wine, you're talking about things that aren't there.' Half an hour later, when Polge showed me two different jasmine samples, one of them warm and exotic, the other more sinewy and delicate, and said to me, 'Do you find tea in the more delicate one? It always reminds me of tea,' I made no comment.

When it comes to wine, what you have in the bottle is the fermented juice of a certain type of grape or grapes. Many readers may not even be familiar with the typical characteristics of the grape in question – and why should they be? Describing 'what is actually there' is not going to convey a very clear sense of what to expect from the wine, though it may work if you are talking to another expert in the subject.

If you were listening to wine pros bitching about bottles, you might hear them say that a chardonnay 'stinks of reduction' or that a sauvignon blanc 'reeks of cold soak fermentation'. They might complain about 'sweaty thiols', or 'brett', or say, 'You can tell the grapes were grown at altitude.' They might whinge that, 'The Australians have gone too far with their skinny, early-picked styles', describe a red as being 'like a cross between a warm climate cabernet franc and a lagrein' or simply put their shoulders down and say with satisfaction that a wine is 'just pure Margaux'. None of this would be of much assistance to anyone not already immersed in the world of wine.

It is much easier with food, because anyone who cooks or eats has some understanding of what makes a dish hang together. It is as if, with food, it is enough to describe its physical characteristics, and the fragrant ingredients, for the reader to *know*. Virginia Woolf did this beautifully in *To the Lighthouse*:

> An exquisite scent of olives and oil and juice rose from the great brown dish as Marthe, with a little flourish, took the cover off. The cook had spent three days over that dish and she must take great care, Mrs Ramsay thought, diving into the soft mass to choose an especially tender piece for William Bankes. And she peered into the dish, with its shiny walls and its confusion of savoury brown and yellow meats, and its bay leaves and its wine and thought, 'This will celebrate the occasion ...'

Those sentences make me almost as hungry for daube de boeuf as if the pot were sitting there in front of me. It is not so easy to be evocative about wine because we must use a vocabulary that has not been created for the purpose. Even if it had been, would it not take a lifetime to learn? There are only 1 million words in the English language, while science tells us that the nose can distinguish between over 1 trillion different scents.

In Roman times, around 100 words were used specifically to describe the taste and smell of wine. Today we embrace a range of approaches and a much wider vocabulary. In some (wine exam) circles there has been a determined and courageous attempt to create a standardized system. This is done by picking out certain key qualities – most of them sense-of-taste-related – such as acidity, tannin and sweetness, and attempting to rank them on a scale. So you might see a tasting note that reads, 'Medium plus tannin, high acidity, bone dry ...' This is fine, up to a point, the point being that it does not get you anywhere, either on smell or on a kind of gestalt appreciation of the whole drink.

One method of dealing with the smell is what has been called the 'fruit salad approach', favoured by the American critic Robert Parker, the BBC's Jilly Goolden and others. It involves listing greengrocery and other items that the wine smells a bit like, so a tasting note might talk about 'white peaches, lettuce, wet stones, thyme and a hint of lemon juice.'

It's a method that has attracted much grouchy ridicule. But here's a thing. As scientific endeavour reveals more to us about the chemical components of a wine, we have found that many of those 'fruit salad' descriptors are more accurate than perhaps anyone initially realized. For instance, Cis-3-hexen-1-ol is an aroma compound found in cut grass, and also in some sauvignon blanc. Rotundone is found in black pepper, and also in wine made from syrah. I could go on.

But lists of 'it smells a bit like' have their limitations, so many writers – and I am one of them – go further. In a – brave? foolhardy? – attempt to create a gestalt impression, a more complete picture of the wine, they take the no-holds-barred route. This is always risky. It can be reminiscent of that scene in *Brideshead Revisited* when raids on the ancestral cellar are accompanied by elaborate, drunken appreciations of the wines – 'Like a flute by still water' and 'It is a shy little wine, like a gazelle.'

But it is not, actually, a remotely radical approach. Writers in other fields have been bending words to new uses and using simile and metaphor for centuries, though admittedly some of them (Shakespeare) do it better and more convincingly than others. Occasionally my tasting notes elicit furious emails of complaint. How can I possibly know what a wet stone tastes like? Have I ever licked one? Well, yes, actually, haven't you? And in any case, I know what a wet stone smells like and it's more or less the same thing. Or, how can it possibly mean anything to say that a wine is 'anorexic and depleted?' I usually write back saying that I agree with every word the complainee has written, and would be more than happy to stick to his or her suggested list of acceptable wine vocabulary if he or she would be so kind as to provide one. No one yet has . . .

III
SIMPLE GUIDELINES

Using this book

For some reason, thinking about what wine to put with what food is often off-puttingly called 'wine and food pairing', which makes it sound complicated and agonized, like a minority sport for which referees and special socks might be required. I am happy to report that this is not the case.

Newsflash: putting food together with wine is supposed to be fun. It is an art more than it is a science. It is interesting to learn about the mechanisms and processes that underpin our senses of taste and smell and which help to explain why a certain combination of flavours might produce a pleasure explosion in the brain, and certain others do not, but when it comes to eating and drinking there is no wrong and no right, simply varying degrees of enjoyment.

I like to savour both wine and food, but my approach to the subject is more broad-brush stroke than nerdish. It has to be, because it is beyond the scope of this book to recommend a particular wine and vintage, which would need to be opened at a particular point in its lifespan, to put alongside a highly specific and carefully tuned plate of food. That is the job of a sommelier in a restaurant. What I have tried to do here is offer guidelines and suggestions for areas of play suitable for those who do not have a Michelin-starred chef in their kitchen and a 5,000-bin cellar at their disposal.

Like a foreign-language dictionary, the book is arranged in two halves. The first takes you from food to wine: look up the dish you plan to make for dinner, or perhaps some of its ingredients, and you will find suggestions for the type of wine that is likely to bring out the best in both the food and the drink.

The second half of the book works in the opposite direction. If you have a bottle of wine and want inspiration for what to eat with it, then look it up by grape (or, in a few cases, by region of origin) and you will find a range of recommendations and tips not just from me, but from winemakers too..

There are also a handful of quick tricks you can use to help you pick a wine without fuss. Here they are:

Picking by mood

Some wines and foods evoke certain moods, so choosing wine to go with the food becomes instinctive. I'm thinking barbecued meat with heavy reds; light summer salads with pristine, chilled whites. If the food is a beach picnic, then ask yourself: is this a relaxed, beach wine or will it taste like wearing a tweed suit and brogues on the beach would feel? If you can imagine the wine and the food in the same setting then you're off. Mixing them up can feel odd, like putting on a fur coat with a ballerina tutu. As in fashion, some people can pull off the gourmet equivalent of a *Vogue* shoot. They have such an innate, creative sense of food and wine that they are able to make an apparent mismatch and inspire gastronomic fireworks. But it's an art that requires flair.

Picking by weight

To play it safe, think about texture and weight. Ask: how heavy is this wine going to taste? How powerful is the food I am eating? Am I setting a shout against a whisper? Look for an even balance so that the food does not drown out the wine (or vice versa). For instance, it's not very fair to pitch a tremulous and faded old claret up against spicy barbecued meat. High alcohol is often an indication that the wine will roar, and be trickier to enjoy with food: a thunking great Aussie shiraz with an abv of 15% isn't the best pick for Dover sole. On the other hand, a light red is a good weight match against meatier fish such as tuna.

Picking by place

The best short cut I know is very simple. Go local. That is, local to the food, not to wherever you happen to be. Think about a cassoulet from Gascony. You might either set this hearty, peasant stew next to a thick black Cahors, or play the other way and open a red Marcillac with lively acidity to cut through the heft and hulk of the rich meat and fat. Either way, both are wines found not so far away, in the same corner of south-west France. And both work.

Sitting in a restaurant overlooking Sydney Harbour ordering crispy soft-shell crab? (I wish I were.) Then try a semillon from the Hunter Valley, a couple of hours north. As for salade niçoise, it is not just south of France holiday longing that makes me say it never tastes better than with a pale pink rosé or a white rolle from Provence. Well, perhaps it is a bit, but it's true anyway.

Putting place with place, region with region, is a trick that works partly because food and wine cultures grow together. It's not just that a winemaker's taste is influenced and shaped by what he or she eats every day (although it is); over the centuries wine has been made to go on the table beside local food and the popular styles would have been the ones that matched the local palate.

Climate also comes into play. Wine made from grapes that have seen a lot of sun has a richer, warmer taste, a sweet ripeness, that can work with food that has also seen a lot of sun. An example? The aubergine and tomato-rich, almost sweet pasta sauces made in the south of Italy taste better with the lusher local reds than they do with a savoury nebbiolo from Piemonte in the north. As for English white wine, with its fierce acidity and keen edges, it suits fish that have swum through our cool rivers, simply poached with watercress and boiled new potatoes.

South Africa is another good example of place harmonizing with wine style. Many South African reds are big-boned and vivid, sometimes with a smoky flavour that goes well with the bold taste of food cooked on a braai. In these vast landscapes, surrounded by the intense red, green, blue of the soil and skies, and the proximity in some places of the roaring ocean, every sense is saturated. Of course, in these circumstances, you would want to drink a wine that was similarly epic.

Because this isn't just about what you eat. We don't just taste and smell with our mouths and noses, but with every sense we have: it's the phenomenon known in the psychology world as cross-modal perception, and in the normal world as, 'This wine didn't taste like this on holiday.'

Which explains why Cape winemaker Chris Mullineux, sounding surprised, told me he found his own wine, Kloof Street Rouge, tasted 'completely different – more South African' when he came to London and opened a few bottles in a series of workshops and meetings in cramped rooms and under grey skies, far away from the smells and sights of the scenery in which it's made.

It also neatly brings in my earlier point, about mood. Sometimes you can't separate the two.

Fine wine and fine food

With smart wine, I like to go as simple as possible with the food. It sometimes feels like a better idea not to bother with food at all on the grounds that, if you have a very complex drink in your glass, anything else is just a distraction, though I would never turn down the chance to eat a plate of truffles and pasta with a glass of even the most perfect nebbiolo.

I often take a similar view when it comes to choosing what to drink with haute cuisine: the dance of flavours in a plate of precision-cooked food is better enjoyed for what it is than matched to a competingly spectacular wine. I tend to stick with water, or order an easy session wine on the rare occasions when I eat this type of food.

It took me a long time to twig that this is the reason why many serious wine drinkers are contemptuous of the idea of wine and food matching. For them, the wine is everything. And they are right – if you have uncorked a 1982 Margaux, frankly whatever else is going on had better not take up too much of your attention.

That said, in the 'From wine to food' section I've made occasional suggestions for food that goes well with old and/or fine wines, but only when I think there is real merit in doing so.

Keeping an eye out for GAME-CHANGER ingredients

A friend of mine runs a supper club. She keeps the menu secret until the guests arrive and I make wine suggestions that are emailed out in advance so that people can bring their own wine. In the early days this didn't always work. I'd show up for dinner, get out a bottle of bright, cherryish dolcetto to go with the bresaola and bitter rocket starter, glance over the menu and notice that Anna had had a creative moment and dressed the whole lot with goat's curd vinaigrette. Both goat's cheese (or curd) and vinaigrette are what I call game-changer ingredients. They seize control of a dish and cannot be ignored. If I'd known about the goat's curd vinaigrette I'd have ditched the idea of drinking red with the bresaola and rocket salad and gone for a fleshy but acidic white – probably an oaked sauvignon blanc from Bordeaux or the Loire.

Other powerful game-changer ingredients include *chilli, garlic, herbs of all kinds, lemons* (and even the tiniest amount of *preserved lemon*), *artichoke, vinegar* and *spices*. I've flagged them up and explained how to deal with these in the 'From food to wine' section, because they make a huge difference to the way you perceive the wine.

Getting more technical: dealing with the big six

As discussed in section II, much of what we think of as taste – from the flavour of a dark pink late August raspberry squashed against the roof of the mouth to the mingle of herbs and spices in a Moroccan tagine – is actually smell. Remove olfaction and we are reduced to managing solely on the data conveyed by our taste buds, which are sensitive only to salt, sweetness, bitterness, acidity, umami, fat (and maybe a few others).

These six tastes have a huge impact on how a mouthful of wine is perceived. If picking a wine to go with a plate of food it helps to take them into account.

salt As any good cook knows, salt reduces the impact of acidity – and vice versa. This is why you can rescue an over-seasoned sauce by squeezing in some lemon juice, or apply the same trick in reverse and soften an overly acidic sauce by adding salt. Similarly, salty food will make a wine with low acidity taste flat and lethargic but get on famously with a screamingly acidic wine. So with salty food look for a sharp wine. For example, with salty feta cheese a citric assyrtiko or Gavi is good and the marine taste of spaghetti vongole goes well with a zippy Valpolicella.

A second and perhaps more surprising strategy is to look for sugar, which can also taste good with salt: think of salted caramel, or a juicy Charentais melon with prosciutto. Sweet wines often match well with salty cheeses.

Another way of looking at this is to think that, if you have very salty food, then whatever you drink is going to taste as if you've also put salt in the glass. If the thought of doing this is very unappealing, then don't serve that wine with that food. Heavy salt can make oaked wines taste odd – this is why oaky chardonnay isn't great with a bag of crisps but a brisk glass of unoaked sauvignon blanc is.

sweetness Sugar can be a real killer with wine. If going to a professional tasting I make sure I don't eat anything sweet for at least an hour beforehand. Also, I always taste wines with any sweetness last: after tasting all the dry wines, my sugar round starts with the champagnes (they don't have much sugar in them but it can be enough to alter your perception of anything you taste afterwards) and works steadily sweeter, through kabinett riesling, on to sparkling moscato, then dessert wines, finishing up with fiendishly treacly PX. Sweetness skews the palate. It can make wine taste almost bitter, as anyone who's ever tried to return to a glass of dry red while eating apple crumble or ice cream will know.

If putting a wine with pudding, pick one that is sweeter than the food. If there's a touch of sweetness – from luscious fruit, perhaps – in a main course, consider a slightly off-dry wine, or at least a rich-tasting wine: a ripe chardonnay, say, rather than a skinny sauvignon blanc.

bitterness A bitter ingredient such as radicchio, chicory or rocket can really throw a wine. I like to put bitter food with bitter wine or, if you can't find bitter wine, then with astringency (tannin) and acidity. For instance, charred bitter radicchio tastes much better with a young Chianti, whose fresh acidity and tannin give it a bit of edge, than it does with a plump, rich Californian merlot. Drinking a ripe, soft, smooth wine with a bitter food can make the wine appear unpleasantly sweet, or leave it looking isolated and helpless, like a child caught in a fierce political debate.

acidity Acidity gets a bad name but it's actually a good thing – a quality that gives wine bite and vim. Acidic food needs acidic wine. If you have a sharp vinaigrette or a lot of citrus on the plate make sure its acidity is matched with a sharp wine. The reason for this is that we adapt to tastes very quickly and eating an acidic food has the effect of knocking out the acidity of the wine (at least, as we perceive it). If the wine is gentle to start off with, it will taste flabby and flaccid after a mouthful of lemon juice.

umami The most potent source of umami is soy sauce, which is rich in the flavour-enhancer monosodium glutamate. This meaty, savoury taste is also found in dashi, the broth made from kelp and dried bonito flakes that is a building block of many Japanese dishes. Human tasters identify a similarly rich taste in mushrooms (particularly shiitake), yeast, aged Parmesan, anchovies, tomato products and Marmite, though laboratory testing for umami does not always back this up. Sake, of course, made from fermented rice, is what you will find on the table in Japanese restaurants. The oxidative taste of dry sherry, or of vin jaune from the Jura, also works well with many of these foods.

fat With fatty food, pick a wine with either good acidity or good tannin (or both) to slice through the fat. An example of this is a young nebbiolo with onions stuffed with a creamy, cheesy mixture. Or a lively young claret with a fatty roast goose.

FROM FOOD TO WINE

An A to Z of Food

In order to make it easier to see what colour of wine is being recommended, the first time a wine is mentioned in each entry or sub-section of an entry, it appears in colour – as red, white or rosé.

abalone This prized mollusc, also known as ormer and ear shell, or oreja de mar (in Spain), is held in particular esteem in Asia and everywhere commands very high prices. A member of the genus haliotis (I can't read that word without seeing halitosis), the herbivorous sea snail lives in a shell with a dull surface and a glistening mother-of-pearl lining. Abalone can grow up to 12 inches across and attach themselves to rocks via a single, muscular foot – which is the bit that is edible. The meat is chewy, often described as having a texture that is a cross between squid and conch. In Japan it is eaten raw, as sashimi, and its marine flavours taste good with a gentle, unoaked chardonnay from Chablis or New Zealand. Abalone that is simply cooked and dressed (say, steamed or grilled) takes on a more meaty taste and texture. Light, fresh wines such as sauvignon blanc and lighter chardonnays still work well. If the abalone is dressed with rice wine and soy sauce, then a lighter sake or the more complex flavours of an oaked, maturing chardonnay are better. In Chinese cuisine, abalone is often braised and may be prepared with shiitake, soy sauce, oyster sauce, spring onions and ginger. These dishes are good with sparkling wines that have been fermented in bottle: richer champagnes, English sparkling wine and chardonnay, pinot noir and pinot meunier sparkling blends from Australia and New Zealand.

aioli This garlicky mayonnaise is often served as a starter with a plate full of crunchy crudités. A dry pale rosé from Provence will happily wash the whole lot down, and complete the picture of a summer evening, but a neutral white wine with firmer acidity might be better if the garlic is fierce. Try needle-sharp aligoté; the clean, Alpine jacquère from the Savoie; or lemony arneis, pecorino or cortese from Italy.

See also garlic.

aligot After holidaying in the Aveyron in the south of France I acquired a serious addiction to this potato purée made with garlic and a lot of Tomme cheese. It is superb with magret de canard and with herby, garlicky sausages and in both cases I wouldn't look much further than wines from nearby. The food is rich and you could go with something that either provides a sharp contrast or that packs a similar punch. Marcillac, made from fer servadou, which tastes of iron, a bit like the blood licked from a cut, is the sappy, cut-across choice. Cahors is the match-heft-with-heft alternative.

anchovies These salty little brown cured fish appreciate a refreshing wine. If they're on a pizza, a good savoury match would be a light Bardolino, Valpolicella or simple Chianti (all from Italy) or a red made with the Spanish mencía grape (look to the regions of Bierzo and Ribeira Sacra). With anchovies on bits of toast or toast and gentleman's relish as a nibble, then a glass of chilled manzanilla or a sparkling wine with some nerve (English or Loire fizz or cava or Franciacorta or a pinot noir-chardonnay sparkling blend from New Zealand or South Africa) goes well. Another killer aperitif with brown anchovies is the olive martini: ice-cold gin (or vodka) with a briny olive is very good indeed with the rich, flaky pastry and savoury fish of an anchovy twist, which is why you so often find these pastries in sleek hotel bars.

The fleshier white boquerones, drenched in olive oil and eaten as tapas, are good with bright white wines such as verdejo, unoaked white Rioja and young Australian Hunter Valley semillon; salty-iodine manzanilla/fino sherry; gentler albariño; rosé; Provence whites; or that ultimate fish wine, Muscadet.

antipasti In Italy you can expect to eat the classic cluster of prosciutto, fennel-seed salami, chunks of grainy Parmigiano, tomato-and-basil bruschetta, insalata tricolore, chicken liver crostini, and all the rest, with either a glass of sparkling prosecco, if everyone is feeling festive, or the local wine, whatever that happens to be. Prosecco is light and airy enough to wash down all of these and with people milling around, picking at this and that while they chat, this is a classic case of a mood match being more important than a food match. I like the softness of prosecco, but there is no need to constrain yourself to Italy when excellent casual fizz is also made in New Zealand, Tasmania, the Loire, Limoux, South Africa, Germany, Spain and England. Anything that would be good at a picnic gets my vote.

artichokes The artichoke is an illusionist among vegetables. It is thought to contain a substance that effectively hacks our taste buds and cons us into thinking that whatever we eat or drink immediately afterwards is sweeter than it actually is. This phenomenon, which has long been familiar to cooks and artichoke-eaters, received scientific attention in 1935 when Albert Blakeslee reported in the journal *Science* that, at a biologists' dinner attended by nearly 250 people, 60 per cent of those who had eaten globe artichokes found that water tasted different afterwards and 'to most, this taste was sweet'.

In 1972, the eminent food psychologist Linda Bartoshuk set out to investigate these taste-modifying properties. In her experiments, she replicated the finding that eating artichokes made water taste sweet and noted that this sweet sensation was unusual in that it didn't arise from having anything in the mouth that was actually sweet, but was an effect apparently caused by temporarily altering the taste receptors on the tongue. Bartoshuk has since speculated that the most plausible explanation for this effect is that a substance found in artichokes (probably cynarin) inhibits the sweet receptors in the mouth. When the taste buds are rinsed by water or another liquid (such as wine), the inhibition is removed, and a message is sent to the brain through the pathways that convey sweet taste, giving rise to a phantom sensation of sugar.

So what to drink with artichokes? It depends how you're eating them. I find the Artichoke Effect is most extreme when you mix artichokes and acid – say, by squeezing lemon juice over them or adding vinaigrette. Try it for yourself by eating a tinned artichoke heart with a bit of lemon juice on it and taking a mouthful of wine afterwards – you get a faint, metallic-sweet taste in your mouth through which it's almost impossible to taste the wine at all. To help counter this, whenever artichokes are part of a dish or salad, whether as raw shavings of hearts or roasted, almost-whole vegetables, look for a white with some astringency and/or acidity. The job is done very well by one of the increasingly fashionable orange wines – white wines that have been left in contact with the skins so that they develop some astringency and a beautiful amber hue. Alternatively, try something Italian and white with a slight hint of bitterness – for instance, vermentino, carricante, vernaccia, ribolla gialla or verdicchio. Manzanilla or fino sherry is another good choice. Reds tend to clash – particularly if they are heavy and oaky. I wouldn't pick a red if artichokes were the main ingredient on the plate, but where red wine fits in best with the other ingredients, you can assuage the artichokes by picking one with a bit of elbow – young and acidic, say Marcillac, Beaujolais or dolcetto or tannic and acidic, like nebbiolo or lagrein.

When artichokes are eaten as a course on their own – boiled and nibbled, leaf by vinaigrette-dipped leaf – I don't serve wine, on the grounds that it's not possible to handle a glass of wine with all that going on. If you do, it had better be something with fierce acidity the better to cope with the vinegar – try aligoté, or a determined, unoaked assyrtiko, or an English white wine (sparkling or still).

asparagus

green Deep green spears of asparagus have an insistent flavour that is well matched by grassy, acidic wines: English bacchus with its taste of hedgerows; Sauvignon de St Bris (the sauvignon blanc from Burgundy); young, razor-sharp, unoaked Bordeaux Blancs; bright young semillon from Australia's Hunter Valley; Austrian grüner veltliner; podded-pea-like sauvignon blancs from Chile; vermentino, arneis or verdicchio from Italy; or herbaceous Loire sauvignon blanc (for specific Loire sauvignon blancs, see the sauvignon blanc entry in 'From wine to food').

Green asparagus has such a clear, soaring flavour that just a few discs of it thrown into a plate of pasta or salad will skew the direction of the dish towards these clean white wines.

A

white Pale cream asparagus doesn't have the chlorophyll edginess of green. It tastes less grassy, more rounded and tender, like white cabbage compared to green. This softer taste goes well with a simple Saumur Blanc from a ripe vintage (especially one that has been in bottle for a year or so to mellow out a bit). The toasty flare of an aged Australian or South African semillon (which sometimes smells a bit like white asparagus, and often smells like salad cream) also goes well. A dry weissburgunder (German pinot blanc) will give the asparagus a bit of punctuation. A just-off-dry German riesling also works very well; pick one from the Nahe, as these rieslings have a taste reminiscent of soft sunshine or backlighting that melds with the soft, alabaster-white fleshiness of the asparagus, or one of the dry but fleshily fruity rieslings made by Joachim Frick in the Rheingau, which have lemony rather than limey acidity, along with a juicy taste of pears and oranges.

aubergine The noble aubergine's finest and foremost features are its plush texture and unctuous richness (at least by the time it's been cooked in lots of oil). These allow it to be drunk with quite weighty wines. Aubergine is a chameleon ingredient, though: it may be cooked with uplifting summer accents that make you want to reach for a fragrant white, or it may be cosied up and made so wintry that only a heavy red will do.

in a dip Aubergine dips are usually eaten as part of a spread of meze and there are wine suggestions in that entry, but a hoppy craft beer like Beavertown Neck Oil will play against the thickly silky, smoky flesh of the blackened aubergine.

with feta and mint If aubergines are being sliced and rolled with feta and mint then, with the chalky cheese in your mouth and the scent of the leaves in your nostrils, a white wine feels fresh as a late spring day. Sauvignon blanc from the cool of the Adelaide Hills is calmer and less attention-seeking than many versions of this grape, a gentle wash of lemon with the herbs. Slightly fuller, more aromatic whites are fun too. Malagousia is a native Greek grape that was virtually extinct until being revived in the late twentieth century. It smells of peaches, prickly pears and jasmine. Greco and fiano, two white grapes found in the vineyards of Campania, also fit the bill; or try an unoaked southern white Italian blend, incorporating fragrant malvasia.

in a salad In a Middle Eastern aubergine salad the squelchy, charred flesh of the star ingredient is combined with fragrant olive oil, tahini, translucent pomegranate seeds, mint or flat-leaf parsley, tomatoes, garlic and lemon juice. As part of a vegetarian meal, I would try this with one of the whites listed directly above. The glorious, burnt, smokiness is also brilliant with a young, barrel-fermented sauvignon blanc or assyrtiko, both of which gleam with the rapier thrust of citrus and, thanks to the oak, have a smoky taste themselves. If the aubergine salad is to accompany grilled lamb or spicy sausages and you prefer to go red, then look for a wine with some pleasingly dirty flavours and a bit of spice. I'm thinking a central Italian sangiovese with a touch of cabernet added to the blend to give it punch; a red from the Dão or Douro in Portugal; a Côtes du Rhône with plenty of syrah in the blend; the baroque syrah that Alain Graillot makes in Morocco; a Lebanese red; or one from Greece or Turkey.

In an Italian salad, the aubergine is more often griddled, and might be put with creamy mozzarella, raw tomatoes, fresh basil and sticky balsamic vinegar. A good match with the sweet-sour of the thick vinegar is Valpolicella Ripasso. If the salad is dressed only with olive oil, you could try one of any number of lighter Italian reds (say, a nero d'avola or simple sangiovese) or a simple Italian white. Moving away from the Italian peninsula, the fragrant breadth of malagousia would be superb here too.

See also aubergine parmigiana, ratatouille.

aubergine parmigiana Flopping out of the dish in great slabs of melted cheese, olive oil, garlicky tomato sauce and soft aubergine, this is comfort food of the highest order. It is great with any of the dusty, earthy wines I affectionately call 'dirty reds' (red blends from the Dão or Douro in Portugal, agiorgitiko from Greece, Lebanese blends, rustic Chianti). Valpolicella from northern Italy is excellent too; a light version cuts through the stodge, while a ripasso, which has been enriched by passing over the skins from an Amarone ferment, has a baroque, cherryish, dusty warmth with a bit of a clip on the finish that is perfect here. Oaked reds from central Italy have plushness but also a mouth-cleansing acidity that makes you ready for the next mouthful – try a Rosso di Montalcino for breadth and spice or a Chianti Classico or a Montepulciano d'Abruzzo. Reds from southern Italy are equally good but perform a different service – warming more than punctuating – try the ripe warmth of primitivo from Puglia, the mineral drive of feral aglianico, or the mulberry swoosh of a nero d'avola from Sicily.

With more modern versions of this dish, like the 'Baked aubergines with tomatoes, tarragon and crème fraîche' in Skye Gyngell's book *A Year in My Kitchen*, in which gooey cheese is replaced with crème fraîche and tinned tomatoes with fresh, it can be nicer not to weigh it down with one of the heavier wines and instead go for a simple Valpolicella or Beaujolais, an unoaked Chianti, or, better still, a Chianti Rufina, which is lighter, edgier and fresher than a Classico. A Douro white would go well too.

avocado Lustrous and green and full of good fat, avocado is surprisingly subtle. If it's the main ingredient in a dish, be careful to pick a wine that doesn't get in the way of its cashmere-soft texture. Pinot grigio may not be as fashionable as the avocado right now but it is ideal to drink with it: smooth enough to provide a neutral frame, but with a subtle, lemony wash. In my student days the best meal I could afford to eat out was salad made with frisée lettuce, smoked bacon, avocado, grated Emmental and hot vinaigrette warmed up in the bacony frying pan. We drank it with a Pinot Grigio delle Tre Venezie that made me think of a stream running over stones and lemons. The combination still tastes good. Other simple, pure wines that work well with avocado include picpoul, Muscadet, aligoté, Soave, Lugana **or a** very young and inexpensive Chablis.

dressed with balsamic vinegar An off-dry riesling from New Zealand is one option: it has a tinge of sweetness and vibrant acidity that reflects and meets those qualities in the vinegar with quite a crackle.

on toast The whites in the general avocado introduction above will work, of course. However, what I really love to drink with avocado

A

on sourdough, sprinkled with chilli flakes and dressed with good olive oil and a squeeze of lemon, is a piercing sauvignon blanc from Marlborough, New Zealand. The wine brings a luminous uplift to each forkful and its hints of nectarine and passion fruit take avocado out of a dimly lit room and back into the sun. My second choice would be a calmer sauvignon blanc from Australia's Adelaide Hills or an exuberant, green capsicum-scented sauvignon blanc from Leyda in Chile.

B

bacalao Salt cod is eaten throughout Spain and Portugal and served in so many different ways, with so many different sauces, that it is most straightforward to say the best wine to go with it is usually the local one. Does that sound like a cop-out? Then I'll add that if you have a soft spot for bacalao with waxy yellow boiled potatoes, Vinho Verde and verdejo are both good.

Or Maria José Sevilla has another option. The director of Wines from Spain in the UK is a bountiful fount of information on Spanish food and drink, with a laser-like instinct for finding the best restaurants in any town – I have never eaten badly in her company. She says: 'One drink is better than anything with bacalao. And that is cider. In the Basque country, after they press the apples but before they bottle the cider, in December, they taste it, and there are three dishes that are always cooked by the cider houses where Basques go to eat and taste. First, bacalao fritto – salt cod just fried in a bit of flour and egg. Second, tortilla, which is made by making a soffritto of chopped onions with little bits of red pepper and then breaking pieces of salt cod into crumbs and stirring them into it and using that mixture in the tortilla. I make this at home using fresh cod, because you can get such good cod in London. I salt it for just two or three hours beforehand; then it gets that magic that bacalao has when it's salted, but it's more delicate. And thirdly, pil-pil sauce, made with cod and garlic and olive oil, where the gelatin in the fish creates an emulsion with the oil in the pan. All of these are good with cider.'

bagna cauda Bright young dolcetto is delicious with this pungent garlic and anchovy dip from northern Italy. Gavi and arneis – two white wines from the same area – are good, refreshing alternatives.

baked beans Beans on toast and a quick glass of wine is up there on the 'too exhausted to cook but in need of a break' list of dinners. Baked beans are so sweet and so processed that it can be best if the wine is too. Just go for a cheapo supermarket red, which is likely to have a smidge of sugar in it. Otherwise open something fantastic and treat yourself. But drink it before and after the beans on toast, not while you eat.

banitsa A Bulgarian dish made by layering a mixture of eggs whisked with spinach and feta cheese between sheets of filo pastry and baking until risen and golden. I love eating this with simple, lemony white wines such as Soave or Gavi or pecorino, which cut across the fat, but it also works with heavier, oaked Bordeaux Blanc or assyrtiko. Rustic reds from Bergerac (for something heavier); from Marcillac or Beaujolais (for something light-bodied); or from Greece, Turkey or Bulgaria itself turn it into a more picnicky and casual meal. And I can testify that banitsa, which goes quite solid when it cools and sets, is very good food for a picnic or eating in the car on a long drive back from Cornwall.

barbecues At big barbecues where all kinds of meat, vegetables and fish will be thrown on to the coals, and there's a long table covered in bowls full of colourful salads, wine essentially needs to behave like a good guest: to have something to say for itself, to rub along well with everyone.

Barbecued food is usually strongly flavoured: smoky from the fire, pungent from the spices and rubs. And it's not just the food that is smoky. If you're standing around waving bellows and tongs, you'll have smoke in your eyebrows and the smell of burning charcoal up your nose. It's not like sitting in the cool of an immaculate restaurant eating food that someone else cooked out the back. It's like standing at a sweaty, shouty rock concert and being handed a hip flask. If what's in the flask is subtle, you won't even notice it under such sensory onslaught. To meet the heat and olfactory noise of a barbecue, go for bold reds from Chile, Argentina, California, Australia, Portugal or South Africa. Or play it the other way and pick a contrast: a refreshing light red, such as Beaujolais, marzemino or a cabernet franc from the Loire, maybe serving it slightly chilled to counteract the brawn of the food.

My go-to barbie red is the Mullineux Kloof Street Rouge from Swartland, South Africa – a loosely knit, open-hearted, liquoricey blend of syrah, carignan, mourvèdre and cinsault. It's not a total party monster, but it doesn't arrive wearing a lounge suit either.

Rosé is always a good barbecue swiller too. If the barbecue flavours are very robust, I like to go for a deeper-coloured rosé; if they are hot, perhaps a raspberry-coloured rosé that is not perfectly dry. This is a book about wine but, of course, it's not just wine that's good at barbecues. For instance, cider is great with juicy pork burgers; a golden ale such as Harviestoun Bitter & Twisted is beautiful with lemon-charred prawns; and a happy jug of sangria will tie the whole thing together.

Marc Kent of Boekenhoutskloof in South Africa, a country where they are rightly proud of their barbecues – or rather, braais – gave me the following recipe for a fiery barbecue sauce. He adapted it from a spicy sauce he first tasted in a rib shack in Anguilla. It can be used as a marinade for chicken wings, ribs or steak, or served as an accompaniment to barbecued meat. It is hot and it is full on and Marc recommends eating it with his Chocolate Block wine – a full on, sock it to 'em bottle of red made in the Cape from grenache, cinsault and syrah, whose tannins will aggravate the chilli in this sauce, which is why Marc likes the two together.

MARC KENT'S SPICY SMOKED BBQ SAUCE
Makes 1.5 litres

- 20 medium tomatoes (preferably Roma)
- 2 onions, peeled
- fresh chillies, to taste
- 8 tablespoons olive oil
- 250ml tomato ketchup
- 250ml tomato purée
- 375ml cider vinegar
- 4 tablespoons aged dark rum or brandy
- 125ml orange juice
- 4 tablespoons mild molasses
- 100g light brown sugar
- 2 tablespoons smoked Spanish paprika
- 4 teaspoons freshly ground black pepper, or to taste
- 8 large cloves of garlic, peeled and crushed
- ground chilli (optional)
- salt

B

Cut the tomatoes in half and scoop out the seeds. Place the tomatoes, cut side up, in a smoker on the opposite side to the heat source. Put the onions and chillies in with them and smoke until tender. Remove from the smoker. Peel the chillies and the tomatoes, saving as much juice as you can. Roughly chop the tomatoes, onions and chillies. Put the oil in a large cast-iron pan and heat until smoking. Add the tomatoes, onions and chillies and all the other ingredients and bring to a gentle simmer. Simmer for 2 hours, stirring occasionally, until the sauce has thickened. Allow to cool, then transfer to a blender and liquidize (you may have to do this in batches) until smooth. Season to taste, adding ground chilli if you want it hotter.

See also beef: barbecue sauce, burgers, chilli, five-spice, sausages.

beef Real traditionalists drink cabernet with lamb and pinot noir with beef, but bordeaux (and other cabernet-merlot blends) is also a favourite with Sunday roasts and chargrilled steaks – as are nebbiolo, Tuscan reds, Napa cabernets, Aussie syrahs, malbecs from Argentina . . . I could go on. In truth it's hard to go wrong when it comes to beef and a bottle of red, but some wines do seem more delicious with some plates of meat than others. The cuisson and the cut both have an impact on the type of wine I like to pick. Beef that is well-done tends to be enhanced by juicy, young wines and richer, riper reds from sunny climates that act as a flavour-boosting sauce for the drier meat. At the other end of the spectrum, the squidgy flesh of rare beef is good with more tannic and also with older wines. So with a well-cooked rump steak I might choose a soft, warm-climate cabernet-merlot to help bring some succulence to the meat, but with a rare sirloin perhaps a prickly young claret or maturing Chianti Classico. I'd put Barossa Shiraz with either.

As far as the cut goes, the fattier the meat the more it suits wines with good acidity and tannin that refresh the mouth in between forkfuls of food. But here are a few more specific ideas.

cuts and cooking styles
bresaola I often put this salty, air-dried beef with a juicy Italian red such as dolcetto or Lambrusco, but its intense beefiness also goes

well with the leather-and-red-berries taste of South African pinot noir. Then again, when it is served on an antipasti plate with rocket and mozzarella it tastes good with white sparkling Franciacorta, and if it's made into a salad with spinach or rocket and goat's curd, then I'd pick an oaked sauvignon blanc with the weight to meet the beef and the lithe fruitiness and acidity to suit the cheese.

carpaccio If there's lemon juice squeezed over the meat, pick a red with good savour, tannin and acidity – a softer red will taste oddly sweet and lacklustre. Italian reds usually have good bite that works well with lemon juice. Young and claret is good too.

chargrilled steak Amplify the smoky-sweet vibe of those caramelized black stripes by pouring a red that tastes of smoky oak.

cold roast beef Leftover beef tastes drier and more solid than it did half an hour after it came out of the oven, so I like to choose a more juicy wine to liven it up. Dolcetto is a favourite with cold roast beef with salads. Pinkish-crimson slices of cold roast topside eaten outside on a hot summer's day are very good washed down with a gorgeously ample, red-berry-scented garnacha from Campo de Borja in Spain; I love the generosity of the garnacha with the tender, cold meat, and this is a brilliant summer wedding combo too. With a dinner of cold roast beef and hot home-made chips, I often open a cosy Aussie cab-shiraz or a Côtes de Bordeaux, Castillon.

daubes, stews and casseroles Long, slow-cooked beef in a rich gravy sauce is one of the most 'friendly to red wines' dinners in existence. Choose any red you like, or look to marry the wine with the other ingredients in the casserole. I often slow-cook beef with thyme and anchovies, and love to eat it with fragrant Mediterranean red blends, such as Minervois, St Chinian, or wines from Corsica. One of my favourite ever dinners was a beef casserole eaten on a cold November night in a Cotswolds gastropub, with a bottle of Côtes du Roussillon that smelt of old leather, bonfires, autumn leaves and dried herbs.

See also boeuf bourguignon and boeuf à la gardiane.

fillet The tender softness of a fillet of beef is beautiful with pinot noir. Pick a luscious pinot from the Mornington Peninsula or

Sonoma to boost the juicy sweetness of a medium-cooked fillet, or a youthful red burgundy to add a slight prickle to one that is crimson in the middle. However it is cooked, fillet of beef also goes well with plush, velvety reds, such as those from Pomerol in Bordeaux, Bolgheri in Italy or Priorat in Spain. Fillet cooked with rosemary or bay leaves or served with redcurrant jelly suits one of the more floral, silky, blueberry-and-violet-scented malbecs from Argentina. This cut is also good with cinsault, and with Loire cabernet franc (Chinon, or Bourgueil or St Nicolas de Bourgueil) from a warm year, particularly if green spring vegetables are an accompaniment.

rib, rib-eye and tomahawk With the feral, earthy, bony flavours of a plainly cooked aged rib of beef; a rib-eye steak; or a tomahawk (a rib-eye steak with the full bone attached), I like an older wine that also has vestigial tastes of blood, soil, decay, tobacco, old leaves or mushrooms. Maturing bordeaux (all kinds of it) comes into its own here. Leathery Madiran, brooding Cahors, top-notch Chianti, Brunello di Montalcino, Barolo and mature northern Rhône reds or earthy syrah from elsewhere are excellent too, as are the malbecs made in Argentina by the likes of Mendel and Achaval Ferrer, which speak more of cedar and smoke than of luscious, bright fruit. If the rib of beef is to be served with sweet roasted root vegetables, or if the meat has less of a feral taste, then a good Rioja or Ribera del Duero will also make a fine accompaniment.

sirloin Sirloin accommodates more or less any red wine you throw at it. Personally, though, I favour wines with savoury notes. Sirloin steak usually has a thick ribbon of yellow fat that flavours the meat and cabernet-merlot blends and also sangiovese go well with this taste.

steak tartare The first time I ordered steak tartare I had no idea what I was doing. After the little patty of raw meat arrived at the table with all its condiments and a raw egg yolk, I politely sat and waited for the chef to come and cook it for me. It was about fifteen minutes before I nervously began to eat it, all the while expecting to be hounded out of the restaurant as a savage. With its capers, shallots, spices, and completely uncooked meat, steak tartare is the beef dish most suited to the firm edges of a claret from the Médoc, ideally one at Cru Bourgeois level. I once had a brilliant steak tartare at the elegant Le Colombier in London, washed down with my share of a bottle of Château Poujeaux. Young, unoaked or barely oaked nebbiolo is another good option.

tagliata Steak (usually either rib-eye or sirloin) that is served the Italian way – chargrilled, sliced, and mixed into a plateful of rocket and Parmesan, dressed with olive oil and lemon juice – needs wine with good acidity and tannin. First choice is a robust red from central Italy – Chianti, Brunello, Sagrantino di Montefalco. Second choice is a red from elsewhere in Italy.

topside (roast) Topside is the cut most commonly used for roast dinners and for me the colour of the meat, the temperature at which it's being eaten and the rest of the dinner play the biggest part in picking the wine. See also *cold roast beef* above.

See cold roast beef (p. 39).

accompaniments, rubs and seasonings
barbecue sauce The sticky sweetness of barbecue sauce, often used as a marinade for beef ribs, needs a loose, fruity wine such as Californian zinfandel or Chilean merlot.

béarnaise The tarragon flavour in béarnaise can be quite strong. It works just fine with cool-climate cabernet blends and is brilliant with the herbal scent of maturing wines from the southern Rhône – Vacqueyras, Sablet, Gigondas, Châteauneuf-du-Pape and so on.

black peppercorn crust Steak cooked with a black peppercorn crust has a beautiful spicy aroma that is reminiscent of violets. Please try this with a bottle of syrah, a grape that can also have a hauntingly floral, black-peppery scent. This profile is (famously) most often found on syrah from and around the Rhône, but I have also found it on syrah from Argentina, Australia, Chile and elsewhere.

See syrah for a recipe for 'Steak with freshly cracked black peppercorns' (p. 352).

celeriac purée The green notes of celeriac taste better with savoury rather than sweetly rich reds – Chianti rather than zinfandel; claret rather than Chilean cabernet sauvignon.

coriander, teriyaki, chilli and garlic rub This is a favourite marinade for either sirloin or a big rib of beef. I make it by mixing equal quantities of teriyaki sauce with Kikkoman less-salt soy sauce, a dash of sesame oil, finely chopped garlic and ginger root, and plenty of roughly chopped fresh coriander, and serve it with either a robust pinot noir from Australia, New Zealand, South Africa, the US or Chile, or with a cool-climate Australian shiraz.

green peppercorns With fiery peppercorns I avoid softer, richer, sweetly ripe reds and look for those with good tannin and acidity – wines from Bordeaux and Tuscany are usually good. With a creamy green peppercorn sauce, there's more latitude, and you can go for herbal reds such as those from the Rhône.

See also barbecues, beef Wellington, boeuf bourguignon, boeuf à la gardiane, burgers, chilli con carne, Chinese, cottage (or shepherd's) pie, meatballs, mustard, ragù alla bolognese, Thai beef salad.

horseradish Fiery accompaniments like horseradish steer me towards cooler-climate red wines, such as cabernet-based bordeaux or rustic Buzet or Bergerac.

mustard Mustard reduces the impact of tannin in a wine, so you can get away with a harsher, greener red – for instance, a tannic, green bordeaux tastes much fleshier and fruitier when you drink it with mustard.

beef Wellington The classic accompaniment is pinot noir, a grape that goes well with both the beef and the mushrooms inside the pastry case. Pick a pinot noir that is savoury rather than sweet. I often see this dish served with St Emilion, perhaps partly because 'beef Wellington' and 'St Emilion' are phrases that have immense celebratory menu appeal – you can just feel Christmas and festivities around the corner. The two do go well together. The slightly fruitcakey right-bank bordeaux has a richness that marries well with the rich food.

beetroot Beetroot's earthy taste is good with earthy versions of pinot noir and it can also go well with those dusty styles of cabernet sauvignon that make you think of the brown husk at the tip of a blackcurrant. There aren't many meals so big on beetroot that you'd be looking to find a wine that went with it, though, as the other ingredients tend to take over. For instance, one popular beetroot dish is beetroot and goat's curd salad, but I'd usually open a sauvignon blanc or a breezy white from the Savoie in France to placate the insistent goat's curd.

See cabernet sauvignon for a recipe for 'Beetroot risotto' (p.212).

beurre blanc I never like to let friends see how much butter has gone into this classic French sauce, which has just four ingredients: shallots, vinegar, white wine and a *lot* of butter. In her *Garden Cookbook* Sarah Raven uses it over egg tagliatelle with a purée of broad beans mixed with tiny, peeled broad beans, the colour of new leaves. I always eat this with Sardinian vermentino because I love the gentle, green flavours in the wine with the rich sauce and the tender beans, but another vermentino would do just as well. When beurre blanc is served with fish, try Chablis; grüner veltliner; Limoux or new-wave Australian chardonnay; sauvignon-semillon from Australia's Margaret River, or a white bordeaux from France. Failing that, find a good version of the consummate fish wine, a Muscadet sur lie, to bring out the more saline, oceanic qualities in the fish.

blinis Buckwheat pancakes with fishy toppings and crème fraîche go down best with ice-cold vodka, knocked back in a shiver of shots. If wine is called for, look for a knife-sharp white, such as aligoté, or a lean, lemony white from Greece, or try Muscadet, a white that likes fish and smells of a cold grey sea. The sur lie versions, matured on their lees, have more texture and a yeasty flavour that works well here.

boeuf bourguignon Don't get into a stew about what to drink with boeuf bourguignon. As its name suggests, this beef casserole is traditionally made and served with red burgundy, but in practice any country-style French red will do the trick, from Fitou or Corbières to a basic claret or Bergerac to a Costières de Nîmes or Côtes du Rhône.

boeuf à la gardiane This slow-cooked beef, red wine and black olive casserole is from the Gard département of France, which takes in the towns of Nîmes and Uzès, as well as the magnificent

B

Pont du Gard Roman aqueduct. It is not only a delicious dish but also a brilliant backdrop to all kinds of French red wine. When I have to do a tasting of different reds from Bordeaux, the Languedoc, Provence, the Rhône or south-west France, I routinely make Elizabeth David's version from *French Provincial Cooking* to eat with whichever bottle I decide to drink for dinner at the end of it.

I cooked boeuf à la gardiane for a wine merchant, Tom Ashworth, one evening, because he had promised to bring a mystery bottle of wine and I knew that this magical dish would see the wine right. Tom told me that his stepfather, Robin Yapp, the founder of Yapp Brothers, which specializes in wines from the south of France, makes the exact same dinner when cooking for friends, and for the same reasons. The stew has a salty herbiness that plays into the wilder nature of those reds that taste of the tinder-dry thyme and olive leaves of the garrigue; sits well with the dark nature of northern Rhône syrah; and allows the emotive fire of a Châteauneuf-du-Pape to flare. And it's kind to the more architectural, structured wines of Bordeaux, which taste calm and intelligent beside it.

bolognese see *ragù alla bolognese*

bone marrow 'I wanted to live deep and suck out all the marrow of life,' wrote Henry Thoreau. Eating bone marrow is an atavistic activity. There is a flavour that stirs something deep within. Eating it with wine that has the vibe of mall music, or a boyband hit, is a horrible thing to do. Open rosé if you want, but make it a rosé from Provence – these wines are more thoughtful than frivolous, even when they are easy to drink. I don't mind white wine either if it's simple and saline, or one of those French country wines that are impossible to describe. But the best wines with bone marrow are reds that taste of the earth and the land, that have a savour or a feel of the farmyard, that taste as if they were made by hand rather than on gleaming production lines. You might find this in the Côtes du Roussillon, in Bordeaux, Chianti, Montalcino, St Chinian or the Douro, among other places.

boquerones see *anchovies*

bottarga The Mediterranean delicacy of salted, pressed and sun-baked roe of the tuna or grey mullet is great with whites such as falanghina, greco di tufo or fiano, which bring out its fruitiness. Ribolla gialla, Verdicchio di Matelica or vermentino will emphasize its marine salinity. These are all Italian wines, but if you want something a bit different go for a fiano made by one of the more experimental Australian producers (Coriole and Fox Gordon both do one). This grape smells of pine nuts, orange blossom and basil and in Australian hands it becomes more rounded and generous, adding an extra swish and a more contemporary feel to the dish.

bouillabaisse This Mediterranean fish stew, a speciality of Marseilles, works well with limpid rosé from Provence; a deeper-coloured and more robust rosé from the Languedoc; or the soft curves of a Rioja Rosado. Spanish verdejo or Portuguese Vinho Verde are thirst-slaking white options. For a wine that gently meets some of the complexities of the seafood broth, try a glass of local Cassis – not a blackcurrant liqueur but a white wine made from marsanne, clairette, ugni blanc and sauvignon blanc. Wines from the AOP Cassis can taste delicate and drily herbaceous at first, but they have concealed might and staying power. Along similar lines, the garlic, saffron and tomatoes in the stew work well with white blends from the Rhône, also made with marsanne and roussanne; and sometimes also with floral viogniers, which taste of almond kernels and hay and waxy white flowers. The nutty, sourdough scent of a dry sherry, or a vin jaune from the Jura, riffs along nicely with the rich seafood broth too. With all those confident flavours, bouillabaisse is forceful enough to survive a red wine such as a young, inexpensive Bandol (don't go for too good a name as the robustness of the young wine will then overpower the food). Tomato-based fish stews also work well with cheaper, rustic reds, such as those from the Dão or the Douro in Portugal, or even a simple Chianti.

Boxing Day leftovers, aka the great Turkey Buffet Now is the moment to pull out the aromatic pinot gris that goes so well with turkey and trimmings, but that you didn't feel like drinking on Christmas Day itself. Suddenly, the day after the excess, a gently perfumed, chilled white, perhaps off-dry (yes – sugar is always a welcome hangover aid), is much more appealing.

'Pinot gris is definitely Boxing Day wine,' says Tim Adams, who makes wine in Clare Valley, Australia. 'On Christmas Day we drink magnums of The Fergus – our grenache, tempranillo, shiraz, mourvèdre blend – and on Boxing Day we open pinot gris.'

Of course, if you've got Christmas dinner wines as well as food to spare they will taste great all over again. Otherwise, bright, young, refreshing reds are good with the firmer consistency of cold meat – think cheap young claret, dolcetto or Beaujolais Villages. In our family, with Christmas Eve turkey sandwiches and Boxing Day leftovers, we like to drink white wines from the Rhône (Côtes du Rhône or white Châteauneuf). These are wintry whites with a hint of warmth, and a subtle taste of ripe pears, white peaches, sushi ginger and heavy blossom, that have a celebratory feel and go well with all the pork products (spicy sausageballs, sausagemeat and chestnut stuffing, chipolatas wrapped in bacon) that we have on our plates alongside the turkey and creamy, clove-scented bread sauce. Failing all those, pull out the prosecco. Its gentle bubbles and slight sweetness are a real perk-up.

See also turkey sandwiches.

braai see *barbecues*

brill If it is simply grilled or fried and plated up with lemon, then chardonnay will do the trick. Brill is often served with a red wine sauce (and sometimes also roasted root vegetables) or with lentils and in this case a good accompaniment is a red wine such as Bierzo from Spain.

broad beans Pale yet also intensely verdant, double-podded broad beans are one of life's great luxuries. The time invested in the second peeling is considerable but worth it. As with peas, wines that work well are those that taste green (of leaves, herbs and grass) and of cool citrus and that remind you of spring. With a broad bean and pea risotto, good options are sauvignon blanc – from the Loire, the Awatere Valley in Marlborough or Leyda in Chile; the scything edge of an Awatere riesling; verdejo from Spain; grüner veltliner from Austria; vermentino, verdicchio, cortese (used to make Gavi) or pecorino from Italy. These wines also go well with crostini piled with mashed broad beans mixed with gratings of Pecorino cheese and mint and olive oil (though I suspect you've probably got the prosecco out for that – good choice).

When eating broad beans with creamy cheeses like ricotta, I lean more towards slightly creamier wines: for instance, a Lugana from north-east Italy or a super-Soave. With the recipe below, a taut, lean, brightly lemony contemporary Australian chardonnay is also good and will illuminate the freshness of the spring vegetables. If you choose a wine that's oaked or, when you open it, marked by the struck-match characteristic known as reduction often found in these wines, then that will also underscore the toasty tang of the sourdough.

BROAD BEAN, PEA SHOOT, ASPARAGUS AND RICOTTA BOWL
Serves 2

- 225g frozen broad beans
- about 10 spears of asparagus
- 4 handfuls pea shoots
- 125g fresh garden peas
- 2 sprigs of mint, leaves removed from stems
- 4 generous tablespoons fresh ricotta
- grated zest of half a lemon
- 2 tablespoons good olive oil
- 4 slices sourdough toast
- salt

Put the broad beans into a heatproof jug or bowl, cover with boiling water, leave for a minute, then drain. Slip the beans out of their skins and put to one side. Trim the hard base of the asparagus stalks and then cook on a hot griddle pan, turning occasionally, until slightly charred but still crunchy. Arrange the pea shoots, raw peas, broad beans, asparagus and mint leaves in two bowls with a couple of spoonfuls of ricotta on the side of each. Mix the lemon zest and olive oil and drizzle over the top. Serve with a couple of slices of sourdough toast per bowl, drizzled with olive oil and salt to taste.

Broad beans also go with red wines that taste of spring, such as young, unoaked cabernet franc from the Loire or a sappy light gamay, perhaps from Touraine, where an edge of earth kicks in with the green.

bubble and squeak My friend, wine hurricane Joe Wadsack, always says that leftovers taste better if you eat them with the person who shared the original dinner. I feel the same way about the wine that might go with this fry-up of mashed potato, leftover sprouts, cabbage and bacon. It should just be something that's knocking around in your kitchen.

burgers (beef) Arguably the ultimate food for red wine, the (beef) burger makes nearly every type look good. Especially if it is home-made with decent, 20 per cent fat, butcher's mince (except for salt and pepper, I don't put anything else in my burgers). And even more especially if it is cooked rare, then its soft, pink middle will snuggle down with whatever delicious bottle you feel like opening, be it a roasted-fruit-scented Central Otago pinot noir, a slightly wild Sicilian nero d'avola, a lightweight Beaujolais or a chunky South African cabernet. If anything provides more of a steer on what you might want to be drinking, it's the garnishes, sauces and side salads.

Melted cheese and fruity ketchup can still handle more or less any red. As soon as you add smoky barbecue sauce, the heat of chilli, blue cheese, punchy gherkins or crunchy slaw made with chipotle mayonnaise, you'll need a red that can match the intensity of these rich flavours. Bigger, fruitier, riper reds that fit the bill include carmenère-cabernet sauvignon-merlot from Chile (I absolutely love Casa Silva's version with home-made burgers); sun-baked reds from Puglia, Italy's heel (for instance, Salice Salentino); and malbec from Argentina. Relaxed American zinfandel, with its high alcohol and smell of raspberries, brambles, cough mixture and dust, is particularly good with chipotle and barbecue sauces, as is carmenère, which has quite a rugged texture. And if you're intending to blacken the meat on a barbecue and use very intense, shouty sauces, then pinotage from South Africa is probably the loudest wine of all.

B

burrata Indulgently soft burrata is a cheese made from mozzarella and cream. It's good with wines that enhance its luxurious texture. Top-end Soaves (or wines from Anselmi, which opted out of the Soave classification) have a savoury custard and nutty-pear taste that adds a touch of gilded grandeur to the plate. An always-discreet Lugana, also from north-east Italy, slips in quietly alongside it. Deep-coloured, just-off-dry rosé will meld beautifully with the burrata and amplify its pillowy texture. At a 'Wine Wars' dinner at Arbutus restaurant in Soho that kicked off with a burrata and compressed watermelon starter, Wine Car Boot founder Ruth Spivey poured a glossy, watermelon-pink Monferrato Chiaretto from Villa Sparina, made from dolcetto and barbera, to go with it. It was a huge hit.

butter Even I would not eat just a slab of butter for dinner, though if you've ever seen how much I put on toast you may argue that I come close. Still, buttery (and creamy) sauces have a richness that leads you away from poky-elbowed, shrill wines like sauvignon blanc or verdejo and towards a more curvaceous chardonnay (oaked or unoaked), marsanne, roussanne or oaked chenin blanc. For instance, sole meunière (cooked in a brown butter sauce) is much better with a white burgundy than with a fresh Loire sauvignon blanc.

An exception is beurre blanc, the classic French sauce made by reducing vinegar with chopped shallots and stirring in huge quantities of melted butter, because the acidity of the vinegar counters some of the richness. The acid in the vinegar needs to be taken care of, so you can still do chardonnay – it needs to be a vibrant one, such as a new-wave Australian chardonnay (low in alcohol, bright with acidity, yet still with curves) – but fresher wines often work better.

See also beurre blanc.

C

Cajun Cajun food is a very broad term that covers a whole spectrum of dishes but, as a general rule, its warmth, in which bell peppers, onions, celery, shrimp and pork mingle with the red heat of Tabasco, doesn't work at all well with cool northern European reds. It prefers the more laid-back, throaty flavours of American zinfandel, primitivo from Italy's heel, Chilean carmenère-cabernet, bonarda from Argentina, the Rhône Ranger wines (red or white) from California, or a Rioja with lots of American oak and ideally a graciano component. Fried shrimp and crab do go well with albariño, though, and spicy fish and white meat can, as ever, work well with off-dry riesling. Beer is also a good bet.

cake A slice of cake really belongs with a good cup of tea or coffee, in my view. But there are a few occasions on which you might want to drink wine with cake, and also a few glorious cake and wine couplings, most of them involving sweet fortified wine. So here is a quick guide.

birthday cake If you are drinking wine and eating cake on a birthday, then you probably have fizz in your glass. The sweeter the better, as dry wine tastes odd after sugar, so prosecco over cava and a sweeter champagne (ideally a demi-sec) over a zero dosage.

chocolate cake A very simple chocolate cake (no icing, no cream) or brownie is lightened by the refreshing neroli scent of a Muscat de Beaumes de Venise. For ideas of what to drink with richer chocolate gateaux and dessert-like tortes, see *chocolate*.

See also chocolate.

Christmas cake Sweet oloroso sherry has a rich, raisin and roasted nut taste that combines well with dense fruitcake. For celebratory occasions, try a demi-sec champagne.

C

fruitcake Fruitcake of all kinds, not just the rich Christmas version, is good with sweeter sherries. Cakes that are more cake than fruit are also lovely with a glass of Madeira.

Madeira cake Plain Madeira cake, made with butter and baked so that the top erupts and crusts over, is good with tawny port, sweet sherries, Marsala and with bual or malmsey Madeira. The simple flavours of the cake act as a canvas for the richer, dried fruit and nut echoes in the glass.

seed cake The St John chef Fergus Henderson introduced the excellent habit of drinking a glass of old Madeira (the proper stuff, not the cheapo supermarket cooking wine) with seed cake at elevenses.

wedding cake All the same suggestions apply as for *birthday cake* and *Christmas cake* above.

See also tarte tartin.

calamares fritos see *fritto misto.*

Camembert This cheese makes red wine taste terrible. Or 'oh-fule', as one Frenchman once put it to me. As in, 'The French tradition of baguette Camembert with red wine is oh-fule.' I'm actually quite happy if there's a big mouthful of crusty baguette in between a tumbler of rustic red, me and the Camembert, but it's not much fun eating a polite little cheese plate of Camembert while drinking red wine. The two seem to curdle in the mouth. A low-acid wine such as a rosé from Provence is a happier option.

capers The salty, vinegary pinch of a pickled caper will floor any wine that does not meet it with confident acidity. Oaked, high-alcohol chardonnay, for instance, tastes fat and flabby and uncomfortable if you encounter it straight after a mouthful of capers. As a quick rule of thumb, you can usually rely on Italy to provide wines with good acidity, both red and white.

capsicum see *red pepper*

C

carbonara Eggy pasta (spaghetti or penne, ideally) with garlicky bacon bits and black pepper is one of the great dishes of Lazio. A relatively neutral white is cleansing against the deep yellow egg yolks and cheese. The local option would be Frascati. A Soave, or a pinot grigio from Italy or Hungary fulfils the same role. The sharp little bubbles of a sparkling wine are also refreshing in between cheesy, eggy mouthfuls. I would go for something like a Graham Beck from South Africa, or for a dry red Lambrusco, which isn't a conventional match by any stretch but hits a mood.

cassoulet This one-pot Gascon dish incorporating haricots blancs, pork, duck or goose confit, Toulouse sausages, lamb and goose fat is French slow-cooking at its best. The local wine options offer a paradigm for food and wine matching guidelines. Want to pick a wine that refreshes and rinses your mouth in between forkfuls? Try a young Gaillac Rouge or a Marcillac, a light-bodied, acidic red made in the Aveyron from fer servadou, which tastes of blood and iron. Prefer a wine that matches the heft and mass of the plate of food? How about a Cahors, young or old, made from malbec, once so dense and dark the wines were known as 'the black wines of Cahors'? Doug Wregg, a buyer at the wine importer Les Caves de Pyrène, is particularly eloquent on this match. In the company's wine list, he writes: 'Eating cassoulet without a glass of wine is like trying to carve your way through the Amazonian jungle with a pair of blunt nail clippers. We should accept that some combinations are meant to be. Cahors is renowned for its medicinal, iodine flavour; it expresses notes of tea, fennel, dried herbs and figs; it has a pleasant astringency and a lingering acidity. Cassoulet is crusty, oozy and gluey, beans bound by fat. The food requires a wine of certain roughness and ready digestibility. Sweet, jammy oaky reds and powerful spicy wines lack the necessary linear quality.'

I also like drinking natural wines with this slow food: as a group, they have an atmosphere and gentle, steady rustic sensibility that work very well here. A syrah or gamay from the grower Hervé Souhaut would be just about perfect. Or a Morgon – Beaujolais's meatiest cru – from Julien Sunier, Domaine M. Lapierre or Jean Foillard.

C

cauliflower cheese There are two ways to go with cauliflower cheese. For maximum snugness, and to emphasize the cosy-blanket aspect to this nursery food, pick a chardonnay whose creamy texture will meld into the cheesy white sauce. It doesn't matter whether the chardonnay is Australian, Chilean, or an inexpensive white burgundy. Go for your comfort chardonnay, and if you don't have one get one. Mine is Domaine Mallory et Benjamin Talmard Mâcon-Villages. For an (arguably) more sophisticated combination that feels like wrapping up in a puffa jacket and woolly bobble hat (that bit's the cauliflower cheese) and going out into the cold snow (that bit's the wine), pick a light red wine with a bit of cut and serve it chilled. Suitable reds here include trousseau or ploussard from the Jura in France; an inexpensive Bourgogne Rouge; gamay; Marcillac; Bardolino; a very light Valpolicella; and Fronsac, that lightest and greenest of wines from Bordeaux.

caviar Vodka, poured ice cold from the deep freeze, is the classic accompaniment to caviar and it does matter what sort. A friend once complained about being given vodka that 'cut my mouth to ribbons'. Was he maybe being a bit hysterical? Well, we are talking about a food that is classically served on special mother-of-pearl spoons, so I think we can also be pernickety about the vodka. It must be wheat vodka, which has a creamy, broad, gentle texture and does not interrupt the sensation of silky little balls moving smoothly across your tongue until they burst in an explosion of salt and sea spray. Rye vodka (Polish vodka is typically made with rye) has a sharper, needling texture. It might not *quite* cut your mouth to ribbons, but it does spoil the luxurious flow. Very good champagne with a high pinot noir/meunier content (for instance, Bollinger) is the celebratory alternative.

celeriac Even when it's only a vegetable with a main, or in a salad, the green flavours of celeriac steer my choice away from sweet or jammy reds or blowsy whites and towards wines with savour and acidity. With roast beef, say, the undergrowth flavours of celeriac would lean me towards claret over a richer, riper cabernet sauvignon or merlot.

C

Celeriac remoulade with Bayonne ham This is particularly good with reds that have some edge and, again, acidity. Examples: Beaujolais Villages, simple young bordeaux, Marcillac. It also goes well with nervy whites. Examples: grassy semillon-sauvignon blends; sauvignon blanc with a touch of oak for body – the ham will thank you for it; grüner veltliner; or, my favourite in this instance, petite arvine which grows in Alpine regions.

ceviche This dish of raw fish, cured in lemon or lime juice and served with chilli and maybe also chopped spring onions, coriander or avocado, needs an acerbic wine to handle the citrus. When guacamole and coriander are involved, aromatic torrontes from Argentina is a good breezy, floral option. Young semillon from the Hunter Valley in Australia works well, as do the rich sauvignon blancs from Marlborough, New Zealand and colombard-ugni blanc blends from Languedoc.

charcuterie A plate of cured ham or a wooden board set out with salami and a sharp little knife so you can hack off chunks screams for a glass of wine. It is hard to pick badly but, as ever, local is always good. A few suggestions: with Teruel ham, a red from Aragon – perhaps a Calatayud; with fatty wild boar salami, a sharp little Chianti; with saucisson sec, the wild buck and kick of a young Cahors; with chewy biltong, the leathery flavours of old-school South African pinotage or cabernet sauvignon. Part of the joy of red wine with charcuterie is that protein softens its tannins and, if you have a feral young red, its acidity is offset by any fattiness in the meat.

White wine is often overlooked as a partner for charcuterie, though, and it is excellent with cured ham. Pick a white that is glossy and has bounce as well as freshness (none of your mean little razor-blade whites) and it will bring out the succulence of the meat. Whites that go particularly well with cured ham include white Rioja (oaked or otherwise); petite arvine (this one's a big favourite – it's an Alpine grape found in Switzerland as well as the Val d'Aosta region of Italy around Mont Blanc); godello; Jurançon sec (from the Pyrenees in France); and Jura whites.

Of course, one of the great cured ham wines is sherry. The salty, iodine riff of manzanilla; the sourdough punch of fino; the intensity of palo cortado . . . Take your pick.

cheese Cheese is eaten enthusiastically with wine but the two are not always the happiest of bedfellows: the creamy fat that coats your mouth can make it hard to taste the wine at all. Often a pint of beer is a much better bet than a glass of wine – especially with the English cheese, vinegary pickled onions and slab of fatty pork pie in a ploughman's lunch. However, beer is not always what you want, so here are a few guidelines to getting the most out of cheese and wine.

cheesy dinners

For many dishes that are rich in cooked cheese (for instance, fondue, macaroni cheese, spaghetti carbonara, banitsa), a white wine with good acidity is the natural choice because the acidity will slice through the gloop. Think bright Gavi or Frascati rather than oaked chardonnay. Light, acidic reds such as Bardolino, Marcillac or Valpolicella will do the same job. With richer cheese and tomato dishes, such as aubergine parmigiana or baked and stuffed onions, try reds with grainy tannins as well as fresh bite, such as nebbiolo, lagrein or sangiovese. I love the prickly feel of acid and tannin as they cut through the cheese.

Some raw cheeses, such as feta or goat's curd, have such a tang that red wine – especially oaked and/or tannic reds – can seem to curdle in the mouth. These cheeses tend to settle better with a sharp white. Think of this if you are adding cheese to a plate of food, because the cheese may change the colour of wine that brings out the best in the food. For instance, I'd probably pick a juicy, cherry-ish red like dolcetto to drink with an autumn salad of lightly dressed spinach, rocket, bresaola and quartered figs. Stick a goat's curd dressing on there and suddenly the red isn't as appetizing as the glossy grapefruit taste of an oaked sauvignon blanc.

If you want to wallow in cheesy dinner with wine, then friends recommend visiting Bernard Antony at Fromagerie Antony in Alsace, where you can book a special dinner at which cheese is served in every course, and wine carefully selected to match. One friend says, 'We often have a first course of Crottins and Cotat. Then we tend to move into Burgundy, and the Rhône, through Alsace,

C

there's always a bit of vendage tardive. You might have one with potatoes, with sublime, wonderfully salted butter ... It's a genius place.' And one that would give you greedy cheesy tummy, I am sure. But probably be worth it.

the cheeseboard

The fantasy of cheese and wine is that a cheese plate is a civilized way to carry on drinking once the main bit of dinner is over. The reality is that much cheese murders much red wine (or vice versa). There are times when this can be a good thing. The old wine trade saying 'Buy on an apple, sell on cheese' isn't based on the idea that cheese flatters wine, more that cheese flatters ropy wine by dulling your ability to taste it at all, which is extremely helpful if you're trying to flog a duff bottle. It's also part of the reason why the field labourer or beach picnicker's lunch of a hunk of cheese with a tin mug of very rough red is such satisfying sustenance.

Once you move up the scale with the wine, the problems begin. Strong cheese is particularly hard on mature fine wine. Hugh Johnson talks about delicate old wine opening out like a peacock's tail, but this is often entirely obliterated by the pong, the acid and the fat, so uncorking a bottle of precious old red with the cheeseboard is not necessarily the greatest plan.

Here are a few guidelines, followed by a short and very far from comprehensive list of happy combinations.

1. Local cheese and local wine often taste great together – for instance, burgundy is good with Époisses – but don't open a special bottle, as the cheese will overpower it.

2. White wine is almost always better than red.

   Eric Monneret, director of Château La Pointe, fulminates that, 'There are only three kinds of cheese for red wine. Old Gouda. St Nectaire from the Massif Central. And Brebis, from the Pyrenees is not bad, though it's better with white.' That's a very Francocentric view. I can think of a handful more, from inside and outside France (including Comté, see below), but the point is well made.

3. Sweet and fortified wines are good with cheese.
   a) The salty pungency of a blue cheese often works well with the luscious, fruity quality of, say, an off-dry pinot gris or riesling, or a properly sweet Muscat de Beaumes de Venise.
   b) Just as dried fruit and nuts go well with certain cheeses, so (with the same cheeses) do the fortified wines that also taste of fruit and nuts. Think sherry (especially amontillado, palo cortado and oloroso), Madeira, tawny port and Marsala.

A few good partnerships:

- grainy Parmesan with old Valpolicella or Amarone
- Mont d'Or and savagnin
- blue cheese with blanc de blancs champagne
- proper Cheddar with white burgundy
- Comté or grainy Mimolette with claret
- Munster with gewürztraminer
- mozzarella's creamy texture is good with succulent wines – try a darker rosé, such as a Chiaretto

See also banitsa, burrata, Camembert, cauliflower cheese, Comté, fondue, Greek salad, jacket potato, macaroni cheese, omelette, Stilton, soufflé.

chestnuts When these starchy nuts are used to flavour a stuffing or polenta I would be more likely to veer towards a fuller-flavoured, earthy wine. They are rarely the dominant flavour in a meal, but wines that go well with chestnuts include reds from Piemonte and the Languedoc.

chicken Roast chicken is anything goes territory. No wine is able to spoil the enjoyment of a good roast chicken (and vice versa). Stick a bird in the oven, baste it every so often with some fat and its own juices, uncork a bottle of a wine you love, and you are off. There is no need to keep to white, either, especially if the roast is a Label Anglais or proper free-range farm chicken that's had lots of chance to run around.

There are a few notably good roast chicken combinations:

- chardonnay with chicken slathered in butter so that the skin is crispy and golden and the juices are sticky and buttery
- white burgundy or oaked semillon-sauvignon from Margaret River or Bordeaux with chicken roasted with tarragon butter massaged under its skin
- light red (Valpolicella; light Chianti; Bourgogne Rouge, Bierzo) with chicken roasted with thyme
- Italian red with chicken roasted River Café 'festive' style, with nutmeg and wrapped in prosciutto
- left-bank bordeaux with roast chicken cooked to Thomas Keller's recipe (it is in his *Bouchon* cookbook), which calls for the bird to be roasted with thyme and then served with a slab of ice-cold unsalted butter and mustard on the table. You eat each morsel with butter and mustard.

Mostly, though, with roast chicken the mood of the drinkers dictates the wine and with other dishes it's the sauces and other ingredients that inform the choice.

coronation chicken This Seventies-tastic dish with its curry spices and sweet raisins really does work with Seventies wine – a medium-dry riesling from Germany.

with forty cloves of garlic An aromatic French classic in which a jointed chicken is cooked slowly with forty whole unpeeled cloves of garlic, thyme, white wine and carrots, so that when the lid is lifted from the pot all the fragrance pours out. Brilliant with a white from the Rhône in France, for choice a simple Côtes du Rhône. These blends of varieties such as marsanne, roussanne, viognier, grenache blanc and clairette tend to be forgotten, but they are gentle, textured and subtle, often with a mild almond-blossom fragrance.

griddled chicken More or less any white, rosé or light red goes (depending on what you're eating the chicken with), but the smoky taste of an oaked sauvignon blanc-semillon blend from Margaret River in Australia or Bordeaux is good with those black grill lines.

Kiev Oozing with garlic butter and covered with crispy breadcrumbs, chicken Kiev goes well with a crisp white such as vermentino, sauvignon blanc or picpoul. A bright young chardonnay, with lowish alcohol and good acidity, will also cut through the fat.

liver For fried chicken livers, still pink on the inside and tossed in a peppery watercress, spinach and bacon salad, dressed with olive oil and vinegar that has also been used to deglaze the pan, open a bottle of light sangiovese (such as a young and inexpensive Chianti, but not one that is heavily oaked or a riserva style). This grape has the acidity to cope with the salad dressing and the earthiness to meet the liver, and it's refreshing too.

smoked chicken Oak-aged chardonnay has the toasty edge that will go with the smoky chicken.

See also coq au vin.

chickpeas Sangiovese and chickpeas both have an earthy taste and grainy feel and they go well together. Zuppa di ceci – chickpea soup, a kind of thick, granular purée eaten with toasted bread drizzled with olive oil – is a classic Tuscan dish and it tastes good with a simple Chianti (made from sangiovese). Chickpeas also turn up a lot in Middle Eastern and Spanish food, such as hummus; salads; and casseroles with chorizo, spinach, squid, garlic, chicken and/or potatoes. They are robust, so a red such as a simple tempranillo, Côtes du Rhône or Bierzo, or a more gutsy wine from Lebanon, Rioja, or Ribera del Duero, often seems more appropriate than a white – particularly if the stew is flavoured with smoked paprika. If opting for a rosé with a chickpea casserole, steer away from delicate pinks from Provence and towards a fuller, weightier Rioja Rosado or Languedoc pink.

chilli GAME-CHANGER It's no exaggeration to say that we don't so much taste chilli as feel it as a blaze of pain. The active ingredient in a jalapeño, Dorset Naga, Trinidad Scorpion or any other kind of chilli pepper (as well as the pepper spray used in riot control) is a compound called capsaicin. It's capsaicin that is responsible for the sensation that your mouth is on fire and it does not activate the taste buds but the nociceptors (pain receptors).

Thanks to the work of Professor David Julius at the University of California in San Francisco, we know that the part of our sensory network that responds to capsaicin is a specific ion channel on sensory nerve endings in the mouth called TRPV1 (it's pronounced 'trip vee one'). This same channel is also part of our warning system for potentially dangerous levels of heat: TRPV1 is sparked into life when it encounters tissue-damaging temperatures above 43.25°C, which is why, when it's activated by chilli (and also, to a lesser extent, garlic), we're tricked into experiencing it as a burn.

The stinging sensation of heat that chilli brings to the mouth, tongue and lips has a strong effect on the perception of everything else we taste while under its influence. Take a sip of wine while your mouth is on fire and you'll barely recognize it as the one you were drinking two minutes earlier. The fruitiness seems to drop out, leaving the wine stripped, featureless and flat. Chilli also heightens perception of tannins, so that even a relatively gentle red wine suddenly acquires a drying astringency and rough sinew.

The question is: when picking a drink to sip with chilli, what do you want to achieve?

extreme chilli
To up the burn factor, go for big, tannic red wines
Aggression in the form of a red-hot, full-on mouth attack. Is this appealing? The ultra-runners of chilli-eating know who they are. They don't think twice about ordering a dish in their local Indian if it is plastered with heat warnings and pictograms of multiple red chillies. Very likely, they board planes with a travel-size bottle of Tabasco rattling around with the toothpaste in their plastic liquids bag. A crime reporter friend of mine munches bags of raw bird's-eyes – I'm talking chillies, not fish fingers – like the rest of us snack on edamame. He would stare at me in slack-jawed incomprehension if I tried to have a discussion about choosing a drink to mitigate the effect of the burn. I mean, what burn? What's the problem?

If ultra-chilli-eaters care at all about what they wash the chilli down with, it's all about stoking the discomfort. To square the burn by adding a clash of violent astringency, then choose a big, tannic red wine. You know how tea tastes less tannic when you add milk? Well, drinking tannic red wine with chilli in your mouth is like taking the milk out of the tea – and then some. Let that astringency loose. A young cabernet sauvignon, spiky syrah or malbec should do it.

softly, softly
To cool things down, there are a couple of options

1. Yoghurt-based drinks such as lassi
   I once popped a padron pepper into my mouth while hosting a food and wine class. It was a hot one. A very, very hot one. I had no choice but to bolt to the fridge, pour myself a large glass of full-fat milk and drink until it was finished. As it turned out, almost all the peppers were hot. Man by woman, my class tried to contain themselves before flinging away their pride and making a grab for the milk carton. One or two tried to tough it out, but the tears streaming from their eyes gave them away. It's the casein – a protein – in milk and yoghurt that soothes the fire of chilli by interfering with the reaction between the pain receptors and the capsaicin. This is why traditional Indian lassi – a yoghurt-based drink that may be flavoured with mango or simply drunk plain – is such a good idea with curried food. And, indeed, why yoghurt-based sauces such as raita are often served on the side.

2. Wines: lighter reds, fruity whites and rosés, and sweetness
   For a more harmonious approach with wine, steer away from tannin and oak and seek out sugar, as this will help to counteract some of the stripping effect of the chilli. For reds, that means softer, lighter-bodied wines, such as inexpensive New World pinot noir, or smooth, fruity wines like bonarda from Argentina, tempranillo, and plush Chilean merlot. Look out, too, for natural reds that have been made using whole-bunch fermentation which often have a rounded, gentle glow that can sit well

C

with the mild warmth of, say, a rich chilli con carne. Cheap supermarket reds often have their fruitiness boosted by a small, hidden quantity (about 5g per litre to be technical) of sugar, and this makes it easier to taste the wine when you are eating chilli.

For whites and rosés, round and fruity is better than piercing and narrow. Chilli blocks out much of a wine's rounded succulence – it can turn a brisk white into a howl of barbed wire, or simply make it disappear altogether, which is not ideal. As with reds, a touch of sweetness, just a little, helps the wine to hold its own. It won't so much taste sweet as leave the wine feeling nicely filled out.

If you want sauvignon blanc, for example, try picking a sweetly fruity example from Chile or New Zealand rather than a stern and steely Sancerre. Whites that have texture and body tend to sit more comfortably against spice than linear whites that are all about citrus and refreshment. Try pinot gris rather than pinot grigio (it's the winemaker's shorthand for the sweeter, more floral style of the same grape). Consider off-dry German riesling – say, a kabinett style, which is sweet like biting into a melon is sweet and can be a real hit with Thai-influenced salads and curries. And don't write off Mateus Rosé, which also has a bit of sparkle (see below) and goes extremely well with Indian takeaways, as well as Vietnamese salads and Thai curries.

the fizz phenomenon
Fizzy drinks of all kinds – lager, G&T, sparkling water, soft drinks, or wine from Vinho Verde to prosecco – also mitigate the burning effect of chilli

Bubbles – a G&T, sparkling wine or lager – are a classic Indian restaurant fallback option and the science behind how we taste helps to explain why. I had always presumed that fizz went well with curry because the physical sensation of bubbles bursting against your tongue acted as a refreshing respite to the heat. This is completely wrong. Carbonated drinks react in the mouth in a number of ways. They taste slightly sour because, when the carbon dioxide reacts with water, carbonic acid is created. But that gentle nipping and pinching at your tongue is not bubbles bursting, it's the carbon dioxide stimulating our pain receptors – and involving the same ion channel (TRPV1) that is used to detect chilli and heat – to create a pleasing tingle. You could say that we experience the fizz in fizzy drinks in the same way as we experience a mild dose of chilli, and perhaps that's why it feels so good to drink fizzy beer, wine or soft drinks with hot, spicy food. For specific recommendations, see individual dishes.

chilli con carne The combination of spice, tomatoes and a meaty sauce enriched with plain chocolate makes chilli con carne a gleaming, bold oil painting of a dish. A similar bold intensity is found in reds that ripen under a warm Chilean, Argentine or South African sun. I like those which have that enveloping richness but also a bit of earthiness to mirror the grainy dust of the red kidney beans. The dried-herbs-and-loose-leaf-tea scent of a rugged Chilean carmenère (or carmenère blend) riffs along with the cumin in the chilli. The smoky, biltong-and-leather smell of an old-fashioned South African cabernet sauvignon makes you feel as if you're ready to saddle up and hit the dusty road after a hearty refuel. An oaked Chilean merlot will bring out the chocolatey smoothness of the sauce; a Chilean cabernet will play up to the meatiness. A South African blend of mourvèdre, syrah and grenache also works well here. As does an easy-going, vibrant bonarda from Argentina or zinfandel from the States. For a more refreshing option, try a Côtes du Rhône, although it risks being drowned out by the fire of the chilli. I usually eat chilli con carne just with rice. If you're going for the full array of guacamole, grated cheese and tortilla, a malty old-school strong ale looks good – how about Fullers 1845, Brains SA or Hogs Back T.E.A.?

This is my brother's recipe for chilli con carne. He adds a square of plain chocolate, which gives a beautiful depth and gloss to the sauce. He also makes it with chunks of meat rather than the traditional mince. I've tried the same recipe with both braising steak and mince and it's much better his way.

C

JONNY'S CHILLI CON CARNE
Serves 4 of my friends, or 2 of my brother

- 2 tablespoons olive oil
- 2 medium onions, finely chopped
- 2 sticks of celery, finely chopped
- 4 cloves of garlic, peeled and chopped
- 1 red chilli, deseeded and finely chopped
- 1 heaped teaspoon ground cumin
- 1 heaped teaspoon paprika
- 450g braising steak, trimmed and cut into small pieces the size of the tip of your little finger
- 1 × 400g tin whole plum tomatoes
- 1 beef stock cube
- red chilli flakes
- 1 square 85% plain chocolate
- 1 × 200g tin red kidney beans, drained
- natural yoghurt
- fresh coriander, chopped
- seasoning to taste

Heat half the olive oil in a small, cast-iron casserole dish on a low heat on the hob. Add the onions and celery and cook, stirring from time to time, until almost soft and translucent. Add the garlic and chilli and continue to fry until the garlic is cooked. Add the cumin and paprika and cook for a further 30 seconds, stirring to mix. Remove the vegetable mixture from the pan and set to one side.

Put the second tablespoon of olive oil in the pan and fry the meat quickly in batches to brown it. Return all the meat and the onion mixure to the pan and add the tomatoes and their juice. Use a pair of scissors to chop the tomatoes in the pan. Crumble in the stock cube, then rinse the empty tomato tin with water and pour this into the pan too. Stir well. Add more chilli flakes to taste. Simmer gently for 2 hours, or until thickened and glossy, stirring occasionally. Add the chocolate and stir in.

The casserole can now be put to one side until you are ready to eat. Add the drained kidney beans just before reheating and when the chilli con carne is hot all the way through, serve with brown rice, chopped coriander and yoghurt on the side.

Chinese Cantonese is the best-known and most prevalent type of Chinese cuisine outside China. It comes from the Guangdong province (formerly called Canton). Christine Parkinson, Head of Wine for the Hakkasan group of restaurants, knows more than most about how Cantonese food works with wine from all over the world. She's been running the wine operation for Hakkasan's restaurants, from London to Shanghai to San Francisco to Mumbai, for years, and is one of the most talented and also punctilious restaurant tasters I have encountered. Parkinson is careful to search out good wines, and meticulous when it comes to trialling them with Hakkasan's food, holding a tasting meeting every Tuesday at which any new candidates vying for a place on the wine list, as well as new vintages of current wines, are tested with at least eight different dishes from the restaurant kitchen, selected to cover the different styles of food (spicy, light and so on). If it tastes bad with any single dish – and, says Parkinson, some wines really do – it's out.

'The single biggest problem with Cantonese food when it comes to wine is that there's a lot of sweetness – a lot of sugar or honey or malt or whatever – and that's a real enemy to tannin and to green notes in red wines,' she says. 'And then of course the flavours are very big. Cantonese cuisine is not particularly shy or delicate. It has robust flavours, which means some wines can get completely lost.'

The heavy use of spice, from ginger to chilli to sichuan pepper to yellow chives, is also an issue, as is acidity in the food, not just with sweet-and-sour dishes, where you might expect it, but also with others that have a strong vinegar component. Chinese chive is also tricky, says Parkinson: 'It's a different variety to the English one. When you see green dim sum wrappers, that's Chinese chive and it is another enemy to wine.'

It's normal to have several different dishes on the table at

C

once, and to be picking and sharing across all those sweet, sour, spicy, vinegar, bold flavours. The chances are you'll be following a mouthful of one with a mouthful of wine with a mouthful of another. So the challenge is to find a wine that still tastes good whether you're eating black pepper rib-eye beef, silver cod in champagne honey, or spicy prawns.

I find the vibrant alertness of English sparkling wine works particularly well with Chinese food, both with dim sum and with main courses. Bob Lindo, who makes wine at Camel Valley in Cornwall, agrees that English sparkling is a good match for the variety of Cantonese food, but even he points out, 'You don't want to drink sparkling wine all the way through a dinner, there has to be still wine in there somewhere.'

From her long years of experience at Hakkasan, Christine Parkinson recommends three mainstream wine styles that can generally (though not always) be relied on to work well: barrel-fermented chardonnay; riesling with a little bit of residual sugar (that is, off-dry riesling); and pinot noir. I find that herbaceous, lean styles of pinot noir – say, from Baden in Germany or a basic Bourgogne Rouge – work particularly well with the umami component in a non-sweet Chinese dish such as beef in oyster and black bean sauce. Off-dry rieslings come into their own with the sweetness of, say, sticky lemon chicken. Barrel-fermented chardonnays are also good with umami, and the texture and spice brought by the wood mean they can deal with richer flavours.

Other wines that work are:

- Lugana from north-east Italy, which is soft, broad and neutral, sometimes with the flavour of savoury custard and orchard fruit. The high-quality wines made by Ca' dei Frati are particularly good.
- ribolla gialla, a white grape grown on the Slovenian border in the mountains of north-east Italy whose wine is tenacious, precise and grips on to your tongue.
- koshu, a white Japanese grape whose wine makes me think of origami. Sipped on its own, it seems as neutral as a sheet of white paper – like a cross between

a very quiet sauvignon blanc and pinot grigio. A bit dull. Sipped with the right food, it pops into shape: you can actually taste it more, as if it has reserves of power that are uncovered only when they are needed. The transformation surprises me every time. Koshu is particularly good with dim sum, but less good with more spicy or sweet food.

- champagne, white or rosé, but non-vintage (NV) – the subtlety of anything finer would disappear amidst the other flavours.
- deep-coloured rosés that are not perfectly dry and which work across the board.
- albariño is great with dim sum but not with dishes that have too much heat or sugar.
- old-vine carignan from Chile is good with heavier meaty dishes and can even take some spice. For example, it works well with star anise.

See also crispy duck pancakes.

chocolate Wine and chocolate together sounds indulgent and hedonistic. I can almost feel the squish of sofa cushions just thinking about it. And that's exactly how it can be, provided that you follow two main guidelines: go high alcohol and, unless the alcohol is so high that you're actually drinking a spirit, go sweet.

Almost any drink that tastes good inside a chocolate truffle is equally good in a glass beside a rich chocolate mousse, creamy chocolate cake or nemesis, chocolate soufflé, chocolate tart or a piece of plain or milk chocolate.

With *spirits*, this means brandy (including, of course, Cognac and Armagnac); rum – especially aged rum, which has a special affinity for chocolate as the sweet fruitiness and the smoky-nutty flavours of the spirit bring out all the cocoa richness; finally, at a pinch, if it's quite a bitter, restrained chocolate, try whisky.

Fruit-flavoured liqueurs work well too – it's almost too obvious to say, but if you pick ones whose fresh fruits you would put with chocolate, that seems to do the trick. The electricity between the bluffness of plain chocolate and the intense tang of bitter oranges is well known, and both Cointreau and Grand Marnier are gorgeous with straightforward chocolate desserts and those with a glimmer

C

of orange. Kirsch, as everyone knew in the Seventies, is brilliant with cream and chocolate. Framboise, too – chocolate seems to exaggerate the berry flavours.

Ordinary sweet wine rarely works with chocolate, though there are exceptions to this rule, such as Brachetto d'Acqui, the sparkling red wine from northern Italy. Usually it's better to look for a wine that has been lightly fortified. Young vintage port has a red-fruited, velvet strength, like the fabled iron fist in a velvet glove, that is especially delicious with, for instance, chocolate mousse cake. Late bottled vintage (LBV) shares the same affinity for rich chocolate puddings. Meanwhile, tawny port, which has been aged in oak, brings a caramelized nuttiness.

Marsala and Madeira can be good too, but when it comes to Madeira pick your wine with care: the drier, lither styles of sercial and verdelho would be buried by some chocolate desserts, but richer, sweeter bual and malmsey can manage almost anything. Sweeter sherries, such as sweet oloroso, cream sherry or PX, are good with chocolate too.

Vins doux naturels are made by adding a small amount of grape spirit to wine before it has finished fermenting, so that it tastes sweet but also grapey. Many of these are gorgeous, but it's an overlooked category, so you can actually feel you are paying the gastronomic world a courtesy when you get out the chocolate and crack open a bottle.

A few examples: Maury is made in the south of France using grenache and it tastes like a pom-pom of liquidized dried figs and plums with a gentle flame of alcohol. Banyuls is another red sticky wine, made in the Roussillon from a blend of grapes, aged in oak, and often very complex.

White vins doux naturels are more refreshing; they lift chocolate in the same way that crystallized kumquats lift a bitter chocolate sorbet. Muscat de Beaumes de Venise and Muscat St Jean de Minervois, for instance, are both reminiscent of orange blossom and honey, while Muscat de Rivesaltes is pale and fresh when it's young, and grows more intense, like honey with baked apricots, as it gets older.

Liqueur muscat is a classic Australian sweet wine that is good with chocolate too. Mahogany in colour, it tastes of figs, dates, treacle cake, molasses and raisins. Try it with chocolate refrigerator cake, chocolate mousse or vanilla ice cream with a chocolate sauce.

The Aztecs believed chocolate was a gift of the gods, who drank it themselves. Wine also has plenty of its own gods – Dionysus and Bacchus, for a start – looking after it. So it seems fair to imagine that putting the two together might sometimes cause hostility. This clash is immediately apparent when you try to drink ordinary dry wine with chocolate. Sweet chocolate has a withering effect on the taste – it sucks the joy out of it, leaving behind an alcohol and acid shell. Eating a smooth, sleek truffle and finding your gulp of red has turned it into an angry tangle, like crash wreckage, is not at all appealing.

Despite this, many producers of red wines remain convinced that their wines go well with chocolate. I think this might be because certain red wines actually taste of chocolate. At least, they do a bit. Putting sweet food and dry wine together never really works, in my view, but if you want to taste chocolate-ish flavours in a dry wine, then have a look at some of the big malbecs from Argentina; southern hemisphere cabernet francs, which are often reminiscent of powdery drinking chocolate; riper St Emilions and also Chilean cabernet sauvignon and carmenère blends, which sometimes have flavours similar to intense, bitter cacao nibs.

Australian shiraz is sometimes also a little bit chocolatey, though it's the taste of cooked raspberries I find more here – which might explain why sparkling shiraz is often enthusiastically matched with chocolate. Raspberries and chocolate are great together. Shiraz and chocolate, not so much, although it does help that sparkling shiraz is often a little sweet.

If you are really intent on eating chocolate and drinking dry wine together follow the advice of Sarah Jane Evans, a Master of Wine who is also a committed chocolate expert and author of the book *Chocolate Unwrapped*, which offers a guide to the top eighty chocolate producers, with tasting notes. She advises picking bars of chocolate 'that have texture: nuts, sea salt, a very fine layer of fruit jelly – this mitigates the tannin disaster'. It does make the combination sit together more happily.

drinking with chocolate at a glance
to lift and refresh the chocolate The light dance and orange blossom of Muscat de Beaumes de Venise or Muscat St Jean de Minervois.

to snuggle into the chocolate Young vintage port, LBV port, ruby port, Maury, Australian Liqueur Muscat, malmsey Madeira.

to pay it the compliment of firewater Rum and brandy.

good combinations
chocolate mousse with prunes The rustic fire of Armagnac sparks off the earthy prunes. This is proper winter fireside, iron-hard frost outside stuff.

nuts (and raisins) and chocolate Those sweet wines that have an intrinsic nuttiness mesh well here. So, chilled tawny port, malmsey or bual Madeira, Australian Liqueur Muscat, sweet oloroso sherry, Moscato di Pantelleria.

sea salt chocolate The iodine smokiness of Islay whisky plays to the marine element in the salty chocolate.

white chocolate bars studded with freeze-dried strawberries Oddly specific, I know, but I have Sarah Jane Evans and her extensive chocolate and wine tasting to thank for this one. 'A delightful girly combo with this chocolate is Californian white grenache from Gallo [a sweetish rosé wine],' she says. 'Great fun.'

frozen berries with hot white chocolate sauce A more sophisticated take on the white chocolate and strawberries bar above, I'd put this with Brachetto d'Acqui.

See also cake.

chorizo The presence of chorizo in a dish immediately moves me across to red wine. Its sweet softness and paprika spiciness particularly suit Spanish wine. In contrast, say, to Italian, which is all elbows, wine made in Spain from tempranillo, cariñena or garnacha is smooth and juicy when young and, as it ages, suggests sweetness, like cooked strawberries, that mirrors that of the chorizo. So with squid and chorizo casserole, I would drink a mellow Rioja. With chorizo sliced into a butter bean and tomato salsa and topped with a lamb chop, I might drink Rioja again, or garnacha from Campo de Borja or a Priorat or a Montsant. If white is preferred – perhaps with chorizo eaten alone as a nibble, or a chorizo, spinach and poached egg salad – then make it succulent and rounded, and consider looking for wine with oak. Oaked white Rioja is the obvious choice. Godello, with its juicy rounded orchard fruits, fits the bill too. The crackle of an oaked chardonnay from Australia, South Africa or Chile would also be gorgeous with a poached egg and chorizo dish, not least because chardonnay is good with eggs too.

chowder This dish is more solid than liquid so works better with wine than most soups. With a mild, creamy vegetarian corn chowder, try a chardonnay. With spicy seafood chowder, consider the texture of a marsanne, the toasty quality of an aged semillon or the cut of a semillon-sauvignon blend from Australia.

Christmas dinner From a food matching point of view, the best way to pick a wine to go with Christmas dinner is to think of it as one more element – a sauce or dish of stuffing – on the crammed table. The turkey may ostensibly be the centrepiece, but it's also a blank canvas. It's the cranberries, the fruity stuffings, the chestnuts, the spicy sausage balls, the prunes wrapped in bacon – all of the other brightly coloured, joyful rattlebag of dishes that need to get along with the wine. Wines that will fall in with this crowd? An aromatic white, such as pinot gris; or a red with cranberry sharpness and bright berry fruit, perhaps a youthful pinot noir (maybe from Central Otago or Martinborough in New Zealand), a Beaujolais Cru, an unoaked carignan, a gaudy garnacha from north-east Spain, or a carignan from Chile.

However. Unless you are particularly in the mood for those wines, picking one would be to miss half the point. Christmas dinner is like the big box of decorations in the cupboard under the steps, filled with gaudy baubles, tasteful baubles, ugly baubles, matching baubles and clashing baubles: a big hotch-potch of family tradition, colour and whim. When you sit down at the Christmas table, the first duty of the wine is not actually to go with the food but to go with your mood: it must be festive and celebratory. The best advice is therefore to drink the wine you quite fancy at the time. Maybe it's classic, reassuring claret, or maybe it's a sturdy, hairy Chilean carmenère.

A good balance between wines that suit the food and the mood might also be struck. How about a richly Christmassy blend of syrah, grenache and mourvèdre from the southern Rhône, Languedoc, California or Australia? Or an Australian bordeaux blend, which will be more vibrantly fruity and hedonistic than a real bordeaux and so go better with the fruity vitality of stuffings and sauces. I love to drink young nebbiolo (ideally a Langhe Nebbiolo) or sangiovese (in the form of a Rosso di Montalcino or Chianti Classico) on Christmas Day, and often tweak the trimmings in a more savoury direction to fit. It's easily done: make stuffings more herby (use thyme and rosemary) than sweetly fruity; use raisins, cranberries and dried cherries rather than apple and apricots; put Parmesan and cream in with the sprouts; and make sure there are plenty of chestnuts, ideally cooked with bacon; and there it is – reimagined for Italian wine.

See also Boxing Day leftovers, cake: Christmas cake, turkey sandwiches.

clams see *fish* for good, generic seafood wines; also *chowder*; *pasta: vongole*

cod Cod is a firm-textured fish and when cooked simply its snowy-white flesh suits medium-weight whites that have some freshness: for instance, Chablis, top-notch Mâcon, godello, white Rioja or Douro whites. Grüner veltliner approaches cod with less roundness and a more chiselled edge.

battered cod see *fish and chips*

black miso cod Silky and umami-rich, black miso cod has a sweetness that is good with champagne. Daiginjo sake would be another obvious choice. Mid-weight pinot noir also works well, as does a nutty white burgundy, say a good-value St Aubin or a Meursault.

brandade of cod This creamy dip is made using salt cod and olive oil. Brisk, salty manzanilla sherry is a pretty perfect match, or try a Rhône white.

cod with green lentils and/or wrapped in air-dried ham Earthy green lentils and/or meaty ham make a light red wine more tempting than a white. Try Bardolino; a light and mineral-edged pinot noir (for instance, one from Germany; or a simple Bourgogne Rouge); zweigelt from Austria; gamay (from Touraine or a Beaujolais); Irouleguy; or a vin de pays de l'Ardèche.

cod with red peppers, tomatoes and onions Once red peppers and onions come into the equation, red wine tastes better than white. Make it a young Bierzo or Ribeira Sacra or a bright Rioja Joven.

xató This tip comes from Ferran Centelles, the Spanish food and wine expert who for a long time was head sommelier at El Bulli. I asked him for an example of a traditional Spanish food that matches well with a non-Spanish wine. He said, 'Cod fish salad with anchovies and romesco [locally known as xató] is a delicious Catalan dish that I love to match with high-acidity and delicate aromatic wine. I had a great experience combining this really savoury food with a verdicchio from Marche in Italy.'

See also bacalao, esqueixada.

Comté If you invite someone who works as a sommelier or wine buyer for dinner and ask them to bring the cheese, there is a very good chance that they will turn up with a slab of this hard, unpasteurized cheese made on the French side of the border between France and Switzerland. Comté is known as one of *the* cheeses that tastes really good with red bordeaux. As always in wine, not everyone agrees. Eric Monneret, director of Château La Pointe in Pomerol, shook his head when I suggested eating grainy Comté with tannic claret. 'Ah, non, I'm from the Jura and so I would have to say that Comté is best with a vin jaune, which also comes from there.' I'd happily drink either.

coq au vin Almost any red blend from southern France, a red burgundy, or a red Côtes du Rhône is good with this bistro classic.

C

My personal favourite is a pitcher of good Beaujolais Cru. On a cold winter's night the combination of piping hot (the coq au vin) and chilly (the wine) feels as comforting as standing by a fire while watching snow fall on the other side of the window. Beaujolais has a slight tang of stone and graphite – girding against the darkness outside.

coriander The leaves of coriander are widely used in Latin American cuisine, and the seeds and leaves in South Asian food. Its smell is divisive; while some experience coriander as a woody and pleasantly fragrant herb, to others it is soapy and metallic. Research suggests that genetic variants in olfactory receptors could contribute to this polarizing effect, and the olfactory receptor gene OR6A2, which is involved in the detection of particular aldehydes, has been implicated. Loathing for coriander is highest among East Asians (21 per cent), those of European descent (17 per cent) and those with African ancestry (14 per cent), according to one study, which also found that the approval rating for coriander was much higher among those from South Asian, Middle Eastern and Latin American backgrounds. For those who dislike coriander, perhaps only an overpowering pinotage can help to remove its sudsy taste. For others, fresh coriander leaves often work well with grüner veltliner, especially when lemongrass, lime juice and cool basmati rice are also involved. The spicy rattle of the seeds might suggest either a spicy and robust red or its antithesis, a soothing off-dry rosé. You need to take into account the whole dish, however.

cottage (or shepherd's) pie Comfort food – and it is perfect with comfort wine. The boldness of a chunky, inky Chilean red (ideally cabernet sauvignon or carmenère, but merlot will do too) suits the rich mince base, all the more so if it's laden with Worcestershire sauce. In the Chilean version of this dish, mashed sweetcorn replaces potatoes, which is lovely with the sweetly fruity ripeness of these southern hemisphere wines. You could also open a Côtes du Rhône, Corbières, Fitou or an inexpensive, chunky Australian or South African red. If the mood takes you, a vigorous young bordeaux or a sumptuous Ribera del Duero would work well too.

courgette 'What wine might go with courgettes?' is a thought that has never crossed my mind. Dinner is never about this subtle green vegetable, it's about everything else – the garlic, the herbs, the tomatoes, the cheese . . . whatever.

fried with garlic and tomatoes, scattered with Gruyère, and grilled to melt the cheese Rosé from Provence; the cut of a pecorino from Italy; the freshness of a white from the Savoie.

ribboned, with pine nuts The lemon-rind flavours of a Gavi di Gavi will bring cool freshness (and underscore the crunch of the courgette if you are serving this as a raw salad). A grillo or greco di tufo will emphasize the more exotic, richer texture of the pine nuts.

roasted and added, with oven-dried tomatoes and parsley, to a garlic and raw tomato sauce for pasta A light sauvignon blanc from Italy or France; Gavi; verdicchio.

stuffed with rice, tomatoes, garlic and thyme An aromatic red (say, meaty Bandol) or white (Cassis or a Côtes de Provence blanc) from Provence or a Provençal rosé hits the spot. Clean Italian whites such as verdicchio or vermentino are palate-cleansing too. If you flip the herb from woody thyme to pungent oregano, however, the French wines are suddenly less happy. The herbaceous Italian whites still play well, as do stonily calm, unoaked whites from Crete.

courgette flowers (stuffed and fried) Again, it's not about the courgette flower, it's about the ricotta, pine nuts, citrus peel, herbs – whatever you have in there. To slice through the fat of cheese and frying oil, and pick up on the brightness of the lemon rind, pick a sharp white that tastes of lemons: Gavi di Gavi, pecorino, assyrtiko, or carricante from Sicily. Other clean whites will have the same refreshing effect: pinot grigio from the north-east of Italy or from Hungary, vermentino, verdicchio or vernaccia. Those 'v' wines also have an astringency that adds a herbal twist. Clean falanghina has an orange-blossom scent that brings another citrus dimension. For a more *Arabian Nights*, perfumed exoticism, choose the crystallized-fruit-tinged fiano, grillo or greco di tufo or the florality of zibibbo – Sicilian muscat. The wine doesn't have to be Italian; Australian fiano or the almond-kernel-and-citrus-peel taste of marsanne from either Australia or France is good too.

crab Chablis – which smells of damp sea fossils and has a glow, as if it's backlit – underscores the marine qualities of the crab while also offering a hint of the lemon you might squeeze into your crab mayonnaise. It particularly suits crab with new potatoes and a little gem salad.

Gently peachy albariño, from Spain's Atlantic coast, is also brilliant with crab, whether the crab is fried in croquettes, freshly picked out of the claws, mixed into a mayonnaise (perhaps with finely chopped coriander stalks or torn basil leaves) or made into a crab sandwich eaten with a view of the beach and the sea air in your nostrils.

These are my two go-to crab wines; the ones I start salivating for the minute I see crab in almost any form on the menu. Riesling also has a substantial following as the perfect crab accompaniment – 'crab and riesling together are part of the Creator's Plan,' writes Hugh Johnson in his *Pocket Wine Book* – though I tend to go for riesling only when certain other ingredients are also involved.

Here are a few suggestions for specific dishes.

crab cakes Cool, hard-edged cava bubbles are cleansing with the crunchy, fatty, crispy outsides of crab cakes.

crab cakes with chilli, lime, avocado, red onion and tomato salad Go for a bright dry or off-dry riesling from Germany, Austria, New Zealand, Chile or Australia.

Thai crab cakes Grassy young Hunter Valley semillon from Australia or the hay and toast scent of more mature Hunter semillon is good here. Otherwise, riesling. The piercing lime of riesling from Clare or Eden Valley (both Australian), a riesling from Chile, or the clean swoosh of an Austrian riesling is good with the lemongrass and ginger of Thai-flavoured crab cakes.

THAI CRAB CAKES
Serves 2, as a lunch

- 75ml mayonnaise
- 1 stick of lemongrass, finely chopped
- ½ teaspoon grated fresh ginger
- 100g white crabmeat
- 75g fresh breadcrumbs
- 2 spring onions, chopped
- 2 tablespoons roughly chopped basil
- 2 tablespoons roughly chopped fresh coriander
- panko breadcrumbs, for coating
- groundnut oil, for frying

Mix together the mayonnaise, chopped lemongrass and grated ginger. Put the crabmeat, fresh breadcrumbs, spring onions, basil and coriander in a separate bowl. Stir in the mayonnaise until the mixture is bound. Divide into four, shape into patties, roll the patties in panko breadcrumbs and shallow-fry in groundnut oil, turning once, until golden and warm.

Serve with rocket or spinach salad, or steamed Asian greens and a glass of Hunter Valley semillon.

deep-fried soft-shell crab The first time I ate this was in a restaurant overlooking Sydney Harbour. On the menu there were lots of wines from the Hunter Valley, some 150 kilometres to the north. So we ordered a semillon. I think it was Tyrrell's Vat 1: an absolute classic, grassy, poised, and beautiful with the crispy, crabby food.

hot crab pots An olden but golden dish which I always find especially pleasing if there are crunchy little bits of shell in the creamy, eggy, hot, crabby pot. It is blissful with oaked chardonnay. I made this recipe when Aussie Larry Cherubino, a winemaking genius (also, an exceptionally talented tidy-upper), was coming to dinner. I thought it would work with the gleam of his Margaret River chardonnay. It did.

C

HOT CRAB POTS
Serves 6

- 4 eggs, beaten
- 400ml double cream
- 200g brown and white crabmeat
- 100g Gruyère, grated
- salt
- butter
- 2 tablespoons chopped chives

Preheat the oven to 180°C/350°F/gas mark 4. Mix the eggs, cream, crab and cheese together. Season to taste and divide between six buttered ramekin dishes. Cook for around 15 minutes until only just set. Sprinkle with chives and serve with really good bread, toasted.

cream Creamy sauces feel like cashmere blankets: luxurious and soft. Sometimes you want to pierce that softness. For instance, the classic French recipe for pork medallions cooked with cream and prunes is so unctuous, sweet and caramelized that it is excellent with the penetrating and refreshing acidity of an off-dry Vouvray. Mostly, though, creamy sauces are more likely to have me reaching for a broad white with rounded edges. Very often that white will be chardonnay, barrel-fermented or otherwise. It might also be a cloud-like grenache gris, oaked chenin blanc, or an oaked white Rioja.

crisps see *salty snacks*

crispy duck pancakes A fruity pinot noir from New Zealand (Central Otago or Martinborough, ideally) or Chile is delicious with the meaty duck, crispy spring onion and just a smear of hoisin sauce. If you are ladling on the hoisin, though, its sweetness will disrupt the wine, so I'd switch to a fruity medium-dry riesling. The same goes for duck spring rolls, which are also very good with sparkling champagne blends – the combination of fat, sweetness, acid and crunch is very moreish.

C

curry Curry is a catch-all term that covers a broad spectrum of spicy food from all over the world. As a general guide, wine with a bit of sweetness helps to neutralize the burning effect of the chilli. Without that sugar, it can be hard to taste the wine at all. A fruity, off-dry rosé or an off-dry sparkling wine holds up well against most curried foods and this, if I'm not pouring a beer or a G&T, is what I open to drink with ready-made Indian-style curries at home.

With curry in a creamy coconut sauce, off-dry pinot gris is extremely good: gentle and softly floral. With lime-scented curries, the lime notes in a riesling play off the citrus in the food – pick an off-dry riesling to counteract the heat of the chilli. When tomatoes together with capsicum are involved, carmenère is good. With the more earthy flavours found in dishes containing lentils and with hearty tomato-and-meat-based curries, red wines with a hint of dust (such as mencía, carmenère again or a Portuguese Dão) are also good. In each case, marry the weight of the flavour with the weight of the wine – and be aware of the impact of the chilli, whose burning effect is exaggerated by the tannin and oak in red wines.

See also chilli, dhal, Indian, Thai green curry.

devils on horseback Sweet-salty prunes wrapped in bacon are great with sparkling wine.

dhal There are many versions of this Indian staple but the earthy flavour of the lentils and some degree of spice are constants. The substantial nature of dhal is more readily matched with red than white wine. It goes especially well with those dusty, dry reds whose flavours align with the lentils: look for inexpensive reds from Turkey, the Dão in Portugal, Lebanon, carmenère from Chile, or sangiovese or montepulciano from central Tuscany.

dill GAME-CHANGER The distinctive aniseed and fennel taste of this herb is disruptive to many flavours, including those in some wines. Unpleasant combinations that come to mind include Rioja and dill, or Crozes-Hermitage and dill – the pungency of the herb curdles the sweet strawberry-ness of Rioja and is aggressive against the tannins of the northern Rhône.

Better to go for herbaceous white wines such as verdicchio, vermentino and vernaccia, or, where small amounts of dill are combined with creamy sauces or crème fraîche, a cool-climate chardonnay (I'm really thinking of white burgundy), which often has gentle notes of woodruff and faint tones of aniseed. My very favourite type of wine with dill, though, and in particular with dill and smoked salmon, is barrel-fermented sauvignon blanc. When it's aged in oak, sauvignon blanc begins to taste of baked grapefruits and pine and sometimes also very gently of dill. Either a straight oak-aged sauvignon or a sauvignon blanc-semillon blend will do the trick, which means that Bordeaux (and in particular the appellations of Graves and Pessac-Léognan) and Margaret River are good places to look.

Incidentally, carvone is one of the main odour compounds found in dill. It comes from the terpenoid family of chemicals and is also present in high concentration in spearmint as well as caraway. This is why Dentinox, the medicine given to soothe colicky babies, appears to smell minty when it is actually flavoured with dill. It also helps to explain the affinity between caraway seeds, rye bread and dill – all stalwarts of Scandinavian cuisine – and, indeed, that much-loved Scandinavian drink aquavit: a perfect match.

dried lime see *lime*

duck Pinot noir is the first grape to think of when it comes to duck. It is a winner with duck eaten any which way – with hoisin sauce; roasted; smoked; with noodles; in a salad.

    With a roast duck, the first decision is whether you're looking for a light, refreshing red to slice through the fat and act like a perky vinous cranberry sauce, or a big, gruff red, as full as the duck is rich, to hunker down with.

    In the case of the former, any of the following light reds are worth considering: gamay (the weight of a Beaujolais Cru might be appreciated, or a rich New Zealand gamay), nerello mascalese from Etna, Bardolino, dolcetto, bobal, mencía, an inexpensive carignan from Spain or France, the warm flow of a Cerasuolo di Vittoria from Sicily, Marcillac, and, of course, pinot noir. It's neither heavy nor light, but Fronsac – a lean and sometimes green-tasting Bordeaux appellation – also has a tannic and acidic cut that is good with duck.

    If you're in search of a more cosy bear-hug of a red, pick one with a hairy chest so as to match the richness and fat with mass and tannic might. Rustic reds go well with duck: a Bergerac Rouge, Buzet, Cahors, Madiran, or a gamey Bandol from Provence will give you a bit of tannic edge. Or try a warm, smooth monastrell from Spain (the grape is known as mourvèdre in France and underpins the Bandol blend, but Spanish incarnations tend to be more fluid, more deeply fruity and liquorice-like). The autumnal notes of Barbaresco or Brunello di Montalcino go particularly well with roast duck and a tray of roasted root vegetables, from parsnips to carrots to red onions, as does the fading strawberry and autumn leaf sweetness of a maturing Rioja or Ribera del Duero. More or less

D

any red from the northern Rhône or the Dão or Douro in Portugal would also be happy here.

Here are a few duck dishes and suggested matches.

casserole One of the hairy-chest reds listed above will meet the weight of the slow-cooked duck.

with cherry sauce Pick a bright, young pinot noir from Central Otago in New Zealand or from California for sweet fruit, or an unoaked young pinot noir from Chile or Burgundy for the taste of red berries wih a slightly sharper edge. A sangiovese or dolcetto from Italy will also taste good with duck and cherry sauce, and give you a bit more elbow.

confit de canard This speciality of south-west France is good with local and local-ish wines. Cahors, Madiran or Bergerac for a big red with grunt; Marcillac or Gaillac for a sappy light red to cut across the fat.

with mushroom risotto balls For a lighter option, pick barbera, juicy dolcetto or pinot noir. Perricone, an unusual Italian grape with a hint of forest floor and mulberryish fruit, is a good mid-weight wine. For more of a growl, try mourvèdre (known as mataro in Australia and monastrell in Spain) or syrah. Barbaresco or Barolo would also be excellent and bring out the autumnal flavours in the mushroom risotto.

à l'orange White wines go well with duck when it's in a citrus sauce. Falanghina from central Italy, which tastes of mandarins and orange blossom and has a refreshing tang, is great with both the fat of the duck and the brightness of the orange. You could also try Australian marsanne; a tangy chardonnay from Chile, South Africa or Australia; off-dry riesling; greco di tufo from Italy; off-dry pinot gris; pinot blanc; chenin blanc or a Rhône white whose almond paste flavours emphasise the exotic side of this dish.

with peas and lettuce Tender pink magrets with a tangle of braised little gem lettuce and fresh peas, perhaps cooked with crispy cubes

D

of pancetta, suits light reds with a similarly spring-like feel. Bright pinot noir (from just about anywhere in the world), Marcillac, Beaujolais or other gamay, passetoutgrains, zweigelt, dolcetto or barbera will all act like a kind of spry, fruity sauce for the duck. Cabernet franc will emphasize the soft meatiness of the duck, while the inherent leafy taste of the grape works with the peas and lettuce. The punctuating tannin and acidity and the energy of a young left-bank claret will also work with both the meat and the green vegetables.

with plum sauce The combination of spice from cinnamon, soy, pepper, ginger, star anise and Chinese five-spice and sweet-sour plums does work with pinot noir, but it needs to be a sturdy wine, and richly fruity, so look for one from Central Otago or Martinborough in New Zealand, Sonoma in the US, or South Africa. Spanish bobal is also good with this dish. Merlot, a grape I have barely recommended in this book, comes into its own here – think of the warm embrace of a big, plush oaked merlot from Chile or the fruit rush of one from Australia. Alternatively, a fruity Argentine malbec.

with Puy lentils Head towards earthier wines. Of the heavier reds listed above, try Buzet or Bergerac for warmth; or go lighter with a Beaujolais Cru or a savoury pinot; or mid-weight with a red made with Spain's mencía (from either Bierzo or Ribeira Sacra).

ragù Duck ragù is easily made by roasting a duck, shredding the meat, then proceeding as for ordinary ragù, perhaps flavouring the sauce with rosemary or thyme or bay leaves and fresh sage. Serve it on pappardelle and eat it with a rich Valpolicella Ripasso or Rosso di Montalcino.

with redcurrant sauce The tingle of redcurrants demands a wine that can match its nervosity. The light reds suggested for peas and lettuce will work, or nero d'avola or Cerasuolo di Vittoria from Sicily.

rillettes For years I have been roasting ducks until the flesh almost melts and picking the carcass to make rillettes, using Delia Smith's

See also aligot, cassoulet, crispy duck pancakes.

recipe, found in *Delia's Winter Collection*. 'I did recently offer it as a lunch for three people with a green salad and some slightly chilled Beaujolais. Magnificent!' says Delia. Exactly so. The shiver of a sappy, minerallic Beaujolais (try a Morgon for one with more weight) is glorious with rich duck. An alternative is a softly fruity, cranberryish unoaked carignan, from southern France, Aragon in Spain (where it is known as cariñena) or Chile.

duck spring rolls see *crispy duck pancakes*

dukkah This Egyptian seasoning has found its way out of the souks of Cairo and into kitchens all over the world. There are many different variations, but essentially it is a mixture of salt, herbs, nuts and spices that have been dry-roasted and pounded. Cumin, hazelnuts, coriander and sesame often play a part, making dukkah a crunchy, dusty, exotic condiment. In small quantities with bread and oil; on vegetables; or sprinkled on dips like hummus or tzatziki, it can work with Lebanese white or rosé or indeed a white wine from elsewhere. A chardonnay with toasty oak picks up on the toastiness of the spices and adds a sunny warmth. A more neutral white refreshes: try trebbiano, with its hints of stone, apple and nuts; or a more sharply lemony pecorino. Alternatively, go for a dusty, earthy red such as a Portuguese Dão; a Lebanese blend; a rustic Italian sangiovese-based red (Chianti, Rosso di Montepulciano, Carmignano); nebbiolo; aglianico; Alain Graillot's Moroccan syrah; a Turkish or Greek red; or a red containing mourvèdre made in Provence (for instance, Bandol).

E

eel (smoked) The principle that when matching wine to food you can either go with the texture of the dish or cut across it is beautifully demonstrated when it comes to smoked eel. Oily and strongly flavoured as well as smoky, the eel tastes good with wines that also have layers and texture. These may be provided by a touch of residual sugar: at Wild Honey in Mayfair, I once ate smoked eel with earthy beetroot purée and washed it down with an off-dry pinot gris. The thick texture of a dry white grenache, which tastes like a heavy late summer's day smells, also works well. So does the dancing texture of an off-dry riesling. At a tasting organized by Wines of Germany the cook Martin Lam, who knows a thing or two about putting food with wine, served warm smoked eel fillets on Jersey new potatoes with horseradish cream with a glittering, just-off-dry (with 5g/litre of sugar), bandbox-fresh riesling from the Mosel. This is a having-your-cake-and-eating-it kind of combination: the sugar gives the wine a fuller texture and the lithe acidity swooshes through the oil of the fish. Bone-dry riesling from Alsace also works in that cutting-across way. If drinking riesling with smoked eel and warm new potato salad, try chopping some chunks of green-skinned apple into the crème fraîche and mayonnaise mixture that binds the potatoes; the sweet-sourness of the apple fizzes pleasingly against the lime of the riesling.

The slice of ice-cold vodka is also refreshing with smoked eel and cool crème fraîche.

eggs Eggs are not a completely natural match for wine, whatever the title of Elizabeth David's book, *An Omelette and a Glass of Wine*, might suggest. As boiled eggs, poached eggs, scrambled eggs, shakshuka, and fried eggs are breakfast items, this is probably no bad thing. The only alcohol it is acceptable to pour first thing in the morning is champagne, and by great good fortune that is a wine

E

that works very well with almost all egg dishes. My second choice would be sparkling wine made elsewhere from chardonnay, pinot noir and pinot meunier. Cava would be the backup.

Where eggs are served as part of a lunch or salad, look at the other ingredients. The sharp acid of salad dressing is better with a simple, unoaked still white, or with the cool, hard edges of cava, than with a warm and toasty champagne.

eggs Benedict Well, maybe a glass of wine for weekend brunch . . . The rounded edges and lemony glints of white burgundy go very well with the combination of eggs and buttery-vinegary hollandaise. Oaked burgundy has a rich toasty scent that fits right in with the eggs. Chablis and new-wave Australian chardonnay (look for one with a lowish alcohol) are particularly successful, as their lemony edges play off the vinegar in the sauce: in fact I find it quite difficult to eat eggs Benedict without craving a cool glass of Chablis. English sparkling wine is also excellent: it is less briochey than champagne and has a brisk citrus edge that feels as if it is helping digestion. A really lovely combination.

fried eggs If the fried eggs are cooked in a tomato, onion, red pepper and spicy sausage sauce, and served with a chunk of bread as a main course, go for a wine that suits the sauce – maybe a young Rioja or barbera, or a rustic young Portuguese red based on touriga nacional. Lacy fried eggs with truffle shavings is another dinner-time classic and nothing goes better with this than nebbiolo.

oeufs en meurette A traditional Burgundian dish, in which eggs are poached in a sauce made from red wine, fried shallots and lardons. It's great with crusty bread and a glass of Bourgogne Rouge.

See also omelette, tapas, tortilla.

empanadas These little savoury-stuffed pastries are a speciality of Argentina and can be made with chicken, spiced meat or sweetcorn. 'Every region of Argentina has their own style,' says Maria Carola de la Fuente of Catena Zapata winery. 'In Mendoza they add olives, in Salta they add potatoes, in La Rioja, dried grapes.' With meaty empanadas, I always like to drink Argentine torrontes. This is a purely Pavlovian response, I think: this very floral white wine is what you have in Argentina, so it feels special to enjoy the two together, and reminds me of warm nights under Argentina's bright stars, hungrily watching empanadas cook in a wood-fired stove. Otherwise, the fleshiness of a young barbera or a bonarda would be tasty and a more obvious choice with the meat.

enchiladas An old Tex-Mex favourite, combining bold flavours, the endorphin-rush of chillies, and stodge. Wines that go well tend to be those that are simple, fruity, soft and safe. Don't spend too much money. With chicken enchiladas, if you want to drink white then pinot grigio, entry-level South African chenin blanc, or inexpensive chardonnay from a sunny place can all be good. Red works well with all enchiladas: try a red blend or zinfandel from California, a primitivo from southern Italy, a juicy and unoaked Chilean merlot, Argentine malbec or syrah, or a simple and unoaked monastrell or garnacha from Spain.

esqueixada This Catalan salad consists of tomatoes, shredded raw salt cod, olives, raw onion, a vinegary dressing, and sometimes also green and red bell peppers and flat-leaf parsley. If it's made using sherry vinegar (and even if it's not), the obvious choice is to drink a cold glass of fino, whose pungent iodine and sea spray scent grapples with the sting of the raw onion and cod. A glass of inexpensive, deep-coloured rosé, ideally made with the so-called workhorse grape bobal, is another good pick. A bone-dry and unobtrusive white can work here too; in Chile one producer farming vines in the stargazers' playground that is the Elqui Valley makes a white using the PX sherry grape that would be perfect here. A grassy verdejo is good too.

F

F

fajitas Wines that taste good with enchiladas also work with the unbaked version of these corn or flour tortillas stuffed with chicken or meat and eaten with salsa, soured cream, guacamole and other accompaniments. I'd also add carmenère to the list, because this grape is so good with the crispy bite of red and green peppers.

fennel Fennel is one of those herbaceous vegetables that can taste odd next to sweetly fruity wines. Its strong aniseed flavour (and that of its darker green, feathery fronds) needs a wine with acidic bite and a savoury personality. Anything from Italy – red or white, from sangiovese to vermentino – usually has a good chance of working with both raw and cooked fennel. Exceptions include red wines from Puglia, which are more rounded, ripe and sun-kissed. Even quite a small quantity of fennel on the plate can make it worth switching to a wine that will accommodate this tricky vegetable. Maybe you are eating roast pork with a side dish of braised fennel, in which case I'd be more likely to open a light sangiovese than a sweetly ripe pinot noir. Or perhaps a mixture of roasted root vegetables that includes a bulb or two of chopped fennel, in which case I'd say the same.

fennel gratin The tricky herbaceous quality of fennel is toned down when it is both cooked and eaten with cream. However, while chardonnay is an excellent grape with most gratins, here it's better to be more selective. Sunny, ripe, yellow, pineapple-and-melon fragranced chardonnay isn't the best with fennel. You want one that smells of woodruff and meadow grass – which leads you to Burgundy or Limoux.

fennel and orange salad (maybe with toasted pine nuts) The warm citrus flavour of orange is brilliant with whites from the south of

Italy's boot, and these will also work with the fennel. Try neroli-scented falanghina; grillo from Sicily, which is reminiscent of candied peel, oranges and papaya; or the slightly tropical greco di tufo.

in salads Slivers of raw fennel in green salads, or with mozzarella and rocket, are best matched with leafy, precise white wines. Verdicchio, vermentino and vernaccia work particularly well. The damp, nettly taste of English bacchus is also good here. A grassy, smoky sauvignon blanc from the Loire can also work, as can the white pepper and grapefruit scent of a grüner veltliner from Austria.

See also fennel seeds.

fennel seeds Fennel seeds are often used with roast pork, to season sausages, and to scatter over roasted root vegetables. Their aniseed hit can be potent and is definitely a strong influence on the overall taste of a plate of food. They are more dusty and less greenly astringent than fresh fennel, but most of the wines that work for the vegetable also work for its seeds. Look for savoury rather than sweetly ripe or jammy wines. Italian reds (or whites), Austrian zweigelt, savoury pinot noir or a savoury chardonnay will do the trick.

fish

the red wine question
'Can I drink red wine with fish?' is a question that comes up over and over again. I am never quite sure what is actually being asked here. 'May I drink red wine with fish?' 'Am I committing a social faux pas if I pour red wine with fish?' 'Will a biblical plague of locusts be unleashed on my family and all my descendants if I offend the fish with a glass of red?'

The idea that red wine with fish is transgressive appears to be a peculiarly Anglo concern that is not shared by other Europeans. The Portuguese unflinchingly pour rustic red wine with oily sardines sizzled with tomatoes and red onions. I've also enjoyed many fishy dinners in Italy with local red wines.

Spanish wine and food expert Maria José Sevilla finds the query odd too. 'We don't have prejudices about red and white wine in Spain,' she says. 'Certain ingredients make a difference to what

F

you might drink with the fish. For instance, cod cooked pil-pil style, where the gelatin in the fish makes an emulsion with olive oil like mayonnaise, is good with red. Or if you add maybe some peppers, you cannot serve these dishes with white wine, they are too substantial.'

A better question, therefore, is: 'When might a bottle of red go on the table with a plate of fish and feel like the best and most delicious wine that could possibly be drunk with it?'

Red wine can be fabulous with fish but there is a time and a plaice for it. And before I start floundering in fish puns, I will salmon up some guidelines and examples.

As with any dish, picking wine to go with fish is simply a matter of not overpowering the food and bearing in mind the other ingredients. For instance, opening a 15% abv shiraz that has been aged for two years in toasty new oak to serve with a delicate Dover sole would just be silly. It would be nearly impossible to taste the sole through such a huge wine. As a general rule, blue (oily) fish such as sardines, trout, salmon and tuna are more robust and therefore more suited to red. But it also depends on where you are, who you are with (mood) and what else is on the plate.

a few happy fish and red wine combinations
cod wrapped in prosciutto and eaten with Puy lentils This goes well with nebbiolo or dolcetto – the nutty, earthy, meaty notes in the food chime with the dust and tannin of the wine.

Sicilian fish dishes Pasta con sarde (pasta with sardines), swordfish cooked in wine with tomatoes, stuffed squid, and all the rest can be brilliant with Cerasuolo di Vittoria, a local light red made from nero d'avola and frappato. A warm night and some ruins in your sight line are preferable, but not essential.

tomato-based fish stew With its sturdy fruitiness, this is good with Dão red from Portugal.

tuna steaks Pink in the middle, these are delicious with sappy light reds such as Sancerre Rouge, Beaujolais Cru or zweigelt from Austria.

white wine choices
Consummate fish and seafood wines include Muscadet, Douro whites (surprisingly refreshing, often made with verdelho, known in the Douro as gouveio), Vinho Verde, white wines from Provence, young Hunter Valley semillon, peachy albariño, and lemony Roussette de Savoie.

rosé wine
Almost always a good idea. Pick deeper-coloured, more tannic rosé with more assertive fish dishes.

These are only the most general of pointers. For more specific recommendations, please refer to individual entries: see *abalone, anchovies, bacalao, beurre blanc, blinis, bottarga, bouillabaisse, brill, caviar, ceviche, cod, crab, dill, eel, esqueixada, fish and chips, fish finger sandwiches with tomato ketchup, fish pie, fish soup, fritto misto and calamares fritos, Goan fish curry, gravadlax, hake, Jansson's frestelse, kedgeree, King George whiting, kippers, lobster, mackerel, monkfish, moules marinière, octopus, oysters, paella, parsley sauce, potted shrimp, prawns, red mullet, red snapper, risotto: seafood, rollmop herrings, salade niçoise, salmon, samphire, sardines, sashimi, scallops, sea bass, sea urchin, skate, sole (Dover and lemon), squid, sushi, swordfish, trout, tuna, zander.*

fish and chips Yorkshireman Ian Kellett, who runs Hambledon Vineyard in Hampshire, has such cravings for what he calls 'proper' fish and chips – 'Haddock, skin off, and cooked in beef dripping, which fries them hotter' – that he sometimes jumps in the car and flogs up the M1 to Wakefield especially to buy them, a round trip of about 760 kilometres. That's quite a mission.

'I buy six times and put the rest in the freezer and warm them up when I want them. I have even been known to get a courier to drive from Yorkshire with them,' he once told me. 'It takes about four hours.'

Kellett is so absolutely focused on the fish and chips I'm not sure he even considers what's in his glass when he's eating them. But, as it happens, the best wine match for all that salt, vinegar, beef dripping and crunchy orange batter happens to be English sparkling wine, like the one he makes. Its vehement acidity and biting bubbles are good with salt, vinegar and fat. A young non-vintage champagne would also work, along the same lines, though I am more drawn to the cleaner swoosh of English sparkling. Personally, though, there is only one thing I would ever drink with this British institution: a pot of tea.

fish finger sandwiches with tomato ketchup Fish fingers are a guilty pleasure and an inexpensive, softly fruity, safe-tasting red is perfect with slightly sweet tomato ketchup and the crunch of the breadcrumbs. Cheap supermarket wines do this job very well – you don't want a wine with intellectual aspirations. A supermarket Fitou is my tried and tested match for fish finger sandwiches (and I never thought, as I cleaned out my freezer one afternoon when I was supposed to be writing this book, that the distraction task would turn out to be actual bona fide research). I also like a very cheap, upbeat Côtes du Rhône or a Californian zinfandel or an Australian syrah-cabernet sauvignon blend. Don't spend too much money. It's best if the wine is bright and as catchy as a pop track.

fish pie Creamy fish pie goes well with chardonnays and fuller-flavoured whites. It doesn't mind a bit of oak either. My ultimate fish pie wine is a good, dry Loire chenin blanc, ideally an oaked Savennières or Montlouis. The acidity is refreshing against the rich dairy and there is an interplay between the smokiness of the oak and the plump pieces of smoked fish. A South African chenin would be a sunnier option, more suited to eggy fish pie than to spinach fish pie. In addition, there are all the usual white-fish suspects, such as picpoul, albariño, Muscadet and white Douro wines.

fish soup One of the few soups with which a drink seems like a good idea. But there's more than one kind.

classic French fish soup The terracotta bisque of this classic, with its hot, garlicky rouille, goes beautifully with the throaty, sourdough taste of a chilled fino sherry. The oxidized style of Jura whites can also work: try a Jura chardonnay or savagnin.

lohikeitto (Finnish salmon soup) Salmon and potato soup flavoured with allspice and dill is a classic Finnish dish; a nourishing blanket of a winter supper eaten among the snowy, twilit, reindeer-stalked pine forests of the Arctic Circle. It's a creamy but robust broth, with chunks of salmon and just-disintegrating potatoes, and it goes well with a wine that also has soft, comforting curves. Try a curvaceous chardonnay, but pick one from a cool climate or with low alcohol, as the tropical flavours of very ripe chardonnay don't go well with dill. A Muscadet aged on the lees (sur lie) also has that lovely soft feeling, and Muscadet is a consummate fish wine. If the soup is very dill-heavy try an oak-aged sauvignon-semillon blend. However, I usually leave the wine alone and go for a shot of vodka or aquavit, ice cold, straight from the freezer.

five-spice Five-spice powder is a mixture of cinnamon, fennel, star anise, cloves and ginger (or sichuan pepper and/or cardamom) – and yes, this adds to more than five. It is used in Chinese as well as other Asian cooking. Cinnamon is a spice I often describe as having a 'jagged' profile. It does not smell smooth. This is probably because cinnamon activates TRPA1, an ion channel that is thought to act as a noxious chemical sensor, and which participates in the production of pain sensations. Of course, cinnamon does not actually make you say ouch, at least not in the quantities in which it is normally used, but it is an irritant, producing a prickling sensation that adds to the pungency of this spice mix. Overly 'clean' wines don't feel right with five-spice; red or white, you want a bit of texture, a bit of rough (I don't mean that in a derogatory way), a bit of jostle. Five-spice is often used as a rub for pork, which works well with both red and white wine, or prawns, for which I'd veer towards white.

For whites, seek out fatter, aromatic varieties such as roussanne, white grenache, viognier and marsanne, all of which go well with pig, or – even better – a blend incorporating one or more of those. Judicious oak can be good, bringing its own spice to the mix. Wines from South Africa, Chile, Australia, New Zealand and the States tend to be more robust – a useful quality where five-spice is concerned.

For reds, I like the loose throatiness of South African red Rhône blends with their hints of liquorice and tar.

MILLTON VINEYARD'S CHINESE PORK BELLY WITH SICHUAN CUCUMBER SALAD
Serves 5–6

The Millton Vineyard is a biodynamic paradise in Gisborne, New Zealand. Annie Millton gave me this excellent recipe for pork belly rubbed with five-spice, which she likes to eat with Millton Vineyard viognier, though she says it's good with the chenin blanc too, and I've enjoyed it with South African blends of chenin blanc, viognier, chardonnay and roussanne. You need to get started in the morning of the day you want to eat it, if not the night before.

for the pork
- 2 cloves of garlic, peeled and finely chopped
- 2 tablespoons brown sugar
- 4 tablespoons soy sauce
- 100ml shaoxing wine
- 4 star anise, ground (or pounded to a grit using a pestle and mortar)
- 1 tablespoon five-spice
- 1 teaspoon white pepper
- 2kg pork belly, skin scored crossways at 2cm intervals
- ½ tablespoon rock salt

for the salad
- half a Chinese leaf, finely shredded
- juice of half a lime
- ½ tablespoon sea salt
- 2 tablespoons groundnut oil
- 2 cloves of garlic, peeled and chopped
- half a green chilli, deseeded and finely sliced
- 2 teaspoons sichuan pepper
- 1 tablespoon rice vinegar
- 1 teaspoon sesame oil
- 2 Lebanese cucumbers, peeled, halved lengthways and cut diagonally into slices (use half a normal

cucumber if you can't find any, but deseed it before slicing)

In a dish big enough to fit the pork, mix the garlic, brown sugar, soy sauce, shaoxing wine, star anise, five-spice and white pepper. Put in the pork, flesh side down, and marinate, keeping the skin dry, uncovered in the fridge either overnight or for at least 3 hours before you are ready to cook it.

About 1½ hours before you plan to eat, transfer the pork to a foil-lined baking tray. Cook in a preheated oven at 220°C/425°F/gas mark 7 for 30 minutes. Remove from the oven, sprinkle the skin with salt, turn the oven down to 180°C/350°F/gas mark 4 and cook for another 30 minutes. Now turn the oven back up to 220°C/425°F/gas mark 7 and cook for another 10 minutes or so, until the skin crackles and blisters. Keep a close eye on it to make sure it doesn't burn. Remove from the oven and rest 10–15 minutes before serving.

To make the salad, toss the Chinese leaf with the lime and salt and put in the fridge for an hour. Heat the groundnut oil in a frying pan and fry the garlic, chilli and sichuan pepper until fragrant. Set aside to cool. Combine the rice vinegar, sesame oil and chilli mixture. Toss with the Chinese leaf and cucumber in a bowl.

focaccia Home-baked focaccia is a treat of a pre-dinner snack and you can customize it to go with whichever wine you're drinking. Olive Hamilton Russell of the eponymous South African winery sprinkles hers with rosemary if she's serving sauvignon blanc (rosemary is also a good bet with sangiovese) and with pine nuts or cashews for chardonnay. My old university friend and ace cook Anna Colquhoun (the Culinary Anthropologist) makes focaccia with balsamic vinegar, sweetly caramelized red onions and strawberries that is to die for (and she might have to if I'm ever going to wrestle the recipe out of her). She made it for a food and wine class we ran together and it was beautiful with moschofilero, a Greek white wine that smells of roses and lemongrass.

foie gras Foie gras, particularly if it is pan-fried and caramelized, has a lustre that is often matched with regal sweet wines such as Sauternes or Monbazillac. I prefer the lighter, more cleansing Jurançon Moelleux, a sweet wine made in the Pyrenees from gros and petit manseng, or an Alsatian Vendange Tardive. Champagne and other French or English sparkling wines also make a good accompaniment, the brisk acidity and the bubbles helping to disperse some of the mouth-coating fat. Also, clearly, champagne + foie gras is a sensational and sensationally indulgent snack. If foie gras is not being eaten by the slab but is part of a more complex dish, such as a terrine or a creamy sauce for chicken, then the curves of an oaked chardonnay or the bosomy, apricots-and-honeysuckle scent of an oaked viognier from the northern Rhône work very well.

fondue A great big pan roiling with melted Gruyère and Emmental, seasoned with garlic, white wine and kirsch and thickened with a spoonful of cornflour – what bliss. Even if you dip crunchy raw vegetables rather than cubes of toasted bread in it, cheese fondue is never going to make it into the nutrition sheets for cardiac care, but it is so delicious. An acerbic white wine from the Alps will give the impression of cutting through the fat in your mouth like Chemmy Alcott spraying snow on her parallel turns. My favourite is the jacquère grape from Savoie. Alternatives include picpoul from the Languedoc, grüner veltliner from Austria, a grassy sauvignon blanc from the Loire or Bordeaux, or savagnin from the Jura. A light, racy red can also work: try Marcillac, with its bloody tingle of iron, made from fer servadou in the Aveyron in France; or a frisky young Beaujolais.

fridge raid Those times when you stand hovering by the open fridge door, with an empty plate and a big appetite, prepared to eat anything and everything. Hopefully you will have a bottle of sherry tucked in there. Even if, strictly speaking, it's a bit too old and has passed into cooking sherry territory, pour yourself a glass to drink with whatever leftovers, chunks of ageing cheese and lumps of raw vegetables end up on your plate.

fritto misto and calamares fritos The crunch of light batter and, inside it, succulent seafood is a treat that goes well with almost any sharp dry white or white sparkling wine, from cava to prosecco to Vinho Verde to arneis. Unoaked white Rioja and floral malvasia are also good. And I love the salty-sea-spray-and-baking-sourdough riffle of a chilled glass of manzanilla sherry. Acidic red can work too.

frogs' legs The primary taste of cooked frogs' legs is usually mild chicken overlaid with garlicky butter. Loire chenin blanc, Muscadet, white Côtes du Rhône or Mâcon or St Véran all go well.

F

G

game see *grouse, partridge, pheasant, pigeon, rabbit, venison*

gammon The salty pink meat of a roast gammon joint is beautifully complemented by the dry sweetness of ripe grenache. I'm thinking less of the pumice and herbal rasp of a southern Rhône wine (although these are good) and more of the baked-mulberry richness of an old vine grenache from Australia's Barossa or the lavish fruit of wines made from the old garnacha vines on the hillsides of Aragon in Spain (Calatayud, Cariñena and Campo de Borja are the DOs to look for). The ripe red berry taste of grenache echoes the kind of flavour explosion you have when you put Cumberland sauce with roast ham and, in fact, the three go together well. Alternatives that work in a similar vein include juicy carignan (from Chile or the Languedoc); Loire cabernet franc (Chinon, Bourgueil, St Nicolas de Bourgueil, Saumur or Saumur-Champigny) from a warm year; or ripe pinot noir from Australia, Chile or New Zealand.

White wines can also be very good with a cooked ham joint. Dry riesling from Alsace, New Zealand, Australia or Austria; white Côtes du Rhône; or Australian marsanne will emphasize the succulence of the meat.

garlic GAME-CHANGER Raw garlic is pungent and if you have ever thought that it also seems to taste hot, just like chilli, you are right. Like capsaicin in chilli, the allicin in raw (but not cooked) garlic activates an ion channel called TRPV1, which is used to detect thermal changes in the mouth, specifically temperatures of over 43.25°C, and this is what causes the burning sensation. Allicin also activates a second ion channel known as TRPA1, which is thought to be used to detect painfully cold (below -15°C) temperatures. So raw garlic elicits sensations of burning heat and burning cold at once. Its effect on wine is to overpower any that do not have sharp acidity or residual sugar, so with dips and dishes that are heavy in raw garlic, I always look for a mouth-cleansingly fresh wine. For instance, guacamole is good with the tingle of sauvignon blanc and aioli goes well with roussette.

Cooked garlic is much less aggressive than raw. In some heavily garlicky dishes, such as bagna cauda or garlicky pasta sauces, the garlic is still burningly pungent as it has only been heated, or partially cooked, and these still benefit from being eaten alongside a wine that has acidic bite. Thoroughly cooked garlic, whether fried or roasted, usually asserts itself in a more aromatic way; it's about fragrance, not attack, which leaves you free to choose aromatic wines that fit in with the whole dish.

gazpacho Fierce raw garlic, pungent onion and the sting of vinegar ensure that gazpacho is a mouthful to be reckoned with. It is a very temperamental dish, easily ruined by the use of rancid garlic, which seems to have become increasingly common and will pollute the plate with an acrid, harsh taste. Still, with good garlic – which can easily be identified by sniffing, though only once a clove has been peeled – this Andalusian dish feels more like a fresh, aromatic salad. The rich tomato base, verdancy of the green peppers, and the bite of alliums and vinegar are best matched with a sharp, cold fino or manzanilla sherry or a fuller, warmer amontillado. The sourdough-like warmth of the sherry acts as an amplifier on the tomato and its tang of sea spray underscores the crisp edges of the vegetables, while the gazpacho makes the sherry taste rounder, more fruity, less austere. A sharp white wine such as a verdejo (Spain's answer to sauvignon blanc) or one of those sauvignon blancs with a spiteful side to them can also be effective. I'm thinking of those sauvignon blancs from the Loire or from the Awatere Valley in Marlborough, New Zealand, or from South Africa that are all about the scent of citrus, grass and green tomatoes rather than nectarines, passion fruit and stewed ripe gooseberries. If you can find a wine with a barbed-wire-like tautness it will really zing against gazpacho.

G

**MRS LEWISOHN'S GAZPACHO
(AN ADAPTATION)**
Serves 6

The best gazpacho, in my view, is made not by blending
but by chopping the vegetables into very tiny pieces.
My knife skills aren't that hot, so I compromise by
blending but using lots of chopped vegetables as a
garnish.

for the soup
- 1½ cucumbers, peeled and roughly chopped
- 500g tomatoes, blanched, peeled and roughly
chopped
- 1 green pepper, deseeded and roughly chopped
- 1 smallish white onion, peeled and roughly chopped
- 1 clove of garlic, peeled and chopped
- 125ml tomato juice
- 3 tablespoons good olive oil
- 2 tablespoons white wine vinegar
- salt

to serve
- 1 good chunk of cucumber, peeled and neatly diced
- 1 green pepper, deseeded and finely diced
- 2 tomatoes, finely diced
- croutons
- 1 small bunch of flat-leaf parsley, chopped
- Tabasco (optional)

Put the soup vegetables in a food processor and
whizz until liquidized. You can also use a hand blender
to liquidize them in a large bowl or pan, but a larger
blender is easier and less likely to spatter your kitchen.
Push the mixture through a sieve into a pan, bowl or
large jug, discarding the pulp left in the sieve. Add
the tomato juice, oil and vinegar (keep tasting, adding
more if you like), stir to mix thoroughly, and season

to taste. Put in the fridge for a couple of hours until chilled, then serve with small bowls of the diced vegetables, croutons and parsley for scattering on top. Add Tabasco if you think it's needed.

ginger As anyone who loves a Moscow Mule already knows, ginger is gorgeous with lime. The two just have something special together. There is no more limy grape than riesling, and there is no more limy riesling than the stuff grown in the Eden and Clare Valleys in Australia. These wines have a rasp, a dryness, a gentle scent of lilac and a sharp cut that's like a steely blade that tastes of intense lime zest, freshly squeezed lime juice and lime blossom. They are wines to put with, say, crispy soft-shell crab fried with ginger and garlic; salad made using chicken marinated in soy, garlic and ginger; or fish cooked en papillote with ginger, lemongrass and chilli.

I sometimes find subtle hints of ginger in dry furmint, which is one reason why it tastes so good with sushi that is accompanied by thin slices of sushi ginger.

gnocchi With gnocchi, it's all about the sauce. See *pasta* for suggestions.

Goan fish curry The creamy coconut and mild spice of this dish from the southern coast of India go well with the aromatic florals of an off-dry pinot gris. My second choice would be a fruity, off-dry rosé, maybe from Anjou or Australia. If a more tangy, citric accompaniment is preferred, then try an off-dry riesling, perhaps from the Great Southern region in Western Australia.

See also chilli, curry.

goose Goose is a fatty bird and the cut of a young claret provides a welcome contrasting edge. It's a great Christmas Day wine too.

goulash The paprika and the peppers in this Hungarian stew are brilliant with carmenère, which often tastes of paprika, dust and red capsicum too. Fighty, robust Greek reds such as agiorgitiko go well too. As do reds from Portugal's Dão or, indeed, Hungarian country wines.

gravadlax The thick fragrance of a dry Alsace muscat or a viognier will work with the fish and the dill. The minute you hit the sweetness of the mustard sauce, however, you run into trouble. An off-dry gewürztraminer can work here. Of course, what I'd really choose to drink is aquavit or vodka, ice cold, in shots.

Greek salad Feta cheese and tomatoes have very tangy acidity and a third ingredient in Greek salad – raw onions – also delivers a sting. Pick a tangy wine to go with them. Grassy sauvignon blanc or grapefruit-pithy assyrtiko are two good options.

grouse The traditional answer to the question of what to drink with grouse is 'a bottle of good, old red burgundy'. This reminds me of the friend who nervously asked for advice on what to wear to a smart ball in Scotland and was told 'a long dress and your good jewels'. Devastating news for anyone who has failed either to inherit any rocks or to marry a man on a diamonds and rubies income.

Burgundy can be the same. Finding a decent bottle that is both older and ready to drink is the devil's work. You need to own it already, and, to do that, to have been in the habit of buying a case or two every year, when it is sold en primeur, for at least a decade.

Happily, I'm not sure the traditionalists are always right. The current fashion for cooking grouse is to serve it practically bleeding. With rare meat, it can be a good thing to have a prickle of tannin, a sense that is more about brightness and crunch than gentle autumn leaves. In other words, with rare grouse look for a young and not a mature wine. A sappy, young red burgundy – even a simple Bourgogne Rouge – would do the trick, as would a young, edgy claret. Save the mature burgundy for well-cooked grouse – the scent of mulching leaves and the earthy sense of place is beautiful with it.

Besides the cuisson, the level of gameyness has a huge impact on the wine. At the beginning of the season, when the birds are eaten fresh, the flavours are milder. Consider an Austrian red; or a good pinot noir from Australia (ideally from Geelong, whose wines are more savoury) or from New Zealand (Central Otago has the most weight and often a background taste of coffee or roasted fruits; Martinborough combines lift with structure).

A well-hung grouse needs a wilder red to meet the pungent

flavours rising from the bird – and actually the wines I am about to suggest will go with grouse of more or less any kind. Mourvèdre can smell quite lived in and is a key grape in Bandol. Dão or Douro reds based on touriga nacional also have a pleasing element of savagery. The Languedoc is a good source of gamey reds (nose out a St Chinian or Pic St Loup) and the northern Rhône (Cornas, St Joseph, Crozes-Hermitage) is rich with maturing syrahs that have exactly the feral, leathery pong you want. An old-fashioned Madiran, made from the tannat grape, also offers leathery austerity and firm, sinewy tannins. Nebbiolo, another mercilessly tannic grape, is a good option as well: I slightly favour Barbaresco over Barolo – it has more brightness and more of a reassuring plume of flavour to meet a well-hung grouse that is served rare. Finally, any red wine infected with a yeast strain called brettanomyces, which makes wine smell a bit horsey, is perfect with well-hung grouse. We used to believe that the niffy farmyard smell of brett was a charmingly French part of terroir. Although it's now considered a fault, it can add pleasing layers of flavour to cheaper wines. All of these wines could also very happily be drunk with a bird that is not well hung too.

G

H

haggis This Scottish speciality made from sheep's heart, liver and lungs, oatmeal, suet and spices is traditionally eaten with mashed neeps and a nip of whisky. My preferred haggis whisky is Talisker 10 Year Old, a single malt from the Isle of Skye that smells like a slap of wild, brisk winter sea air with a tinge of woodsmoke in it. The piquant, peppery notes in the whisky meet the seasoning in the haggis as if they were made for each other.

Whisky aged in sherry casks has a gruff warmth and soft breadth that sidles up to the sweetness of the accompanying neeps. Try the warm spread of Macallan 10 Year Old Sherry Oak, or Kilchoman Machir Bay, which has the precise edge and peat of an Islay whisky but is also enriched with a few weeks in old oloroso butts. Japanese whiskies – the closest you get to Scotch outside Scotland – are also excellent with haggis as well as in their own right. Look for Yamazaki whiskies.

As for wine, the grape that works so well with pepper, not least because it tastes of cracked black pepper itself, is syrah. Go northern Rhône, or to cooler parts of Australia or South Africa.

hake Lightly fried in flour with perhaps a touch of egg, hake is gorgeous with chilled fino sherry. In Spain, the personality of hake seems to change from region to region, depending on how it is cooked, and the local wine – either red or white – is almost always the one that works the best.

ham see *charcuterie, gammon*

hangover I drink Lucozade and endless cups of tea with a hangover. The hair of the dog cure is overrated. But see Javier Hidalgo's comments in *sherry*.

harissa The fiery, red North African chilli-based paste is often used as a marinade or rub on chicken, quail and fish. This works well with aromatic off- or medium-dry whites such as blossom-scented pinot gris or a floaty riesling from the Mosel or Nahe. Rose harissa, in particular, is very pretty with the floral fragrance of a pinot gris.

An off-dry rosé will have a similarly soothing effect on the chilli fire of harissa. When this paste is smeared over charcoal-grilled lamb it can be pleasing to stoke harissa's heat by drinking red. A Lebanese or Portuguese blend is a good option.

herbs GAME-CHANGER Herbs are powerful ingredients that have a huge impact on the flavour of a dish and therefore also on what wines taste good with it. There is a real potential for clash here – but also for great synergy.

H

See also coriander, dill rosemary, tarragon, thyme.

hollandaise This buttery rich sauce works well with the curves and soft edges of barrel-fermented chardonnays, and also unoaked chardonnays.

I

ice cream Cream, frozen or otherwise, is good with rich, warm-tasting spirits such as brandy and rum. Vanilla ice cream also works well with other drinks that channel Christmas flavours – nuts, spice, dried fruit and caffè mocha. And of course a vanilla ice cream base can be customized to go with just about any sweet flavour you like. There are a few ways to do this.

in

Arguably the best way to mix alcohol and ice cream is to do it right from the beginning. The most obvious delicious examples are rum and raisin; Baileys; and eggy, Marsala-lashed zabaglione. Being experts in both wine and ice cream, the Italians can't resist turning practically every drink made on the peninsula into gelato, but I draw the line at gelato flavoured with nero d'avola (the red wine grape found in Sicily) and Strega (a violent yellow, bitter herbal liqueur).

over

Slosh alcohol over a couple of scoops of dairy vanilla and serve it in a tall sundae glass like a boozy affogato. One wine that's good for pouring over ice cream is pedro ximénez, known as PX for obvious pronunciation-difficulty reasons. This viscous sherry is possibly the sweetest wine in the world, loading up to as much as 450g of sugar per litre. Thick, and a very dark, treacly brown, it looks and tastes like molasses might if molasses had had fat, juicy raisins liquidized into it. Ice cream and PX is one of the quickest, easiest and best-received desserts I have encountered. My granny used to go nuts for it. In fact, a slim half-bottle of PX is a very good granny stocking filler.

with

quick suggestions Stick to ice cream in the vanilla-chocolate-nuts-crème brûlée-coffee-fudge spectrum and there are many wines – most of them fortified – that will taste good in a glass beside it. Try Australian liqueur muscat, the indulgent fortified wine that's reminiscent of demerara sugar, caramel and dried fruit; sweeter Madeiras – wines from the volcanic island between Africa and the European mainland that have such longevity they are virtually immortal (bual and malmsey are the grapes used to make sweeter styles); Marsala; tawny port; Maury (a red vin doux naturel made in the Roussillon in southern France from powdery grenache); and chocolate liqueur. My pinnacle ice cream and booze experience (to date) was at Penfolds' Magill Estate in South Australia. There for lunch, I passed on dessert, only to enrage my neighbour by eating half of hers. It was an incredibly elaborate ice cream, made with roasted almonds, chocolate, macadamia nuts, caramel and raisins that had been marinated in Penfolds' Grandfather Tawny – a rich, fortified Australian alternative to port. With it, we drank a glass of Penfolds' Great Grandfather Tawny, a more refined, intense version of the wine in the ice cream. It is easy to make an approximation of this gorgeousness using a good recipe for vanilla ice cream as a base and either an Australian fortified wine or an aged tawny port for the drinking and the raisin-soaking (this always makes me think of Roald Dahl's *Danny the Champion of the World* – do not include sleeping tablets). Claudia Roden uses a similar raisin and sweet wine combination in a favourite recipe in her book *The Food of Spain*. Also, she likes to put the booze in the ice cream as well as passing it round to drink with it.

more elaborate ideas In theory, any sweet wine could go with any ice cream, if the dessert has been put together so that the flavours reflect and complement the wine. Only remember that if your mouth is very cold you will not taste as many nuances in the wine. I once drank Tokaji, the rich, sweet golden wine from Hungary, with ice cream made with figs and orange peel stewed in sweet wine – a real hit. On another occasion an old bottle of Château d'Yquem, the famous Sauternes, was opened to go with vanilla ice cream served with slivers of fresh coconut and pineapple with Cape gooseberries and kumquats. A very clever combination.

Indian India makes wine but is neither a wine-drinking culture nor a wine-with-food culture.

'I learnt very quickly on arriving in France that people will stand for fifteen minutes with an aperitif, then spend three hours over dinner with wine,' Indian-born sommelier Magandeep Singh told me at a tasting of Indian wines. 'In India, the opposite. You call people for 7 p.m., they'll turn up at 8 p.m., spend three hours talking and grazing over a buffet, then rush through dinner in twenty minutes and be home asleep by midnight. Food and wine pairing is a bit lost on us, because we don't do it outside a hotel or a restaurant.'

The exploration of wine flavours with Indian food has therefore largely been left to cooks who have emigrated and set up restaurants in Britain, Australia, the US, and elsewhere, as well as Western eaters and drinkers pouring wine with food they have cooked from recipe books at home, ordered from the takeaway or are eating in a restaurant.

This means that we're always thinking about versions of real Indian cooking – adaptations and approximations, and a dilution of regionality – as we tend to have dishes originating in completely different parts of India on the table at once.

Westernization brings another shift in emphasis. Dimple Athavia of the Indian wine-making company Grover Zampa tells me their off-dry viognier is very popular – the aromatics play into the spicy scents and the slight sweetness acts as a buffer against the burn of the chilli. These are the kinds of flavours I would choose with spicy dishes. However, while 70 per cent of Grover Zampa's produce is sold on the domestic market, much of it is drunk in restaurants in the big, more international, cities of Mumbai, Delhi and Bangalore. Many Indians I speak to who do enjoy drinking wine with food say they love not off-dry whitess but oaked reds, the very wines I steer away from with heavily spiced dishes, as heat and spice make the tannins (from both the wood and the grape) feel tough and harsh. I had always presumed this reflected either a higher tolerance for chilli and spice, or a preference for that clash. Magandeep makes a different point: 'In India, we don't have side plates. The bread goes at the six o'clock position on the plate with the other dishes ranged around it. Every time I have a mouthful, I'm starting with the bread, or the rice, and dipping into the others. Eighty per cent of each mouthful is carbs. This has a softening effect on the spices.' In other words, when eating from the same table, an Indian's experience of the food is different from the richer hit of mostly sauce, spice and protein a Westerner might enjoy.

The world of Indian food is large and sprawling, but if you are sharing food, with several dishes on the table at once, finding a wine that tastes good with it is always going to be an art of approximation. That's why I have written at most length about the effect of *chilli* and talked about the generic dish we call the *curry* as well as giving entries for just a few of the best-known Indian foods.

See also dhal, Goan fish curry, rogan josh, tandoori.

J

jacket potato (with cheese) When the potato is cooked in bonfire embers, or in the oven without being wrapped in foil to keep the skin tender, so that it has a crisped, smoky-smelling thick jacket, try a smoky oaked St Chinian, which sometimes smells of chestnut skins. A bottle of claret is another cosy match. Ditto a cabernet sauvignon-syrah blend from Australia. If you want to posh it up, then nebbiolo, Barolo or Barbaresco is great with the buttery cheese and the smell of fire. But of course anything goes with this kind of comfort food.

jambon persillé This jellied ham terrine made with pork hock and parsley and served in thick slices with bread or toast is delicious as a starter or snack. A cool, lightly oaked white burgundy is perfect.

Jansson's frestelse Literally, Jansson's temptation – a Swedish dish that is traditionally eaten at Christmas – this is a kind of fishy dauphinoise made with potatoes, onions and 'ansjovis'. Ansjovis are sprats that have been cured in spiced brine and have a sweet, mellow, clovey taste – unfortunately, substituting Mediterranean anchovy fillets does not work. Jansson's frestelse was first cooked for me by the human gastronomic tornado that is the half-German, half-Swedish (by parentage), English-raised Joe Wadsack. Joe made it using Abba ansjovis imported from the homeland, which, despite being packaged in a tin, must be kept refrigerated. The spice mix used in these is a secret but it is said to include cinnamon, sandalwood and ginger. An ice-cold shot of vodka (bison-grass Zubrówka, for choice) acts like a palate cleanser in between mouthfuls of this salty-sweet-spicy-oniony potato gratin, but aquavit is an even better choice as its spices play off those in the food.

In fact, said Joe, as we sat discussing ansjovis, 'the more I eat

Jansson's frestelse, the more I think you have to drink aquavit with it'. He then proceeded to give me a rapid lesson in aquavit styles: 'Swedish aquavit – the best-known brand is O. P. Anderson – is typically very pristine and sleek and fresh, with herby dill and fennel overtones. Danish aquavit – Aalborg is the big brand – is similar but softer, not so crisp, a kind of fino to O. P. Anderson's manzanilla, and the caraway flavours are stronger. In Norway, you have Linie, which is sent out to sea in oak sherry casks. You have the unusual humidity, and the rocking motion of the boat on the waves, so it's softer still, like aged rum, and a different drink to the other two.'

A wine that is equally clean and needle-sharp – say, aligoté or the Alpine jacquère – and served at a fairly arctic temperature is a good alternative.

jerk (chicken, goat or pork) Rum (with soda) is best with this hot and spicy Caribbean dish which contains thyme, fresh ginger, allspice and brown sugar. A slightly sweet beer is next best. For wine, go for an unpretentious, deep pink rosé that isn't perfectly dry.

K

K

kebab Home-made kebab is a favourite way of using up leftover roast lamb, but I eat these so quickly and so greedily and so messily – garlic and chilli sauce oozing out of the pitta, shredded lettuce and bits of tomato spilling all over – there is never any chance to take a sip of wine. I do know, though, that lamb kebabs in pitta are fantastic with a robust rosé (maybe one from Lebanon), or a robust red with a bit of fight in it (from Greece, Turkey, Lebanon or Portugal). Chicken kebab needs an inexpensive, neutral white.

kedgeree I have never got on with any wine with this mixture of smoky fish, egg and rice with cumin. Also, it's a breakfast dish. Lapsang souchong tea, whose leaves are smoked over pine wood fire, matches the intense smokiness of the fish and seems to me the only way to go.

King George whiting The delicate white flesh of one of Australia's finest fish, the King George whiting, is superb with young, fresh Australian riesling. The piercing lime flavours of the dry wine are gloriously refreshing in between mouthfuls of (ideally barbecued) fish on a sunny day close to a beach.

kippers Smoky kippers and buttered brown bread cry out for a cup of English breakfast, Lapsang Souchang, or Earl Grey tea. The only alcoholic alternative is a nip of peaty Islay whisky.

L

lamb Lamb is blessed by having a grape seemingly made precisely to go with it. That grape is cabernet sauvignon. This means that a classic match is red bordeaux, preferably one from the left bank, where cabernet sauvignon usually forms the backbone of the blend. At the high end, this might be a top growth from the commune of Pauillac in the Médoc, which you could drink with rack of Pauillac lamb conveniently raised nearby; sheep in the region, as well as wine, have protected designation of origin status from the EU. On an everyday level, stick a chop on the griddle and open the most miserly, scratchy claret you can find – anything will do, as long as there is cabernet sauvignon as well as merlot in there. When you drink and eat, a piece of magic will occur. A wine that tasted as dusty, threadbare, green and tannic as black tea is transformed, becoming riper and more succulent. It's practically a party trick and a brilliant way to make cheap wine sing.

Cabernet sauvignon does not, of course, have to mean bordeaux. There are great, slightly more rustic, versions in nearby Bergerac and in Buzet, as well as further south in the Pays d'Oc. Nor does it have to come from France. There are superb examples and blends from the Napa Valley, Argentina, South Africa, Tuscany and Australia, and that's just for starters.

Cabernet sauvignon is also far from being the only red that is absolutely gorgeous with lamb. I've lost count of the number of times I've put a butterflied leg of lamb, smeared with a mortar and pestle paste of garlic, anchovies and rosemary, in the oven and not just because it's an easy dinner. The aromatic flavour of this dish is good with so many red wines that I had to ban winemakers from recommending it in the second half of the book, otherwise that's all you'd have read about. Lamb is also fantastic with red wine from Rioja and Ribera del Duero (particularly slow-cooked lamb); Portugal; Provence, the Rhône, Madiran and the Loire (France again); Greece and the Lebanon. To get the most out of both wine and food, it's worth paying attention to how the lamb is cooked (barbecued, roasted, griddled, casseroled), for how long (seared versus slow) and what other flavours are involved. Has it been rubbed with hot spices or covered in fresh green herbs? Is it going to be eaten with bright pomegranate seeds, smoky aubergines and hummus, or with stuffed Mediterranean vegetables? Or has it been barbecued over smoky coals? There are suggestions for all of these, and more, below.

Is there any red wine that lamb doesn't go with? Well, yes, actually. At an extensive tasting of pork, beef and lamb with Argentine wines at the Gaucho Grill, I was surprised to find that lamb and malbec are the sort of bedfellows who would probably approach each other awkwardly from across the central mattress chasm, bicker over the tog rating of the duvet and end up sleeping in different rooms.

There is no need to stick with red, though. Rosé is also delicious. A glass of palest pink from Provence with new-season lamb is a real treat; the heavier and richer the accompaniments, the darker and sweeter you can afford to go with the wine. Don't rule out white wine either. Lamb stuffed with herbs, capers and olives and served with potatoes cooked Greek-style with vigorous lemon and oregano can taste great with a vibrant assyrtiko from Santorini or an oaked white bordeaux.

See also cottage (or shepherd's) pie, curry, kebab, Lancashire hot pot, moussaka, tagine.

cuts and cooking styles

barbecued The big flavours of meat cooked over smoky coals or burning wood demand wine with substance and courage. If you're picking bordeaux, go for one that's young and vital, or youngish and more expensive (more expensive = more concentrated). Otherwise, this is a good moment to bring out a northern Rhône or a New World red: for instance, a smoky syrah from South Africa or an exuberant Barossa Shiraz. The ingredients in the marinade or rub will also determine the direction (see below).

braised shank Peasant reds with soft flavours suit the rich, melting texture of this cheaper slow-cooked cut. Reds from the Languedoc-Roussillon – Corbières, Fitou, St Chinian – fit the bill. A Lebanese red blend or an inexpensive South African cabernet, syrah, merlot or cinsault would also be good.

cold roast The more solid texture of cold slices of meat goes well with young, fruity wines with a bit of edge (acidity) and little or no oak. Try a Côtes du Rhône; Coonawarra cabernet sauvignon; Beaujolais Cru or Villages; basic claret (perhaps a Côtes de Castillon); or a bright, focused Italian red such as barbera.

kidneys A soft, light pinot noir from Australia, or a country French pinot, will meet the soft texture of the kidney.

liver The tang of sour cherries is good with lamb's liver and this is found in young dolcetto, barbera or gamay. If lamb's liver and kidneys are being eaten together, then try the herbaceous tautness of a German pinot noir. An alternative is a strongly flavoured red such as Chilean carmenère or South African cabernet or pinotage.

milk-fed Tender and subtle, this merits a more distinguished, older bottle, such as a mature bordeaux or burgundy, whose flavours will be complex but also much more delicate than those of a bright young wine.

pink Pinot noir or the leafy redcurrant and new-school-pencil taste of cabernet franc from the Loire is lovely with pink lamb, particularly if served with a tangle of peas, lettuce, baby carrots and other spring vegetables.

roast With a plain roast, you can go almost anywhere. See the list at the top of this entry for suggestions from left-bank bordeaux to Supertuscans.

slow-roast Shoulder is the cut that most often comes in for the slow-roast treatment and it is at home with Spanish reds such as Rioja or Ribera del Duero. Try them young, for the contrast between the falling-off-the-bone meat and the bright strawberry and straw flavours in the wine, or with more oak, and older, when the wine

L

begins to mellow like autumn leaves and will melt right into the soft lamb.

with
anchovies, rosemary and garlic The Mediterranean/Italian flavours suit wines from the same place. With leg of lamb, basted or slits stuffed with this salty mixture of condiments try, Bandol or red from another part of Provence, Languedoc reds (Corbières, Faugères, St Chinian, for example), Rhône reds, north or south – both have a wild, herbaceous, sometimes almost menthol, smell that picks up on the rosemary. Central Italian wines such as Rosso di Montepulciano or Montalcino or Chianti are good too. Be extra-smart and bring in a cabernet sauvignon element by opening a Domaine de Trevallon, a red wine made in Provence from syrah and cabernet, or a Supertuscan, or a Chianti that has a small amount of cabernet bolstering the majority sangiovese in the blend (Querciabella and Fontodi are two Chianti Classico estates that use a percentage of cabernet in one of their cuvées). Italian + cabernet is a particular winner if you're putting the anchovies, rosemary and garlic in a white bean side dish – brilliant with griddled lamb steaks.

chilli/spicy rubs Try a warm, ripe hug of Australia's great syrah-cabernet blend or a bright, fruity red from Chile or South Africa.

couscous (as a side dish) With a rich, raisined couscous, try the woody, plum and tobacco flavours of a Rioja Reserva. Lamb with spicy couscous studded with pomegranate seeds can be good with cabernet sauvignon from Coonawarra in Australia, pinot noir from Central Otago in New Zealand or a roar of an Australian syrah, maybe from McLaren Vale or the Barossa. Couscous with sharper flavours, such as radish and spring onion, served with pink lamb prefers a cabernet franc or an unoaked Costières de Nîmes.

feta, lemon, capers and/or green olives The high acid and salt here need a wine that can fight back with some acidity/astringency of its own. Barbera would work, as would a Lebanese or Greek red, or a very young, keen-edged red bordeaux without too much oak on it. If the feta, lemon, capers and olives are very heavily represented either in the stuffing or accompanying salads and potatoes then a white – say, an oaked white bordeaux with its baked grapefruit, lemon pith and woodruff flavours, but choose a young one, or an assyrtiko from Santorini, would be good too. Diana Henry combines many of these flavours in her glorious, Easterish recipe for Greek-influenced lamb – lamb with caper, parsley and preserved lemons stuffing which you can find in her book *Food from Plenty*.

herb crust On a simple chop, a rack of lamb, or leg, the leafy, crunchy crust calls for a cabernet of some sort – either sauvignon or franc. Head to Bordeaux, the Loire or Coonawarra in Australia.

lavender and rosemary Butterflied leg of lamb scattered with rosemary and lavender is delicious with Côtes du Rhône (Villages), either from the generic appellation or from a village that has been promoted to its own appellation – such as Gigondas, Vacqueyras, Rasteau.

Mediterranean vegetables (aubergines, tomatoes stuffed with thyme and garlic, red peppers) We're back in Provence. One of their vanishingly pale rosés would go well. Or I might be tempted north, just slightly, for a syrah from the northern Rhône or grenache-based blend from the southern Rhône.

meze/Middle-Eastern flavours If you're eating lamb as part of a dinner with many other meze dishes, there is likely to be a lot going on: a crowd of green parsley, salty olives, tangy sumac, earthy chickpeas and spices. A wine needs growl to stand up to these boisterous flavours. Crozes-Hermitage and St Joseph from the northern Rhône do this well. Deep coloured rosés are good too. As are the more rustic, tannic reds coming out of Eastern Europe or the (much-finessed in the last few years) blends from Lebanon. A clever solution is the throaty syrah made in the heat of Morocco by Crozes-Hermitage star Alain Graillot. Or try Stellenbosch cabernet sauvignon.

mint sauce The violent vinegar and mint need a cheap, acidic bordeaux.

redcurrants and other sweet, fruity accompaniments With red berries on the plate with lamb, I veer towards bright, young reds from the Loire (cabernet franc is very good with lamb and redcurrants) or riper reds from Argentina, South Africa, Chile, New Zealand and Australia. If there's an earthy tinge – say, lentils or hummus – on the plate too, then you can take a bit more oak.

skordalia For wines to go with lamb as well as this lemon and almond mash see the *feta, lemon, capers and/or green olive* entry above.

Lancashire hot pot Any number of reds go well with this dish but I particularly like inexpensive tempranillo, from Rioja or elsewhere, as its mellow quality is good with both the lamb and the sweetness of the cooked root vegetables.

lasagne Lasagne to most means what the Italians call lasagne alla bolognese – pasta layered with meat ragù and béchamel sauce. There are many interpretations, from those that are light and scented with bay leaves to the cheesy, gooey Anglo versions. All go well with Italian red wine, most of which have the acidity to cut through the creamy sauce, as well as the savour to match the meat. Sangiovese is a good catch-all; pick a Chianti Rufina if you want the wine to be more refreshing. I like young (unoaked or barely oaked) nebbiolo with the less creamy, more herbaceous versions. But Italy has many other red wines that will do a good job with lasagne, from easy-drinking Biferno Rosso to nero d'avola from Sicily. Look at the entry for *ragù alla bolognese* for more ideas.

Of course, lasagne is simply the name of the type of pasta. It takes only a glance at the index of *The Silver Spoon*, the bestselling Italian cookbook, to see that there are many regional variations, including lasagne alla napoletana (made with beef, mozzarella and slices of hard-boiled eggs), lasagne with radicchio, with leeks and black truffles, with aubergine and ricotta, and so on. Add to this the number of different veggie lasagnes developed outside Italy and lasagne would probably fill a book on its own. Baked pasta dishes from lasagne to cannelloni to pasticcio are usually richer and heavier than boiled pasta dressed with a sauce, but the filling remains the best guide. Any lasagne, veggie or otherwise, made

L

using tomatoes will usually go well with sangiovese. A radicchio lasagne demands a wine with astringency. Seafood and tarragon lasagne is good with sauvignon-semillon blends. Mushroom lasagne with almost any rich, meaty red wine. And so on.

lemon GAME-CHANGER Lemon is an ingredient that demands attention. It's just so piercing and acidic, which can make some wines taste flat. Watch out for lemon-dressed salads, or baked dishes that include whole lemon slices: for example, one-pot chicken with chickpeas, green olives and lemons, or fish roasted with thinly sliced lemons.

If you are having a lemony salad with meat – say, steak and spinach with lemon juice and olive oil – then you can count on an Italian red wine to have enough acidity to deal with the issue. Otherwise, it is simple: look for whites that taste of lemons or other citrus fruit, as they will often have vibrant acidity. Good examples include Gavi, arneis, sauvignon blanc, riesling, verdejo and assyrtiko.

See also preserved lemon.

lemon tart Dessert wines made from riesling have a tingle that is perfect here; look for a beerenauslese or trockenbeerenauslese from Germany.

lemongrass This tropical grass with a woody base has an energizing citrus fragrance that dovetails with aromatic white wines made from riesling, sauvignon blanc (especially the pungent sauvignon from New Zealand or South Africa or Chile) and grüner veltliner. A word of warning, however. Lemongrass is often used in Thai cooking and when chilli, which prefers sweeter wines, gets involved ignore it at your peril. Still, there's such a natural affinity between those aromatic wines and lemongrass that, if cooking Thai, I often open a bottle of dry riesling or Marlborough sauvignon blanc to drink in the kitchen during the chopping and chatting part of the evening. Bone-dry Hugel riesling from Alsace – which tastes at first like just-squeezed lime juice washing over stones, then starts to swell out like peaches and clementines – is a favourite bottle to open while making a giant bowlful of 'Chicken, lime and lemongrass soup' from Tom Parker Bowles's book *Let's Eat*.

See also chilli.

lentils The presence of earthy, small dark green (they may not necessarily be Puy) lentils, or the little brown ones you find in Umbria, shuffles a plate of food towards a red wine. It might be a chunk of cod with pancetta and lentils, or honey-roast gammon with lentils cooked in the ham stock and mixed with chopped rosemary, garlic and a spoonful of cream, but either way red usually appeals more at this point than white. I usually go with whatever wine is suggested by the other ingredients on the plate: maybe a nerello mascalese from Sicily with the fish, perhaps an Aussie grenache with the ham. If you're looking for a wine that shares the same earthy register as the lentils, then consider mencía from Spain, Dão from Portugal or a farmhousey Chianti.

See also dhal.

lime As with lemons, the acidity has a strong impact and, if there's lots of it, it's best to choose a wine that has decent acidity too. There is one grape that both tastes of lime and also has very vibrant acidity – riesling.

See also lime (dried), South-East Asian food.

lime (dried) Dried limes are used in Middle Eastern cooking. They are intensely aromatic and the lime comes through in a very dusty and earthy, rather than in a sharp, way. They have a tendency to take over a dish, and when that happens I look to reds that remind you of soil and heat. Those from Greece, Lebanon, Turkey and Portugal often work well.

Here is an adaptation of a classic Iranian dish. I love the strong flavour of the limes in it so much that I break them up and squeeze them over the food on my plate to get even more of the dusty limeyness out. If dried limes are an alien flavour, maybe just use one the first time you make this, as the taste is quite powerful.

KHORESH GHEIMEH
(LAMB, DRIED LIME AND TOMATO CASSEROLE)
Serves 3–4

- olive oil
- 1 onion, peeled and chopped
- 3 cloves of garlic, peeled and finely chopped
- 500g lamb, diced

- 1 pinch of saffron, mixed with 2 tablespoons warm water
- ¼ teaspoon ground cinnamon
- ¼ teaspoon ground cumin
- ½ teaspoon ground coriander
- 1 teaspoon turmeric
- 1 × 400g tin tomatoes (whole)
- 2 tablespoons tomato purée
- 3 dried limes, pierced a couple of times with a metal skewer or corkscrew
- 150g split yellow peas, rinsed in cold water
- 500ml water
- 1 aubergine
- plain yoghurt to serve (optional)

Put 2 tablespoons of olive oil in a small casserole dish, heat gently, add the onions and fry until they are almost soft and translucent. Add the garlic, stir and continue to cook until both garlic and onions are pale gold. Use a slotted spoon to take them out of the pan and set aside. Now brown the lamb in the same pan, turning up the heat and adding more oil if necessary. Return the onion mixture to the pan and stir in the saffron, cinnamon, cumin, coriander and turmeric. Cook for a couple of minutes, stirring. Add the tomatoes, breaking them up with the edge of the spoon as you stir, and the tomato purée. Pour some of the water into the tomato can, swirl it around and then add all the water to the pan along with the dried limes. Simmer gently, partially covered, for 45 minutes. Now stir in the split yellow peas and carry on simmering, partially covered, for 45–60 minutes. Check to make sure the casserole does not simmer dry, adding more water if necessary. While the casserole is cooking, slice the aubergine and cut into strips. Fry these in oil until they are golden and cooked, then put them on a plate, layered with kitchen roll to absorb the grease. The stew is ready when the pulses are completely cooked through and the sauce has

L

thickened. Serve with rice studded with little chunks of cold butter, and the aubergine strips scattered on top, with a dish of yoghurt on the side if you like.

liver Chicken livers (served either in a spinach and bacon salad, or fried and chopped with capers on crostini) are a natural with sangiovese or Beaujolais. Seared calf's liver and bacon goes well with barbera, red bordeaux, Beaujolais, Chianti or Valpolicella Ripasso.

See also chicken: liver.

lobster With hot grilled lobster, open a white burgundy – as good a bottle as you are prepared to pay for – or an oaked Bordeaux Blanc whose substance, taste of baked-citrus, and pine tree scent are perfect with the sweet lobster meat. Bordeaux Blanc is particularly good if the lobster has been grilled with lime rather than plain or lemon butter. With cold lobster mayonnaise (perhaps with freshly torn basil leaves and halved cherry tomatoes mixed in), a cool glass of chardonnay is perfect for its creamy texture. Pick one that's not too heavy: go for one from Chablis or from elsewhere in Burgundy; for one of the new-wave Australian chardonnays from the Mornington Peninsula or from other, cooler, Victorian regions; or champagne.

M

macaroni cheese For a white that's refreshing against all that gooey cheese, pick piepoul or one of the citric unoaked Italian grapes (such as arneis, cortese, vermentino, slightly spiky vernaccia). But this is old-fashioned nursery food, and an old-fashioned glass of red bordeaux – youngish (for the refreshing edge), and with plenty of cabernet in it – is also satisfying.

See also cheese, pasta.

mackerel Choose a bracing white or red with this oily fish. Say, Gamay de Touraine or Marcillac for a red, Vinho Verde for a white.

meatballs There are many different styles of meatballs, so be guided by the seasoning. With Italian flavourings – basil, Pecorino, fennel, fennel seeds – choose an Italian wine. Nero d'avola, Teroldego Rotaliano or Cerasuolo di Vittoria (a blend of frappato and nero d'avola from Sicily) is a lovely summery match with Pecorino and basil porkballs in a milky tomato sauce. With spicier cumin and coriander meatballs, pick a throatier wine, perhaps a red from Lebanon. With straightforward beef meatballs in a tomato sauce, you can very happily drink almost any cosy red.

melon Heady, fragrant and sweet-fleshed gallia and charentais melons taste of summer. Ripe halves of these, with the seeds scooped out and the hollow filled with sweet liquor, are a brasserie staple with a markedly retro vibe. In the area around La Rochelle, in western France, where pale green striped charentais melons are grown, they fill them with Pineau des Charentes, a drink made by mixing sweetly ripe, tangy fresh grape juice with the burn of eau de vie. It's a hedonistic marriage. The glow of the nectar-like Pineau is blissful with the perfumed melon and I can't imagine why we don't drink more of it. A happy alternative is port – white or, even better, tawny, which is oak-aged, so that it takes on the relaxed flavours of caramel, dried fruit and roasted hazelnuts. In both cases the port tastes better chilled.

melon with air-dried ham Often the instinct is to pour red with charcuterie, however it is served. But a fruity or aromatic white brings a juicy succulence to prosciutto, serrano or other air-dried hams, counterpointing their salty savouriness. Perfumed whites such as viognier (all heady honeysuckle and apricot skin) and muscat (grapey and floral) also play to the hedonistic qualities of the melon. These effects are enhanced if the wine is off-dry – the sweetness of the melon hides the sugar in the wine so that you barely discern it. In fact, if there's a lot of melon then you *need* a white with some sugar in it, otherwise the fruit sweetness will completely knock out the wine so that it tastes arid, like putting sand in your mouth. No need to go overboard with a super-sticky dessert wine – an off-dry or medium white or pink will do the job. Try a non-dry chenin blanc from the Loire, scented like wildflower honey and quince: Vouvray or even the cheapest white Anjou will slide beautifully up against the ham and melon. The innocent, apple blossom waltz of a kabinett-level German riesling (go for one from the Mosel or Nahe – wines from the Rheingau are often too stern and earthy for melon) is also a good option. For a little more sweetness, try a gently effervescent moscato. This style originates from the north-west of Italy where the joyful, floral, stones-and-peach-skin frippery that is Moscato d'Asti is made. This is still the best as well as the most delicate and subtle moscato. But sparkling moscato is also big in California (the mammoth E.&J. Gallo makes it) and Australia (Innocent Bystander sell their bubbly rose-coloured moscato in wine bottles, lager-sized bottles and also by the keg. Yes, it's that big).

meze The earthy grittiness of chickpeas; the smoky burnt aubergine dips; the tahini, the fried little balls of spinach and spicy sausages, the piles of green tabbouleh with their radish and toasty crunch; the crackle of the thin sheets of charred taboon flatbreads … Very often with a table full of food exuding Middle Eastern flavours I will pour that 'sling it with everything' of wines – a rosé. It's not imaginative, but it works extremely well. If choosing a white wine, hold back on buttery New World chardonnay or vengeful sauvignon blanc and look instead for a less cartoon-like grape, such as a plain, stony bianco Terre di Chieti from Abruzzo in Italy or a fresh, citric roditis from Greece. For reds, sangiovese has a wonderful, gritty taste that is excellent here. Also ideal are reds from Greece, Lebanon, Morocco and Turkey and darker, heavier reds from Portugal or a brooding Languedoc blend, such as a Corbières, Fitou or St Chinian. For something a bit lighter, stick a bottle of Bardolino or Valpolicella in the fridge for twenty minutes and drink it with an edge of cold on it.

mince pies The crumbling pastry and luscious dried fruit of mince pies suit the molten raisin flavour of a sweet oloroso or cream sherry. It somehow works with dry sherry too, though pick one that's robust – an amontillado or a punchy fino rather than a manzanilla. Mince pies are also gorgeous with the sweet, floral Moscato di Pantelleria, made on the island of Pantelleria, a speck of Italy that lies between Sicily and Tunisia.

monkfish One of the most meaty-textured of all fish, this can happily be drunk with white wine – say an oaked Rioja or an albariño – but it is often cooked as part of a casserole, or with rice, flavoured with saffron or tomatoes or artichokes, in which case a red from Rioja or Ribera del Duero is a fine accompaniment.

moules marinière With a garlicky, fishy broth and the indigo shells of moules marinière (with or without cream), I am never really happy if I don't have a glass of Muscadet de Sèvre et Maine (ideally sur lie for extra texture and flavour). It's a classic combination and nothing beats it.

moussaka The heavy layers of minced lamb, béchamel sauce and aubergine are good with the prickle and tannin of agiorgitiko from Greece. Other good reds are Montepulciano d'Abruzzo or a simple sangiovese from Italy; smoky pinotage or cabernet sauvignon from South Africa; dusty carmenère from Chile; blends from Lebanon; or Bierzo from Spain. In summer, moussaka is good with rosé. Rather than choosing a subtle pink from Provence, go for a deeper-coloured wine from the Languedoc, Italy or Spain.

mushroom Because mushrooms are a meaty vegetable, if you have made them the star of the dish the instinct is to reach for a red. Fragrant, earthy reds are the best bet. Pinot noir is a natural with almost any mushroom dish. Porcini and chanterelles – simultaneously both powerful and delicate – are very good with nebbiolo (Barolo or Barbaresco) from north-west Italy and sangiovese (such as a Chianti from Tuscany). For mushroom mixtures, or the juicier, more grounded flavour of flat, button and chestnut mushrooms, you can afford fleshier reds, such as a gutsy blend from the south of France, mencía from Bierzo and dusty reds from the Douro or the Dão in Portugal. Pinot noir (or, along similar lines, trousseau), Pomerol and aged Ribera del Duero or Rioja accentuate the autumnal savouriness when mushrooms are an accent to game or pork. If the dish is more concentrated, perhaps intensified with yeast extract or beef stock, then a richer wine such as a cabernet sauvignon or a pinotage from South Africa makes a sturdy, wintry accompaniment.

If you want to emphasize the umami component in the mushrooms, then certain whites will do the job even better. Oak-aged chardonnay (from Limoux, the Jura, Burgundy or elsewhere), oaked white bordeaux and oak-aged white Rioja will underscore the umami and make mushrooms taste more bosky. These are a good accompaniment to, say, garlic mushrooms on toast (with a spoonful of cream in the sauce) or chicken or pork casseroled with mushrooms in a creamy sauce.

I especially like duxelles of mushrooms with lemon thyme, spread on toast or put in vol-au-vents, with white bordeaux, Australian semillon-sauvignon or champagne. If the wine is young and vigorous serve the toasts with bright, lemon-dressed endive. If the wine is aged, and beginning to smell of mushrooms itself, keep the citrus accents gentle.

Good claret is also excellent with mushrooms on toast: an opportunity to turn a tired late-night supper into a sneaky feast.

See also lasagne, mushroom risotto, omelette.

mushroom risotto Any of the wines that go with mushrooms, from chardonnay to left-bank claret, will also work with risotto. Risotto recipes vary, though, and it's best to try to match the heaviness of the risotto with the heaviness of the wine. For instance, if the risotto is a very rich one, seasoned with beef stock, sherry and Bovril, don't put it with a light French pinot, give it a smoky South African one.

mussels see *moules marinière*

mustard GAME-CHANGER As with chilli, cinnamon and garlic, we don't just experience mustard through the taste receptors in our mouths and smell it via the olfactory receptors in our nose, we also feel it as pain, thanks to ion channels that run through a branch of the trigeminal nerve, which is responsible for sensation in the face and also for communicating the motor commands that allow us to chew. Mustard is a kind of miracle worker when it comes to tough, hard red wines. When mustard meets red wine, it calms down the tannins. If you eat mustard with steak or roast beef, you will notice that the red you drink with it tastes even softer than it does with the beef alone. This means that a wine that tastes prickly and hard when drunk alone – a Madiran or an inexpensive green claret, for example – suddenly becomes much more approachable and delicious. It also means that a fruity, soft wine you were enjoying before you had a mouthful of mustard might now begin to taste a bit floppy and boring.

So, in short, with mustard look for wines that have a bit of poke in the form of tannin (especially) and/or acidity. Also, young wines will fare better than old. As well as sinewy Madirans and astringent young clarets, consider young sangiovese, Cahors, or peppery cool-climate syrah – any of these reds would go well with classic mustardy dishes such as lapin à la moutarde. If you're after a wine that is more refreshing, and where fighty tannin isn't involved, then try bright, young, dry wines with a good flash of acidity. Gamay is the trailblazer here for reds – Beaujolais works really well with calves' liver with a mustard sauce, for instance. For whites think about grapes such as arneis, cortese, verdicchio, vermentino, and so on – these can work really well with heavily mustardy salad dressings.

M

octopus Dressed with olive oil and sprinkled with paprika, Galician octopus is one of the great seafood delicacies of north-western Spain. It is at its best when washed down with the salty-apricot taste of a glass of albariño, but a chenin blanc (or chenin blanc blend) from South Africa is also fruitily satisfying.

olives Gin and tonic goes well with olives. So does a vodka martini. And a glass of chilled manzanilla or fino sherry is near perfect with a small plate of them. If olives are part of a dish, then the salt and astringency will tilt you towards more savoury wines. Black olives tend to be savoury and rich, green ones more acidic and sour. Sangiovese, for instance, has no problem with black olives. Nor do most of the reds from the south of France (from Bandol to Corbières to Fitou) or from the Rhône. Green olives tend to demand a bit of acidity in a wine. Again, sangiovese can offer this, as can many white wines.

omelette

plain or cheese The regal toastiness of Bollinger, a champagne that is matured in oak and majors on the pinot noir grape, is a real treat with the rich yellow of a Burford Brown omelette with or without gooey strands of melted cheese. Cava is a good second choice. The softness of a Lugana or Soave (especially one of the richer, more nuts and savoury-custard types of Soave) or albariño, or a lighter chardonnay, either unwooded or with some but not too much oak, melds with the dairy but gives a fresh backdrop too.

aux fines herbes A light red, even one verging on the under-ripe, makes a sappy complement to the green herbs. Try a gamay from Touraine. For a white, try a pinot blanc from Alsace.

with bacon The floral perfume of a pinot gris mingles well with smoky bacon and just-cooked egg.

with mushrooms A chardonnay would be good here – this is a grape that works well with both eggs and fungi. Limoux makes wines that have just the right weight. Otherwise, a humble white burgundy, perhaps a Bourgogne Blanc, Mâcon or nutty Montagny.

See also tortilla.

onion tart A barely set savoury custard mixed with soft, tangled long strands of golden onion in a crunchy, cheesy pastry is one kind of onion tart. Onion tarte tatin, all caramelized allium and rich base, is another. Both of these are beautifully offset by a not-quite-dry pinot gris from Alsace. Alsatian pinot gris is not a fashionable style. Fragrant and feminine and roiling with criss-crossing undercurrents, these wines are the anti-aperitif. They don't come at you like a gleaming blade or a piercing shot of cold citrus, and in this case that's a good thing. Pinot gris melds gently with the sweetly caramelized onions, and it has an ample texture that sits comfortably with the cream and the eggs. Other whites that work well include aromatic Côtes du Rhône, Alsatian muscat or glossy Jurançon (with both kinds of tart) or a simple French viognier or Alsatian riesling (with the eggy version).

What I really love to drink with onion tart, though, is red wine made from nebbiolo (the Barolo grape). I love the sensation of nebbiolo's tannin and acid cutting through the richness. The wine comes in like coal dust with pinking shears, nibbling away at the dairy, creating a pleasing contrast. Nebbiolo loves a bit of eggs, cream and cheese; and eggs, cream and cheese love nebbiolo too – they take a wine that, tasted alone, might appear thin and hard and mean, and they plump it out, rounding its edges. The firm backbone of both Irouléguy and Madiran also works well with a creamy onion tart. Because I like drinking sappy, light-bodied wines in cold weather – a bracing reminder of the new shoots of spring – I'd also pour a glass of Marcillac with a nice, hot slice of onion tart to eat beside the fire on a cold winter night.

O

ONION TART
Serves 4–6

for the pastry
- 175g plain flour
- 100g cold butter
- salt
- 50g Gruyère cheese, finely grated
- 1 egg yolk, beaten with 2 tablespoons ice-cold water

for the filling
- 50g butter
- 2 tablespoons olive oil
- 775g white onions, peeled and finely sliced
- 3 sprigs of thyme, leaves removed from stems
- 2 eggs
- 1 egg yolk
- 150ml single cream
- salt and pepper

To make the pastry, sieve the flour into a large bowl. Use a knife to cut the butter into small rough cubes and rub into the flour with your fingertips. Keep going until the mixture resembles fine breadcrumbs. Stir in a pinch of salt and the cheese. Add the egg yolk and water and mix with a knife and then with your hands until it's bound. Wrap the dough in cling film and pop it in the fridge to rest. For the filling, put the the butter and the olive oil in a large, heavy pan and heat gently until the butter has melted. Add the onions and cook gently for 20–30 minutes, stirring occasionally, until they are soft and just beginning to colour. Heat the oven to 200°C/400°F/ gas mark 6. On a floured surface, roll out the pastry and use it to line a greased deep 20cm or shallow 23cm flan dish. Cover the pastry with a circle of greaseproof paper weighted down with baking beans. Wrap in a damp tea towel and refrigerate until the oven is hot enough before baking blind for 15 minutes. Remove the paper and beans and cook for 5 more minutes to dry the pastry out. Meanwhile, sprinkle the thyme over the cooked onions, stir in the eggs, egg yolk and cream, and season generously. Pour the eggy onion mixture into the pastry case and cook for 15–20 minutes, until the filling is just cooked – it will still seem slightly wobbly. Serve with a salad of bitter leaves.

oranges Some dishes rely heavily on the flavour of oranges. For instance, Ottolenghi's 'Saffron, orange and chicken herb salad', which uses syrup made from a whole boiled orange (I found the recipe online); fennel and orange salad; or clementine pork steaks. With these I often open a pinot blanc or a falanghina. Both are refreshing whites that have a faint taste of oranges and orange blossom that plays to the taste of the food.

osso buco Reds from Piemonte are the obvious choice – nebbiolo, barbera and dolcetto. But a sturdy white from the Rhône can also be very good, as can a lighter or older Chianti.

oysters I think every oyster-slurper has his or her own favourite raw oyster wine. You can go sharp and piquant, with manzanilla sherry, English sparkling wine, Vinho Verde, bacchus, Sancerre, or non-vintage champagne. Or slightly gentler, with piepoul or Muscadet. Or gentler still, and more succulent, with Chablis. If you are eating the oysters with shallots and red vinegar, be sure to go for one of the sharper wines. A pint of porter is, of course, another traditional accompaniment.

O

P

paella With this Spanish rice dish red wine is just as good as white. Or rosé for that matter. But paella is a hugely movable feast. *The Oxford Companion to Food* reports that the traditional ingredients for the authentic Valencian dish are 'rice, chicken, rabbit or lean pork, green beans, fresh butter beans, tomato, olive oil, paprika, saffron, snails (or, a curious alternative, fresh green rosemary), water and salt'. The wine to drink with this (and with vegetarian versions) would be a local red, though the following would work equally well: an inexpensive Côtes du Rhône, a simple tempranillo from elsewhere in Spain, a young cabernet franc from the Loire, a young Bierzo, or a more internationally styled red from Somontano. Many incarnations of paella exist. Made with chicken, artichokes and oloroso, it's good with white Rioja, verdejo or sherry. With pork, chorizo and spinach, then more or less any red Rioja or Ribera del Duero suits the sweet chorizo. With artichokes, monkfish, fat prawns and saffron, try a young Rioja Crianza or other young tempranillo without too much oak; a mellow (older) Rioja Reserva; or an older (older because it will be softer and gentler than a brash, youthful wine) Ribera del Duero. Adapt the wine choice to the star ingredients in the dish.

paprika Smoky, earthy paprika is made from dried and ground chilli peppers and gives a soft warmth and a rustic dustiness to the food it seasons. Often found in Hungarian and Spanish cooking (chorizo is full of it), this dusty component can trip up elegant or thoughtful wines, so look for something hearty. When paprika is prominent in an ingredient list, Spanish wines can be a good option. Albariño and white Rioja (oaked or unoaked) have fragrance and acidity but also a hidden power that can handle the spice of the paprika, whether it's sprinkled over a cold octopus carpaccio or dressing a piece of hake served with olive oil and boiled potatoes. Where paprika, in particular smoked paprika, is added to a more meaty dish, or present in the form of chorizo added to a chicken or chickpea stew, a Bierzo, red Rioja, Ribera del Duero or Ribeira Sacra would make a suitably robust partner. It's no surprise that Hungarian reds are good with paprika too. The grape blaufrankisch (also known as kekfrankos) has a spicy, dried-tomato taste also found in paprika. The Austrian red grape zweigelt (a cross between blaufrankisch and St Laurent) is an easy, lightish-bodied, cherryish grape that goes well in a sluicing-down-a-hearty-stew kind of a way. Chilean carmenère, which is rugged in texture and smells of black tea leaves, roasted red peppers and dried tomato, is another excellent partner.

See also goulash.

parsley sauce White sauce with curly parsley is an old-fashioned but delicious accompaniment to poached white fish such as haddock or cod, and usually eaten with boiled potatoes. It suits an equally plain white wine. An inexpensive cool-climate chardonnay is perfect with the slightly damp taste of the parsley. Try an unoaked Bourgogne Blanc or Mâcon.

partridge An excellent option with this game bird is a generous pinot noir – 'I had partridge with Pommard last night. Finesse, class, ahhhh,' said Sebastian Payne of the Wine Society when I saw him at a recent tasting. Other good ideas include Rioja (especially graciano-rich Rioja) and juicy rustic reds that aren't too tannic, maybe a wine from the Languedoc, or a Montepulciano d'Abruzzo or a country syrah.

pasta Italy is the first place to look. Italian wines, both red and white, usually have good acidity that fits well with the angular feel of pasta made tangy with concentrated tomatoes, salty with Parmesan, anchovies or olives, or hot with garlic. Their refreshing bite also cuts cleanly through olive oil and cheese. If I were to give just one pasta-wine-picking guideline, it would be to drink red Italian with any sauce that incorporates cooked tomato and white Italian with 'white' (non-tomato) or raw tomato sauces. But I can immediately, of course, think of about a dozen exceptions.

For pasta dishes that have been anglicized or Americanized the world opens up more readily. I'm thinking of macaroni cheese,

P

so unctuous and rich it will rejoice in an acerbic white from any mountainside; or intense, almost barbecue-like meatballs with pasta that seem more at home in a burger bar than in a trattoria and will go well with a smooth, ripe red from California, South Africa or Chile.

Contemporary recipes that take inspiration from Italian flavours but play them into a lighter, more nuanced expression also suit wines from beyond the Italian peninsula. For example, a particularly clean and refined version of linguine al granchio brought home in a doggy bag from Trattoria Nuraghe in Tufnell Park in north London was delicious with a Japanese white wine made with the koshu grape.

But even if you stick to Italy, picking a grape from a country with over 3,000 registered varieties (even the extremely thorough *Wine Grapes* by Jancis Robinson, Julia Harding and José Vouillamoz deals with only the most important 377, from abbuoto to vuillermin) can be quite an adventure.

pasta dishes and suggested wines
amatriciana and arrabiata (the hotter version) Suits a basic red with some guts from Tuscany, Emilia-Romagna or Umbria.

broccoli and garlic orecchiette Pinot grigio is cleansing against the garlic and bitter broccoli. For a better class of pinot grigio, look to the pristine wines made in Friuli, in the north-east of Italy, on the mountainous border with Slovenia.

cacio e pepe A classic Roman dish, just peppercorns, spaghetti and Pecorino Romano, so in theory it would be blasphemous to have anything but a wine from Lazio. Frascati is the obvious choice. Good alternatives include Vernaccia di San Gimignano and verdicchio.

crab linguine A white with a slightly creamy texture but a cool, calm profile offsets the crabmeat. Chardonnay is good but it needs to be the right sort of chardonnay: a white from a humble burgundy appellation (one of the Mâcons or a Bourgogne Blanc), Chablis or a linear chardonnay from northern Italy or Australia. Soave would also do it, but I prefer Lugana. This northern Italian white is a camel cashmere cardigan among wines – never coveted but has a quiet sophistication that brings a dinner (or an outfit) together. Timorasso, a white grape from Piemonte, revived only recently after nearly dying out, is used to make gloriously textured wines that are nutty and aromatic and play against the brown as well as the white crabmeat. If you want to go Spanish, head for an apricotty albariño, which is light and fragrant; or try a more clean, neutral wine such as a white from the Marche region of Italy; or go for a squeeze of citrus with pecorino or Gavi. When cream is involved (as in my recipe below) I prefer the slightly heavier, more closely textured options of chardonnay or Lugana.

CRAB LINGUINE
Serves 2

You can also use spaghetti for this crab dish. The secret is the mixture of gentle white and full brown meat.

- 2 tablespoons olive oil
- 2 shallots, chopped
- 1 clove of garlic, chopped
- 175g linguine
- ½–1 red chilli, depending on heat preferences, finely chopped
- 3 tablespoons full-fat crème fraîche
- 100g white and brown crabmeat
- 3 tablespoons flat-leaf parsley, chopped

Heat the olive oil in a small pan. Add the shallots and fry, stirring, for 5 minutes. Add the garlic and continue to fry until soft and golden. Bring a large pan of salted water to the boil and add the pasta. Add the chilli to the onion mixture, fry for a couple more minutes, then turn off the heat. When the pasta is almost al dente, add 2–3 tablespoons of its cooking water to the shallot mixture and stir in the crème fraîche and the crabmeat over a gentle heat. Drain the pasta as soon as it is al dente and mix it with the hot crab mixture. Divide between two serving dishes and sprinkle with chopped parsley.

P

garlic, chilli and parsley (aglio, olio e peperoncino) For a red, a light Bardolino or Valpolicella. For white, any of the crisp, herbaceous Italian whites – verdicchio, vermentino, vernaccia and so on.

pea and spring onions The spring vegetables need a bright white such as vermentino, arneis, pecorino or young Hunter Valley semillon.

pomodoro crudo Simple raw tomato sauce works well with a crisp, unoaked white wine. Vermentino, verdicchio, pecorino, soave … Also good is a light sauvignon blanc, not too shrieky – say, a basic unoaked white bordeaux or bottle from the Pays d'Oc.

prosciutto and radicchio Dry-fry some prosciutto until it's crispy, stir shredded, wilted radicchio into a garlic and cream sauce and you have a superb winter dinner. One problem: radicchio is so bitter it will nuke almost any wine. As ever, Italy to the rescue: they make wines that go with their food. For red, try dolcetto, barbera or a young nebbiolo. For white, verdicchio. I also enjoy two Spanish reds, Bierzo and Ribeira Sacra, with this.

puttanesca This full-flavoured, olive, anchovy and cooked tomato sauce (*puttana* translates as whore) is a southern Italian dish, though no one can agree on exactly where it's from. It is attracted to the almost lasciviously fruity reds made in the heat of Puglia – for example, Salice Salentino and Brindisi.

salsiccia More or less any Italian red tastes great with sausage pasta.

con sarde This Sicilian dish made with raisins, pine nuts, sardines and chopped fennel tops sounds strange on paper but is delicious in practice. For a white, fiano works. For red, frappato.

vongole My brain tells me I ought to drink white with this salty clam pasta, but for some reason I always want a glass of nervy Valpolicella. My white choices, if I ever drank them, would be simple and unoaked so as not to interfere with the fish and salt – pinot grigio, albariño, Muscadet, picpoul, Frascati, verdicchio.

See also bottarga, carbonara, lasagne, macaroni cheese, meatballs, pesto, ragù alla bolognese, ravioli, truffles.

pâté For any kind of pâté, rustic reds from Spain, Italy, Portugal and France have my heart.

peaches The best way to have peach with wine is to slice it into a simple but delicious glass of cold white wine (Côtes du Rhône or vermentino for choice) and eat it in the bath. With the door locked. I discovered this piece of food and wine heaven as an au pair in Florence, charged with the care of three-year-old twins, and relished every second of getaway.

If raw peach is a prominent ingredient – in, say, a salad or on crostini – remember that it brings sweetly juicy acidity that may require you to ramp up the acidity and/or the sugar in the wine. For instance, I make a salad using peaches, marinated in lime juice, olive oil and salt, with mozzarella or burrata and rocket. It's great with just off-dry riesling or a very ripe Marlborough sauvignon which itself tastes of nectarines. Chenin blanc is a good grape to consider when peaches are involved in savoury dishes too.

peas and pea shoots Peas have a fresh, green taste that is redolent of spring. I like them with bright, unoaked white wines that share the same vibe. For example, Gavi, vermentino, verdicchio, vernaccia, young Hunter Valley semillon, assyrtiko, roditis, gros and petit manseng, white wines from Crete, piercing dry young Loire chenin blanc, sauvignon blanc.

Sauvignon blanc from Chile and New Zealand has a luminous quality that is particularly suited to freshly podded peas, snow peas and mangetout, while the sinewy taste of pea shoots is mirrored in the sauvignon blancs from the Awatere Valley in Marlborough.

Any of these wines would be perfect with a salad made from acidic feta cheese, fresh peas and pea shoots, dressed with olive oil and grated lemon zest.

See broad beans for a recipe for a 'Broad bean, pea shoot, asparagus and ricotta bowl' (p.47).

penne see *pasta*

peppercorns Syrah grown in a cool climate, and in particular syrah from the Rhône Valley, often has the earthy, floral fragrance

P

of freshly cracked black peppercorns. This helps to make it a beautiful match for steak with a peppercorn crust or steak served with a green peppercorn sauce. I also like tannic young red bordeaux, or Beaujolais Cru, with green peppercorn sauce – the wine has a vigour (from acidity and astringency) that fits well with the bite of the peppercorn. Or, to put it another way, both of them pep you up.

See syrah for a recipe for 'Steak with freshly cracked black peppercorns' (p.352).

pesto This garlicky, basil and pine nut sauce originates in Liguria, where the local white grape is the herbaceous and green-tasting vermentino. It's a perfect match. Alternatives are vernaccia and verdicchio. But watch out: wine tasters are wary of pine nuts because of a phenomenon that has been called 'pine mouth'.

See also pine nuts.

pheasant If the bird is in a casserole, claret or Madiran or Bergerac. If it's roast, then red burgundy will help bring some succulence to the dry meat.

picnics These occasions are more about mood than food. Pink fizz is a sheer delight – find a good cava rosado or hunt out something more obscure, such as the Rosé Frizant made by Mas de Daumas Gassac in France. Everyone is always pleased to see a chilled bottle of fine Sancerre (or Pouilly-Fumé from the opposite side of the river) at a picnic. Or go with a light red such as dolcetto, a good Loire cabernet franc or a Beaujolais Cru, which as well as capturing the sappy promise of spring will feel like the right thing to be drinking when you're sitting on the grass and have the damp, sweet smell of turf up your nose. By chance, all of those reds happen to go extremely well with a spread of different picnic foods. So-called 'natural' or 'low-intervention' wines are another good option at picnics. They often have an atmosphere and sense of the outdoors that just works. Finally, I have never seen anyone complain if you arrive at a picnic with a bottle of champagne.

pierogi These small, half-moon-shaped Polish dumplings can be made with a variety of fillings and may be served boiled, or boiled and then fried in butter and onions. I asked Polish wine writer Wojciech Bońkowski for his recommendations.

pierogi z kapustą i grzybami: pickled cabbage mixed with forest mushrooms The sour tang of the pickled cabbage is not great with heavy reds. Bońkowski suggests pinot noir for a red, or 'a rustic white wine – chenin blanc, for example'. Zweigelt from Austria would be an interesting match here.

pierogi z mięsem Bońkowski says, 'The traditional ground veal filling is often spiced with marjoram and peppercorn. This is a good dish to match with light- and medium-bodied red wines; look for acid rather than oak.' I suggest unoaked barbera, Bardolino, zweigelt or an unoaked, cool-climate syrah.

ruskie: cottage cheese and potatoes Bońkowski says, 'These are often served plain boiled with no sauce, and go well with a dry or off-dry riesling, or with unaromatic dry white wines such as sylvaner, Soave, or a light furmint.'

pigeon Lodovico Antinori, the septuagenarian scion of Tuscany's most famous and powerful wine family, likes to drink one of his own Supertuscans with pigeon. 'Colombaccio sui crostini – pigeon casseroled and then served on croutons – is good with our Insoglio del Cinghiale, which is made from syrah, cabernet franc, merlot, cabernet sauvignon and petit verdot. Pigeons taste much better in Italy because, when they fly to us, they're in the wild, they eat acorns. You know for sure because when you shoot one you can always find seven or eight acorns in their stomach. In England they eat cabbage.' A Supertuscan – a red wine made in Tuscany using bordeaux grapes – is an excellent choice with this wild bird: structured but also spicy and rich and generous. Pigeon served pink and bloody is also good with the tang of Chinon or Bourgueil from the Loire.

pine nuts Eating pine nuts can trigger an effect known as 'pine mouth', a mysterious condition that temporarily alters your sense of taste, leaving an unpleasant astringent or metallic taste in

P

your mouth. I've never experienced it, but those who have report that the sensation may kick in straight away, more usually begins twelve to forty-eight hours later and may persist for as long as three weeks.

The cause of this effect is unknown. Research conducted by the FDA (America's Food and Drug Administration) found that sufferers of pine mouth did not notice any unusual flavours in the pine nuts, and had usually eaten the pine nuts raw (frequently in pesto or in a salad), though whether that reflects a higher preference among Americans for eating raw rather than cooked pine nuts, or relates more directly to the pine mouth effect is not known. Other researchers have pinned the blame on certain batches of *Pinus armandii* imported from China, which are shorter and plumper than the slim European versions.

If you have pine mouth, I'm afraid wine will not taste good. If not, what wine you pick will depend more on the overall dish than on the presence or otherwise of pine nuts.

See also courgette flowers (stuffed and fried), pesto.

pissaladière One could happily drink rosé from Provence all day long with this niçoise pizza topped with caramelized onions, salty anchovies, olives and garlic. Provence rosé now also comes in bubbly form – delicious and decadent. Lebanese rosé, which often also includes a bit of silky cinsault in the blend, is a more emphatic, equally delicious partner. A simple inky red is also pleasing: for instance, a Provence red or a country syrah with a bit of bite.

pizza On the one hand, I want to say, 'Pizza is street food, it is sofa food, it is fresh out of the wood-burning stove and eat it in the garden, casual, happy food. Please, eat it with anything.' On the other, there's a Paulie Gualtieri from *The Sopranos* inside me, twitching away, moments from picking up a dangerously heavy glass ashtray and saying, 'I know I said anything, but why did you have to go and drink something that wasn't Eye-talian?'

Look, I spent a year living in Italy and, as a result, am pre-programmed to favour Italian reds with pizza. To be fair, they are particularly successful because, as a general rule, Italian reds have a bite that meets the bite of the tomato and the heat of any spicy cured meat. But while I was writing this book I got a Facebook message from lovely Emily O'Hare, an Italian wine expert and former River Café sommelier now living in Florence. She was canvassing opinions on what wine to drink with pizza – because all the Italians she knows drink beer. Figurati!

My go-to at home pizza reds are sangiovese or Montepulciano d'Abruzzo or a particular wine a friend has christened 'The Mighty Biferno' (its real name is Biferno Rosso, and it's made in Molise from aglianico, montepulciano and trebbiano). I also like wines from Puglia. Ole Udsen is an expert on southern Italian food and wine who goes for something more unusual: 'Pizza is traditionally paired with the young, lightly sweet and sparkling Peninsola Sorrentina Gragnano red wine from the Sorrento coast (if not with beer). Otherwise, much depends on the topping in terms of wine choice. I would generally go for a light, sappy red wine.'

Beyond Italy, cabernet-carmenère blends from Chile are chunky and pleasing with pizza as well. Lebanese reds or rosés work with slightly burnt wood-fired pizzas eaten outside. Any of the inexpensive, rustic, unoaked, swill-it-back reds you find in France, Spain, South Africa . . . everywhere will work, provided the wine you pick is not too sweet with the topping. I have reservations about tempranillo with anything but a chorizo pizza. I'd steer clear of South African pinotage unless you have a strong meat like biltong on the pizza. You get the idea. Pizza is one of those foods that most suits what you most feel like drinking (as already mentioned, for many Italians this is not actually wine but beer). The one wine–pizza combination that would really fox me, in a toothpaste and orange juice kind of way, is top burgundy. I'd have a little drinking session, then an eating session, then drink a bit more. They just don't bring out the best in each other, like friends you wish you'd invited round on separate evenings. Though both are fabulous.

There are just a couple of pizzas that might tempt me to open certain types of wine. With anchovies and olives on pizza, Venetian reds – a light Valpolicella or Bardolino – have a cool edge that is good. With the sweet flavours of spicy salami and pepperoni mixed with caramelized onion and red and orange peppers, I love the sweet flow of a riper red from the south – examples include Salice

P

Salentino, Copertino and Brindisi, and grapes to look for are primitivo and negroamaro.

plum and almond tart The sweet taste of cooked plums (or prunes) with ground almond frangipane, and slivers of toasted almonds calls for Armagnac.

pork Pork is at least as happy with white wine as it is with red. Actually, I'll go further and say that a pork chop or joint of roast pork with crackling is even more succulent and tasty with white: try riesling, chenin blanc, chardonnay (especially white burgundy), Australian marsanne, white Rhône blends (from the actual Rhône, or from the US, South Africa or Australia), viognier, godello or fiano. If you're after a red, then pinot noir (from anywhere), tempranillo (perhaps Ribera del Duero or Rioja), an Etna red, cinsault, carignan and the hard to pronounce xinomavro (from Greece) are all pretty good too.

When shoulder of pork is slow-roasted and unctuous, then I veer towards the red wines in that list, and in particular the mellow wines from Rioja. With slow-roast shoulder of pork, I also like the juicy quality of good natural red wines such as those made from syrah and pinotage at Lammershoek in South Africa, or the gamay and syrah of Hervé Souhaut in France.

with apple sauce or caramelized apples or apple pommes boulangère With a generous helping of sweet apples alongside the pork, an off-dry riesling or off-dry chenin blanc (say, a Montlouis or Vouvray) from the Loire really sings with the fruit. Alternatively, if the fruit isn't over-sweet, try dry versions of those grapes. The lusciousness of the apple also goes well with hedonistic viognier; with the orchard taste of chenin-based blends from South Africa; with white Rioja; and with white Rhône blends (incorporating some of roussanne, marsanne, viognier, bourboulene, grenache blanc) from anywhere in the world.

with apricot or other stone fruit stuffing Albariño, chenin blanc, white Rhône blends, and riesling all celebrate the juicy sweetness of the fruit.

with bay leaves, garlic, anchovies and sage, slow-cooked in white wine and served with chard This is a Stevie Parle recipe that I fished off the internet (it appeared in the *Daily Telegraph* in 2011). It's gorgeously savoury and tastes good with dry rosé (don't limit yourself to Provence, think also of the fuller, slightly tannic but still-dry rosatos from northern Italy). Slightly astringent whites work well with the savoury herbs – say, verdicchio and vernaccia. Godello and good verdejo offer a glossier approach. White burgundy, with its undertones of woodruff and toast, is superb. I also enjoy this dish with red: ideally an unoaked or barely oaked nebbiolo.

(pork loin) with calvados cream An old-school match with this creamy, appley sauce is an off-dry or medium-dry riesling. But cider also goes really well and is probably my favourite here. Just close your eyes and think of the Seventies. Perhaps even get things going with a Kir or Kir Royal first.

(belly of pork) with cinnamon, star anise, five-spice, ginger and cloves Pork belly cooked with Asian spices is fantastic with the leaping florals of viognier, as well as with blends incorporating roussanne, marsanne, viognier, clairette and grenache blanc (and chenin blanc if the wine is from South Africa).

with fennel seeds White burgundy often has a faintly aniseed tinge that works well with fennel seeds. Italian whites go well too, as does the prickle of sangiovese if you're after a red.

stir-fried with lime and cashew nuts Dry riesling has the limey-zing to go with this.

with prunes and cream Pork medallions cooked with sweet prunes in a thick double cream sauce are brought to life by the ripe pear sweetness and cleansing acidity of a medium-sweet Vouvray.

with quince Chenin blanc mirrors the floral-orchard taste of quince and is lovely here in combination with pork, and perhaps also roast parsnips in maple syrup. If there's a lot of sweetness on the plate, go for an off- or medium-dry wine (the Loire has plenty to offer, from

Vouvray to Montlouis to Savennières). Otherwise try a dry chenin blanc from South Africa or one of the Loire appellations, or one of the wines suggested as a match with apple sauce.

with roasted root vegetables I tend to opt for the reds listed in the introduction to this piece when there's an autumnal tray of roasted onions, parsnips, carrots, pumpkins, turnips and beetroots on the table.

pork pie I can't help feeling that pork pies are beer more than wine territory – a pint of Black Sheep Best, perhaps? But a simple red would also be good, maybe the sour cherry-burst of a rustic bobal from Spain.

potted shrimp Teeny little shrimps with lots of butter – chardonnay or albariño, please.

prawns There are so many seaside wines to choose from, from Vinho Verde (whose alertness is great with garlic prawns) to rosé, delicate Cassis, sauvignon blanc from San Antonio in Chile or peachy albariño, a classic seafood white that brings out the best in succulent pink prawns.

With buttery, fried prawns or prawn mayonnaise, then chardonnay (from Burgundy or elsewhere, Chablis is the classic; Mâcon also has a good balance of curves and edge).

prawn cocktail in Marie Rose sauce mixed with halved cherry tomatoes and shredded lettuce A good pick is Coteaux du Giennois, a sauvignon blanc from the Loire that has a softer, lemon-meringue pie edge compared to some of the sauvignon made in neighbouring appellations. Alternatively, Sancerre or Reuilly for a grassy, herbaceous cut.

prawns fried with garlic and a generous squeeze of lemon Try rosé, inexpensive fizz (I like the teeny bubbles and alka seltzer taste of txakoli from the Basque country) or a refreshing dry white, perhaps with a lemony-flavoured edge such as pecorino or Gavi di Gavi from Italy, young Australian semillon, or assyrtiko from Greece. An old favourite is Torres Viña Esmeralda from Spain – a floral blend of muscat and gewürztraminer that sings of holidays and summer time off.

with Thai flavours (lemongrass, chilli, ginger and so on) Look to luminous sauvignon blanc from Marlborough, or to the piercing lime of New World riesling – maybe a glittering, pure riesling from Washington State; a clear-edged riesling from Chile; the lime rind and lilac scent of an Eden or Clare riesling from Australia; or the tangerine and lime fragrance of riesling from Australia's Great Southern region. Consider increasing the sweetness of the wine to balance the heat as the *chilli* is ramped up; there are some gorgeous non-dry rieslings made in Marlborough, New Zealand.

preserved lemon GAME-CHANGER The pithy taste of preserved lemon is powerful and acerbic, far more so than the bright tang of a fresh lemon, and just a small amount of it can alter the balance of a dish. You could try any of the lemony wines mentioned in the lemon section, but I particularly like assyrtiko from Santorini, which is grown in volcanic soil. It has some weight, and you can almost taste the black lava that the roots of the vines have grown in, as well as feel a kind of voltage charge. Gavi di Gavi (as opposed to the lighter Gavi) is also good as it often has a thick taste of lemon and grapefruit rind. Don't be afraid of oaked whites either – the baked grapefruit flavours in oaked sauvignon blanc and oaked assyrtiko really resonate with preserved lemon.

pulled pork Xinomavro (it's pronounced zeeno-mavro) from Greece is an unorthodox wine to drink with the sweet fruitiness of pulled pork with a barbecue sauce, but it tastes really good. This red grape is reminiscent of nebbiolo, if nebbiolo also tasted of squashily ripe wild strawberries, and the combination of warmth with astringency is gorgeous with a mouthful of sweet burger bun, coleslaw and pork. The slack, ripe warmth of Californian zinfandel also goes down well with pulled pork, as does the brightness of cheaper Chilean pinot noir. Red or white Rhône blends made outside the Rhône (in California or South Africa) have the easy-going exuberance and ripeness to work too. Alternatively, a bottle of cheap American beer is just great.

P

pumpkin and squash Pumpkins and squashes are chameleons, on the one hand very rich, their orange flesh almost sweet; on the other surprisingly watery.

richer pumpkin and squash dishes, perhaps roasted and spiced Roasting gourds has a concentrating effect on flavour; it brings out a sunny, sweet opulence. To play into this, choose a fleshy, bold wine – white or red – such as an oaked chardonnay or a juicy merlot, perhaps from Chile, or a full-throttle zinfandel or primitivo from the US or Puglia. All of these will work with pumpkin that is pimped with spices (for example, cumin, cayenne, star anise) and chilli flakes too (including with spiced pumpkin soup, with the caveat that soup and wine – liquid against sloshy liquid – are not really ideal together). A luscious pinot noir, perhaps from California or Chile, can also have the same effect and is particularly sumptuous when the pumpkin is being served with roasted duck.

If you want to savoury things up a bit, then pick a leaner red, with tighter tannins. This might mean choosing a more sappy pinot noir, a mencía from Spain or Italian reds such as nebbiolo from Piemonte or sangiovese from central Tuscany, whose tannins reign in the splurgey flavours. Actually, the sangiovese can bring the best of both worlds as it can be rich and warming as well as prickly and tannic. These Italian reds are especially good when pumpkin is roasted with pancetta, sage, garlic or thyme.

P

See also ravioli (and other filled pasta), risotto.

quail If the quail is coated in sage and salt, roasted until it's crispy, and served with spinach leaves and a garlicky dressing, then I like Brunello or Rosso di Montalcino or nebbiolo. If the bird is simply seasoned and roasted without herbs, then mencía, claret and pinot noir all make fine accompaniments.

R

rabbit If simply braised (and perhaps eaten with cheesy noodles) this lean white meat bounds along with a light to medium-bodied red wine such as one made from cabernet franc (from anywhere in the world; in France look to the Loire appellations of Chinon, Saumur, Saumur-Champigny, Bourgueil and St Nicolas de Bourgueil); gamay (Beaujolais); a light and rustic sangiovese (try Chianti Rufina); or one of the lighter South African pinot noirs. Other good options include Marcillac (with its tang of iron); a taut Irouléguy; or a fuller-bodied rosé such as Tavel. A nutty chardonnay from the Jura would also work well.

with broad beans and pancetta in a creamy casserole, served with mashed potatoes This was the first dinner I ever cooked for an (ex-) boyfriend who was horrified to be fed bunny, ate it politely at the time, and refused ever to touch it again. The cossetting cream and mash make a rounded white a good pick. I like gently oaked chardonnay or aromatic viognier or a blend of viognier/roussanne/marsanne (from the Rhône, California or South Africa).

with mustard sauce (and bacon) Any of the light reds at the start of the entry will work, but heavier wines are better and tannic wines go well with the mustard. Try a richer sangiovese-based red from Tuscany (a Chianti Classico, Carmignano or a Rosso di Montepulciano); an aglianico or nebbiolo from Italy, a hairy red from Provence; the fresh edges of a young bordeaux from the Médoc; or a smoky cabernet sauvignon blend from South Africa that will underscore the smokiness of the bacon.

ragù on pappardelle An Italian red with some astringency – say nebbiolo, aglianico or Sagrantino di Montefalco.

stew (with the cream) and served with cheesy noodles A bracing riesling from Alsace is good against the rich dairy; for reds try a sappy, light Marcillac or a simple, grainy sangiovese.

stew (without the cream) Many winemakers, from Italy (sangiovese) to Australia (syrah), vengefully tell me they love to eat rabbit stew with their wines. Hop to it!

radicchio The dramatic carmine and white-veined leaves of the radicchio are bitter as well as beautiful. The more the radicchio is cooked, the more this bitterness is minimized. Particularly watch out, therefore, for the shock of raw radicchio leaves. They are really horrid with sweetly fruity, oaky white wines; lean, herbaceous whites (such as vermentino, arneis or vernaccia) are a better counterpoint.

Italian reds – from just about anywhere in the country – hold up to radicchio's astringency better than most. With a radicchio salad, I like the fine balance of a nebbiolo (especially a more rustic nebbiolo from Ghemme or Valtellina). Other Italian reds I'd be tempted to open include barbera or dolcetto also from northern Italy, or a relatively raw young sangiovese, perhaps from Chianti Rufina.

Radicchio that has been braised or chargrilled goes well with the Italian reds above but also with Bierzo from Spain and zweigelt (it's a cross of St Laurent and blaufrankisch), a kind of light-bodied, Austrian alternative to pinot noir. The bitter-sweetness of blackened radicchio that has been dressed with sticky, dark balsamic vinegar is mirrored by a sweet-sour, cherry-and-dust scented Valpolicella.

See also risotto.

ragù alla bolognese (with pasta) There are many, many versions of this meat and tomato pasta sauce but the original takes its name from the city of Bologna in Emilia-Romagna, where it is often washed down with a glass of dry red Lambrusco (yes, dry, you read that correctly). This sparkling wine, often a deep violet colour with a slightly earthy smell, has recently experienced a fashion renaissance in the bars and restaurants of east London. It is best served by the tumbler and makes a great casual accompaniment to a bowl of penne con ragù.

In Piemonte in northern Italy, where they serve ragù with tajarin, a sort of hand-cut tagliolini made with a lot of eggs and whose edges seem very soft in your mouth, they like to eat it with barbera. Something about the combination gives both the wine and the food a very silky feel. If you visit the village of Barbaresco, go to the Trattoria Antico Torre. The restaurant is named for the medieval tower next to it, which was built a thousand years ago to defend the village against the Saracens, and it is famed locally for its excellent, egg-rich home-made tajarin. Order this and a bottle of Bruno Rocca barbera.

Other good options for ragù are central Italian reds such as Chianti, Rosso di Montalcino or Montepulciano d'Abruzzo. A generic sangiovese (the Chianti grape, with its classic, crenellated feel and sour cherries and dust notes) or a softer, fruitier red such as a Salice Salentino from Italy's heel offer more budget options. Such a simple plate of food can also be a good occasion to showcase a fabulous Italian red: a good Brunello di Montalcino, perhaps.

Of the non-Italian reds, a cabernet sauvignon-carmenère blend from Chile is a really good choice.

ratatouille The laid-back aromatics of this Provençal vegetable stew relax into red wines that also smell of herbs and sun. Whether eating ratatouille as a main course on its own with slices of crusty baguette or dauphinoise potatoes, or putting it with merguez sausages, roasted leg of lamb or lamb casserole, wines I'd look to include Chianti, Bandol, Palette (and other reds from Provence), St Chinian, agiorghitiko from Nemea in Greece, Vacqueyras, Gigondas, Douro reds and the peppery depth of the syrahs from the northern Rhône. A friend who insists on making ratatouille without the courgettes, which results in a richer and more unctuous aubergine and tomato stew, reports that it goes extremely well with the warm embrace of Australian shiraz. Finally, on a summer's evening the wine it's always hard to avoiding opening with ratatouille is palest pink rosé from Provence.

ravioli (and other filled pasta) Mostly I go with the same types of wines that I'd drink when the sauce was on the outside rather than the inside of the pasta. However, filled pasta is usually (though not always) fresh and that sometimes makes a difference: the softer texture feels completely different in your mouth to the flick-flack of spaghetti cooked very al dente. Plus, there are a few fillings that you don't find as sauces.

pumpkin With butter melted on to it and Parmesan grated on top, a verdicchio or vermentino will provide a punctuating textural contrast, while a clean (oaked or lightly oaked) chardonnay or the luscious flavour of an upmarket Soave will play into the curves. I more often serve pumpkin pasta with just-brown butter and fried sage leaves and then I'm chardonnay or Soave all the way for whites, but also like the herbal cut of a light red such as an unoaked or barely oaked Chianti Rufina.

ricotta and spinach For a white with a lemon tinge go for Gavi. More herbal but still citrusy options include vernaccia, verdicchio and vermentino. To go gently with the softness of the pasta, pick a Soave.

red mullet Red mullet is one of those fish that is particularly comfortable with red wine but happily moves from red to white depending on what you put with it. At The River Café in London I once ate red mullet with tomatoes and black olives, which was perfect with a Valpolicella – Ca' Fiui from a producer called Corte Sant'Alda. With fennel and olive oil, red mullet is good with a red from Etna or a nero d'avola. It also works with pinot noir as well as with the subtle aromatics and warmer feel of Rhône whites and fresh rolle/vermentino from Provence/Italy.

red pepper The intense paprika-like fruitiness of red peppers that have been thoroughly cooked in a casserole or a hot oven has a natural affinity with dusty Chilean carmenère but it also goes well with bold reds from South Africa (in particular Rhône blends and tobacco-scented cabernet sauvignon); cabernet sauvignon from Chile; and also some of the more exuberant Spanish reds from Rioja, Ribera del Duero and Navarra. The leafy taste of crunchy raw red peppers is good with rosé made from cabernet sauvignon and also rosé from Navarra in Spain. It also goes well with the freshly

R

podded pea and grassy taste of sauvignon blanc from Robertson or Darling in South Africa, and with the sweet snow pea taste of sauvignon blanc from Chile. Red peppers that have been partly blackened on a grill (perhaps as part of a kebab), barbecue or griddle often strike a halfway mark between the sweet power of cooked peppers and the more acidic brightness of raw and I like them with both groups of wines, as well as with bright reds such as gamay (the Beaujolais grape) and barbera.

red pepper filo Roasted red pepper filo is good with any of the wines listed above. Pick the wines that are better with raw red peppers if the filo is made with acidic ingredients such as feta.

stuffed peppers If they are loaded with rice, courgettes, fresh tomatoes, olives, thyme and garlic (and lamb), then head to Provence, the Rhône or the Languedoc (white, red or pink, it doesn't matter), or to the Rhône blends of South Africa. With the more tangy flavours of feta and oregano, I look for a more bracingly assertive, acidic wine such as sauvignon blanc, a Greek island wine (the pithy grapefruit and lemon flavours of assyrtiko are perfect) or pecorino for whites or barbera for a red. The aromatics of xinomavro from Greece, which smells like dried thyme with ripe wild strawberries, are also good here. If the peppers are stuffed with fat-grained rice enriched with stock and flavoured with an onion and pepper soffritto, tomato purée, and perhaps some saffron, then try the mellow smoothness of tempranillo – say, a Rioja Crianza.

red snapper The sweet, firm flesh of this tropical fish is often cooked with fragrant herbs and spices. I've eaten it baked en papillote with lemongrass and fresh coriander, barbecued with lime and chilli, and grilled and served with cumin and fresh coriander potatoes. With all of these dinners I'd pick similar wines – lithe whites with a lift of lime, lemon or bergamot zest that also carry the scent of lemongrass, starfruit, or nectarines. Riesling (from South Africa, New Zealand, Chile, Washington State in the US, or Australia – say Eden Valley, Clare Valley, Great Southern or Tasmania) will play into the green lime; sauvignon blanc from Adelaide Hills in Australia has an understated taste of Meyer lemon and starfruit that underscores the succulence of the fish flesh; sauvignon blanc from Leyda in Chile will bring in a vibrant taste of crunchy snow peas and green capsicum; a young semillon from Australia will lift it with a meadowgrass and citrus flavour; and an oaked semillon-sauvignon blanc from Margaret River brings a waxy texture with hints of lemon, papaya and toast. For a wine with cool clarity and a hint of orange, try pinot blanc from north-east Italy or Alsace. If the fish is cooked with heavier spices and/or more chilli (for instance, with jerk seasoning), then seek out a wine with more sweetness, perhaps a riesling from Germany or one of New Zealand's sweeter offerings. In all cases, as so often, another good choice is rosé.

rillettes With goose or pork rillettes on a baguette with cornichons, the wine I really love to drink is a Cornas or St Joseph. Those black northern Rhône syrahs taste granitic and gravelly, like having your bare feet on pebbles; then you get the milky white softness of the bread; then the chippy, argumentative wine; then the cold creamy butter; then the vinegary cornichons; then the proud, stony wine again. It is pure bliss. That is the really gorgeous match. Failing that, a simple French red, what used to be called vin de pays, or its equivalent from Italy, will do.

risotto The wine I pick to go with risotto very much depends on what ingredients have been added to it. The classic risotto is the almost naked milanese (made with shallots, chicken stock and saffron). A traditional match would be a local red – barbera, say, or a light nebbiolo or dolcetto – and I like these because they have an earthy savour that showcases the delicate powdery taste of the rice. Milanese also goes well with limpid Soave, Frascati, Lugana or a light, cherryish Valpolicella, all of which have a transparency that allows you to taste the rice. With an absolutely plain risotto (no saffron), the controlled, teasing style of a dry Pfalz riesling or a subtle pinot bianco is refreshing. With more complicated risottos, as with any other plate of food, the richer the ingredients, the richer the wine can be. I prefer not to drown the rice, though: it deserves to be the star of the dish, not an invisible flavour-carrier. Here are a few ideas.

R

asparagus The cool geometry of grüner veltliner from Austria and the pithy lemon of arneis from Italy are favourites, but any wine that is good with asparagus would naturally be splendid.

chicken Invigorating light reds are good with a brothy chicken risotto: say, the transparency of Valpolicella, or a summery, chilled Beaujolais Cru. For whites, Lugana and Soave are subtle options. This is also an opportunity to get out the chardonnay, which will go especially well with a more dairy-rich chicken risotto, into which you've perhaps stirred some crème fraîche and gone particularly heavy on the butter and cheese; try a Mâcon for a chardonnay with a cool, crisp cut, or a grander white burgundy for indulgence. Limoux chardonnay is underrated and perfect here too.

fresh tomato A grassy Loire sauvignon blanc with a raw tomato risotto makes for a lovely outdoor summer's evening dinner. A very precise pinot grigio from the Collio or Colli Orientali region of Italy, or a lemony white from Crete, will also play into the fresh edges of the tomato. You could use lemon thyme in the risotto too. With raw tomato and oregano, a herb that has warmth, I'd be tempted to try the more opulent, spicy greco di tufo from Campania in Italy.

mushroom This has its own entry, as it's such a popular dish.

peas (risi e bisi) A Venetian classic that really does go well with the local wines (Lugana and Soave) as well as with pinot grigio. I also love risi e bisi with that rare creature, Beaujolais Blanc, a very gentle and refreshing chardonnay.

primavera (with peas, broad beans, and all things fresh and green) If there's asparagus in the dish, go with asparagus choices. Otherwise pick any crisp, clean white, from pinot grigio or verdicchio to Soave or an unoaked viognier.

pumpkin The glow of roasted pumpkin risotto is delicious with oaked chardonnay from almost anywhere in the world or with a white Rhône. If the pumpkin has not been roasted it will be more subtle in taste; squash and pumpkin often taste surprisingly aqueous in a risotto, like a dawn tribute to the lagoon of Venice. Try the soft but rice-grainy texture with round-edged, gently nutty Italian whites such as posh Soave. A very light, unoaked chardonnay, such as a Bourgogne Blanc, also matches the delicacy of this type of risotto, and, again, it has no corners so doesn't jab at the silkiness of the squash. Prosecco is a good alternative.

radicchio and pancetta The bitterness of the radicchio and the salty-meaty bacon is most delicious with a red: barbera, nebbiolo, sangiovese and dolcetto will all do you proud. As will a Valpolicella Ripasso. A touriga nacional from Portugal is a more inky, heavy partner. País from Chile also works well.

red wine with chestnut mushrooms and sausages Any of the reds that go well with a radicchio and pancetta risotto will also work here. Alternatively, pick a Beaujolais Cru, a Spanish red made from mencía, or a light, cool-climate pinot noir (stern German pinot works well here) to be refreshing against the risotto stodge or a rustic syrah for heartiness. Take care not to use a sweet wine when you are cooking this; you'll ruin the risotto. I speak from bitter experience here. Many cheap red wines do contain sugar and it sticks out even more on the plate than it does in the glass.

seafood There are many different versions of fish and seafood risotto. The best I have eaten were all in the lagoon city of Venice, where the plate of rice and stock is often very liquid. A glass of limpid prosecco makes a fine accompaniment but it must not be one of those cheap, commercial wines that taste of boiled sweets. Instead look for a cool, crisp prosecco that tastes of stones, hard pears, and winter mornings, and has been made with care by a small-scale producer. Other Venetian white wines that work well include Bianco di Custoza and Soave. I also like the earthy taste of Crémant du Jura (a sparkling wine made in eastern France from chardonnay) and the clean lightness of Crémant d'Alsace. Otherwise, find a relatively transparent white wine that does not have obtrusive fruit. Muscadet, piepoul, trebbiano, or pinot grigio are all ideal.

R

with truffles I feel cheated if I don't have nebbiolo, in one of its many forms, with truffles.

rocket Rocket is such a bitter leaf that it makes gentle, sweet or plump wines wilt. Oaked chardonnay or jammy shiraz or sweetly ripe pinot noir are not the answer. Bite – in the form of tannin or acidity – helps. Earthiness does too. Try a citrusy white with a simple, dressed rocket salad; vibrant oaked sauvignon blanc with a rocket and cured ham salad or a rocket and blue cheese and pear salad; sangiovese or nebbiolo with tagliata and rocket dressed in lemon and olive oil; mencía with fig, rocket and ham. And so on.

rogan josh This aromatic, tomato-based dish is often made with lamb and goes brilliantly well with the rugged capsicum scent of Chilean carmenère. Melvin D'Souza of Soul Tree wines says that with rogan josh he likes to drink his own shiraz-cabernet, a smooth-fruited red made from grapes grown in India that's aged in oak barrels.

rollmop herrings Herrings that have been gutted, boned and rolled (sometimes round pickled cucumber) and preserved in vinegar or a mixture of vinegar and wine that might have been flavoured with dill or other herbs and spices are pungently flavoured. They are at their best not with wine but with a cold shot of vodka or aquavit.

Roquefort, pear and endive salad The spice of the blue cheese and juiciness of the pears needs a succulent white with good acidity. A glossy dry Jurançon, made from gros and petit manseng, with a tang of white grapefruit and taste of sunflower seeds will do it, as will an oaked sauvignon blanc. With blue cheese, bitter leaves and the sweetness of the pears I particularly enjoy the tangy, floral notes of oaked sauvignon and semillon blends such as those made in Bordeaux and in Margaret River in Australia.

rosemary Rosemary's heady fragrance sends you first to the Mediterranean, where the blue-flowered herb grows wild in the garrigue. The pumice-dry reds from the southern Rhône (Vacqueyras, Châteauneuf-du-Pape, Gigondas, Sablet and Cairanne, as well as the more generic Côtes du Rhône blends), which smell like a dry, stony hillside on a hot day, are made for rosemary. The herbal reds of Provence (including Bandol) also complement rosemary's soaring scent. Chianti reds from Montepulciano and Brunello di Montalcino play well with this herb's pungency, particularly when meat is involved. For instance, these Tuscan reds are good with rosemary focaccia but really shine with braised rabbit with rosemary potatoes; rosemary and juniper-rich wild boar stew or ragù; or lamb roasted with rosemary and eaten with white beans with rosemary and garlic. Rioja can also work well with rosemary, but its youthful strawberry taste isn't quite such a natural fit as the earthier grenache-based wines of France, so I tend to choose a slightly older Rioja that has begun to melt and mellow and take on autumnal flavours. The eucalyptal notes of shiraz from McLaren Vale in Australia and the earthy base notes of shiraz from Heathcote, Australia, also resonate with rosemary.

R

S

saffron Saffron is a subtly powerful spice with notes of hay and iodine that gently yet firmly tilt the flavour of a whole dish. It doesn't have an obvious wine partner but it never fails to make an impact. In a vegetable, chicken or seafood paella or other rice dish, for instance, saffron's steady presence can open the door to serving a substantial red rather than the more obvious white: think of monkfish and artichoke saffron rice with Spanish tempranillo; or one-pot chicken cooked with rice, olives, chickpeas, cumin and saffron eaten with a feral Bandol. Conversely, with saffron-scented side dishes such as raisin and pine nut couscous, I often open a floral white wine such as viognier, or a white Rhône blend, even when they are being eaten with red meat such as grilled or tagined lamb. Viognier has an *Arabian Nights* charm that dances seductively around calm saffron.

Perhaps a general principle is that, where rosé and white are concerned, quietly forceful wines tend to work well with saffron. Examples include rosé from Provence (it's subtle, but with understated power and a spicy sandalwood tone); orange wines (made from white grapes, but with extended skin contact giving them tannin and hold and a pale amber hue); Douro white blends; and Rhône blends (floral and almond-blossom-scented).

With fishy dinners containing saffron, such as bouillabaisse or barbecued sea bass with a saffron aioli, manzanilla sherry has a salty, bready edge that zings against the spice.

salade niçoise The sight of the runny egg yolks, tuna, black olives, anchovies and green beans of this salad from the Côte d'Azur instantly evokes in me the desire to drink the pale pink rosés of holidays in Provence. It might be a Pavlovian match but it's one I stick by: rosé ought to be mandatory with niçoise salad. As a backup, perhaps consider a white from Bandol or elsewhere in Provence, or the herbaceous riff of a vermentino from Corsica.

salads Watch out for the dressing. The acidity of a lemon and olive oil emulsion or of vinaigrette can make low-acid, oaky wines taste quite odd. Dressings that are high in mustard, raw garlic or salt can also have a distorting effect on the perceived flavour of a wine. Of course none of this matters if you are just eating a small side salad, or if (like me) you heap the salad on to an empty plate as a palate cleanser after the main course, but if the salad is a big, or the main part of a meal, then it might be worth choosing a wine that will still work. To balance the effects of raw garlic, lemon juice, vinegar or mustard in a dressing, look for a wine that is high in acid.

A few other powerful ingredients in a salad (or its dressing) that are worth taking into consideration include blue cheese, goat's cheese or goat's curd, bitter leaves (see below), chilli, herbs and anything sweet (for instance, sugar, maple syrup or honey in the dressing or sweet fruit in the salad itself – also see below).

bitter leaves and radish sprouts Chicory, watercress, rocket, radicchio and fiery radish sprouts need reds that have some astringency or a red or white with refreshing bite. Italian wines are an easy solution. Arneis, vermentino, verdicchio, vernaccia, and cortese are vibrant whites that will do the job. Nebbiolo, dolcetto, sangiovese, sagrantino, montepulciano and sometimes nero d'avola work for the red team.

crunchy Thai salads It doesn't really matter what vegetables – crunchy carrots, snake beans and so forth – are in the salad because it's the sweet-sour-heat of the palm sugar, lime juice, green papaya and chilli and also the coriander and mint that drive the flavour. The happiest match here is medium-dry riesling. Its aromatics play beautifully with the vibrancy of the herbs and lime, its acidity works well with the pungency of the citrus, and its sweetness has a calming effect on the heat of the chilli. Off-dry pinot gris is another option.

S

sweet dressings and salads containing other sweet ingredients, such as quince cooked in syrup, or sweetly ripe fruit, such as pears or peaches It's best to balance the sweetness in the salad with sweetness in the wine. This might be as subtle as choosing a just off-dry, juicy rosé or chenin blanc from the Loire to drink with a salad containing sweet figs, quince or juicy pears. If the sweetness is very noticeable – for instance, if the salad is coated in a honeyed or maple syrup-rich dressing – then a medium-dry wine (try a riesling from Germany or New Zealand) will feel more comfortable than one that is bone dry.

salmon The classic salmon dinner is a pale pink poached fillet with a big pile of buttery new potatoes and hollandaise sauce, and the roundness and gloss of a chardonnay goes beautifully. Chardonnay's curves perfectly cushion and cosset the salmon, emphasizing the soft luxury of the hollandaise. Pick anything from the scale, from a richer wine, all toasty, barrel-aged and fat, to the taut, matchstick-scented new-wave Australian chardies with their refreshing flashes of lemon, to a Chablis, to the limpid, apple-blossom crispness of a young, unoaked Mâcon.

Simple, fine ingredients are the best way to enjoy more serious bottles. I can hardly think of a more exquisite dinner than a piece of wild salmon with a heap of Jersey Royals scattered with fresh herbs and a good white burgundy. Among other wines that are beautiful with salmon with potatoes and/or a plain salad are whites from Provence and the Rhône and pale rosé.

If the salmon is fried rather than poached, then try godello or an Australian semillon whose grass and hay and lemon flavours buzz against the crispy, fatty skin.

As the texture of chardonnay works well whenever creamy sauces, eggs and butter are involved, it's also a good pick when salmon is served with poached eggs, spinach and hollandaise; richly buttery rösti; mayonnaise; or as salmon en croute. Chenin blanc, from South Africa or the Loire, is a fine alternative as it combines vibrant citrus, which acts like a squeeze of lemon, with curves.

Different accompaniments might send you to different places. For instance, I sometimes make a hot potato salad, maybe mixed with cucumber or wild garlic or dressed with dill vinaigrette.

These are punchy ingredients: aniseedy dill, wild garlic or the heat of a mustardy-vinegary dressing demand a wine with at least a bit of elbow. The woodruff flavours found in some burgundies can still dovetail beautifully here, but I veer towards one with a youthful kick, the better to cope with the vinegar of the dressing. A more refreshing, herbaceous acidic white, such as verdicchio, vermentino, or grüner veltliner, will pick up on the aniseedy notes in the dill, while a Loire sauvignon blanc or a Bordeaux Blanc (oaked or unoaked) will provide a grassy backdrop. These wines are also good ones to pick for salmon with asparagus.

As salmon is quite meaty it can also be delicious with light, tensile reds. Pinot noir seems to underscore the pinkness and sleek muscularity of the fish. If you are chargrilling salmon on a barbecue or griddle pan, so that the skin is crispy and black, those fuller flavours make red wine a very stylish option, be it a Bierzo from Spain, a nerello mascalese from Etna, a gamay, a cabernet franc from the Loire, or a lighter (say 11.5–12.5% abv) syrah such as the textured wines made by Craig Hawkins in Swartland, South Africa; or the low-intervention wines made by Hervé Souhaut in the Ardèche, France. With nutty lentils as a side dish, definitely go red, and ideally a red that is more earthy than fruity – say, to a pinot noir from Germany or one from the excellent Puy de Dôme co-operative in France, or a Bardolino from northern Italy.

Side dishes of salads containing hot, peppery radish sprouts or mustardy micro-herbs and Ottolenghi-style salads or soy, chilli and coriander marinades provide more excuses to head towards light reds – gamay (the Beaujolais grape) is a good choice here. Put the red in the fridge for 20–30 minutes and the chill will give it more definition and a bit of cut.

blackened salmon with miso aubergine My top choice would be champagne, but steer away from harsh zero dosage wines, and other styles that are dagger-like in their directness, as these will cut into the beautiful silky texture of the food and rip it to shreds. Fruitier champagnes like Canard-Duchêne would be lovely with that glutinous sweetness. Sake is clearly an option too, or try a medium-dry Vouvray.

fishcakes With clouds of potato and Anglo ingredients, try chardonnay or chenin blanc. With Thai flavours – lemongrass, chilli, ginger – aromatic riesling, semillon, and sauvignon blanc really sing.

hot-smoked salmon and horseradish The heat of the horseradish and the smoky fish are perfect with an aged Australian semillon. These wines begin to taste like toast as they mature – you'd swear they had seen the inside of a barrel even when they've lived in stainless steel.

scrambled egg and smoked salmon This feels like a breakfast dish to me, so it's too early for anything but sparkling wine, which happily goes very well.

smoked salmon Zesty, citrusy wines such as sauvignon blanc from Sancerre to Marlborough or Gavi from Italy or gruner veltliner from Austria act like a squeeze of citrus over the smoked fish. I prefer fuller versions, where some of the wine has been enriched by time in barrel, as this meets the oily texture of the fish. With buttery bread (and the butter does make the salmon taste better – fat is such an effective flavour-enhancer), the roundness of Chablis (or another white burgundy or chardonnay from elsewhere) is appealing and, of course, Chablis also has a dash of lemony zip. A favourite choice with the richness of smoked salmon is chenin blanc from the Loire. Go for anything from Vouvray to Savennières to a Saumur blanc. Dry, off-dry or even medium, these wines have a winning combination of texture and acid that brings succulence to the fish. The smokiness of the fish is also well matched by the toasty edge of crisper whites that have been fermented in oak barrels – sauvignon-semillon blends from Bordeaux, Margaret River, and elsewhere have a smoky taste of hot grapefruit that spritzes and hums with the citrus squeezed on the fish and the salmon's own smokiness. Likewise, the peaty-bonfire-iodine smell of Islay whisky, reminiscent of sea and land at once, brings out the smoky-savoury salmon flavours. Maybe water it down, one part water to three parts whisky. If the salmon is on rye bread, the strong caraway scent of a tot of ice-cold rye vodka or aquavit draws out the savoury, aromatic smokiness of both bread and fish.

tartare of salmon For raw salmon, move away from buttery chardonnay. The cool, sinewy flesh is good with bracing wines with cut, such as sauvignon blanc, chiselled grüner veltliner and chenin blanc, though there is one caveat. High-acid wines can also change the texture of the fish, 'cooking' it like ceviche in your mouth. For tartare served with pickled cucumber, I like greener-tasting herbaceous wines (such as verdicchio or vernaccia) or a wine with some sweetness – for instance, a chilly medium-dry Vouvray, reminiscent of stewed apples and wild honey. Pinot gris from Alsace is another interesting, textured choice, while the clean cut of a pinot grigio or other white (say, ribbolla gialla) from Collio or Colli Orientali in north-east Italy brings cool precision and calm.

teriyaki The brightness of a young, unoaked new world pinot noir plays well with the sticky ginger and soy flavours. Sake, koshu or a fino or manzanilla sherry would also work and seem to boost the umami flavours in the sauce.

See also gravadlax.

salsa verde Look for a wine with bite to stand up to the piquancy of the sauce. If the salsa verde is to go with white fish, then white wines that will do the job include Loire sauvignon blanc, Spanish verdejo, arneis, Gavi, assyrtiko and young dry Loire chenin blanc. Salsa verde seems to like oak, so you could look for an oaked assyrtiko or white bordeaux. These oaked white wines also hit the spot if the salsa verde is to be eaten with lamb and lots of salads, ideally outside on a hot evening. With lamb, however, you may already be thinking about red bordeaux and that's a very good idea. Vinegary salsa verde and lamb have a miraculously redeeming effect on clarets that are green and tannic, which makes this the perfect opportunity to open a bottle of more astringent young claret, or perhaps a Fronsac.

S

salt Food that is very salty, whether because it's rich in anchovies, salted capers or brined olives, or simply because it's been very highly seasoned, needs a wine, red or white, with good acidity. This is because salt reduces our perception of acidity, so a wine that's rounded and low in acid from the start can taste flabby and flat. There are loads of wines with good acidity, from champagne to sauvignon blanc to riesling. Reds from northern and central Italy can usually be relied on to have a good spine of acidity too.

saltimbocca alla romana With this classic dish of veal escalopes wrapped in sage leaves and prosciutto, fried in butter and drizzled with a sauce made by deglazing the pan with Marsala, try the prickle of a nebbiolo from Valtellina or the Langhe; the savour of a lagrein from the Südtirol; a dusty dry red Lambrusco; a leathery Montepulciano d'Abruzzo; or a Chianti Rufina. For whites, Frascati would be the local match, but I also like the seltzer, just-floral taste of sparkling chasselas from Switzerland – if you can find one.

salty snacks I'm happy to say that one of the very best vinous accompaniment to crisps and other salty snacks is champagne. Seriously. Champagne has high acidity, which is good with salt. English sparkling wine, too. And most other dry sparkling whites. Sauvignon blanc is also perfect with lovely vinegar as well as salt and fat.

samphire A breezy Vinho Verde is good with salty samphire. Douro whites and Muscadet work too – both are classic fish wines and samphire is almost always served with fish. Nettley-tasting English bacchus also has an affinity for this slightly damp-tasting sea vegetable.

sardines Cooked with red onion and chunks of tomato on a beach barbecue or under a fierce grill until the skin blisters, golden and crunchy and black, sardines scream to be washed down with a glass of rosé. I wouldn't pick a pale, almost invisible rosé, but one with more guts and colour. Try Spanish rosado, from Rioja or Navarra, or one made with bobal from the unglamorously named region of Utiel-Requeña. Alternatively, a rosé from the Dão or Douro in Portugal or a Lebanese or Chilean rosé with some cinsault in the blend. This oily fish is also fantastic with red wine. With the sweet red onions and smell of basil, a young, inky inexpensive Ribera del Duero (not too much American oak) might not be the first wine you'd think of but it is a great match. Alternatively, a sangiovese di Toscana; the bright and slightly smoky smell of an unoaked pinot noir from Chile or South Africa; a cheap nerello mascalese, frappato, or Cerasuolo di Vittoria from Sicily; a red from Portugal's Dão. Intensely bright, lemony whites also work to sluice the mouth in between forkfuls – for instance, Roussette de Savoie.

sashimi The very best matches I've found with raw fish, served Japanese-style, with daikon, wasabi and a soy-based dipping sauce on the side, are unoaked white wines made from the koshu grape; fino or manzanilla sherry; sake; and champagne or English or other sparkling wine made from a combination of chardonnay, pinot noir and pinot meunier and fermented by the traditional method. With leaner fish, the precision and keen edges of grüner veltliner from Austria can also be wonderfully refreshing. Fattier fish such as the richer parts of tuna meld better with the softness of koshu and sake.

See also sushi.

sausages Isn't every red wine good with sausages? From tough tannat to light dolcetto to Barossa shiraz, it's hard to think of one that's not and so picking a wine becomes more about scene-setting. Here are a few combinations that I enjoy.

On a cold winter's night I love a chilled, juicy, granitic Beaujolais to rinse down mouthfuls of buttery mash, onion gravy and bangers. Solid Chilean reds are cosy and comforting, but rather than the usual cabernet sauvignon, carmenère or syrah, why not open a bottle of a less mainstream grape, such as país or carignan?

In summer, outside with a plate of salads, give me the redcurrant-leaf scent of a chilled Bourgueil or Chinon. Garlicky sausages or sausages cooked on the barbecue or eaten with ratatouille are beautiful with herbal Bandol, which will recall the heat of a Provençal summer even if the sun's not shining. They go similarly well with the thunder of a Lebanese red. With barbecue-blackened sausages I also have a weakness for Australian syrah-cabernet sauvignon blends.

The dried herbs and figs, and the scent of wild hillsides covered in tinder-dry herbs that you find in Languedoc reds such as St Chinian, or the wild, flaring fire of a Côtes du Roussillon seem to suit late summer or autumn evenings when the nights are closing in. If there's a Tuscan vibe – maybe herby-garlic-fennel sausages, and a dinner that begins with crostini and follows up with potatoes

S

cooked in rosemary and olive oil or a borlotti bean salad – then how about a hearty Rosso di Montalcino, a Chianti or a Supertuscan?

With sausages on the menu you can go in any direction. And, obviously, while a simple dinner is always a good opportunity to bring out a bottle of good wine, sausages and mash are also fantastic with beer. A pint of London Pride would be ideal.

scallops There is an intrinsic sweetness to scallops which makes them a natural with chardonnay (I'm thinking expensive white burgundy), particularly if they have been fried so that the edges brown and caramelize. Tweak the wine according to the accompaniment. For instance, with pea purée pick a younger, fresher chardonnay, and with woody parsnip purée or with scallops with chorizo choose a richer, oaked chardonnay.

Other wines that are generally good with seared scallops include ageing white bordeaux and also champagne. Also surprisingly good: a shot of frozen Cognac.

For scallops with fresher-tasting ingredients, such as pea purée, pea shoots, micro-herbs, lime, or coriander, sauvignon blanc can work very well. I prefer to pick a riper sauvignon blanc that tastes of nectarines and has a heavier, softer feel in your mouth and usually look for wines from Marlborough, New Zealand; the Adelaide Hills or Margaret River in Australia; or Chile. These sauvignon blancs often also have a luminous quality that suits the plate of food.

With scallops with beurre blanc, an off-dry riesling, say Donnhoff, can be just right as the zing and sweetness of the wine play against the vinegar in the beurre blanc. With scallops with chorizo or wrapped in bacon or prosciutto, it's hard to beat champagne; a sparkling wine elsewhere made from the champagne grapes (chardonnay, pinot noir and pinot meunier); or cava. Oaked white Rioja works too. With carpaccio, that sweetness still survives, and the tender, white translucent slices of scallop have an almost meadow-flower mood that goes well with colombard-ugni blanc blends from south-west France or with Spanish muscat.

sea bass A delicate fish that suits whites with either elegant finesse or a light touch. If served plain, then try Rhône whites; pinot bianco (weissburgunder) from either north-east Italy (or Germany); or a fine pinot grigio such as one from Friuli-Venezia Giulia in north-east Italy, or a pinot grigio ramato, which is made by leaving the grape juice on the skins so that the wine is coppery pink in colour, a rosé, and has a faint taste of dried acai berries. If introducing sharper flavours on to the plate, then perhaps up the ante. Sea bass served with roasted baby vine tomatoes is good with a precise pinot grigio too, but the cool green notes and barbed-wire feel of sauvignon blanc from Awatere in New Zealand will boost the bright intensity of the tomatoes. With lemongrass, lime and ginger sea bass, try the streak of a young, limey riesling from Clare or Eden Valley in Australia or Martinborough in New Zealand. If chilli is involved, you could also try an off-dry riesling.

sea urchin The intense seawater and iodine taste can be very good with sharply aromatic, floral wines. I have vivid memories of a plate of sea urchin pasta, eaten on a broiling evening at a pavement café in Palermo with a glass of dry zibibbo (muscat) made by Sicilian producer Marco de Bartoli.

shepherd's pie see *cottage pie*

skate A pungent and closely textured, meaty fish, skate goes well with stony dry riesling from Alsace, saline Muscadet and also sauvignon blanc blends from Bordeaux. The classic dish of skate with capers and brown butter sauce works well with Vernaccia di San Gimignano; verdicchio; or pinot blanc from Alsace.

skordalia This Greek purée of potatoes and almonds is very garlicky so I usually put it with a fierce white wine such as assyrtiko from Santorini, whose pithy citrus and high-voltage energy fire back at the garlic. Gavi from Italy would be a good lemony alternative.

slaw Home-made slaw – a world apart from the tired, pre-prepped stuff you buy in a little plastic box – is crunchy and hearty with a sweet-and-sour vibe. It will kill a subtle wine, but it's unlikely that a delicate dinner is planned if coleslaw is in the mix. Coleslaw is more often eaten with highly flavoured food, such as pulled pork, barbecued meat or vegetable kebabs, strong marinades, burgers or

S

cold roast gammon. Everything else on the plate will probably be leading the wine choice here, but with the bite of raw onion and the peppery heat of the mustard in the dressing, perhaps veer towards a wine with more acidity and/or more tannin or just one with a bit of punch. For example, I'd pick a riesling rather than a Chablis; an awkward, young red rather than a fine old bordeaux. Mustard has the magical quality of calming down a difficult wine, so slaw will actually make an imperfect, tannic, green red taste more expensive – a good time to uncork a difficult, young claret – though don't do this if there's chilli or heavily flavoured sauces in the rest of the meal.

made with chipotle and paprika The smoky, fruity warmth of chipotle is good with the high-alcohol-burn and cough-mixture-scent of American zinfandel. It's also good with ripe Chilean, Australian and Argentine reds and upfront wines that have a ton of oak. The charred vanilla and sweet strawberry taste of young, modern Ribera del Duero fits right in here, especially if you're eating the slaw with pulled pork.

snails The squeamish might be tempted to choose a wine big enough to obliterate any hint of mollusc. In reality, the sauce, generally vibrating with garlic, tends to do that for you. In Alsace I once ate snail pizza, which was a bit of a shock as I had presumed those smooth-looking grey-brown chunks nestled among the melted cheese were actually mushrooms. The pizza was washed down with sparkling pinot blanc. It was fine, though I won't recommend it as a match that will make your toes tingle. Escargots are good with almost any young French red. They can work with the lightness of young Chinon or Saumur from the Loire; with entry-level red burgundy such as Mâcon Rouge; with a simple Corbières or Fitou; or indeed with any wine of indeterminate origin (but from somewhere in France), of the type that is sold in a brasserie by the carafe or from a petrol-type pump at which you fill your own bottle/saucepan/bathtub.

sole (Dover and lemon) A good white burgundy is a beautiful accompaniment for Dover or lemon sole, either grilled or fried with butter.

soufflé With cheese soufflé, try a chardonnay, served not too cold; a red burgundy; a mature claret; or a nebbiolo (especially good if truffles are involved). With the prickly pungency of a blue cheese soufflé, how about the precision of a ribolla gialla from north-east Italy, a minerallic greco di tufo from southern Italy, or the texture and florality of a malvasia from Istria in Croatia?

soup Soup is tricky with wine. Liquid + liquid just do not go brilliantly together. However, one wine that does taste very good with many kinds of soup, from gazpacho to mulligatawny to fish soup, is dry sherry. Fino (slightly punchier and more yeasty) or manzanilla (finer and more delicate) provides an edge that garlicky soups can rest against, and has a savoury, umami-like richness that works well with stock. Sherry also acts as a flavour-intensifier for tomato-based soups, in the same way that a slug of amontillado improves a Bloody Mary. Either serve the sherry on the side in a glass or add it to the soup. Both fino and manzanilla need to be poured chilled and from a freshly opened bottle.

See riesling for a recipe for 'Riesling soup' (p.310). And see also fish soup, gazpacho.

South-East Asian food This area encompasses Thailand, Vietnam, Singapore, Cambodia, Indonesia and Malaysia among others. It might seem peculiar to lump the cuisines of such a vast area together but in contemporary kitchens the ideas and ingredients behind them have been reinterpreted, cross-pollinated and redeveloped. In most places where a large choice of wines is available you're likely to be eating a version of the originals, not the real thing. These foods are often shared, too, with several dishes placed on the table at once, and there is a common thread in terms of the sorts of wines that drink well with the ingredients often found here.

Now that disclaimer's done, a quick look at the ingredients likely to feature.

Chilli is the first one. Unless the aim is to ramp up the jangle and discomfort factor, wines with low tannin, no oak and a touch of sweetness are best.

The sharpness of lime juice, tamarind, green papaya and green mango calls for wines with good acidity.

Flavours such as Thai basil, lemongrass, mint, lime leaves, fish

S

sauce and galangal or ginger demand wines that have a seamless brightness. Don't hamper them with the dust, incense and jagged texture of, say, a Chianti, or the farmyardy brett of some Old World red wines.

Wines that work here are ones that have 'Good acidity, natural fruit sweetness, and either a light touch with oak or no oak at all,' advises Sam Christie. He is a former sommelier and now managing director of his own four restaurants, including Longrain Melbourne, which serves beautiful South-East Asian food and has an excellent wine list.

Christie says that wines that work with the food at Longrain include 'really crisp Austrian and Australian riesling. I love that acidity and pristine river stone taste. We have a lot of pinot noir too, both Australian and New Zealand but also French. Once again I'm looking for cleansing acidity and no clumsy overtones. Often rosé goes well with the more spicy food – sweeter Spanish or Australian styles work best as you're looking for a bit of residual sugar to wrap up and meld with the spice.

'In terms of specific dishes, look for synergy with the herbs. Fresh green peppercorns are particularly tricky – make that a nightmare – with wine. Coriander and lemongrass work well with herbal styles of riesling, chenin blanc or sauvignon blanc but not so well with chardonnay. Mint can go quite surprisingly well with red wine, as long as the red is soft and juicy. Grüner veltliner from Austria is good with Thai basil and lemongrass too. Viognier is good with herbs but not with chilli. Pinot blanc, semillon and new-wave taut, lean Australian chardonnay are also worth a try.'

You're really looking here not for a wine that is a perfect 'match' but one that gets in the way of the food as little as possible, and isn't nuked itself by what's on your plate. Once chilli gets involved, you really need a bit of sweetness in the wine. If chilli is minimal, then besides Christie's recommendations, I would also consider Adelaide Hills sauvignon blanc, pinot gris, albariño, unoaked Australian semillon, sekt and nerello mascalese.

spaghetti see *pasta*

squid In its simplest form, grilled or griddled and dressed with lemon, garlic and olive oil, squid will go very happily with almost any rosé or bright, young, unoaked white wine. A few examples: South African sauvignon blanc brings a grassy freshness, Gavi di Gavi from northern Italy underscores the lemon, young semillon from Australia adds zip and vibrancy, albariño brings a tickle of apricot stone and marine salinity, and so on.

cool cucumber, cumin and squid salad There's a recipe for this in Leith's Cookery Bible. It's very good with a neutral dry white, such as a Terre di Chieti from Italy or a piepoul from France.

grilled with lime and chilli Riesling is superb with lime and the joyful clarity of a dry or off-dry wine from Australia, Chile, Washington State or South Africa really hits the spot.

salt and pepper squid (and salt and chilli squid) I've only ever eaten this nose-ticklingly aromatic snack, lunch or starter in restaurants, but Nigella writes that it is 'unexpectedly easy to shop for as well as easy to cook'. Her recipe is on her website, nigella.com. If you want wine, pick a dry white with a snap of acidity, perhaps also with bubbles to slice through the crunchy batter. Cava will do it. Pink fizz is good too; sparkling gamay made in Touraine in the Loire has a delicious bracing freshness, though any dry fizz will do the job. But I'd be making a saketini by shaking two parts of ice-cold Tanqueray Ten gin with one part of chilled daiginjo sake and ice, and straining the mixture into a cocktail glass.

squid ink risotto Emily O'Hare, an Italian wine expert and former wine buyer and head sommelier at The River Café, has the best advice here: 'Soave is just heaven with it and is exactly what I had when I ate it at the caff. I mean a straightforward Soave, nothing flashy-fruity, as it's such a subtle dish, all about texture and that squiddy flavour and colour. You don't want the distraction of anything too up itself. Otherwise, possibly a Ligurian pigato, or one of those Cinque Terre whites – they've way improved.' Another serious foodie friend – Joe Wadsack – remembers once enjoying a softly floral white Graves with squid ink risotto – an unusual non-Italian match.

S

stewed with chorizo and red peppers The paprika and the peppers lend themselves more to red than to white wines. Try a soft-cornered Spanish red, either one made from tempranillo or one from Navarra.

Stilton The traditional match with this blue veined cheese is port. I've never been entirely convinced by the combination of tannin which puts up a vigorous fight against strong blue cheese but it's such a festive pairing that I'm slowly coming round to the idea. The sweetness certainly helps. The classic choice would be an LBV, or a vintage port with some age on it but the mellow sweetness of a tawny makes for a gentler combination. Blue cheese kills delicate mature claret but it can go very well with an older cabernet sauvignon from Australia or Napa – the brighter fruit and age-softened tannins hold up well against the mould. In the depths of winter a glass of oloroso sherry is also good. My favourite match of all was suggested to me by the wine and food expert Fiona Beckett whose website matchingfoodandwine.com is a superb resource. Beckett points out that a nip of sloe gin is delicious with Stilton.

strawberries
hold the cream
One of my life's perfect lunches was eaten on a chilly June day in the Loire, in the garden of septuagenarian (and totally not looking it) winemaker Paul Filliatreau. We drank his Saumur Champigny, made from cabernet franc, tasting of leafy summer berries, with lamb barbecued over burning vine trunks, but the pièce de résistance was the pudding: a huge bowl of strawberries with Saumur Champigny poured over them. Red wine – cabernet, to be precise – and strawberries is one of those quirky and unexpected marriages. It works with cabernet franc from the Loire or cabernet sauvignon from Bordeaux and not much else. The strawberries need to be good (wild and other outdoor-grown strawberries flourish; big, watery Dutch greenhouse strawberries flounder) and the wine is better if it has noticeable tannin and not too much overt oak. Fragrant Margaux is particularly fine with strawberries. Ice-cold rosé (from almost anywhere) is also good to drink with, as well as to pour over, strawberries. Pick dry Provençal rosé for berries that

have not been sprinkled with sugar, darker and sweeter coloured rosé for those that have.

As for white wines, for sheer razzmatazz champagne is hard to beat; demi-sec champagne is not fashionable, but it is sybaritic. For lazy summer afternoons and early evenings, a glass of moscato is an inexpensive alternative. This effervescent, sweetish wine smells of blossom and peaches, a heady combination with the sweet, fragrant strawberries. Moscato has recently enjoyed a nightclub renaissance thanks to its appearance in hip-hop tracks (fans include Lil' Kim and Kanye West). The original and best version is Moscato d'Asti from Piemonte in Italy; but moscato is made elsewhere too. Soundtrack optional.

and cream
Cream transforms the strawberries into a full-blown dessert. I tend to prefer puddings without wine but many disagree, and a properly sweet wine such as Jurançon moelleux or a floral Muscat de Beaumes de Venise will hit the spot. Grand Marnier and strawberries is also a match made in heaven – add the Grand Marnier to the cream, or drink it separately and enjoy the fusion of the intense orange with Cognac and red fruit.

stroganoff If you want to do this properly, go for Balkan refosco or kekfrankos from Hungary. Ideally you want a red that is rustic and prickly and tastes like it's drunk out of chalices. Greece and Turkey are good places to look for wines that still have prickle and an air of the untame.

suckling pig While ordinary roast pork can be rather dry, the meat of roast suckling pig is tender and juicy. It goes well with all the whites suggested for roast pork, but a red is my favourite match, and because the meat is succulent, you can afford the savoury tannins of a serious wine, from the Douro, say, or from Bordeaux. Rioja and Ribera del Duero are both excellent too. Says Ferran Centelles, a Spaniard and former sommelier at El Bulli: 'Tempranillo Crianza and suckling pig is a classical match, but I also love suckling pig with the intensity and power of a Médoc wine, especially if it is slightly aged.'

See also pork.

sushi It's normal to eat several different types of sushi at once, so the wine choice is necessarily quite general. Sake very obviously works beautifully and Western palates usually prefer the lighter daiginjo style, which is drunk chilled. The Japanese grape koshu, like a cross between pinot grigio and sauvignon blanc, with subtle flavours of starfruit, is brilliant here. It's a wine that tastes almost invisible when drunk on its own, but swells and blossoms with food. Look for chiselled, calm wines such as dry furmint (which often has hints of sushi ginger and Japanese pears), pinot blanc from Germany or north-east Italy, albariño, pale rosé, grüner veltliner, Loire sauvignon blanc (Menetou Salon and Reuilly are particularly good), aligoté, Pfalz or Rheingau dry riesling, verdicchio, rosé champagne and English sparkling wine. Pinot gris is more floral and softer but also good with the rice element. Red can work too – think German pinot noir or gamay.

swordfish The robust white flesh of swordfish is among the most meaty of fish. With lemon garlic sauce or the anise flavours (fenugreek, aniseed, fennel tops or Pernod) with which swordfish goes so well, try oaked sauvignon blanc-semillon blends and oaked assyrtiko, which also have tinges of fennel and baked-lemon flavours. Powerful yet fresh Douro whites are good here too, as is South African semillon and oaked white Rioja. If you are treating swordfish like a steak and serving it with, say, Café de Paris butter or mixed peppercorn butter, then think more steaky on the wine too, with a young and unoaked red such as Côtes du Rhône, or garnacha from Calatayud in Spain. Plain swordfish dressed with just a squeeze of lemon and a slick of olive oil also suits red wine, but go for a little more tartness with young gamay or Marcillac.

T

tagine The combination of heat, spice and fruit is a difficult one for wine. Provided that the chilli is not too hot and the spice not too strong, with lighter, chicken, vegetarian or pork-based tagine, then aromatic viognier, which smells of honeysuckle and apricots, has a suitably Scheherazade air to it. With heavier meats, I like the warm spice of Lebanese reds or the fading splendour of an old Gran Reserva Rioja or silky Montsant. All too often what I actually end up opening, however, is rosé: dry and pale for a low-chilli tagine, deeper and sweeter the more spice-heat there is.

tandoori With tandoori you retain the juiciness and succulence of the meat or fish and this becomes the core that goes with the wine, unlike with a wet curry, where the sauce almost overwhelms other flavours. Tandoori monkfish or sea bass is great with dry muscat, if you can find a good one. There are an awful lot of cheap perfume horrors around but I've had a few excellent ones from Spain, with a hint of orange blossom woven into the florals and with which the lightness of the wine dances around the spice. Dry furmint is a good alternative. Tandoori prawns are beautiful with an aromatic gewürztraminer. Tandoori chicken works well with a very bright but not too oaky chardonnay from South Africa, Australia or Chile. The warmth found in the wine glows with the heat but is limpid enough for the spice. Succulent tandoori lamb is good with red, but as tannins have the effect of concentrating the dried spices, go for one that's smooth: for example, an inexpensive Mediterranean pinot noir or a blend from the Midi. A Turkish red can also work, though the spices might taste more aggressive.

tapas A glass of manzanilla, fino, tempranillo or cava is the classic accompaniment to the different flavours on a table loaded with tapas. But go with your mood.

tarragon This herb has a powerful, slightly aniseed taste. It's best friends with semillon (in particular, with barrel-fermented semillon), which makes a white bordeaux a good bet with, say, roast chicken with tarragon butter under the skin. In such simple dishes tarragon also works well with the woodruff taste of young, oaked white burgundy. In salads where tarragon is added as a raw herb, it's usually better to stick with the vibrant tang of a sauvignon-semillon blend. With tarragon mustard (in a hot dog) I like the herbal vigour of a young German pinot noir.

Aged syrah – say, a mature Cornas or Hermitage or older Heathcote syrah from Australia – can also be superb with tarragon.

See also beef: béarnaise.

tarte tatin Caramelized orchard fruit in a buttery pastry – tarte tatin is one of the few desserts that really plays up to a dessert wine. The obvious choice is a beerenauslese or trockenbeerenauslese riesling whose own luscious apple-strudel flavours mirror those of the tart. Sweet Loire chenin blanc, and the saffron and crystallized fruit flavours of Sauternes, as well as other sweet sauvignon-semillon blends (Monbazillac, Loupiac and so on) are good too. The golden-brown sugar in the tart underscores the honeyed flavours of the wines.

Thai beef salad Steak seared so that it's pink in the middle and smokily charred on the edge; the scent of torn Thai basil, mint and coriander leaves curling up your nostrils; threads of crunchy raw shallots; the grit of the rice powder; and the sour lime of the dressing ... eating Thai beef salad is a very fragrant, and intense, experience. And I haven't mentioned the chilli.

See chilli.

A hot version of this will nuke wine. My favourite match for a very mild Thai beef salad is Marlborough pinot noir, silky and perfumed. Failing that, a young pinot noir from elsewhere in New Zealand, or from Australia or from Chile. You could also try one of the soft, lusciously fruity old-vine carignans coming out of Chile; the white pepper and soft mulberry of a cinsault from South Africa; a brambly, unoaked Fitou or Minervois or Costières de Nîmes; the cranberry and tea flavours of an unoaked Chilean carmenère; or the warm pom-pom of strawberry that is a simple and unoaked Spanish garnacha. Put the bottle in the fridge for 20–30 minutes and drink it slightly chilled to give it a refreshing edge against the herbs and lime.

Thai green curry The piercing, almost luminous, quality of a sauvignon blanc from Marlborough, New Zealand, plays off the fresh lime, the burst of the pea aubergines and the crunch of the snake beans but fares less well up against chilli. I often open a bottle to drink as an aperitif, or while cooking, as it anticipates the dinner beautifully. With the food, an off-dry wine is better. Non-dry riesling from Australia, Chile or New Zealand (first choice) or Germany (second choice) will counteract the chilli heat and float along with the aromatic coriander and lime. A pretty pinot gris or Chilean gewürztraminer with an edge of sweetness is a good choice too and its gentle florality will cosy up to the coconut milk.

Thanksgiving You can expect there to be a turkey on the Thanksgiving table. Depending on family and cultural traditions, there might also be sage, sausages, chestnuts, cranberries, sweet potatoes, bacon, apples, raisins, mashed potatoes, corn on the cob, cornbread, homity and squash. The overall effect is one of sweet abundance, with sweetness coming not just from the dried and fresh fruit or the sweet cure of fatty bacon, but also from the corn and sweet potatoes. For a white, go for more ample styles of chardonnay in which you can taste sun, butter and oak. For reds, a luscious and supple pinot noir (perhaps from Sonoma) will harmonize all those flavours; and the fruity roar of a zinfandel wraps the whole feast in fruity warmth. Cinsault and carignan (particularly natural styles of these wines) also work well. Randall Grahm, whose winery in Santa Cruz makes superb Californian wines using Rhône grape varieties, tweeted, 'Just a reminder: virtually every Bonny Doon wine seems to go very well with turkey.' Indeed they do: the aromatic qualities of most Rhône-style blends, both red and white, from the Rhône itself and elsewhere, mesh beautifully with the many flavours on the plate.

As the original point of Thanksgiving was to give thanks for the blessing of the harvest there is good reason to drink native wines, but looking further afield, a Beaujolais Cru will act as a pert counterpoint in much the same manner as the cranberry sauce.

T

More alternative suggestions: an Etna red for its flow and light-bodied refreshment; a trousseau or poulsard from the Jura for its elegance; a chenin blanc (or chenin-roussanne-marsanne blend) from Swartland, South Africa, for the scent of warm orchard fruit and texture that go particularly well with mashed sweet potato and corn.

See also Christmas dinner, turkey.

thyme Woody and aromatic, thyme is not a tricky herb with wine but it does have a tendency to make commercial (fruity and slightly sweet) reds and whites taste trivial and embarrassingly simple. Thyme has a special affinity with pinot noir. It also suits those Mediterranean red wines, from Collioure to Bandol to Cannonau di Sardegna, that seem to smell of sun-baked slopes covered with dried scrub and herbs.

tofu Not exactly abundant in flavour itself, wines that go well will be those that take their cue from the other elements of the dish. Tofu is often used as a substitute for chicken, or another meat, in which case look up that dish and use those guidelines.

tomatoes The cool zing and green aromatics of sauvignon blanc really pick up on the refreshing bite of tomatoes (especially raw ones). It's quite a special match, though of course not the only grape that tastes good with a tomato. The main point about tomatoes is that they are super-acidic, which changes the balance of a plate of food and can make a low-acid wine taste flabby and dull, so it's best to look for one with a bit of nip. Here are a few of my favourite tomato and wine experiences.

fresh tomato salad, pan con tomate, insalata tricolore If I were in Barcelona, I'd hope to be sitting on the waterfront with an open bottle of Torres Viña Sol, a quintessential slug-it-back holiday wine made from cava grapes. Cava would also do very nicely. With a lunch or outdoor dinner of warm roast chicken and a big plate of sliced tomatoes sprinkled with freshly chopped chives or basil, or with an insalata tricolore (tomatoes, mozzarella and basil), I'd look to meet the cool green herbs with a grassy Loire sauvignon; a South African sauvignon blanc; one from the Awatere in New Zealand; a generic Touraine sauvignon; a Coteaux du Giennois; or a Sancerre or one of its satellites (Pouilly-Fumé, Quincy, Reuilly, Menetou Salon). Herbaceous Italian wines – vermentino, verdicchio – do well here too. As does young Loire chenin. For red wines, think Bardolino, Beaujolais (or gamay from elsewhere), or just a young red with low alcohol (say, 12% abv), which indicates that the grapes were likely to have been picked with plenty of acidity in them.

oven-dried tomatoes Halves of tomatoes dried slowly in the oven at a low temperature until the flavour intensifies to a piercing burst can take richer, more demanding wines. Consider ripe sauvignon blanc from New Zealand that tastes of nectarine and passion fruit; the warm gooseberries and white currant of a Chilean sauvignon; the broad, pink grapefruit-tinged fumés from California; or a more premium Loire sauvignon with a bit of barrel-fermentation. Look at the other ingredients too; all of these wines go particularly well with dried tomatoes in, say, a salad of peaches, mozzarella and rocket. Chenin blanc and also carricante from the slopes of Mount Etna in Sicily can also be good alternatives, depending on the dish. For instance, chenin blanc is good with a combination of oven-dried tomatoes and goat's cheese. Carricante works well as a palate cleanser with very savoury dishes, such as pasta with oven-dried tomatoes, garlic and olives or oven-dried tomatoes with fried white fish and capers.

salsa cruda For a raw tomato pasta sauce, perhaps with flat-leaf parsley chopped in, as well as fried courgettes and Parmesan gratings, I pick watery, inexpensive French sauvignon blanc, whose grassiness will mesh with the chlorophyll without overwhelming the delicate sauce. The wines mentioned in the entry for *fresh tomato salad, pan con tomate, insalata tricolore* above will also work here.

tomato gratin In her (sadly out of print) book *Modern British Food*, Sybil Kapoor has a recipe for tomato gratin – tomatoes cooked in cream with a cheesy topping – that is the very definition of heavenly summer eating with cold roast beef or chicken. The creamy sauce absorbs much of the acidity, so I pick pinot noir with beef and with chicken, light chardonnay – a Mâcon or one of Australia's twangy, low-alcohol new chardonnays.

tomato tart Layers of thinly sliced tomatoes, laid on a puff pastry base, garnished with capers, olives and anchovies (for those who like them), then gently baked in a slow oven is really a version of pissaladière. The following recipe was first made for me by my friend Stephen, on a villa holiday in Provence during which a copy of F. Scott Fitzgerald's *Tender is the Night* was making an increasingly factor 30-smeared round of the sunloungers by the pool, hence 'Dick Diver's Tart'. This is a much-repeated recipe in my house. I often make it to cut into tiny squares as a pre-dinner G&T or V&T snack, but everyone always eats so much that the main course becomes almost superfluous. The wine needs to be savoury with all those salty-vinegary additions. White (or pink) wine from Provence or Loire sauvignon blanc or Gavi or arneis or one of the Italian V-grapes mentioned under *fresh tomato salad, pan con tomate, insalata tricolore* is just delicious.

DICK DIVER'S TOMATO TART
Serves 3–4 as a main or 6 as a starter

- 350g ready-made puff pastry
- 3–4 tablespoons passata (if you like you can fry some garlic in olive oil until golden, then cook a larger quantity of passata gently with the oil until the flavour is infused, and use this garlicky passata to spread on the tart)
- 1.5kg medium-sized tomatoes, washed and evenly sliced (about 5mm thick)
- a handful of capers (optional)
- a handful of black olives (optional)
- salt and freshly ground black pepper
- 1 tablespoon olive oil
- fresh basil (optional)

Heat the oven to 200°C/400°F/gas mark 6. Roll the puff pastry out into either a 30cm circle or a rectangle, roughly 20 × 35cm. Spread a very thin layer of passata over the pastry, then lay the tomatoes on top, in circles or lines, according to whether you are making a round or rectangular tart, so that they overlap. They will shrink a lot when cooked so ensure that there is a good amount of overlap. You need to overlap both the slices in each row and the rows themselves. Scatter with capers and black olives if using. Season. Drizzle with the olive oil. Bake for 25–30 minutes, keeping an eye on the tart to make sure it doesn't begin to burn, then turn the oven down to to 150°C/300°F/gas mark 2 and cook very slowly for about 45 more minutes or longer if required. The tomatoes need to dry out and the base to become crisp. Take out of the oven, scatter with fresh, torn basil leaves (if using) and that's it.

Well done, as Stephen would say.

tomatoes in cooked sauces The acidity is the reason nippy Italian reds are so good with pasta sauces. Cooked tomato sauces are richer than raw ones and so they can take heavier wines.

See pasta and individual pasta entries for more detailed suggestions.

tortilla Sparkling wine is often a winner with eggs, and cava or champagne or a sparkling pinot-chardonnay from elsewhere in the world is a very cheery way to wash down a deep, runny-centred tortilla. Sherry – manzanilla or fino for choice – is also a good option.

tortilla española (with potatoes fried in olive oil) Any of the above sparkling wines go nicely with this. The earthy potatoes make red wine appealing too. A young, unoaked Navarra or a bright Rioja Crianza feels casual and hearty. A Spanish friend once cooked the best, most melting tortilla española I have ever eaten. She served it with home-made chips fried in a gigantic Le Creuset and a green salad. Her husband opened a cru Bourgeois – it was Château les Ormes de Pez. So, a left-bank claret and a Spanish omelette. Unorthodox but brilliant. It was a clever way of turning a humble tortilla into a highly prized Saturday dinner with friends. I was curious to know what Spaniard Ferran Centelles, who was the sommelier at El Bulli from 2000 to 2011 and specializes in matching wines to high-end food might like to drink with tortilla, so I asked him. He said, 'Eggs are always difficult to pair. However,

T

if you use onions and potatoes and really cook them well the tortilla will be easier to match. I love to eat the tortilla with a sort of oaky rosé wine produced in Navarra, but a delicate rosé from Provence is also a great match.'

See also omelette, tapas.

trifle If it's a sherry trifle, then sherry is what you must drink with it – ideally the same stuff that has been used to make it, which in our house is always cream. Cream sherry is a throwback, but so is our family trifle. Made with bright layers of pink packet blancmange and wobbly yellow Bird's Custard, it is a thing of beauty that no one else seems to understand. 'As natural as a nuclear reactor,' said the last person I tried to feed it to. But we love it, and we love it with the rich raisin taste of cream sherry too.

With more delicate fruit trifles, perhaps made with fresh custard and fresh summer berries, ratafia champenois is delicious. This is quite rare, because champagne grapes command such a premium when they're made into fizz. It's made by mixing fresh grape juice with alcohol, so has a sweetly grapey taste. The Ratafia de Champagne from Dumangin is particularly good – it's aged in solera (in barrels) and smells very gently of dried figs and spices, and buttery, sugar-crusted Madeira cakes baking in the oven, as well as having a luscious melon sweetness and kick of spirit.

trout This delicate river fish shies away from wines that are too fierce. Fresh trout is lovely with Austrian grüner veltliner, with the cool hedgerow flavours of English bacchus, with dry furmint, or with simpler, unoaked burgundy such as Mâcon or Bourgogne Blanc. Hot smoked trout is good with refined, non-shouty riesling from Austria, or from Pfalz or Rheinhessen in Germany.

truffles The scent of truffles is both captivating and giddying. At least it is to some of us; 25–50 per cent of the population (depending on which study you read) can't smell them properly or, in a few cases, at all. I pity those people. For others, like me, the smell of a truffle is so intoxicating that even the thought of one is enough to bring on heart palpitations and a kind of meerkatty alertness.

The specific cause of all the olfactory excitement has been the centre of much debate. Around fifty volatile odour-carrying components have been identified for the black Périgord truffle, *Tuber melanosporum*, and more than 200 across all species of truffles, a number that keeps on going up as increasingly sensitive instruments for identifying the volatiles become available.

Back in 1981, three German researchers published a paper reporting that truffles contain a steroid, androstenone, that has a musky smell and is a main component of boar pheromones. As well as being found in boar saliva and truffles, androstenone also occurs in the armpit sweat of men, in bacon and, unexpectedly, in celery. The scientists speculated, not unreasonably, that this must be the smell that attracts wild pigs to nuzzle and paw at the ground until they have unearthed a dirty, smelly tuber, and which causes humans to sigh in contentment. However, later students of truffles demonstrated that it does not appear to be androstenone that draws boars and dogs to buried scent caches but another compound present in truffles – dimethyl sulphide (DMS), which has been described as 'the smell of the sea' or, less attractively, when present in higher concentrations, 'the smell of rotting cabbage'.

What effect does androstenone have on humans? Women find it more appealing during ovulation, according to one study, so perhaps appreciation of truffles also changes through the female cycle. My own never flags. Indeed, it is so intense that for a moment I seriously considered acting on a friend's suggestion to organize the world's first wine and truffle matching championship – 'Just think how many you will get to eat, and what fine wines!' – before I realized that he was teasing me. A small part of me still wonders if it might be possible to pull this off. The realistic side says otherwise.

Magnificent with truffles at most times: nebbiolo, in all its guises; vintage champagne; white burgundy; Pomerol.

white truffles The three best ways to eat white truffle, in my opinion, are shaved on to thin strands of eggy pasta with butter, shaved on to a fried egg, or in fonduta. White truffles are of course also used to flavour risottos and puréed squash. They are shaved on to carpaccio of beef with rocket, and also on to tartare of beef or veal, and all manner of other foods. In all these cases, the dried rose and sandalwood scent of nebbiolo (Barolo or Barbaresco or one from Valtellina, Ghemme or a simple Langhe nebbiolo) is the best possible wine to be drinking. The fragrance is heavenly. Also, with dairy-rich, creamy, eggy dishes, nebbiolo's fine, sinewy tannins offer a bit of a workout in between those dizzying mouthfuls of fat and fragrance. You will have invested heavily in the truffle so it's worth making a bit of effort with the wine. Either young or old is fine, but don't open a super-grand bottle that is also young, as it's likely to be so oaky, and so powerful, that it's not pleasant to drink and drowns out the truffle. Failing nebbiolo, seek out another wine from Alba, such as barbera.

There is also a synergy between white truffles shaved on to seafood/fish and vintage champagne.

black Périgord truffles Mature Pomerol has a soft, sumptuous texture, and it smells gently fungal, which resonates with, say, black truffles stuffed under the skin of a roasted chicken. A maturing red burgundy would also be good here. The luxe of white burgundy is also gorgeous with black truffles with chicken, as well as black truffles when they are put with seafood.

At a Noble Rot lunch at The Clove Club in east London, I once ate carpaccio of scallops with black truffles, sudachi (a Japanese fruit with a citrus twang) and hazelnuts with a glass of young Jacques Carillon Puligny-Montrachet. The wine was the perfect counterpoint for the sweetness of the scallops, the crunch of the nuts and the scallop shavings together with the subtle burst of citrus. It was a genius plate of food with a genius wine beside it.

other truffles: English summer truffles, Australian truffles, black Istrian truffles Milder in flavour, these truffles need a more subtle wine. Rosé champagne is perfect, as I discovered after going truffle hunting at a secret location in the south of England with the cook and restaurateur Roger Jones and his Manchester United-loving son Richard, who was then eleven and as good a truffle hunter as any Périgord pig. He said he could feel them through the soles of his trainers. Once we'd unearthed a few dirty truffles from among the roots of the trees, Roger whipped out a little camping stove; fried some turbot; sliced subtle, nutty and freshly unearthed English summer truffles over them; and opened a bottle of rosé Gosset. Both food and wine were delicate, elegant and blissful. White champagne works too, as does white burgundy, as long as it's not too heavy. In Istria, Croatia, local truffles are a speciality that goes with the fragrant, floral, textured local white wine made from malvasia. The Istrian version of the summer truffle is glorious with filled pasta, foraged wild asparagus and a carafe of local wine.

tuna Of all fish, tuna is the most likely candidate for eating with red wine, so much so that I can't actually remember the last time I ate cooked tuna with white. Seared so that it's brown on the outside and a translucent stained-glass window pink in the middle, it is lovely with chilled light or medium-bodied reds, such as Beaujolais; Cerasuolo di Vittoria; Etna reds from Sicily; zweigelt from Austria; crunchy pinot noir from Chile, Burgundy, Germany or Austria; cabernet franc; Bierzo; dolcetto; Valpolicella; Bardolino; lagrein and so on. If you are cooking it with a crushed-peppercorn crust, then consider a lighter cool-climate syrah, such as a young St Joseph that has been sparingly oaked.

carpaccio of tuna Drizzled with olive oil and scattered with slices of spring onion, carpaccio of tuna is excellent with a lemony white such as cortese, assyrtiko, or a lemony sauvignon blanc. I once ate this dish with a fantastic sauvignon made by Sevilen in Turkey.

turkey A juicy or aromatic wine, whether red or white, helps to combat turkey's tendency to dryness. Dolcetto, Beaujolais, pinot noir, unoaked Spanish garnacha, grillo and falanghina are all happy contenders, while the soft aroma of pinot gris brings a succulence to the meat. What you're eating with it makes all the difference.

See also Boxing Day leftovers, Christmas dinner, Thanksgiving, turkey sandwiches.

turkey sandwiches A festive favourite, often eaten in an over-indulgent stupor while surrounded by scrunched-up wrapping paper and relatives. Crack open a bottle of dry, red Lambrusco, a superb and underestimated sparkling wine from the Emilia-Romagna region of Italy. It's sparkling, slightly earthy and dusty and often tastes of cranberries, which makes it perfect if sausage-meat stuffing, cranberry and bread sauce are also involved in the sandwich-making.

See also Boxing Day leftovers, Christmas dinner, Thanksgiving, turkey.

veal A versatile meat that can go with both red and white wines, though I more often pick a red. The perky acidity and fine delineation of north-western Italian wines made from nebbiolo, dolcetto and barbera are always a good bet, or, in the same vein, a sangiovese. I also like the reds from the Italo-Alpine region of Alto Adige made from lagrein or teroldego, or a chilled Valpolicella from the Veneto. With veal chop or roast, simply cooked with no sauce, besides the wines mentioned above, try the frisson of claret (a lighter, inexpensive wine, or one from the left bank; not St Emilion); a Marcillac; or a simple, young pinot noir. The earthy tones of mencía (from Bierzo or Ribeira Sacra in Spain) also work well, as do older, fine red wines from Brunello to Rioja to burgundy, that have mellowed with age. The accompaniments make quite a difference, however.

with braised fennel or with sage, rocket and white bean salad Those edgy reds with good acidity go well with tricky fennel: sangiovese, frappato, nebbiolo, gamay, or at a pinch barbera. For whites try a more complex Gavi, oaked white burgundy, white bordeaux or greco di tufo.

with creamy sauces With a richer, creamy sauce, either stick with one of those Italian reds mentioned above, which have the acidity to cut through the fat, cleansing the mouth between forkfuls, or pick a richer, heavier wine from Bordeaux to match the weight of the food.

escalope, fried in butter with a squeeze of lemon A white wine would be just as good as a red, perhaps a fuller-flavoured Gavi di Gavi or a Chablis.

meatballs made with pine nuts and Pecorino A northern Italian red or a richer Italian white, such as fiano or greco di tufo.

veal parmigiana Brought to the US from Italy and enriched over the generations, this dish has become an Italian-American classic. Its layers of cheese, tomatoes and veal escalopes are heavy and comforting. Choose sangiovese, frappato or dolcetto to cut through the clag or a rich primitivo or zinfandel to roll with it.

veal milanese see *wiener schnitzel*; also *osso buco, saltimbocca alla romana, vitello tonnato*.

venison This meat has forceful flavours that can take (and sometimes demand) big red wines.

rare steak or loin Here, however, pinot noir can be a good choice. A plumper wine from New Zealand or Oregon will bring juice and ease in a similar way to a dollop of redcurrant jelly on the plate. This is also a good pick if the venison is served with sweet red cabbage or a rich jus. The compressed red fruit flavours of a youthful Châteauneuf-du-Pape or grenache-based Côtes du Rhône also make a good counterpoint to pink venison. With more savoury accompaniments, such as mushrooms, you could try a stern German pinot noir, or a mature burgundy. An oaky barbera, Montepulciano d'Abruzzo or even a younger, fruitier St Joseph, or young Australian shiraz, works well here too.

venison burgers with redcurrant jelly With these, play into the sweet fruit with an Australian, North American or New Zealand pinot noir, a Beaujolais Cru, a juicy young unoaked or barely oaked syrah from pretty much anywhere in the world, or a fruity carignan.

venison casserole or braised venison When slow-cooked with herbs and, possibly, bacon and juniper, the feral scent of venison is at its most pervasively intense. It's time to call on the big boys: try a gamey syrah, old or young, from the northern Rhône (Cornas, Côte Rôtie, Crozes-Hermitage, Hermitage or St Joseph); an earthy or eucalyptal Aussie shiraz (perhaps from Heathcote or McLaren Vale respectively); a savage touriga nacional from Portugal; a herbal oaked carignan; a St Chinian; or the smoky flare of a Côtes du Roussillon. Mourvèdre is an especially good match as this grape

V

has a gamey flavour, which makes red Bandol another good option. Venison casserole also likes a bit of brett – the yeast that can make a wine taste of old leather horse saddles, or stables – so if you have a bretty wine (maybe a Bandol or a claret or a Rhône), then bring it out now. Wine aside, the bitter flavours of a dark beer can be utterly superb with the dark, dense flavours and meaty perfume of venison casserole. Look for either rich, smooth, malty, fairly strong old-school brown ales or fresh, fragrant, thymey, hoppy black beers with acidity and a bitter-chocolate finish. Try Fullers 1845, Beavertown Black Betty or Yeastie Boys Pot Kettle Black.

vitello tonnato Pick the clean bite of verdicchio, a vermentino or a lemony Gavi or arneis if you like white wine; a sangiovese rosato for a pink with a prickle of tannin; or a Provençal rosé that tastes more of herbs than it does of strawberries. My favourite wine to drink is actually red: a chilled Valpolicella or lighter nebbiolo or, failing that, a dolcetto or barbera.

V

W

Waldorf salad The cold crunch of green apple, the brisk bite of celery and the cold slap of mayonnaise go very well with a fresh, unoaked Saint-Véran from the Mâconnais in Burgundy. However, it's not often anyone eats Waldorf salad without a plate crammed with so many other foods (quiche, slices of ham, pork pie, pickles, rice salads – all those classic Seventies buffet staples), so the choice of wine isn't too important, though I'd happily drink a Saint-Veran with all of that as well.

walnuts If you were sitting by a fire, cracking open walnuts, with a glass beside you, you might want that glass to contain a rare, old Madeira. Madeira is a wine that is almost immortal: it still tastes good when it is not just decades but more than a century old, and it has flavours of dried fruit and nuts, all of which make it a perfect, meditative combination with walnuts.

Otherwise, it's unusual for walnuts to play an insistent enough part on the plate to steer the wine choice. This is partly because walnuts are friendly to most white wines. Crisp, fresh, fruity whites provide a similar pleasing contrast to that found between apple and walnut in a Waldorf salad. More complex, oaked whites, perhaps with extended skin contact, which gives them texture and tannins, from dry to sweet like those rich old Madeiras, draw out the more complex flavours, as dried figs and raisins do with most nuts.

There are times, though, when walnuts, along with other ingredients, haul a plate of food in a very savoury direction: for instance, Diana Henry's recipe for 'Jerusalem artichokes and chicken with anchovy, walnut and parsley relish' (found in *A Bird in the Hand*). In these cases, good matches are savoury red wines such as those made from mencía (for example, Bierzo or Ribeira Sacra) or blends from the Dão in Portugal.

See also Waldorf salad.

wasabi Much commercially available 'wasabi' contains only a small proportion of the real stuff, consisting mainly of horseradish and a pale green-coloured mustard. It can still produce explosive effects, however. I once put a whole teaspoonful in my mouth, presuming it was guacamole (I was in South Africa and not a Japanese restaurant, so perhaps the mistake is understandable). A few seconds later, a burning in my nose and a kind of electric slicing at the front of my head, similar to what you might expect to feel if you dived into a pool of iced water, alerted me to the error. Wasabi activates the trigeminal nerve, which carries pain sensations in the mouth. Its pungency can be tricky with wine. The best advice is to go easy on the wasabi if you want to be able to taste the wine too, but with small amounts then zesty whites such as grüner veltliner are good.

See also sushi.

watercress This cool, peppery leaf suits the chilly, damp nettles-and-hawthorn taste of English bacchus – a good option for a white to go with watercress salad with trout. I often eat watercress in a salad with papaya (have you noticed they share a similar flavour?) and also feta, in which case a white with good acidity is key. Bacchus can certainly supply that, but I like a white with a bit more gloss – a dry Jurançon or a white St Mont is ideal. Watercress salad with steak would make me look for a red that is prickly or leafy rather than mellow – sangiovese or peppery syrah or cabernet franc or claret in place of warm Rioja or mellifluous merlot.

wiener schnitzel The crispy, fried-breadcrumb crust around this veal escalope demands a white wine with some edge. A refreshing grüner veltliner or dry riesling is the obvious choice for this Austrian dish. A measured sauvignon blanc, such as a Reuilly from the Loire, or a sauvignon blanc from Australia's Adelaide Hills, is good too, as are the precise and clipped wines of northern Italy: Gavi or arneis will act like a squeeze of lemon, while friulano and ribolla gialla are more aromatic.

Z

zander When it has been pan-fried and served with simple flavours, this lake and river fish also known as the pike-perch is good with dry white chenin blanc from the Loire, riesling from Alsace, or dry Jurançon. In the Loire it is sometimes cooked in red wine, in which case choose a Loire red to drink with it.

See sauvignon blanc for a recipe for 'Filet de sandre aux agrumes' (Fillet of zander with citrus, p.333).

FROM WINE TO FOOD

An A to Z of Wine

T his part of the book is for those times when planning food begins with a bottle: the wine is chosen and what's wanted is inspiration for what to eat with it. As far as possible, I have organized things by grape, starting with aglianico and ending with zinfandel. To make it easier to navigate, a short list on the next page will direct you to the right entry if a wine is looked up by the appellation on the label. For instance, searching for Chinon (red) will send you to cabernet franc.

It's not an exhaustive list. To keep things concise, I have not included regions of origin where it is usual to find the grape name stated on the label. The expectation is that a reader faced with a bottle of Sauvignon de Touraine, Vin d'Alsace Riesling or Coonawarra Cabernet Sauvignon, for instance, will have no difficulty in figuring out which grape entry to turn to. Nor have I attempted to create a gazetteer of, for instance, Burgundy, though a few well-known names are included.

Of course, many wines are made from a blend rather than a single grape. Where it seemed to make sense to do so, I've discussed the blend under the umbrella of its main grape. For example, Châteauneuf-du-Pape is contained within the grenache entry. In some cases, an appellation or style has sprung its own entry – for example, Priorat elbowed its way out of grenache and cariñena to stand alone. There are also entries for both rosé and orange wines, both of which are defined only by their colour.

A few grapes are covered in multiple places. For instance, sauvignon blanc is discussed under the sauvignon blanc header, and additionally under dry sauvignon-semillon blend and Sauternes, as well as a miniature entry for Sancerre.

As far as possible, I've tried to stick to the most commonly found wines and grapes and allowed the material to shape the book.

Foods appear in bold so that you can scan rapidly for ideas.

For the 'what the winemakers' eat sections I asked the producers of wines I admire to share what they like to eat with their own wines.

GRAPES AND WINES

Listings in **bold** have an entry; those not in bold refer to the entry where they are discussed.

aglianico

albariño

aligoté

alvarinho, see albariño

Amarone

amontillado, see sherry

Anjou (blanc), see chenin blanc

Anjou (rouge), see cabernet franc

arneis

assyrtiko

Bandol, see mourvèdre

Barbaresco, see nebbiolo

barbera

Barolo, see nebbiolo

Barsac, see Sauternes

Beaujolais, see gamay

Bergerac, see cabernet sauvignon,
    sauvignon blanc-semillon blends

Bierzo, see mencía

Bolgheri, see Supertuscans

bordeaux (red), see cabernet franc,
    cabernet sauvignon, merlot, Pomerol

bordeaux (sweet), see Sauternes and other
    sweet sauvignon blanc-semillon blends

bordeaux (white), see sauvignon blanc-
    semillon blends (dry)

Bourgueil, see cabernet franc

Brouilly, see gamay

Brunello di Montalcino, see sangiovese

burgundy (red), see pinot noir

burgundy (white), see chardonnay and
    also aligoté

cabernet franc

cabernet sauvignon

Cahors, see malbec

carignan

cariñena, see carignan

carmenère

Carmignano, see sangiovese

cava

Chablis, see also chardonnay

champagne

chardonnay

Châteauneuf-du-Pape, see grenache noir
    and also mourvèdre

chenin blanc

Chianti, see sangiovese

Chinon, see cabernet franc, chenin blanc

Chiroubles, see gamay

claret, see cabernet sauvignon, merlot,
    Pomerol

Condrieu, see viognier

Cornas, see syrah

cortese

Côte Rôtie, see syrah

Côtes du Rhône, see grenache, syrah,
    Rhône – white blends

Crozes-Hermitage, see syrah

dolcetto

Douro reds

English sparkling wine

fer servadou

fino, see sherry

Fitou, see Languedoc-Roussillon reds

Fleurie, see gamay

gamay

Gavi, see cortese

gewürztraminer

Gigondas, see grenache

graciano

Graves (white), see sauvignon blanc-
   semillon blends (dry)

grenache

grüner veltliner

Hermitage, see syrah, Rhône – white
   blends

Juliénas, see gamay

koshu

Lambrusco

Languedoc-Roussillon reds, see also
   cinsault, grenache, syrah

Mâcon (and Villages, Uchizy and so on),
   see chardonnay, gamay, pinot noir

Madeira

Madiran, see tannat

malbec

manzanilla, see sherry

Marcillac, see fer servadou

marsanne, see also Rhône – white blends

Médoc, see cabernet sauvignon

mencía

Menetou-Salon, see sauvignon blanc

merlot

monastrell, see mourvèdre

Monbazillac, see Sauternes

Montlouis-sur-Loire, see chenin blanc

Montsant, see Priorat

Morgon, see gamay

Moscato, see muscat

Moulin-à-Vent, see gamay

mourvèdre

Muscadet

muscat

nebbiolo

nerello mascalese

nero d'avola

oloroso, see sherry

orange wine

palo cortado, see sherry

palomino, see sherry

pedro ximénez, see sherry

Pessac-Léognan, see cabinet sauvignon,
   sauvignon blanc-semillon blends (dry)

piepoul

pinot blanc

pinot grigio

pinot gris, see pinot grigio

pinot noir

pinotage

Pomerol

port

primitivo, see zinfandel

Priorat

Prosecco

Quincy, see sauvignon blanc

Reuilly, see sauvignon blanc

Rhône – white blends

Ribera del Duero, see tempranillo

riesling

Rioja, see tempranillo and also graciano

rosé

Rosso di Montalcino, see sangiovese

Rosso di Montepulciano, see sangiovese

St Amour, see gamay

St Emilion, see merlot

St Joseph, see syrah

St Nicolas de Bourgueil, see cabernet
franc

Sancerre, see also sauvignon blanc

sangiovese

Saumur (blanc), see chenin blanc

Saumur (rouge), see cabernet franc

Saumur-Champigny, see cabernet franc

Sauternes

sauvignon blanc

sauvignon blanc-semillon blends

savagnin

Savennières, see chenin blanc

semillon

sherry

shiraz, see syrah

Supertuscans

syrah

tannat

tempranillo

torrontés

touriga nacional, see also Douro reds,
port

Vacqueyras, see grenache

Valpolicella

verdejo

Vino Nobile de Montepulciano, see
sangiovese

viognier

Vouvray, see chenin blanc

zinfandel

A

aglianico

what it tastes like: This native red grape of southern Italy makes dark red wine that is savoury, gamey, firm, and deep, a real sleeping monster, with uncompromising tannins and licks of black lava (it's often grown on volcanic soil), smoke, salami rind, dried cherries and liquorice root. It's found in Campania and Basilicata, where its most famous incarnations are Aglianico del Vulture and Taurasi.

what to eat: Aglianico is good with **rich, meaty, tomato-based pasta, sausage, beef braciole in tomato sauce, liver, middle Eastern lamb dishes, youvetsi** (a Greek dish cooked with leftover lamb, tinned tomatoes, cinnamon, risoni pasta and Parmesan), **balsamic vinegar, sticky dark stews, salami** and **hard southern Italian cheeses**.

> *what the winemakers eat*
> **Luigi Tecce of Luigi Tecce, Campania, Italy:** 'For the bigger, fuller wines which have aged and are mature – braised meat, game, boar. A typical plate is lamb's liver that has been wrapped up in lamb intestines. For simpler, young wines, simple dishes – pasta with pork sauce, ragù. But always the food of the land, not the sea.'

albariño
also known as alvarinho
what it tastes like: From the Iberian peninsula, this peachy white grape is known as albariño in Spain, and alvarinho over the border in Portugal, where it can make up all, or part, of the breezy Vinho Verde blend. Albariño also turns up quite unexpectedly elsewhere – I've tried very good albariño from Uruguay and New Zealand – but its heartland is the north-western corner of Spain, Rías Baixas (pronounced Ree-ass By-shass – it means 'lower

estuaries'). Holiday here at your peril. This is no sun-drenched Costa but a place of frequent downpours as the weather systems from the Atlantic dump their rain as soon as they hit land mass. This climate is bad for bikinis, but good for making refreshing, light white wines that taste of white peaches and lime blossom with, sometimes, a hint of salt or stony minerals. In Spain there's a trend for producers to experiment with sobre lias (on the lees) expressions, which turn albariño into a sort of aromatic, juicy, papaya-apricot-kernels-and-lime version of Muscadet sur lie. Portuguese versions tend to be less peachy and more searing, with accents of green apple and brighter citrus.

what to eat: Refreshing albariño, served by the tumbler or carafe, is found in clattering tapas bars across northern Spain (though not so much in the Basque country, where you see a lot of txakoli). It is also good for all those other, ad hoc, lunches and dinners when there are lots of different plates of food on the table; an **anytime wine** useful for those moments when you just want a lovely white wine to drink with a salad or an omelette or even posh Chinese that won't clash and everyone will enjoy drinking and to hell with precision planning. Its real friend, though, is **seafood**. More than that, it is *the* **white wine for shellfish**. The delicate white of **crabmeat** is enhanced by the peachy nudge of albariño, while its salty-citrusy side is refreshing against richer brown crabmeat. Albariño loves **crustaceans** in almost any form, whether you're eating seaside **crab sandwich**, picking at **lobster claws**, or tackling **fat pink langoustines** fried in butter, garlic and lemon, or enjoying **prawns** made into an old-fashioned cocktail. It is gorgeous with **chipirones**, the baby little squid often served as a tapa, or tender, thin slices of **octopus**, spread across a whole plate, drizzled with olive oil, dusted with russet paprika and served with a waxy yellow potato salad. The subtle marine flavours of albariño also play well with **plain, grilled white fish**, from cod to sea bream to hake. And if you are in a restaurant and ordering one of those big cake stands filled with **crushed ice and shellfish**, albariño is the wine to look for.

A more zesty, crisp Vinho Verde makes a refreshing contrast to the heaviness of, say, **fritto misto** or richer crabcakes.

Because Spanish albariño is not a sharp-edged wine, it also goes well with the soft, almost sweet taste of rice and this, together with its ocean freshness, makes it a good match for **sushi rolls**, particularly when crab or salmon is featured.

If you travel to Rías Baixas, be sure to drink it with some of the superb Atlantic seafood with which albariño goes so well.

Ben Henshaw of specialist Spanish importer Indigo Wine recalls a research trip on which he stopped at Cambados, a coastal town with a big shallow bay, lots of restaurants and bars, and a large beach. 'I was meeting Eulogio from Bodegas Zarate, so we were drinking his wines and there were these **local clams**, just picked out of the bay itself, quite different to the clams I'd seen before, much bigger, served raw like oysters. They were sweet and plump and the Zarate albariño was so good with them. It was quite a special moment.'

It's hard to find these fresh clams in many places outside Spain but they are available in tins – the Spanish do very high-quality tinned seafood.

Albariño also goes well with **Vietnamese fresh summer rolls**, which I sometimes make with juicy prawns and kumquats (the apricot of the wine and the zesty orange go well together).

The peachy, apricotty taste of albariño is pleasing with **pork and summer roasts**. Try a **slow-grilled pork chop with a chickpea and spinach or fennel and orange salad side**, or **pork loin stuffed with apricots and shallots**.

aligoté

Burgundy's forgotten grape makes white wine that is nippy and brisk, like sharp bone needles. Aligoté is *the* wine to add to Crème de Cassis (blackcurrant liqueur) to make a kir – the still version is so much better than the fizzy royale one – which I drink as an aperitif, no food needed.

Aligoté is a consummate fish wine – I'm thinking **white fish** (maybe hake), plainly cooked, in butter or with oil and lemon. Its piercing quality and lack of obvious fruity flavours mean it is good when a clean, acerbic white is required as a **palate cleanser,** say with **cheese fondue** or with **fried whitebait**.

Amarone della Valpolicella

This mighty red wine from the Veneto has all the grandeur, depth and richness of a High Renaissance Venetian altarpiece or the shimmer of gold on a church fresco. It's made mostly from three grapes, corvina, corvinone and rondinella, which are first dried to raisins, and then fermented almost dry, meaning that the wine is incredibly complex, with flavours of dried cherries, figs and cigars. The Italians call it a *vino da meditazione* – a phrase that is only reduced by translation. I would never pour this with dinner, but drink it afterwards, in a comfortable chair with **a hunk of top-quality, grainy Parmesan cheese**.

arneis

The sharp, clean taste of lemons defines this white grape from northern Italy. As with Gavi, drink it where a squeeze of lemon would be appropriate on the food. For instance, with **shellfish** or with **ricotta, mint, pea and pea shoot salad**.

assyrtiko

Assyrtiko is a bracing white grape from Greece, most famously grown on the volcanic island of Santorini, where the branches of its vines are woven together to protect the fruit from too much sun. Here it produces fierce, acidic wines that taste like an electric shock, all mineral with an eruption of grapefruit and lemon pith.

The zesty flavour is wonderful with **white fish with lemon juice, carpaccio of tuna, fritto misto, or lemony Greek potatoes**. Its rich barrel-fermented incarnations, which smell of cooked grapefruit and pithy lemon, as well as wood spice, are excellent with **barbecued swordfish steaks** and with **salsa verde**, served with either fish or lamb. Assyrtiko's vibrancy is also good with **green asparagus; preserved lemons; jointed chicken roasted with quartered lemons and olive oil**; and **Moroccan baked chicken with olives, chickpeas and rice** (the recipe is in *Delia's Winter Collection*).

B

barbera

what it tastes like: Barbera makes wine that is comfortably soft with a nippy acidity. It tastes, as so many Italian reds do, of amarena cherries, and also strawberries, and sometimes has a mace-like spice. It is neither weedy nor heavy, can be surprisingly sturdy when it comes with a lot of oak, and has a pleasing richness of flavour.

what to eat: Barbera is the second red grape of Piemonte (after nebbiolo) and suits many of the local foods, such as **agnolotti del Plin** (tiny parcels of fresh pasta filled with roasted meat – rabbit, veal, pork – and finished with Parmesan, nutmeg and a gravy made from the roasted bones). Its smooth softness makes it the perfect match for **ragù alla bolognese** served with the silky local eggy pasta and also for **pumpkin and sage**-filled pasta. The combination of rosewood spice and tartness is good with all kinds of **red meat** and **game**, especially slower braises and roasts. It loves **sage, rosemary, porcini, nutmeg, mace** and **richer boozy sauces, such as those made with red wine, Madeira or Marsala.** Examples of dishes include **pappardelle with rabbit or lamb**; **pot-roast pheasant**; herby Italian **sausages braised with small brown lentils**; or **beef casseroled with chestnuts, red wine, mushrooms and pancetta**.

cabernet franc

what it tastes like: Cabernet franc is distinguished by its fragrance. It is a princess and the pea grape in the best possible way. Even when cabernet franc forms only a small part (as little as 10 per cent, say) of a wine you still catch its breezy, uplifting perfume. It's like brushing past a large flowering redcurrant bush so that its leaves squeeze their scent into the air – floral and a bit green and also reminiscent of red summer berries and freshly turned earth.

Cabernet franc's heartland is the Loire in France where, unblended, it makes wines under the appellations of Anjou (soft and smooth, and frequently too shallow); Saumur and Saumur-Champigny (more interesting); and the highly regarded Chinon and St Nicolas de Bourgueil and Bourgueil (often more complex and weighty). Here its wines have a similar, organized structure to the cabernet sauvignon-based wines of Bordeaux, but without the stern tannin and might. They are like girlish, springtime versions, which is perhaps surprising since, in genetic terms, cabernet franc is actually the parent of cabernet sauvignon, not vice versa.

The highly praised warm vintages of Bordeaux are not always, in my view, the best, but I do very much like the warmer years of Loire cabernet franc (for example, 2003, 2005, 2009 and 2014). This is because cabernet franc is a grape with bright acidity that can taste thin and slightly green if it doesn't get enough sun but that, given more warmth, is generous and more ample.

Cabernet franc is also grown in Bordeaux, most notably in Pomerol, where it is riper and more sumptuous than in the Loire, and its beguiling garden scent plays a key role in the blend. It is also important in Castillon, Côtes de Bordeaux and for some properties in St Emilion.

Beyond France, cabernet franc is also found in California,

Argentina (Pulenta Estates makes a rather gorgeous one), Australia and Chile. It is also an increasingly important and respected grape in coastal Tuscany, home of the Supertuscans, where it seems to have found a particular affinity with the climate and soil. In these warmer climates it grows lusher and plusher still, like thick crimson velvet, and tastes warmer and plummier, sometimes almost like drinking chocolate.

what to eat: Cabernet franc tastes delicious with lamb. But whereas with cabernet sauvignon any lamb will do, cabernet franc especially suits **tender, pink lamb**. Neat little racks cooked so that they are still juicy and raw in the middle. Its red berry taste goes beautifully with **new-season chops charred black on the griddle pan but still pink inside**. The bright fruit of cabernet franc emphasizes the succulence of the rare flesh. Its summer-pudding taste is also delicious with lamb and redcurrant burgers and, if chilled for half an hour or so in the fridge, it's also refreshing with **seared tuna** or **baked trout**, or just to wash down a simple **poulet- or bavette-frites**, maybe with **tabbouleh** or a simple parsley, olive oil and salt salad on the side (the leafiness of a Loire cabernet franc is especially kind to parsley and other herbs).

With its lively acidity cabernet franc is also a good match for the bite of **salsa verde with lamb** (I prefer the fuller flavour of mutton with maturing claret) or **chicken** or **grilled salmon**.

The vegetables you most want to serve with young, herbal Loire cabernet franc are green and leafy: **peas cooked with a buttery tangle of little gem lettuce,** or a **summer vegetable casserole of broad beans, peas, new potatoes and carrots and mint** (with chicken in there too for non-vegetarians).

More serious, older wines can take heavier food: perhaps a **rabbit, broad bean and bacon casserole with a pile of mashed potato; a roast guinea fowl;** or **cold fillet of beef with a lemon and herb butter.**

Cabernet franc does not have fierce tannin and those plusher, softer versions grown in warmer climates are good with **roast beef** and can also take meat with a little bit of spice, cushioning and cosseting, for instance, **lamb with a cumin and coriander crust**.

These warmer expressions are also good for barbecued food.

C

I wouldn't put them with barbecue sauce, but the fuller, smokier flavour of food cooked outdoors suits them down to the ground.

At a rather chilly outdoor lunch at the Saumur-Champigny producer Filliatreau we were given, first, lamb cooked over a fire made from burning vine cuttings (Saumur-Champigny in our glasses), followed by **a bowl of strawberries**, sprinkled with sugar, halved and with Saumur-Champigny poured over them. Cabernet franc with strawberries is a very fine dish.

Finally, food aside, my main feeling about cabernet franc is that it goes with a springtime mood. As it ages, its scent does become more autumnal, but prettily so, in a way that leads me to it more in an Indian summer than in deepest winter.

what the winemakers eat
Jean-Philippe Blot, Domaine de la Butte, Bourgueil, Loire, France: 'With our Bourgueil, I like a juicy beef roast.'

Philippe Vatan, Château du Hureau, Saumur, Loire, France: 'One of my favourite recipes is veau marengo [veal stew with mushrooms and tomatoes], which I cook myself and like to serve with a delicate and rich red wine, like Tuffe 2013 or 2014, or Fours à Chaux 2011 or 2014.'

cabernet sauvignon
what it tastes like: The telltale scent of cabernet sauvignon is a waft of blackcurrant, or cassis. The former recalls the fruit; the latter the deeper, sweeter, softer scent of the liqueur.

This king among grapes also has a remarkable ability to make wines that can age; these wines are all about structure and form; thanks to the fact that the grapes have thick skins, cabernet sauvignon is not short on tannins.

Cabernet sauvignon's spiritual home is Bordeaux, where, with merlot (as well, sometimes, as cabernet franc, malbec and petit verdot), it forms the red bordeaux blend, with cabernet providing the backbone and merlot the fleshier infill.

The grape is grown throughout the region but in the gravel of the Médoc, on the left bank of the Gironde estuary, and Graves, to the south of the city, it makes the most prestigious cabernet sauvignon-based wines in the world. These smell not just of cassis but also of cedar, pencil shavings, cigar boxes, dried tobacco and old leather saddles. They feel reassuring, and have a measured dignity and frame, like classical architecture – these wines recall the Pantheon, the Colosseum, the Acropolis. The grace of their lines, proportions and elegant form is at least as important as the flavour; the very best have the ability to age for many decades.

In the Médoc, the four communes of St Estèphe, Pauillac, St Julien and Margaux produce wines with distinctive styles: St Estèphe tends to deep, black fruit and can be darkly austere; Pauillac is patrician, as if wearing a fearsomely expensive hand-tailored suit; St Julien is often reminiscent of fine antiques, and a comfortable room in a very well-appointed farmhouse; Margaux is the most feminine, finer-boned and often with a perfume of violets.

In Bergerac, on the Dordogne and further inland from Bordeaux, and Buzet, to the south, you find more rustic versions of the bordeaux blend.

Cabernet sauvignon is also found in many of the other wine-producing regions of France and is widely disseminated around the world. Depending on where it's grown, it can take on minty, leafy or eucalyptal characteristics, and sometimes tastes of green capsicum or red fruit.

Looking at the most important areas: it is much-loved in America, particularly in California, where the Napa Valley is Bordeaux's most serious challenger. These wines can be higher in alcohol than their counterparts in the Médoc, with more succulence and perhaps a trace of vanilla and rich black fruit.

It is very important in Chile, where heavy, ambitious 'icon' wines sit alongside the everyday. The taste here is typically assertive, with ample fruitiness sometimes reminiscent of wine gums and often also a tinge of green pepper.

In Australia, the key cabernet sauvignon regions are Coonawarra in South Australia and Margaret River on the west coast. In Margaret River, the bordeaux blend is particularly successful, making wines that often have a tinge of graphite allied to a smooth, berryish brightness – more restrained than a Napa cabernet but juicier than a French one. In Coonawarra this grape thrives

C

on the red terrarossa soil, and it makes earthy wines that have extraordinary length and seem to carry you with them, like potholes heading towards the centre of the earth. See also *syrah* for more on Australian cabernet sauvignon in the great Australian shiraz-cabernet sauvignon blend.

In South Africa, cabernet sauvignon can also be extremely good, with a sturdy, full flavour and sometimes a slightly leathery taste. It is also used here to make excellent bordeaux blends, some with a pleasingly leathery flavour and some of which have an extra dollop of South African smoke and roasted coffee because they also contain pinotage.

Spanish cabernet sauvignon is often broad and generous and can taste slightly of Chewits. And in Italy, cabernet sauvignon is a vital ingredient in Supertuscans such as Tignanello and Sassicaia.

In essence, if pinot noir is all spirit and soul, cabernet is cerebral – a massage for the neurons – and, unlike pinot noir, which soars when it is bottled alone, cabernet sauvignon responds well to the massage of a blending partner.

See also syrah.

what to eat: Cabernet isn't often the first wine that comes to mind when I'm thinking about what might go with food, but, if starting with the wine, it's often the bottle I want to drink; bordeaux, in particular, is a consummate occasion wine.

With cabernet sauvignon – and its blends – I stretch first for red meat. **Lamb** in all its forms, whether cooked rare, slow-roasted until it drops off the bone, barbecued, or casseroled, is delicious with cabernet sauvignon. If you have a slightly dull, green cabernet (perhaps a cheap claret from a cool year) then **a simple lamb chop** can perform an almost magical transformation on the wine, making it taste less mean and dusty and more three-dimensional.

Almost any cabernet is enhanced by the **classic roast leg of lamb incorporating garlic, rosemary and anchovies**. Fleshier, fruitier wines are often better suited to brighter accoutrements: try a **lamb and redcurrant jelly burger** with a cabernet-merlot from Margaret River or put lamb with peas and other spring vegetables with a young, alert wine. A more robust wine, such as a South African bordeaux blend, can take spicier flavours, such as **lamb with a coriander and cumin crust**, or **curried lamb kebabs.**

Pinot is the classic match for beef but I enjoy cabernet with it too – it's a mood thing. Here if you are opening the grandest wines the simplest dinners are best: **sirloin steak, roast rib of beef** or **roast fillet of beef** make a princely banquet for a bottle of claret or sumptuous Napa cabernet. Well-cooked beef is often better with younger wines, and/or wines from warmer climates that have the juice to hydrate the drier meat. I also like to put earthier wines with earthier cuts of meat: for instance, the deep savour of rib of beef mirrors the savour of a claret, smoky Cape cabernet or a Chianti containing a dollop of cabernet sauvignon; while the atavistic scent of **bone marrow** really needs the undergrowth, cedar and tobacco of a proper claret. There is probably no cabernet sauvignon that would not go well with **bavette-frites**.

The sweet smell of **root vegetables** – carrots and parsnips – in a beef casserole is good with claret and with Coonawarra cabernet, in particular. The fatty flesh of a **pink cheeseburger** is juicy perfection with the cheery fruitiness of an inexpensive Chilean cabernet; add some caramelized onions and maybe go for one of the cheaper Californian cabs. The bolder the flavours in the food, the bigger and brighter a wine I look for. **Slow-cooked smoky beef ribs** with a large helping of coleslaw suggest an opportunity for a cabernet from Chile, the US, Australia or South Africa. These rich and robust wines from warmer places are often good with the richness of slow-cooked dishes, especially those with fruity, or at least bright, spicy or sweet accents. Other examples include **braised lamb shank with redcurrant and rosemary jus**; **spicy barbecued lamb**; **roasted duck breast with pecan sauce**; or **slow-roasted Moroccan lamb shoulder with pomegranate couscous**. I like **lamb that is braised with green and red peppers** with Chilean cabernet sauvignon, which sometimes has a tinge of capsicum to its flavour.

The perky fruitiness of young, inexpensive cabernet, from Chile, the US or South Africa, can be pleasing against the squeak of **spicy-marinated halloumi cheese served with blackened pepper kebabs**.

In the restaurant at Xanadu in Margaret River, they have beef slider with zucchini pickle, caramel onion and aioli and also beef served with chimi churri, smoked potato and red pepper on the menu: either would be perfect with the bright, berry scent of the home-grown cabernet-merlot blends.

Young claret can be good with fatty birds such as **duck** or **goose** because its acidity and prickly tannins offer some resistance to the glide of the fat. It is also a happy choice with many of those dishes that invoke the spirit of Robert Carrier, such as **pheasant roasted in red wine**. One of the parts of my job that I love the most is the annual spring trip to Bordeaux to taste the bucking young wines from the previous year's harvest *en primeur*, while they are still in barrel. This is also an opportunity to eat the best food that the best cooks in Bordeaux can come up with to showcase the wines. Or it ought to be. I realize it won't invoke much pity if I say that getting up at 5 a.m. (to 'do emails' and write) then tasting, talking and driving around until well into the evening does not leave you in much of a fit state for dinner – I am usually grateful for pizza and beer. There are exceptions, such as the time my tasting companion and I were alerted to the fact that 'the best caterers in Bordeaux' were 'doing lunch' at a large tasting at Château Soutard in St Emilion. We made an accidental approach across the vineyards – sallying confidently forwards, a lone car crossing the landscape, until we arrived at a narrow flowerbed, in front of which stood an unimpressed parking attendant who patiently redirected us out of the vines and back to the drive. The food was good, though.

On the left bank, food frequently offered to make the most of the wine includes, again, **lamb**, in all its forms (heavier dishes with younger wines). Also, **meaty terrines** (for young wines), **guinea fowl, side of beef with sauce bordelaise (made with red wine, bone marrow, shallots and butter)** and neat little **confits de canard with green salad and dauphinoise potatoes** (this works particularly well with wines that are younger, maturing and/or more powerful, in other words, wines that still have a decent amount of oomph and edge).

The following dishes also often appear on menus in châteaux and they work particularly well with the delicacy of an old bottle of mature claret, so one for your fine wines, as well as with the poise of a younger wine that is either lighter or more elegant: **veal stuffed with truffles**; **veal chop, perhaps with mushroom sauce**; **pan-cooked veal sweetbreads with porcini**; and roasted **quail**.

One of my favourite matches for a not-too-old – I like the wine still to have edges – claret of Cru Bourgeois quality is **steak tartare**. The tannins and acidity of the wine are beautifully crisp against the softness of the raw beef and also perky enough to deal with the seasoning.

Inexpensive young clarets, and also the slightly more rustic Bordeaux blends such as reds from Buzet and Bergerac go well with **rough pâtés, cold (and hot) sausages**, and **beef sandwiches (hot or cold)**. Cabernets from warmer climates can work here too, bringing warmth and juice to the plate, though if going down the gherkin track then I'd pick a more acidic, cooler-climate wine for its edge.

I always struggle when looking for food to serve vegetarians when cabernet sauvignon is being drunk. This is so much a grape that works with meat. However, there are some foods that work. I have a rather seventies recipe for something called **Gruyère roulade** – a kind of eggy, cheesy mixture that is cooked in a Swiss roll tin and then rolled up around halved cherry tomatoes, green salad and mayonnaise. It actually goes really well with lighter unoaked or barely oaked red bordeaux (the sort an earlier generation would have referred to as luncheon claret) as well as with fresher, crunchy-fruited, unoaked New World styles, particularly those from Chile that have a tang of green capsicum. Recipes containing **Gruyère** often seem to go strangely well with cabernet – try dauphinoise potatoes or putting a slice of this cheese on your burger (or veggie burger). The savoury taste of **dark green lentils** is good too. Another option is to cook mushrooms: **stuffed mushrooms**, or a **shiitake mushroom sauce** (try this on beef too), or a mixture of **wild mushrooms and garlic on toast** will go well with the mushroomy flavour of older or more savoury cabernet sauvignons.

As Vanya Cullen points out on the next page, the earthy blackcurrant flavours of this grape also work very well with beetroot.

If looking for a cheese to give you an excuse to have another glass (or two) after dinner, then the one to go for is aged **Comté**. Also very good (and, again, a common sight in Bordeaux) is a slice of **Mimolette**, the aged cheese produced around Lille and which is bright orange like a Belisha beacon. And while I think the delicacy of a mature claret is wrecked by blue cheese, and that the tannins of a younger one curdle against it, an aged Australian and Napa cabernets can be good with **Stilton**: there is a strange synergy between the creaminess of the cheese and the faded bright fruit of the wine.

what the winemakers eat

Vanya Cullen, Cullen Wines, Margaret River, Australia: 'Our cabernet sauvignon is fantastic with beetroot, you just get that earthiness in both the beetroot and the wine. We're a biodynamic wine estate and we grow all our veggies biodynamically too and I love to get beetroot from the garden and use it to make a risotto. I love to eat this with a side of root vegetables and one of watercress.'

BEETROOT RISOTTO
Serves 4

- The amount of stock you need will depend on the rice you use, so you may need a little less or a little more.
- 400g beetroot
- olive oil
- 1.25 litres vegetable or chicken stock
- butter
- 1 large onion, finely chopped
- 4 anchovy fillets in olive oil, drained and chopped (it's fine to omit these)
- 175g Arborio or Carnaroli rice
- a small glass of red or white wine
- 10 black olives, quartered
- 2 tablespoons chopped chives
- 1 handful of flat-leaf parsley, chopped
- 1 handful of sage leaves
- salt

Preheat the oven to 200°C/400°F/gas mark 6. Peel the beetroot and cut into 1cm dice. Put half on a non-stick roasting tray, drizzle with a little olive oil and season, then roast until tender, about 20–30 minutes.

C

Put the rest of the beetroot in a pan with the stock, bring to a simmer and cook until just tender, then scoop out with a slotted spoon. Leave the stock on a low simmer. Heat a tablespoon of olive oil and a knob of butter in a wide, shallow sauté pan. Add the onion and cook until soft and translucent, then add the anchovies and cook for another couple of minutes. Add the rice and cook for 3 minutes, stirring until it is coated in the buttery mix. Tip in the wine and bubble away until it has almost gone. Add the simmering stock a couple of large ladlefuls at a time. Keep stirring now and again until the liquid is absorbed, then add more stock. When the rice is almost tender stir in the boiled and roasted beetroots. To finish the risotto stir in the olives, chives and parsley, a splash of stock or water, and another knob of butter and season. Put on a lid and leave for 5 minutes. Heat another knob of butter in a small frying pan until foaming. Add the sage leaves and fry until crisp. Serve the risotto in warm bowls topped with the sage leaves.

Véronique Sanders, Château Haut-Bailly, Pessac-Léognan, Bordeaux, France: 'I enjoy quail with a fine and fruity red like our second wine La Parde Haut-Bailly. It brings freshness and spices. It is also nice with fish like the regional speciality "lamproie [lamprey eels] à la bordelaise" and other dishes with red wine sauce.

'Our in-house chef likes to pair Haut-Bailly wines with poultry, veal or beef and a lovely "truffat de pommes de terre" – a pastry filled with potatoes, cream and truffles ... a winter delight! A perfect Saint-Nectaire or a vintage Comté is also a great pairing ... I agree with Steven Spurrier when he says, "The joy of a wine cellar is that there should be a wine to match the mood, which won't offend the food."'

Duncan Meyers, Arnot-Roberts Wines, California, US: 'We work with several different vineyards for cabernet and the wines are distinctly different from each other, reflective of their

C

sites. In particular our Fellom Ranch cabernet sauvignon from the Santa Cruz Mountains displays vivid herbal and savoury undertones intermixed with dark currant and bittersweet chocolate notes. The wine is deep, dark and structured from the tiny berries that grow on this austere mountaintop. I think that our Fellom Ranch cabernet pairs well with grilled pork or lamb served with a mild salsa verde or herb butter to match with the herbal qualities inherent in the wine. The acidity and tannin cut through the fat of the lamb and pork nicely to create a great match.'

Christian Seely, Château Pichon Baron, Pauillac, Bordeaux, France: 'Here is what I do with Agneau de Pauillac (there really is a producer of lamb here). One gigot (leg) and one épaule (shoulder). I like doing both because I think the tastes are a bit different. Make several holes in each with a sharp knife. Insert in each hole a clove of garlic and a salted anchovy. Lots of holes, lots of anchovies. Then cover both shoulder and leg with olive oil and roll them in fresh thyme.

'In the meantime you have lit a barbecue with lots of charcoal, which has had time to die down but there remains a thick layer of red coals. Then barbecue both bits of lamb, cooking them quite slowly for quite a long time. When it is ready add more fresh thyme and a bottle of Pichon. We had a magnum of the 2008 with this recently and it was great.

'Nuance to make it all perfect is garlic sauce. Boil a large lamb bone for a while to make stock. Then you take about four whole heads of garlic, peel all the cloves, cut each clove in two and remove the slightly indigestible middle bit in each clove. Blanch the cloves in boiling water for a minute or two to remove harshness. Then throw the blanched cloves into the stock and simmer and reduce for a long time. After a while the garlic mashes into the stock and produces a wonderful sauce with the consistency of apple sauce. It is disastrously delicious and the next day you awake with garlic emanating from every pore, so it is very important that this is a dish to be shared with the person you love if you are going to see them the next day.'

C

carignan

also known as cariñena, mazuelo, samsó

what it tastes like: Cranberry juice, dried figs and sometimes also salami skins and tindery herbs are the flavours I most associate with carignan. The dusty fig-roll smell is a particular giveaway; it streams out of the wines from the likes of Corbières and Fitou in the Languedoc-Roussillon, even when carignan only forms a small part of the blend alongside syrah, cinsault and grenache. In the south of France, carignan is not considered a quality grape and for decades now has systematically been uprooted to make way for more syrah. It is more prized in Catalonia in north-east Spain, where it is an important constituent in Montsant and in the velvet warmth of *Priorat*. And old-vine carignan has won niche appreciation in California, as well as in Maule in Chile, where a wine revolution has seen the fruit of ancient, wizened dry-farmed bush vines transformed into textured and impressive wines that feel like artefacts and are reminiscent of black olives as well as red fruits and herbs.

what to eat: The youngest, simplest, cheapest carignans taste as bright and fresh as cranberry juice and make a tangy accompaniment to rich and **fatty meat** such as **duck or pork rillettes**. Carignan goes well with **slow-roasted pork shoulder** or a **fatty belly of pork** too. Pick a French carignan for meat roasted with savoury fennel seeds; a plusher wine from Chile, Spain or California can take the more exotic spice of star anise or five-spice. These fuller wines are also good with **Christmas or Thanksgiving turkey and all the trimmings**, and they happily melt into the sweetness of roasted squash, pumpkin or sweet potatoes. Herbs and spices that go well with carignan include crushed **cumin** and **coriander seeds, thyme, rosemary** and **za'atar** – especially when they are mixed with roasted gourds, rubbed over roasted duck, put in spicy lamb meatballs, or used as a marinade for lamb that is blackened on a barbecue or griddle. The more savoury wines (look to France again and also Chile, where the herbal characteristics tend to be stronger) also work with **roasted red peppers with tapenade**, and are comforting with **beef, thyme, anchovy and carrot daube**. Try the close texture and richness of a Chilean carignan with **black**

C

bean chilli, **sausage and mash** or **a steak sandwich**. The cheapies are good to wash down **corned beef hash**.

what the winemakers eat
Derek Mossman Knapp, The Garage Wine Co., Maule, Chile: 'I enjoy carignan, with its freshness, savour and those exotic herby-floral notes, with foods that we have been taught to think are too rich for us. With a glass of lifted Maulean carignan, we can enjoy such fare guilt-free and without the tummy ache. Richer food goes with fresher wine.

'Moreover, as we learn to eat less "high-on-the-hog" many forgotten cuts of meat such as tapabarriga or palanca [thin flank/flank steak/belly muscle] are being shown the love and care needed to make things very tasty. Stronger in flavour, richer and perhaps with a bit of candied fat, we need a wine with lifted acidity. Where is that bottle of carignan I have been saving!'

See also Priorat.

carmenère

what it tastes like: Carmenère is Chile's signature red grape so it is surprising to learn that as recently as 1996 there was officially no carmenère in South America at all. It simply didn't exist. Not one single vine.

This peculiarity can be explained by a major administrative screw-up. The first cuttings of carmenère arrived in Chile in the nineteenth century, and they came from some of the best estates in Bordeaux, where plantings of carmenère were then widespread. Most vines are distinguishable to experts not only by the taste of the grapes they produce, and the size and shape and level of compression of the hanging bunches of berries, but also by the wiggling edges of their leaves. It happens that carmenère leaves look exactly the same as merlot leaves. Before long, carmenère in Chile had a new name: merlot chileno. Chilean merlot. Confusion set in.

This is how it came to pass that when Chilean wine exports began to boom in the late twentieth century much of the stuff that was labelled merlot was actually carmenère. No wonder it tasted so good.

Merlot is smooth and plummy (boring, say its detractors).

Carmenère is textured and rustic. It has a riffle of tea and the swell of red capsicum. It smells of paprika and sometimes also of roasted coffee. It's herbaceous, tobacco-scented, tarry, earthy. How could winemakers possibly not notice the difference?

In his book *The Wines of Chile*, Peter Richards argues that growers always were aware of the distinction between what they called 'merlot merlot' and 'merlot chileno'. Considering the huge global demand for international varieties, perhaps a little ambiguity suited everybody. The ampelographer Jean-Michel Bourisquot put a stop to that in 1994 when he identified merlot chileno as carmenère. DNA analysis backed this up in 1997 and the following year carmenère was given legal status as an official grape variety of Chile.

How much so-called Chilean merlot still contains a proportion of carmenère is debatable. Winemakers are adamant that the issue is in the past and it is certainly the case that those producers using both grapes produce two distinctive wines. That said, occasionally I do come across a bottle of Chilean merlot that tastes more interesting than it ought.

what to eat: Its rustic nature makes carmenère a good choice for **salami-and-bread Saturday lunches** as well as **long, slow braises – especially when beef is involved**. Because it is spicy it also goes extremely well with **spicy sausage, 'nduja, chilli con carne** and **spicy beef stews,** such as the popular Chilean pot roast **plateada**, which is often served with a vivid salad of tomato, onions, cabbage, avocado and celery and spicy bean purée. My favourite match of all, though, is **Hungarian goulash**, because the flavours of paprika and peppers in the wine play off the ones in the cooking pot: there is definitely a lick of paprika to the taste of carmenère. Similarly, **Basque chicken**, made by cooking chicken pieces with red peppers, sherry, paprika, chorizo, thyme, onions and tomatoes, is also a big hit with carmenère.

The spiciness of carmenère can also work well with **mildly spiced Indian** or **Indian-inspired dishes**, such as **venison marinated in Rajasthani spice paste; curried lamb, tomato and red onion kebabs** with **baba ganoush;** or **lamb bhuna**. The combination of carmenère with the scrape of **Indian spices, blackened onions and green peppers** is particularly tasty. The ruffled scent of this grape finds a resonance with the rattle of **coriander, cumin** and **cardamom** – just be aware that the tannins in the wine will clash with chilli so you get the most out of the spice match when the chilli rating is mild.

cava

Cava is a sparkling white (and sometimes rosé) wine made in many parts of Spain, but particularly in Penedes in the north-east. Many different grapes are authorized for its production (from the local xarello and parellada to the international chardonnay and pinot noir) and as a consequence styles and quality vary tremendously. Cava is known as a cheap drink, but more recently boutique producers making seriously good wine have also emerged. It's a great way to wash down **tapas** or **pinchos** of all descriptions. The easy-going and neutral nature – of the inexpensive wines in particular – mean it doesn't clash with bold or competing flavours and the bubbles are good at cutting through the fat of, say, fried **croquetas** or **calamares fritos**.

Chablis

In Burgundy, growers often serve their wines with freshly baked **gougères**, still warm from the oven. The smooth curves and lemony tang of a chilled glass of Chablis go beautifully with the cheesy, choux-pastry balls, which are unexpectedly easy to make. I like this combination so much that I've allowed Chablis its own entry especially to highlight it. Needless to say, as Chablis is made entirely from chardonnay, there are more food suggestions in *chardonnay*.

GOUGÈRES
Makes about 20 gougères

- 125ml water
- 50g butter
- a pinch of salt
- 50g plain flour
- a pinch of cayenne (optional)
- 2 eggs, beaten
- 75g Gruyère, grated

Preheat the oven to 200°C/ 400°F/ gas mark 6. Put the water in a pan with the butter and salt and bring to the boil. Remove from the heat and add the flour and cayenne if using. Beat in the flour with a wooden spoon. Allow to cool for a couple of minutes, then add about a third of the eggs and beat in thoroughly. Repeat until all the egg is incorporated, then add the cheese and stir until the mixture is smooth. Using two teaspoons, put walnut-sized balls of the mixture on to a sheet of baking parchment on a baking tray. Make sure to leave plenty of space between the balls as they will rise when they cook. Bake for 20–25 minutes until golden brown, remove to a cooling tray and eat while still warm.

what the winemakers eat
Didier Defaix, Domaine Bernard Defaix, Chablis, France: 'We have three appellations in Chablis: straight Chablis, which is fresh and easy; 1er Cru, which has a lot of minerality and is a bit straight at first but opens out with time in the glass or in the bottle; then the Grand Cru, which is always more powerful with more structure and richness. The straight Chablis goes with grilled fish, or guacamole made with lemon juice, which goes with the citrus in the wine. Our 1er Cru Côte de Léchet has a lot of minerality and quite a salty finish, so you can put some spice with it. I like to make rice with chicken and coconut milk and curry spices – though not too much chilli. A client of ours serves this wine with turkey escalope cooked with lemon, which is also very good. For our Chablis Grand Cru Bougros, which has some smoky aromas, then maybe a fish cooked en papillote with crustaceans in the sauce.'

See also chardonnay.

champagne

what it tastes like: Words frequently used to describe this most luxurious of sparkling wines include brioche, lemon curd, honey, acacia blossom, creamy, toasty, spicy, biscuity, hazelnuts, and almonds. As this list suggests, champagne has a richness that not all sparkling wines possess. This rich grandeur is developed through ageing the wine on its lees (dead yeast cells) – it's no

C

flight of fancy that makes 'yeasty' another descriptor that often pops up.

Each of the three main champagne grapes brings different qualities to the wine in the bottle. Chardonnay offers elegance and creaminess; pinot noir has a sappy vitality that drives the wine; and pinot meunier has a broad, rich spiciness. The three may be blended, or not, as the winemaker sees fit, though a blanc de blancs is made only from chardonnay, while a blanc de noirs is made only from black grapes, and might be entirely pinot noir, all pinot meunier or a mixture of the two.

Non-vintage (NV) wines are blended from 'base wines' made in different years. I think of the chef de cave like the conductor of a fifty-piece orchestra. He will be playing with varying sizes of vats of wine made from different grapes, grown in different sites, in different vintages, each one with its own personality and sound. He might bring in a tiny dash of precious old pinot meunier as a spicy bass, a particularly creamy chardonnay to smooth, and so on. In most cases, and especially with the big, well-known names, the aim is to achieve consistency from one batch to the next. A few producers take a different view and aim instead to create the best wine each time, even if this means it has a very different personality to the previous batch. Jacquesson is one grower notable for this approach: every blend is numbered so that drinkers know when they are buying a different one.

Vintage wines are produced only in very good years, using grapes from a single harvest. These are usually released much later than NV wines. The best have the potential for long ageing and might taste firm and impenetrable when young, only mellowing to unlock the full depth of their flavours with time, which will make them taste gentler and bring out accents of smoke, dried apricots, honey, mushrooms and dried flowers.

The level of sweetness of a wine also has a big impact on the way it tastes, as well as how it interacts with food.

The very driest (and currently highly fashionable) champagne style is known as 'zero dosage', 'pas dosé' or 'brut nature'. It has no added sugar. Champagne is already notably acidic and, without the buffering sugar, zero dosage feels to carve through your mouth.

Extra Brut has less than 6g of sugar per litre. Brut is the most common style of champagne and may have up to 12g per litre. In practice, superior brands are often tighter and hover around 6–8g , while cheaper supermarket wines go for the maximum 12g. Sweetness, like make-up, covers a multitude of sins, and it's easier drinking too, which makes for more crowd-pleasing wines.

Extra Dry has 12–17g of sugar per litre. The confusingly named Sec has 17–32g. Demi-Sec has 32–50g. Doux is the sweetest, with more than 50g.

One final point: champagne is occasionally used colloquially as a generic name for sparkling wine, but champagne is only champagne if it comes from the demarcated region around Reims and Épernay in France. The Champenois protect their naming rights with vigour to ensure that if you see the word 'champagne', then that is precisely what you can expect to be drinking. A very busy and resolute legal team makes hundreds of representations every year to make sure that the word 'champagne' is not used inappropriately: for example, for Japanese wine; to describe the colour on a mobile phone case; or to sell a bottled water as 'the champagne of mineral waters', as Perrier once attempted to do.

what to eat: A bottle of champagne is usually cracked open as an aperitif. If snacks are also required, then no more strenuous action needs to be taken than opening a bag of **crisps** or **roast, salted nuts**. I'd steer away from strange flavours or the penetrating pong of bright orange reconstituted potato (especially with a good glass in my hand), but salted crisps or cashews are ideal as the salt is a good foil for champagne's fierce acidity. Other easy small bites include **gougères**, the **cheese star biscuits** from Nigella Lawson's book *How to Eat* and, in particular, **cheese straws**: the yeasty depth of champagne is perfectly met by the rich savour of **Parmesan cheese**.

Champagne also goes well with fish, especially those nibbles that are softened with bread or potato and/or dairy. It's good with **prawn, crayfish or crab mayonnaise** (served on toast or in lettuce leaves); **rillettes de la mer** on slices of baguette; **hot-smoked salmon** or **lumpfish caviar blinis**; oysters (especially **oysters served with a slice of fried chorizo,** whose meaty spice plays up to champagne's richness); **scallops wrapped in prosciutto** and baked until the prosciutto is crisp; and **hot little new potatoes topped with cold crème fraîche and caviar** (or lumpfish caviar).

Chicken might not sound very inspiring but it also works well with champagne, especially with blanc de blancs, and it's easy to make 'on toast' snacks from chopped smoked chicken mixed with, say, basil, capers and home-made mayonnaise.

Visitors to Reims and Epernay are often served champagne all the way through dinner. Producers often showcase their wines with main courses of fish or chicken with morels in a creamy sauce. I've eaten some fabulous food as a guest of champagne houses. Food and drink combinations that ended up starred in my notebook include **smoked pork with fig** with rosé Veuve Clicquot; **turbot with roasted girolles, black truffles, salty fried slices of potato** and Moët & Chandon 1993 – the developed flavours in the wine were superb with the fungal notes in the food; and the rich, nutty Collard Picard Essentiel 2006 with **foie gras**.

Similarly, wealthier champagne houses often collaborate with top chefs to produce dinners at which the food has been precisely matched with one of their wines. Giles Cooper of fine wine merchant BI told me about one such dinner at Andrew Fairlie in Gleneagles: 'We ate **half a lobster in tarragon butter**. The lobster had been steamed to set the meat, then removed from the shell. The shell was then smoked, and the lobster meat put back in, so the lobster was almost on a smoked plate, and we ate it with aromatic Krug Grande Cuvée. It blew my socks off.'

Krug also produced a book of recipes from chefs around the world whom they had asked to create recipes involving potatoes that would go with Krug. I can guarantee I will never make Ryan Clift's recipe for ratte potatoes with crispy layers of algae and a truffle dressing made by passing ultrasonic sound waves through a solution of oak chips, chardonnay vinegar and black truffle, but I am sure it is very good. Likewise I would probably not attempt Tsuyoshi Murakami's Kappo Sweet Potato, made by filling a hollowed-out Persian lime with sweet potato purée topped with yuzu and salmon roe and decorated with edible flowers, but maybe it would taste good in a restaurant, and I think all these ingredients paint a picture of the types of flavours that champagne suits. I'd also add **truffle** to that list. And **mushrooms** – when you put champagne with mushrooms the flavours in both seem to amplify.

Sommeliers often like to match zero dosage champagnes with food. The exhilarating briskness of the wine acts as a brilliant palate cleanser between mouthfuls and their precise geometry can be especially good with **bisquey seafood flavours** and with **morels**.

My very personal preference when it comes to drinking champagne all the way through dinner, though, is for more casual food and a mood of exuberance. Earnest food matching with starchy linen, Michelin stars and bubbles gives me stomach ache. But I love to have lots of friends round a kitchen table eating **sausage, mash and onion gravy** and washing it down with a pinot-based NV champagne. Or go out à deux and order **lobster and basil salad**, or **grilled lobster and fat chips** with a bottle of the best blanc de blancs we can afford. Or graze on **sushi** or **dim sum** with rosé champagne. Rosé champagne is actually a superb food wine and great with posh Chinese. Bigger, brighter, young crunchy rosé champagnes that have an emphatic taste of red berries go very well with **pork**. The more subtle, elegant pink wines suit delicate fish in combination with bosky flavours. I once drank rosé Gosset outdoors, in a clearing in an English wood, with **turbot in a creamy sauce with slices of freshly dug English summer truffle**. It was cooked up on a little camping stove by the chef Roger Jones and the marine taste of the fish with the fungal accents of the truffle was just superb. A meal that has stuck out in my mind ever since.

Many people also love to eat **salt-and-vinegar-laden fish and chips** with champagne. It does work – but I prefer a cup of tea.

what the winemakers eat
Benoît Gouez, chef de cave at Moët & Chandon: 'We like to play with crunchiness in the food. To me there's an echo with the effervescence of the wine. The perception is not the same. One of the things we think is key with champagne is salt. I have a personal theory – I don't think harmony comes from opposition but from completeness. In a glass of champagne you have sweetness, umami, acidity, bitterness – the only taste missing is salt. So you need to have salt in the food.'

Olivier Collard, co-owner of Collard Picard: 'With our champagnes I really appreciate top-quality produce simply cooked. For instance, scallops or lobster just steamed, no special creamy sauces.'

Jérôme Philipon, President of Bollinger: 'My wife and I host a lot of people so we eat and drink a lot, but when I'm on my own for the weekend, and I want to eat less, I like to have Bollinger with hard cheeses. Old Comté – two- year-old or three-year-old – is always spectacular. Sometimes we serve that at the office too, with a piece of each on the plate. Beaufort, from the Alps, is also good. So cheese, with a good piece of bread, one of our white champagnes – Grande Année or the Special Cuvée – and a salad afterwards is a fantastic treat.

'Prior to joining Bollinger, I spent twelve years living in Asia – in the Philippines, South Korea and Thailand. I still love to eat Asian food and when you go to a Chinese, Japanese or South-East Asian restaurant, then a really good match with most of the food is a bottle of rosé champagne.'

chardonnay

what it tastes like: Chardonnay is a chameleon grape that may be lean or rich, plain or voluptuously complex, and is responsible for some of the world's best still as well as sparkling wines. As the second-most planted white grape in the world (according to 2010 figures; it is beaten to first place by airén, of which there is loads in Spain), it is also widespread. Here I'll consider only the still wines, but even within this category chardonnay is still a versatile shape-shifter. Taste-wise, you don't always know what you are getting. It's a grape with depth and breadth, curves and rounded edges, that can move from understated and chic to busty and loud. At one extreme, it can taste almost invisible – like white sheets of paper perhaps with the gentlest tinge of lemon. At the other, in sunny, warm places, if the grapes are left to get very ripe, and aged in brand-new toasty oak barrels, the wine turns a deep yellow and tastes buttery and fat, with a twang of pineapple cubes and tropical fruit and rich wood spice. Then there are all the wines in between.

C

Chardonnay reaches its pinnacle in Burgundy in France, where alterations in the geology create huge taste differences, not just from one subregion to another but also from one village to another, and from one vineyard to the next. Lemony Chablis tastes of the compressed oyster shells and marine fossils on which it's grown (if you doubt this, go stand in one of the underground cellars in Chablis, break off a chunk of wall and see if you don't find the same damp limestone smell in the wine). Montagny is nutty, reminiscent of hazelnuts. Meursault is also on the richer, nuttier side, with more breadth and subtlety than Montagny. Mâcon and St Véran taste of green apples and honeydew melon. The finest wines, such as Puligny-Montrachet and Chevalier-Montrachet, have great majesty and detail. Some producers (Patrick Javillier, for instance, in Meursault) make wines that have an astonishing, heavy perfume and smell of woodruff and dried meadow flowers and rosewood.

Other notable French chardonnay-producing regions include Limoux in the foothills of the Pyrenees (underrated and brilliant, making wines that are nuanced like almost-burgundy, but a bit more emphatic, with gentle mushroom undertones) and the Jura (nutty, oxidative sherry-ish styles are rife here).

Flavours around the rest of the globe are extremely hard to generalize, partly because winemaker influence is so strong, partly because of the refinements and stylistic changes made over the last decade or two. However, extremely good chardonnay is also found in a number of places. For a start, New Zealand, particularly in Marlborough, on the South Island, where the taste is luminous, just as it is for the more famous sauvignon blanc of the area. Marlborough chardonnay often has a lemon-blossom or lemon-meringue-pie quality. Noteworthy chardonnay is also made by Neudorf in Nelson and by Kumeu River on New Zealand's North Island.

Australia may have given us the oaky pineapple-chunk chardonnay soup that caused chardonnay overload in the Nineties but things have changed there. Much Australian chardonnay is now invigorating: lean, twangy, cooler grown, earlier-picked and low in alcohol (say, 12% abv). It often has a whiff of struck match and gleams with bright-lemon curd flavours. I love it. Look for wines

C

from Margaret River; Victoria – including Yarra Valley, Gippsland, Henty, Mornington Peninsula; Adelaide Hills; Tasmania.

South Africa is making serious chardonnay, structured, with quiet opulence. Californian chardonnay has a tendency to be golden-coloured, sweetly high in alcohol, voluminous and rich – even the new-style, earlier-picked versions planted in cooler sites. Oregon is cooler, so chardonnay here has a twang of white peaches. In Washington State, too, the acidity is bright. In Chile more chardonnay is being planted in cooler, coastal areas, as well as the northerly valley of Limarí. It is less tropical and heavy than in the past, with lemony edges and often a hint of putty.

Chardonnay is a wine that, at its best, can be aged for years and decades. As it matures, it begins to open out and smell less of bright fruit and more of mushrooms and soil, while some wines – in particular New World styles – often begin to smell of honeycomb, like Crunchie bars.

what to eat: Chardonnay is a brilliant and hugely sociable food wine but its biggest friend is **chicken**. The gentle white meat is great with chardonnay's creamy breadth. That goes for any style of chardonnay made anywhere in the world; it's actually impossible to imagine one that wouldn't taste fantastic with a simple roast chicken, ideally **slathered with butter** rather than olive oil.

Think of the simultaneous glow and twang of, say, an early-picked Australian chardonnay with **roast chicken and roast carrots and sweet potatoes**; or the limpidity of a young, unoaked burgundy with **chicken thighs casseroled with fresh peas, broad beans, potatoes and mint** (there's a recipe in Tamasin Day-Lewis's *Simply the Best*).

Imagine chicken soaked in buttermilk until it's tender, then cooked in a spicy paprika and cayenne batter – **southern fried chicken**. Chardonnay is the wine you want to drink with it. Pick one from a warmer climate than Burgundy (Chile or Australia or the US or a bright Languedoc chardonnay with some oak) with low or medium alcohol (13.5% abv or under). These wines have some of the warm amplitude that comes with sun to go with the spicy batter, but also the vibrancy of youth and a jangle of lemony acidity to slice through the fat.

A **room-service club sandwich, all bacon, chicken and**

mayonnaise, is great with a crisp glass of Mâcon. **Chicken and avocado salad** (the siky texture of the avocado slides against that of the wine) goes with an inexpensive, unoaked or lightly oaked chardonnay from anywhere.

Dairy – **cream, cheese, milk and eggs** – also suits this creamy-textured grape. Try a richer chardonnay with **cheese soufflé**.

Eggs are notoriously tricky with wine but chardonnay, in particular Chablis, is so gorgeous with **eggs Benedict** (with ham and hollandaise) and **eggs fiorentina** (with spinach and hollandaise) that it tempts me to drink at brunch time. Actually, it's really the hollandaise that is doing the work here: creamy, buttery sauces from **béchamel** to **mayonnaise** to **hollandaise** are always a hint that chardonnay could be a good accompaniment.

Put a cool-climate chardonnay with **roast trout, hollandaise, new potatoes and spinach salad**. Any chardonnay you love will taste good with **poached salmon with hollandaise**. Actually, chardonnay, especially Chablis, is extremely good with salmon and a big pile of new potatoes with or without the hollandaise.

A good burgundy or Limoux chardonnay melds with the butter of **sole meunière**. New-wave oaked Australian, coastal Chilean or Limoux chardonnay, or a nutty Montagny or rich Meursault are all superb with **creamy hot crab pots**.

See crab for a recipe for 'Hot crab pots' (p.78).

For **white fish with parsley sauce** pick a cool-climate (Burgundy or Limoux) chardonnay with minimal oak because the vegetal greenness of the parsley tastes odd with the tropical flavours found in a riper wine. Creamy and buttery **fish pie** is also lovely with chardonnay; the more smoked fish there is in it, the more I like taut, reductive styles of wine (which smell of struck matches). There's no way of identifying one of these unless you know it already, but lower-alcohol (say, 11 or 12% abv) Australian wines are a good place to start – they will at least have the twang.

A full-on chardonnay – warmer climate and plenty of toasty oak – is beautifully offset by **chicken with chipotle mayonnaise**. Most chardonnays will also go very well with **roast chicken leftovers stirred into a béchamel sauce and baked inside rolled-up pancakes**, or **just-warm roast chicken, hand-shredded and eaten with home-made mayonnaise and crusty bread**.

Likewise, most **gratins** are excellent with chardonnay. I like creamy

C

tomato gratin with tarragon or lemon thyme, which can accompany chicken or be served with nutty brown rice and a green salad as a meal in its own right, and is great with edgy new-wave Australian chardonnay or a young, modern, minimally oaked burgundy.

Sometimes you only need a spoonful of cream to make the chardonnay go down. Chardonnay wouldn't be my immediate choice of drink with tagliatelle with prawns and a raw or just-cooked tomato and fresh basil sauce – unless the tomatoes were mixed with crème fraîche or a splash of double cream, in which case I'd look for an unoaked or barely oaked wine that wasn't too dark in colour. Lighter and unoaked chardonnays go well with a plain seafood risotto, but stir in a tablespoon of cream and even weightier chardonnays become convincing options. Creamy sweetcorn, chicken and bacon chowder is also great with a lightly oaked chardonnay. Come to that, sweetcorn is always great with chardonnay – think of a corn on the cob, blackened on the barbie, slathered with butter and washed down with a lovely, oaky, ripe wine.

Following the cholesterol trail, chardonnay and shellfish is another natural match, all the more so, again, if there's a little bit of dairy present. Think lobster, plain grilled with butter or mixed with home-made mayonnaise, chopped tomato and torn basil. Make sure the chardonnay isn't too heavy or oaky: burgundy is blissful; new-wave Australian or South African is fine; colour of long-haul urine sample is not.

Bright, lucid chardonnays from Chile, Australia, South Africa and New Zealand like crayfish, in mayonnaise or in salads, as well as fried prawns dripping with butter and garlic. Lemon and seafood are lovely with the vibrant New World styles, whose acidic twang mirrors the citrus.

Crab is another classic. What could be better with a plain dressed crab than a good burgundy or a stylish Limoux? Chablis and piercing New Zealand chardonnays are also gorgeous with a mixture of brown and white crabmeat stirred with mayonnaise, a squeeze of lemon and chopped coriander stalks, and spread on brown or sourdough toast.

Chardonnay can be outrageously good with pork, but let your choice take its cue from the ingredients going with the meat. If there are fennel seeds, then the notes of woodruff and fennel tops in a white burgundy will mirror those in the herbs. Pork that has richer flavours around it is going to need a sunnier wine.

Mushrooms, too, have a synergy with chardonnay. Notes of brown chestnut mushrooms can often be found even in young chardonnay from Limoux and Burgundy, and as chardonnay ages that mushroom smell grows dustier and more pronounced. Put some of the above pointers together and make a **mushroom omelette**, or a **chicken and mushroom casserole with a creamy sauce**, and there you have two more perfect chardonnay plates.

The curves of chardonnay suit **pumpkins** and **squash**, as well as the richness of **sweet potato**. Try one with a **roasted butternut squash risotto** with lots of cheese stirred in; with **pumpkin pie**; with **a chunky roast onion squash, chilli flake, stock and sourdough toast mixture so thick it's more stew than soup**; with **pumpkin and Pecorino ravioli**; or with **roasted sweet potato** slathered with butter and melting grated cheese. Choose a lighter, more lemony chardonnay grown in a cooler place, or at least one that's earlier-picked (an indicator of this is that the alcohol level will be lower), if you want to freshen up the plate of food. The golden sunniness of a riper, and/or more oaky wine will play more into the richness of the dish.

A more unexpected match with toasty, oaked chardonnay is **chicken liver pâté on toast**, especially tasty if you put tiny slivers of date on the pâté to pick up on the richness in the wine.

Chardonnay is also a very good cheese wine. Vegetal burgundy is my favourite thing to drink with a **proper Cheddar** from Keen's or Quicke's.

If you've got a special bottle to drink consider preparing lobster, crab or roast chicken in as simple a way as possible. My best-ever burgundy dinner was at the now-defunct Café Anglais, with a guy I was head-over-heels in love with. No starters, no messing, just buttery **grilled lobster and chips** with a bottle of Jacques Carillon Puligny-Montrachet.

what the winemakers eat
Josh Bergström, Bergstrom Wines, Oregon, US: 'Classic pairings for Oregon chardonnay are local Dungeness crabs when they are in season, as well as fresh local oysters which are small and sweet. However, one of my favourite things to eat with our Sigrid

Chardonnay is a home-made summer pasta that I make with as many ingredients from our garden as possible. First I fry some bacon, not too crispy. Then I cut up some fresh tomatoes, mixing larger red and small sweet orange and yellow cherry tomatoes. Then I finely chop some chives, French tarragon and mint.

I also lightly steam some sweetcorn, put it in an ice bath so that the kernels are still crunchy and cut it straight off of the cob. I then boil some pappardelle pasta al dente, toss all of the ingredients together with a little bacon fat, a small amount of olive oil and a small amount of cream. Top it off with some finely shredded Parmesan and voilà! A dish that goes well with the herbal, fruity, acid, sweet and toasty side of chardonnay.'

Alex Moreau, Domaine Bernard Moreau, Chassagne-Montrachet, France: 'I like to drink our Chassagne-Montrachet and our St Aubin when it still has the taste of fresh fruit but isn't completely young – the perfect window is four to eight years old. The other day I cooked dinner for a friend and we had oeufs en cocotte [eggs baked in ramekins] with morels and a bit of cream and Parmesan, and I opened a Chassagne-Montrachet 1er Cru Les Grandes Ruchottes. We then had sweetbreads, so I opened pinot noir to go with that, but then we returned to chardonnay for cheese. More and more I like to drink chardonnay with cheese. It works better than red. Also it's good to go back to a white when you have a long dinner, more refreshing. Our chardonnay goes particularly well with goat's cheese and it's also very good with Cîteaux – a very small production cheese made at Cîteaux Abbey using milk from Montbéliarde cows. That night we drank a wine from 1995, a very small vintage that everyone said was too heavy to age well, but which did because it had great energy.'

Judy Finn, Neudorf Vineyards, Nelson, New Zealand: 'We have a wooden bach [summer house] at Awaroa in the middle of the Abel Tasman National Park. We share the bach with friends and barged the timber for it up the coast ourselves, so you can imagine it's a very minimal affair. We can walk in across the inlet or boat in. No power. No cellphone coverage. Life revolves around the tides for fishing, gathering mussels and rock oysters and dredging for scallops. Tradition demands the first scallop we haul up is opened and slurped with just seawater. The rest of the scallops come back to land to be rinsed, opened and cleaned. Hot pan on the fire, knob of butter and a glass of Neudorf Chardonnay in my fist. That's it. Simple. But joyful.'

Rozy Gunn, Iona Wine Farm, Elgin, South Africa: 'I really rate egg dishes. Ridiculously simple, a beautiful little dish of baked eggs is a most underrated companion to our chardonnay. The eggs of course must be top drawer – we use our own free-range eggs from the hens who spend their days scratching up my garden. We use fresh-foraged horse mushrooms – thick and meaty, they keep their shape well and have the most incredible flavour. Any – non-poisonous – brown-style mushrooms would make a good substitute.'

IONA BAKED EGGS
Makes 10

- 300g bacon, diced
- butter, for greasing and frying
- 150g firm brown mushrooms, roughly chopped
- a handful of fresh herbs, such as parsley, chervil or tarragon, finely chopped
- salt and freshly ground black pepper
- 10 eggs
- 60ml mascarpone cheese

Preheat the oven to 200°C/400°F/gas mark 6. Dry-fry the bacon until crisp and divide among ten generously buttered ramekin dishes. In a very hot pan, fry the mushrooms with a little butter so that they seal and colour without steaming. Divide between the ramekins. Sprinkle the herbs over and season lightly. Break a raw egg into each ramekin on top of the mushroom mixture and follow with a teaspoon of mascarpone in each one. Bake in the oven until the eggs have just set. Serve with crusty bread.

Mike Aylward, Ocean Eight, Mornington Peninsula, Australia: 'We make two chardonnays at Ocean Eight and they are quite different in style. Both have plenty of natural acid – in fact we grow the grapes so that we can make the wine without any acid addition and because of this the wines just cry out for food. They match well both with delicate subtle flavours or richer heavier foods to which they provide a counterbalance.

'Our Verve Chardonnay is sharp, full of crisp citrus and a bit steely on the finish. It is suited to freshly shucked oysters, particularly when they are enhanced with a Japanese-inspired dressing of yuzu vinegar. It's also great with goat's cheese, as well as with delicate seafood like scampi, Balmain Bugs or Moreton Bay Bugs. These are all small lobsters and suited to subtle treatment in the kitchen: simply cook them however you please, and toss them with some butter and herbs, or serve in a delicate broth flavoured with lemongrass and a spike of chilli.

'Our Grande Chardonnay has aromas of white flowers and stone fruit combined with a mouth-filling richness and a lingering soft and dry finish. The richness of scallops that have been baked in their shells and drizzled with olive oil and fresh herbs is almost a perfect match. It's also great with full-flavoured fish like salmon or ocean trout that has been poached and served with a white wine and cream sauce. If looking for an alternative to seafood, the wine is just fine with chicken in a boisterous, herby pho.'

Julien Barraud, Domaine Daniel Barraud, Mâcon, Burgundy, France: 'Mâcon is a wine to drink young, between two and four years old, so it's an aperitif wine, and good with crevettes and also oysters. Our St Véran Les Pommards is different, more substantial, more like Pouilly-Fuissé. You have to wait at least three or four years for it and then it's a wine you can drink with white meat or a dry cheese like goat's cheese.'

Laurent Pillot, Domaine Fernand et Laurent Pillot, Chassagne-Montrachet, Burgundy, France: 'Last New Year's Eve we had friends round and we had a lobster roasted in the oven for just 15 minutes with butter and lemon. Beautiful. We drank Chassagne-Montrachet 1er Cru Vide Bourse 2004.'

Vasse Felix, Margaret River, Australia, gave me the following recipe, which they serve in their winery restaurant with their chardonnay.

**RICOTTA GNUDI WITH ARTICHOKE,
BROAD BEAN, HAZELNUT AND LEMON**
Serves 3 as main or 6 as a starter

- 250g ricotta, drained overnight (broken up before draining if firm ricotta)
- 75g Parmesan, finely grated
- salt
- 2 eggs, beaten
- 1 egg yolk
- 1 tablespoon flour
- 500g plain flour
- 4 globe artichokes
- 1 lemon
- a knob of salted butter
- 1 tablespoon olive oil
- 1 large or 2 small radicchio, separated into leaves
- 100g broad beans, shelled weight, blanched (double-pod them if you like)
- 1 preserved lemon, cut into julienne
- 100g hazelnuts, roasted and roughly chopped

Put the drained ricotta, Parmesan, a pinch of salt, eggs, egg yolk and the tablespoon of flour in a large stainless-steel bowl and mix until well combined and dough-like in consistency. It is important that the mixture is as smooth as possible in order to make neat gnudi. Transfer the mixture to a piping bag. Spread about 350g flour about 3cm thick on a tray. Make holes in the flour with your thumb – the mixture will make 20–30 gnudi and you need a hole for each one – and pipe

C

gnudi mixture into each hole. If you don't have a piping bag you can pass the mixture between two tablespoons to make a smooth oval shape, like a quenelle. Each gnudi should be made from about a tablespoon of mixture. Cover with the remaining flour and refrigerate for 3 hours.

To prepare the artichokes, snap off the tough external leaves and keep going until you reveal the pale yellow heart. Cut off the top leaves to expose the thistly choke. Remove the choke using a teaspoon and a sharp knife. Rub the artichokes with lemon to prevent discoloration, place in a pan of simmering water and simmer for 20–30 mins, or until cooked.

Remove the gnudi from the fridge, shaking off the excess flour and place on a floured tray until required. When ready to eat, put a large pan of water on to simmer (you may need more than one pan). In another pan, heat the olive oil and butter. Add the artichokes and cook until golden. Now add the raddichio to the same pan, along with the broad beans and preserved lemon. Season with a pinch of salt and keep warm.

Place the gnudi in the simmering water and cook for about 3 minutes. Remove with a slotted spoon, drain and place on bowls or plates, decorating with the vegetable mixture and the nuts. Drizzle with a small splash of juice from the vegetable pan and a squeeze of lemon.

See also Chablis, champagne, English sparkling wine.

chenin blanc

what it tastes like: At its simplest level, chenin blanc is a straightforward white with accents of apple and pear. It can also be beautifully scented, like the floral smell of quince, and makes more complex, exhilarating wines, sweet or dry; still or sparkling, in both the northern and southern hemispheres. The Loire Valley and South Africa are its two main homes for good-quality wine.

Chenin blanc has become South Africa's signature white grape, covering 18 per cent of the country's vineyards. It's planted in abundance for mass-market, everyday wines, but there are also old, wild vineyards, such as those found under the big skies of

Swartland, where gnarled bush vines upwards of eighty years old flourish amidst the empty mountains and dry plains. South African chenin is distinctive and different from its French counterpart: more rounded, more beeswaxy, sometimes a little reminiscent of fiano, tasting more of riper fruits like glazed pears, sharon fruit, apricots and honeydew melons with the golden glow of an autumn sun. When oaked, and aged, it can become rich with the flavours of vanilla and honeycomb.

In the Loire, chenin's acidity is very keenly felt. Young wines can taste savage and searing (this can be a good thing). There is also enormous variety of styles as chenin blanc is vinified dry, off-dry, medium-dry and sweet. The climate here is cooler than South Africa's and you can taste it. There's more citrus and green apple. A mineral bite, a scent of wildflower honey, complex vegetal notes, the taste of quince and sometimes also damp hay or wet wool. Navigating the Loire demands an understanding of the appellation contrôlées. Anjou Blanc tends to be softer and smoother. Savennières makes intense, savoury, autumnal dry wines. Montlouis is a very dynamic appellation, with young winemakers creating a real buzz, and its wines are often intensely detailed and mineral. Vouvray is the best known, making wines in all styles and of variable quality, with much commercial wine produced. Alone or as part of a blend, chenin blanc also makes refreshing sparkling wines reminiscent of apples and hedgerows. In Bonnezeaux, Quarts de Chaume and Coteaux du Layon, it can develop the ugly rot known as botrytis that enables the making of highly prized sweet wines.

what to eat: **Seafood** is a natural fit. The salty slither of **oysters** is cut through by a young Loire chenin with its direct acidity and crab-apple sourness. Sluice down a plate of prawns, or a **prawn and avocado salad with a nice lemony dressing**, or a **pink-sauced prawn cocktail** with a chenin blanc from just about anywhere. Or eat a brown and white **crabmeat sandwich** with an inexpensive, uncomplicated chenin blanc straight from the fridge.

Slow-cooked or barbecued pork is often put with apple sauce and the two also go well with the orchard-fruit taste of chenin. If you have access to a wood-fired pizza oven, spike some jacket

C

potatoes, leave them in the back of the oven to bake and absorb the smell of woodsmoke, then use their flesh to make smoky mashed potato and serve with roast pork and an oak-aged chenin blanc.

Oak, age and climate all make a big difference to the way wine plays with food. As a shorthand, young and unoaked chenin is brisk and crisp; think of it as being like adding a squeeze of citrus. The curves and weight of oak, and age, are softer landings; a richer wine that fits well with richer, creamier food. There will still be acidity, but it refreshes rather than slicing aggressively. Pick a cooler-grown chenin blanc, which at its extreme means Loire chenin blanc from a cold vintage with more savoury, earthy, cool citrus flavours to accompany dishes such as **pan-fried salmon with sorrel and spinach**.

A warmer-climate Californian or South African chenin has warmer, more exotic fruity notes (starfruit, apricots, melon, orange rather than lemon) and a glow that works with **autumnal vegetables – squashes, gourds and sweet potato**. So, for instance, the tan edges and sweet white insides of **caramelized scallops** pick up the subtle, honeyed notes of chenin from South Africa or a fuller wine from the Loire (one from a warmer vintage, or with a bit of age, or a touch of off-dryness).

Fish pie, which mixes juicy prawns, smoked and pink fish in a creamy white sauce under buttery mash, is gorgeous with almost any kind of dry chenin. But if it has a base layer of spinach and you want to serve a salad of bitter winter leaves, then I'd look for a barrel-aged Loire chenin from Montlouis, Vouvray, Jasnières or Savennières, whose savoury complexity will unfold beautifully against the clouds of mash and fishy cream sauce.

For **prawn with little gem lettuce**, I'd go for the spring-like brightness of a young, unoaked Loire chenin blanc; if there's **warm coriander chopped into the prawn mayonnaise**, then I might be more tempted towards the exotic warmth of a South African chenin blend or at least a Loire wine that has been aged in oak.

With **smoked salmon and crème fraîche**, the vivid energy of a young Loire wine counterpoints the texture like a squeeze of lemon; an older one will play into it, adding layers of weight, smoky oak and quince.

With a **roast chicken**, perhaps with **a sweetcorn stuffing**, or piled around with **roast butternut squash and roast sweet potatoes**, I love the warmth of a South African chenin, which plays to the sunny opulence. The more assertive flavour of **chicken blackened on the braai** is another good excuse to open chenin blanc from the Cape.

South African chenin, and also blends incorporating chenin along with some or all of viognier, roussanne, marsanne, chardonnay and clairette, are gorgeous with pork and spicy rubs, pork chargrilled on the braai or **slow-cooked pulled pork** – especially if they are served with a big spread of **colourful salads**.

South African salads are something else. I've often been wowed by them on tasting trips to Cape winelands. I know this sounds odd, but it's not just me. When I asked Claudia Brown in the UK office of Wines of South Africa what food she had really enjoyed eating with South African chenin, she emailed me photographs of **barbecued parsnips** and an 'orange salad' consisting of blackened sweetcorn, celery tops, nasturtium flowers, clementine segments and baby carrots along with green lettuce, clustered in groups on a plate. There is a vibrancy to the flavours that really suits the local wine. I love **hot chickpea and tomato salad** with South African chenin (with pork, chicken, fish or just other salads). While Marvelous Wines suggest serving their Yellow (that's the name of the wine) with a smoked potato salad and a fennel and orange salad, and cured salmon, which sounds just about perfect.

By contrast, the fierce acidity, citric glide and vegetal notes of dry Loire chenin blanc are good with entirely savoury salads, such as **chicory and rocket salad** or the bitter walnut, cool celery and icy green apple in a **Waldorf salad**. If you've got something cool but sweet in there, such as quince or other fruit, maybe pickled pears, then think about picking a gentler wine, either from South Africa or one that is not perfectly dry.

Young, unoaked Loire chenin blanc is also good with **asparagus**. Older, oaked Loire chenin blanc can be beautiful with **firm fish cooked with truffles and served with white asparagus**. A dry Loire chenin that has begun to mellow is also lovely with **white asparagus and Gruyère tart**. In winter, an oaked Loire chenin works well with another tricky (with wine) vegetable – the savoury taste of **gratin of Jerusalem artichokes**, perhaps served with roast pork, or made into a vegetarian dinner with a spinach side salad.

Off-dry chenin blanc has a great affinity with fruit and is good

C

with plates that combine those sweet fruit flavours and pork. For instance, an off-dry Vouvray is ideal with that old French classic **pork noisettes cooked with prunes**. I also recommend it to those who ladle a lot of sweet apple sauce on to their roast pork.

I should talk about **quince**. There is a remarkable consonance between quince and chenin blanc. The floral and orchard flavours of the fruit are reflected in the wine, making it a natural partner, whether on the cheeseboard as **membrillo** or poached and served either in a salad or with meat. At the north London home of Anna Colquhoun, the food expert known as the Culinary Anthropologist, I once ate a **poached quince, white chicory, Stichelton, watercress and toasted walnut salad** with Mullineux White Blend, a chenin blanc-based wine made in Swartland that uses small amounts of viognier and clairette for extra aromatics. They were lovely together. Slow-roast a pork shoulder; glaze it with quince; serve it with **spicy, sweet pickled quince** and some sweet roasted root vegetables, and you have a great chenin blanc dinner.

A succulent, medium-dry chenin blanc is also perfect with juicy slices of **ripe melon and prosciutto**.

Then there's **cheese**. Hard white cheeses and membrillo work with more complex chenin, whether dry, off-dry or sweet, according to your taste. Bright, lithe, young Loire chenin blanc is lovely with soft white cheese, including **soft goat's cheese**. One of my happiest cheese and chenin experiences was simply **toast spread with soft goat's cheese and topped with juicy peach slivers** with a young bottle of Domaine aux Moines Savennières La Roche aux Moines from a warmer, slightly later-picked vintage. The wine tasted of nectarines and wild honey and had a sleek acidity that rinsed your mouth in between bites of pungent cheese.

If you have a bottle of properly sweet chenin blanc, perhaps a Coteaux du Layon or Bonnezeaux, then as well as cheese and membrillo, its taut sweetness and orchard overtones are lovely with **baked apples stuffed with honey and raisins and spices** or **tarte tatin**.

what the winemakers eat
Adam Mason, Mulderbosch, Marvelous and Yardstick, South Africa: 'Recently I have begun experimenting with a smoker

I made from a recycled metal dustbin. Don't worry, I gave it a proper scrub before commissioning it. I seem to have got the method down pat for a 2.5kg smoked shoulder of pork.

'The process begins with brining overnight in an 8 per cent salt solution (plus a few extras like diced onion, celery, carrot and bay leaf), which is then followed by 2 hours of direct smoking using chipped raw oak. This imparts a lovely, savoury smoky quality to the meat. Once finished the shoulder is then wrapped in foil and "finished" off for 6–7 hours of low-temperature (approximately 60–70°C) cooking to bring the meat to the point where it falls from the bone. We serve this with freshly baked potato flour rolls, and a few colds such as traditional coleslaw with home-made mayo, a spicy salsa using corn, sweet peppers and coriander and a little lime and of course a little hot sriracha sauce.

'Imagine diving into your freshly constructed bun, and biting through layers of still-steaming, juicy pork, tangy mayo, crunchy slaw and a little slap on the wrist of chilli, then washing it down with a gulp of generous, succulent (Mulderbosch of course!) chenin blanc. With its vast array of flavours, succulent fruit acidity and generous palate weight I can think of no better variety to pair with this communal comfort food.'

Tessa Laroche, Domaine aux Moines, Roche aux Moines, Savennières, France, does what so many winemakers do when you ask what they like to eat with their wines; she talks about vintage. '2013 with oysters,' she says, picking a wine that, at the time of speaking to her, was both lean and young, angry with acidity, and taut. '2012 – not with oysters.' She is now wagging a finger at me. '2012 with lobster.' This wine is more buttery. 'Older vintages, I like with riz de veau, veal with girolles. And when it's in between, around five or six years old – cheese.'

Andrea Mullineux, Mullineux & Leeu Family Wines, Swartland, South Africa: 'Shellfish with more exotic flavours (think ginger and saffron) is an obvious combination with our chenin blanc. The sticky, warm, clovey nuttiness you get from

C

marinated pork belly is a match made in heaven too. I think our whites have a good body without high alcohol and a spice as opposed to a primary fruit focus, which to me broadens the food spectrum that works with them.'

Jean-Philippe Blot, Domaine de la Taille aux Loups, Loire, France: 'Our Montlouis Sec Clos de Mosny is good with oysters, but oysters with a lot of body, not fine de claire. I also like it with scallops, just seared and served with morels.'

cortese

This brisk and crisp white grape from north-west Italy is used to make Gavi and tastes of fresh lemon juice and preserved lemons. As a clean white it's a useful refresher, and is one of those wines that will go with almost any food that might have lemon in it or squeezed over it. For instance, to wash down a **prawn brochette**; or with a **chicken, parsley, mint, grapefruit and pistachio salad with a yoghurt sauce**; or with **white fish and lemony Greek potatoes**. At Tenuta la Giustiniana in northern Italy, I was once given a glass of Gavi as an aperitif and, to accompany it, **sage leaves crisped in a very light tempura batter**. Beautiful.

D

dolcetto

Poor dolcetto. It's such a jolly grape – vibrant and alert, with a ping of refreshing acidity and a smooth, darting taste of black cherries. If it grew anywhere other than north-west Italy it would be better known and better regarded. Unfortunately, in Piemonte, it's the third-string red, grandly and easily bested by nebbiolo and pushed even further down the pecking order by barbera. Or, as first-generation wine producer Manuel Marinacci puts it when I ask what he likes to eat with his own wines, 'You know how it is in Alba. Dolcetto is a quotidian grape. So for me dolcetto with **salami**.' Dolcetto, to be fair, is great with salami. It delivers juice and makes your mouth water in between chewy, stretchy bites of meat. It's also good with **simple risottos**. If you want to put it with smarter food drink it with **roasted duck**, as it will cut refreshingly through the fat. I also like it with **torn roast chicken, dried cherry and bread salad**, or with **bresaola and rocket salad** (like most Italian grapes, it's not shy of bitter leaves). Dolcetto is also a great **picnic** and **leftovers** wine – it has the juiciness to perk up slightly rigid cold meat and can get along with a great spread of food. It works wonders with a **Boxing Day turkey buffet** too, not least because the bright fruit in the wine acts like another fruity sauce or stuffing.

Douro reds

what it tastes like: Of all the vine-growing places in the world, the Douro in Portugal is one of the most spectacular. To reach it, you follow the Douro river inland from Oporto. As you go deeper in, its banks rise vertiginously, sheer cliffs of schist that have been dynamited to form terraces and patamares, some of them so narrow there is space only for a single row of vines before the slope climbs up again, rising more than the height of a man, then another row, and so on. It feels remote here – wilderness that has been civilized, but only just. And that's exactly how the wines taste.

The Douro is best known for its fortified port wines, but in the last couple of decades more and more producers have begun to focus on making 'normal' wines (most of them red, some white) too. The reds are diverse but the biggest fashion is for blends based on the main port grapes: touriga nacional, tinta roriz, tinto cão and tinta barroca. These wines have a firm, claret-like structure but are higher in alcohol, deeper, more earthy, darker-coloured and more savage. They may have a skein of flavour reminiscent of granite and dried herbs. I often recommend them to those who enjoy red bordeaux but want to try something different (or something that's better value).

what to eat: Local dishes are heavy and rustic. There is a lot of **cabrito (goat), pigs' trotters, cabbage soup and coelho estufado (stewed rabbit)**.

With Douro reds, steer away from dainty cuts of meat such as beef fillet. Instead go for **hearty stews** and **slow braises**, and do not shy from **herbs** (**thyme** and **rosemary** especially), **spices** (the pine-like smell of **juniper** works well) and lashings of black or white pepper. Good dishes include **venison and juniper casserole**; **pulled pork with a fiery sauce**; and **lamb leg rubbed either with garlic, rosemary and thyme**, or **with a cumin, coriander and garlic crust**. The tannin of Douro reds also cuts nicely through goose fat and, as they are robust and warming but also filled with fruit sweetness, the right one would make a wonderful Christmas Day wine with **roast goose**.

what the winemakers eat

I arrived at Quinta do Noval, an old estate high above the river, guarded by a huge cedar tree, one hot afternoon to be greeted by **Christian Seely, Managing Director of AXA Millésimes**, which owns Quinta do Noval. 'I hope you don't mind,' he said, 'but it's just the two of us for dinner so I've ordered my favourite food. Roast suckling pig.'

Only Christian could commission roast suckling pig for

two. I ate gigantic quantities of roasted, crispy-skinned piglet that night, with rice and the Seely special pepper sauce, washed down with the red wine from both Quinta do Noval and Quinta do Romaneira. The pepper sauce is apparently made by simmering six cloves of garlic, salt, half a bottle of white wine, 125g rendered pork fat, an entire tub (30g) of white pepper, a small bunch of parsley, dripping from the roast pig and lots of black pepper until it seems ready, a recipe I have not attempted but which tastes very good up in the Douro.

Francisco Ferreira, Quinta do Vallado, Douro: 'Strong meats, for example goat, are really good. Or pork.'

E

English sparkling wine

what it tastes like: Most English sparkling wine is now made not from the likes of seyval blanc, huxelrebe and reichensteiner as it once was, but from the champagne grapes of chardonnay and pinot noir. The quality of the wine has improved immeasurably over the past decade and more of the South Downs, Hampshire and Kent are planted with vines than ever before. England's wine industry can now count itself a serious contender on the world stage, but national production is still tiny in global terms, making this a rather patriotic entry. The average annual production is a mere 5.27 million bottles – of which around two-thirds will be sparkling wine.

The salient feature of English sparkling wine is its acidity, which reverberates like a spade hitting frozen ground, and gives the wine a mouth-cleansing freshness. It can taste relatively simple and plain, but better versions have a very attractive sophistication and creaminess.

what to eat: I think sparkling wine is most often drunk for pure and unadulterated pleasure rather than with dinner, but the rosés in particular do go very well with Asian food – the purity and gentle berry flavours along with that refreshing quality work extremely well with assortments of **sushi**, as well as Western versions of **Cantonese** and South-East Asian plates. English sparkling wine is also a winner with **fritto misto** or **fish and chips** because, thanks to the acidity and the bubbles, it can fight its way through all that fat and salt. And, as Bob Lindo of Camel Valley points out, 'It makes sense in so many ways, especially economically, in that you can have a relatively cheaper meal with a relatively more expensive wine.'

In terms of nibbles, as with champagne, **chicken and prawn-based snacks** work very well with any fizz containing chardonnay. **Parmesan crisps** and **cheese straws** also make good small bites.

Julia Stafford, who runs the Wine Pantry, which specializes in English wine, says she loves sparkling rosé with cold tomato soup; dry sparkling white with a fry-up (that sounds like a hair of the dog hangover cure to me) and a demi-sec with apple and rhubarb crumble or spotted dick.

what the winemakers eat

I asked **Brad Greatrix of Nyetimber in Sussex** what he liked and it took him weeks to reply: 'I think I psyched myself out trying to remember my ultimate moments. But actually what I love most of all and have most often at home with Nyetimber is Scottish smoked salmon in various combinations. Tartlets are my favourite, but easiest at home is to use blinis or savoury biscuits topped with a touch of crème fraîche, smoked salmon, sea salt and (sometimes) a tiny bit of fresh dill.' Perfect.

Bob and Annie Lindo have shared the recipe for the grissini they make to serve to visitors **at Camel Valley**. According to Annie, 'These tasty breadsticks are easy to make and provide the perfect accompaniment to a nicely chilled glass of Camel Valley "Cornwall" sparkling wine. Originally from Turin, this is our own recipe for the grissini we serve at our wine tastings, and they are always very popular for pre-dinner drinks as they don't curb the appetite. As optional extras you can add a sprinkling of fennel seeds or sesame seeds at the end along with the sea salt.'

ANNIE'S GRISSINI
Makes 40

- 275ml warm water
- 2 teaspoons dried yeast
- 500g strong white bread flour, sifted
- 1 teaspoon salt
- 3 tablespoons olive oil
- semolina for rolling out
- a little beaten egg to glaze
- salt crystals

Place 125ml of the water in a food processor, sprinkle on the yeast and stir to dissolve. Leave for about 10 minutes until frothy. Add the flour, salt and olive oil and the rest of the water, and mix on pulse several times until well combined, smooth and elastic. Leave with the lid on in a warm place for 1–2 hours until well risen. Preheat the oven to 200°C/400°F/gas mark 6. We cook ours on the lowest set of runners in the Aga, turning after 5 minutes. Mix the dough again, then turn it out on to a worktop sprinkled with semolina. Divide into four portions and roll each into a rectangle about 12 × 25cm, using a little more semolina on top. Brush with beaten egg and sprinkle with a few salt crystals, then roll lightly so they stick to the dough. Cut into ten strips with a sharp knife and place about 1cm apart on a silicone baking sheet. Leave in a warm place while you prepare the other portions in the same way. By now the first batch should have risen a little. Bake for 15 minutes and cool on a wire rack. Irresistible when warm, they will keep for a few days in a tin, or can be frozen when cold.

F

fer servadou

This light-bodied, tangy red grape is from the south-west of France, where it is used to make Marcillac, among other wines. It tastes of blood and iron and sluices the mouth, cutting through the heaviness of the local food – confit de canard, cassoulet, aligot and so on. It's also good with steak, casseroles and merguez sausages.

G

gamay

what it tastes like: Gamay is a light and sappy French bistro classic best served chilled. Good gamay is reminiscent of red summer-pudding berries and graphite. Bad, cheap gamay smells of bubble gum and bananas – try to avoid that. This grape is found in the Loire in France, and in the environs of the Rhône, and is famously the red grape responsible for all Beaujolais. Beaujolais comes at four different levels, from low to high as follows:

- Nouveau is the wine rushed out on the third Thursday in November, straight after the harvest, and it can taste astringent and harsh
- Beaujolais is the standard stuff, the equivalent of Economy Class
- Beaujolais Villages is a bit better, so Economy Plus
- Beaujolais Cru – the equivalent of Club Class – is the best of all

Ten villages have earned the right to be Beaujolais Cru. Each makes a distinctive style and is allowed to put its name on the label. They are Brouilly (the biggest, so there's most of it); Chiroubles (the highest village in altitude and the wine is correspondingly chirpy and tart); Fleurie; St Amour; Juliénas; Morgon (the most masculine, with the darkest fruit and an undertow of rock); Moulin-à-Vent; Côte de Brouilly; Chenas; and Regnié.

Gamay is not seen much outside France, although some is found in Switzerland, and Te Mata in Hawke's Bay, New Zealand, deserves an honourable mention because it makes a fantastic one, plusher than French gamay, but still redcurrant-fresh.

what to eat: It's often presumed that because gamay is light it is a summer wine, but I like it best in the dead of winter, in the new year, when the earth is iron-hard but snowdrops are about to burst through. Gamay has a sappy freshness that also reminds you that spring is on the way. It's great chilled, poured from a carafe, with steaming dishes of **coq au vin** and jacket potatoes; with **boeuf bourguignon**; or with **home-made duck rillettes and a peppery watercress salad**. Put it with **bavette-frites**, or a **chunky terrine**, or **sausage and mash with an onion gravy**. Or, if you do drink it in summer, have a **tuna steak** just-seared so it's translucent red in the middle, or a **roast chicken with new potatoes**, or put it with **swordfish steaks with a squeeze of lemon and black pepper and a big bowl of couscous with parsley, mint and tomatoes** chopped into it. For a November celebration of 'BojoNuvo' at Galvin Bistrot de Luxe recently, head chef Tom Duffill put together a menu of country terrine with cornichons and sourdough and roast whole poussin with caramelized quince, consommé and garlic sausage. While I spotted andouillette on the Facebook feed of Beaujolais Queen Anne-Victoire Jocteur Monrozier. Gamay is also good with **cold meat** and **leftovers**. Its brightness stands up to the rapier jabs of **peppery leaves** (rocket, watercress, radish shoots), so one of these salads brings freshness to the table.

> *what the winemakers eat*
> **Edouard Parinet, Château du Moulin-à-Vent, Moulin-à-Vent, Beaujolais, France:** 'Our Cuvée Château du Moulin-à-Vent is light but it's still powerful so it can support a light meat with a sauce. I like it with chicken with a mushroom sauce. A less obvious match that I ate in a restaurant in Paris we were working with and that tasted really good is monkfish cooked in a red wine sauce.'

gewürztraminer

what it tastes like: This giddily perfumed grape smells of rose petals and lychees and can be dry, off-dry or very sweet. The most celebrated examples of gewürztraminer are grown in Alsace, where you can find wonderful wines at all the levels of sweetness, including the very sweet Vendange Tardive (made from late-harvested grapes). Gewürztraminer is also grown in Germany and Eastern Europe. There is only a little bit in Chile, but I am very partial to the one made by Cono Sur – drunk chilled, it tastes like a glacial, wine-strength rose and lychee cocktail. New Zealand and Oregon are other good places to look for this cleaner and more floral style – quite a contrast to some of the spicily heavy, massage-parlour versions.

what to eat: The received wisdom is that gewürztraminer is *the* wine to order when you're eating oriental food: for years I never ate Chinese without a glass of it on the table and vice versa. Now I'm not so convinced by this match. Most gewürztraminer is too OTT for most Chinese food – the heavy aromatics in combination with all the food spices are just exhausting.

There are exceptions: the heady fragrance of a dry gewürztraminer is extremely good with **white fish with spring onions and ginger**, for example, not least because gewürztraminer itself can taste and smell of green ginger and this picks up on the hot ginger in the food.

And in fact, while Chinese food might not always be the best accompaniment, many oriental ingredients do go very well: **ginger, coconut milk, galangal, cardamom** and **lemongrass** are all good gewürztraminer flavours. Perhaps this helps to explain why the Alsatian wine company Hugel surprisingly says it sells tons more gewürztraminer in Asia than it does riesling. I particularly like off-dry gewürztraminer with **chilli Thai beef and ginger**, as well as with **coconut milk Thai curries** – especially with red Thai curry, which is sweeter and richer than green.

In Alsace, gewürztraminer demonstrates a curious affinity with **smoked meat** and rich food. It is poured with stinky **Munster**, the local washed-rind cheese; **Gruyère and onion tart**; **eggy quiches**; **choucroute**; **tartiflette** (a gratin of potatoes, Reblochon cheese, onions and lardons). Floral, yet also oddly sturdy (it can get quite oily), gewürztraminer can also work with the kind of cheesy, cabbagey, smoked meat mountain stodge you find in the Alps. Think **cheesy polenta with mushrooms**; **white pizza made with melted Taleggio**; **penne with fontina cheese**; **Tyrolean dumplings** made with speck and served with melted butter and grated cheese. I once watched in slavering restraint at a lunch at The Wine Society as Alsace buyer Marcel Orford-Williams served Humbrecht Clos Windsbuhl Gewürztraminer 1999, a graceful wine with the beauty of a rich but subtle perfume. Apparently it was delicious with the wonderfully smelly **Epoisses**. And with the **pâté**. I was pregnant, so had to stick to crisps and water.

The spicy rose and lychee of a sweeter Vendange Tardive (late harvest) gewürztraminer from Alsace makes a hedonistic accompaniment to a slice of lemon tart.

graciano

Graciano is the unsung grape of Rioja, where it may be blended with other varieties or bottled on its own. It is throatier and spicier than tempranillo, and often also reminiscent of dried tobacco and mulberries: it has the same saturating quality as that squashy fruit, which can barely be picked without leaking its colour and juice. There is sometimes also a smear of eucalyptus or mace. Graciano's mellow combination of intense colour, autumnal savour and roasted dark plums goes well with **slow-cooked lamb** or **pork** and can also take a bit of spice in the meat – for instance, **star anise**, **cinnamon**, **juniper**, **cumin** or **coriander seeds**. This grape also has enough about it to go with **game**, such as **partridge**, **woodcock** or **pheasant**, and it can suit **meat cooked or served with cooked fruits such as grapes, figs or dark berries**. Try it with **game pie**, or spicy rich **meat terrines** served with fruit compotes. Graciano also works with **roasted root vegetables** – and you can afford to fling in the spices.

what the winemakers eat
Jesus Madrazo, Contino, Rioja, Spain: 'Over the years, I have come to understand the graciano grape. This is not a straightforward variety; it's trickier and more challenging than tempranillo, but it has fantastic potential. To my blended wines it brings deep colour, acidity and freshness, but I also make a single varietal graciano. This grape works so well with spicy food. It's perfect with Mexican mole (mole poblano or black mole from Oaxaca), with some curry sauces, and with Chinese food – our graciano is listed in the Hakkasan restaurants in London. It's good with partridges too; I like to drink it with partridges with salsa española.'

grenache

also known as garnacha tinta

what it tastes like: Young grenache (garnacha in Spain) tastes of sweetly bright, crushed red berries, melting to confit strawberries as it ages. It is not a neat grape. It has a layered, powdery feel and it's often high in alcohol and careless with its colour, starting out as a deep crimson and fading rapidly to a tawny shade.

It can be found alone in a bottle but is more often blended. Syrah and mourvèdre (monastrell in Spain) are its key collaborators – if you see the acronym GSM on a label, that's what it stands for. To my taste, grenache almost always performs better in combination with other grapes; I itch to add 5 per cent syrah or mourvèdre to even some of the best single varietal wines.

Grenache is the grape that gives the red blends of the southern Rhône their distinctive character. Here in northern Provence, where cicadas sing and the mistral blows, grenache smells not just of red berries but also of sun-dried wild herbs – thyme, olive leaves and tindery undergrowth – and often also tastes dry like pumice, reminiscent of the craggy limestone of the nearby Dentelles de Montmirail.

In Châteauneuf-du-Pape, grenache might be bottled neat or combined with up to seventeen other different grapes, but it almost always drives the wine, its alcohol flaring like flames of a fire to give a spicy warmth. Similar flavours are found to varying extents in the villages of Gigondas (which has a particularly red-fruit personality), Vacqueyras (often more solid and black-fruited), Vinsobres, Rasteau and Cairanne, as well as in the more grenache-heavy versions of Côtes du Rhône and Côtes du Rhône Villages.

Grenache is also found in the Languedoc-Roussillon, where, again, it is often blended with syrah, as well as carignan, mourvèdre and cinsault. In Maury and Banyuls, it is also used to make gloriously sumptuous sweet red wines – vins doux naturels.

As cannonau, in Sardinia, grenache is wilder, broader and more herbaceous still, sometimes with a feral hint, like dry old sausages and wild fennel seeds.

The dry, grainy feel of grenache is often less apparent in Spain, where it thrives as garnacha and makes wines that tend to more plumpness. The DOs of Calatayud, Cariñena and Campo de Borja in the north-east, just to the west of Zaragoza, are rich with old vineyards whose gnarled and ancient vines grow grapes that are deep in flavour and have a juicy succulence.

In Priorat and Montsant it is combined with cariñena (carignan) and other grapes to make luscious red wines that are reminiscent of thick crimson velvet.

Álvaro Palacios, who makes celebrated wines using high proportions of garnacha at Bodegas Palacios Remondo in Rioja, as well as in Priorat, talks about this grape as if it is the elixir of life: 'Garnacha is the most musical, poetical, the most delirious Mediterranean grape, and it transforms in the heat into a very refreshing grape. It can be hot and the garnacha vine is there looking like, *¿qué pasa?* Bright and green. People believe I am crazy only about garnacha. I am not. I don't mind pinot noir. In Priorat garnacha has a spirited, mysterious super-special strength [he goes on tiptoe and points at his glass], but sometimes it doesn't have the musicality of pinot noir.'

Certain regions of South Australia, too, are notable for the luxuriance of their grenache. It's frequently blended but sometimes also bottled as a single varietal. The warm Barossa Valley has some extraordinary old vine grenache. It's sumptuous, redolent of raspberry jelly and cooked mulberries and baking heat, with just a tinge of liquorice. Also worthy of note is McLaren Vale, 100 kilometres south of Barossa, the other side of Adelaide, where the grenache blooms into a thick pom-pom of a red wine – high in alcohol but also high in flavour.

In the US, grenache again has bigger bones and less herbal savour than it does in France, but it is combined with syrah and mourvèdre to make some extremely good GSM blends, most notably in California but also in Washington State.

Rosé/Rosado Grenache/garnacha is also the linchpin in many rosé blends. It contributes to the pale, dry pink wines of Provence; underpins the rich, deep colour and taste of Australia's most famous rosés (Turkey Flat and Charles Melton's Rose of Virginia, both from the Barossa); and in Navarra, in northern Spain, garnacha makes strawberries-and-cream flavoured, highlighter-pink rosados.

what to eat: Perhaps the most perfect and certainly the easiest grenache dinner is a **leg of lamb rubbed with pounded-up garlic, rosemary and anchovies**. It's good butterflied and scorched for 15 minutes in a hot oven, so that the outside browns and the inside remains bloodily pink – I particularly enjoy young, savoury wines, such as a young Vacqueyras or Gigondas, with very rare lamb. A slow and slightly more cooked joint is perfect with almost any sort of grenache from France (the herbs pick up on the herbaceous quality of the wine) or Spain (the juicy sweetness underscores the melting softness of the meat). I sometimes scatter the meat with **lavender** or **thyme** when drinking a grenache blend from the Rhône, or serve it with **tomatoes stuffed with rice, thyme, courgette, and garlic**.

Norrel Robertson, a Scot who makes wines in Calatayud (see below for more of his food ideas), suggests a Spanish twist to the lamb-and-garlic idea: 'Ternasco de Aragón – young lamb shank or shoulder (remember that the Spanish call anything over 18 kilos mutton, so it really is infanticide here) is best slow-cooked with garlic on top of a bed of patatas panaderas – thinly sliced potato with stock and a little bit of white wine and a splash of cream, done in the baker's oven after he has finished his bread for the day.' Obviously he drinks this with one of the glorious garnachas from north-east Spain whose juiciness melds so well with the slow-cooked meat and the glossy potatoes, but it would go well with French versions too, or Australian versions, come to that.

Grenache that smells of dried herbs, such as those sunny grenache blends from the southern Rhône and some of the more savoury versions from Australia, goes well with **Provençal stuffed vegetables**, and also picks up nicely on the Mediterranean flavours of **ratatouille**.

Beef Wellington is a classic with young or old Châteauneuf-du-Pape. **Roast grouse** also works well with Châteauneuf, which can be gamey and feral, especially if there's some mourvèdre in the blend. **Crispy-skinned, dark-fleshed roast duck with roasted root vegetables** also rejoices in the warm spice of a grenache or grenache blend. And grenache blends – from Gigondas, Côtes du Rhône or Costières de Nîmes to an Aussie GSM – are cosy with **cold-night**

stews and **daubes, slow-cooked meat** and **hearty braises**. For instance, **daube de boeuf with a sliver of orange peel** works well with the sort of grenache that look luscious when young and dry when old (in other words, savoury French styles and cannonau from Sardinia). A rich **venison casserole** goes well with the dark fruit and herbs of a grenache-syrah blend from the southern Rhône or Languedoc.

I also serve aromatic Sardinian cannonau with Sardinian dishes such as **mixed grilled vegetables (incorporating aubergines, fennel and celeriac) with buffalo mozzarella scattered with pine nuts** (I like the scratchy feel of the cannonau against the silky cheese). Or **Sardinian sausages** or **malloreddus (traditional Sardinian pasta) with a tomato and meat/sausage sauce. Pasta with a tomato and 'nduja sauce** is good too. 'Nduja is a soft, spicy, red peppery pork sausage that actually comes from Calabria, but the streaks of heat play up to the fiery, flaring side of cannonau.

More juicy, bright grenache from, say, Navarra or Campo de Borja in Spain has a clean lucidity that is lovely with **jambonneau** or **Teruel ham**. Continuing on piggy lines, there's a lovely Skye Gyngell recipe for '**Slow-cooked pork shoulder with celery and braised rhubarb**' that is great with garnacha from north-east Spain, and most grenache is lovely with a simple pork chop. Black pudding is also good with dense grenache or grenache blends. And **home-roasted joint of gammon** is especially good with the deep richness and baked-raspberry scent of Barossa grenache, which seems to enhance the succulence of the ham.

The tannin content of grenache is low, so with those softer, juicier styles you can even get away with food that is spiced, perhaps with a bit of coriander and cumin seed, or with cinnamon. Think the gentle Moroccan spice of a **tagine with prunes and lamb**, or the sweeter Claudia Roden recipe for '**Slow-cooked lamb shoulder with couscous and orange-blossom water, cinnamon, almond and date stuffing**' from her book *Arabesque: A Taste of Morocco, Turkey and Lebanon*. Either of these would be lovely with a garnacha from north-east Spain.

Asian pork is lifted and tickled with a juicy old-vine Australian grenache blend, such as the ones made by Spinifex in the Barossa. Even a **Jamaican goat curry** could enjoy the softer, sweeter unoaked grenache from, say, Campo de Borja.

G

The fruitiness and spice of those riper versions – or of GSM blends from California, Australia or elsewhere – play well when there is a sweet sauce or vegetable on the plate. A few ideas: with the **turkey and cranberry** of a Christmas or Thanksgiving dinner; with **Moroccan chicken wings and a lentil salad with a pomegranate molasses dressing**; with **sweet potato mash**; with the sweetness of **roasted root vegetables**; with **pumpkin pie**; with a **baked, buttered sweet potato and a salad with a hot-sweet-sour dressing**.

As for those dessert wines, the Maury and the Banyuls – they are perfect with **chocolate**, ideally the sleek gleam of **chocolate parfait** or an unctuous **mousse** or rich, **cherry or strawberry or raspberry chocolate gateau**.

See also Languedoc-Roussillon reds, Priorat, rosé.

what the winemakers eat

Emilie Boisson, Domaine du Père Caboche, Châteauneuf-du-Pape, France: 'With our red Châteauneuf-du-Pape Domaine du Père Caboche, I really enjoy lamb cooked in the oven, with some Provençal herbs, potatoes and courgettes. With our Châteauneuf-du-Pape Elisabeth Chambellan Vieilles Vignes, I really like grilled côte de boeuf with a bordelaise sauce (butter and shallots) and French beans. And with our red IGP Pays de Vaucluse Le Petit Caboche: lasagne, but also grilled meat and pizzas.'

Stephen Pannell, S. C. Pannell, McLaren Vale, Australia: 'I am a mad cook. At this time of the year [the end of March], at the end of vintage and the beginning of autumn, the quinces are ripe and while I am visiting vineyards I stop and pick them at the side of the road and make lamb tagine. My favourite recipe is the lamb, chickpea and quince tagine that you can find online at delicious.com.au. It has an Asian twist on the classic Claudia Roden recipe. I think the perfume of the quince with the gamey lamb and the cumin, turmeric, saffron and cinnamon spice mix works perfectly. After tasting young ferments/wines all day at work I cooked the tagine and opened my '06 grenache with some French friends and they couldn't believe how youthful the wine was.

'There are many other things that go with grenache and game is one of my favourites, not because it also starts with G.

Duck is always a winner – especially Peking duck – and I also love deep-fried five-spice quail with a hint of chilli; try Justine Schofield's recipe at everydaygourmet.tv.'

Norrel Robertston is El Escoces Volante – a Scot making wine in Calatayud in northern Spain: 'Anything which combines good quality pimentón [Spanish paprika], garlic and meat usually works as a good foil to garnacha. I like pinchos morunos – cubes of pork loin on skewers, normally marinated with a healthy dose of pimentón, cumin, garlic and oregano then done on a hotplate or barbecue. No doubt these are North African in origin, where lamb would originally have been used. The thinking man's kebab, if you like.

'I also like garbanzos and bacalao – a great dish using desalinated salt cod, chickpeas, pimentón, ground almonds, lots of golden toasted cloves of garlic and breadcrumbs. José Andres Puerta has the best recipe I have found for this.

'Morcilla – black pudding – is good too. I actually favour morcilla de Burgos, which will have a bit of rice, pine nuts and cumin rather than the cinnamon which is more commonplace in Aragón. Heavenly when toasted properly.

'Finally – haggis, for which garnacha is a match made in heaven. It cuts through sheep fat, handles the gameyness of the pluck and synergizes with the white and black pepper and other herbs you want to throw in. We make our own every January and the Spanish whom we invite usually flip out.'

Justin Howard-Sneyd, Domaine of the Bee, Côtes Catalanes, France: 'Wild boar! After what they are already doing to our grapes a month from harvest. Or beef stew – or rather daube de boeuf.'

Randall Grahm, Bonny Doon Vineyard, California, US: 'When I first started selling Le Cigare Volant (a blend of grenache, syrah, mourvèdre and cinsault), the category of red Rhône blends was largely unknown in the US. I had my first big sales trip on the East Coast – this was maybe 1987 or '88 – and I had a number of lunches and dinners planned at (mostly) fancy restaurants. The chefs all wanted to know what they should prepare to complement Le Cigare Volant. This wine is often a bit fruitier and higher-toned than Châteauneuf-du-Pape, but also has a certain gameyness/savouriness as well, which seems to play on a number of elements of venison. (Also tends to go well with lamb, quail, partridge, guinea fowl, and other game birds.) Anyhow, I told the chefs that the wine would go very well with venison, and, to my chagrin, I ended up being served venison for lunch and dinner for perhaps eight days in a row. I had to take a bit of a break from venison after that for the next ten years. But the wine still goes well with venison (and the other items mentioned – also pepper-crusted ahi tuna, for some reason). Also, any of the meat/bird preparations that incorporate wild mushrooms in the sauce (morels, in particular) seem to work exceptionally well.'

grüner veltliner

what it tastes like: Austria's signature white grape makes refreshing wine that has acidic verve and is not overtly fruity. Its flavours are a subtle mingle of white pepper, white and pink grapefruit and radish or sushi ginger. There is often also a gently spicy note that can be reminiscent of orris root. Many grüner veltliners have an almost crystalline texture; in your mouth they feel as svelte and precisely metred as if they have been diamond-cut. Some are broader and plumper, perhaps with accents of nectarine, but still with a punctuating prickle.

what to eat: Grüner veltliner is one of those glorious grapes that go reasonably well with nearly everything with which you might want to drink white, and particularly well with some of the foods that often cause problems for wine. For instance, it is good with **fresh asparagus**, both white and green. It can also take on **artichokes**, either alone or as part of a salad or other dish. Skye Gyngell makes a great vegetable tray bake using braised artichokes, saffron, fennel, preserved lemons, tomatoes and black olives: all those herbs and powerful ingredients are tricky for any white wine, but grüner veltliner can manage it. This wine is also a friend to **bitter greens**, so goes well with **chicory**, the peppery bite of fricasseed **sprouts** or **rocket** salads.

In the same way that gari brings vibrancy to raw fish and rice, the zesty citrus tang and tingly heat of grüner veltliner work well with **sushi rolls**. These qualities also dovetail with some of the **ingredients found in South-East Asian food** (especially Vietnamese and Thai): grüner veltliner is good with **lemongrass, Thai basil, mint, fresh coriander, galangal, lime juice, bok choy, green mango, Chinese leaf** and **water chestnut**. As with many other dry wines, though, it is less good with the heat of chilli. Try grüner veltliner with **pork and prawn dim sum**, or a **crunchy Vietnamese salad**.

In Austria, grüner veltliner is often poured to wash down **wiener schnitzel**. Its cool crispness feels revitalizing with the crispy fattiness of the fried breaded veal escalope. In the same way, grüner veltliner works well with **stodgy dishes** and **creamy sauces**: for instance, **macaroni cheese**; **kärntner kasnudeln** (a traditional Austrian dish consisting of pasta filled with potatoes, onion, cheese, soured cream and herbs); or **semolina and saffron dumplings with a creamy vegetable stew**. It's good with **pork, smoky ham** and **veal**, responding particularly well when bright Asian ingredients or creamy sauces or fat is involved. Good dishes include **spaghetti carbonara, veal escalopes cooked in butter, belly of pork with Asian greens, pork chops with rösti potatoes, pasta with blue cheese and toasted walnuts**, and **Tiroler Gröstl** (the Alpine potato, bacon and onion fry-up sometimes served with a fried egg).

It's also lovely with **sweetbreads** and, thanks to its good acidity, goes well with **seafood and fish**. Try grüner veltliner with **fried prawns**; with **sea bass cooked en papillote with lemongrass and coriander**; with **river trout and a cool watercress salad**; or with **pancakes filled with creamy seafood and chives**.

what the winemakers eat
Martin and Anna Arndorfer, Arndorfer, Kamptal, Austria: 'Beetroot carpaccio with olive oil, fleur du sel and fresh horseradish works really well with GV Strasser Weinberge … pretty easy to "cook" and super delicious.'

K

koshu

Koshu is a delicate white grape that is widely grown in Japan but whose origins are an enigma. It tastes a little like a cross between a very quiet sauvignon blanc and pinot grigio – peaceably neutral with a faint stirring of citrus and a gentle fragrance. Drunk alone it may seem nearly invisible: koshu doesn't say anything unless it is asked. Put it with food and a piece of magic happens: koshu emphatically stands up to things, acquiring power and mysterious substance. An excellent wine to drink with **sushi, dim sum, soba noodle dishes, plainly cooked fish served with Japanese-dressed salads,** and **fish and vegetable tempura**. It likes dishes that have fresh notes – say, **cucumber spaghetti** – in combination with **oily fish** or **rice** (koshu is brilliant at underlining the ricey flavour of rice). It is also a winner with **chicken and saffron kebabs**, as well as with good old **fish pie**.

L

Lambrusco

Once known as a slightly naff wine that tasted more like pop – fizzy and luridly sweet – these days Lambrusco is loved by the cognoscenti. Its grown-up incarnations are delicious: expect a dark, purplish-red, dry sparkling wine that tastes deeply but aridly fruity, and of sour cherries, salami and dust. It's wonderful drunk by the tumbler with food from its homeland of Emilia-Romagna in Italy. Try it with a spread of antipasti – **raw mushrooms dressed in olive oil, lemon juice and salt and pepper** and left for half an hour before serving; **figs and prosciutto**; **tomatoes stuffed with parsley, basil, spring onions and garlic**; with **pasta with Gorgonzola sauce** or with **ragù alla bolognese**. It's also fantastic with a chewy chunk of **dried salami**.

Languedoc-Roussillon reds

The robust red blends from the Languedoc-Roussillon often have a waft of scent reminiscent of the herb-covered scrubland of the garrigue. Typically made from syrah, carignan, grenache, cinsault and mourvèdre, they are good everyday wines for drinking with meaty, herbal Mediterranean dishes as well as simple meat-based dinners. Good bets include **daubes** and **casseroles** scented with **rosemary** and **thyme**; roasted **leg of lamb with rosemary**; **merguez sausages** served with **roasted red peppers and tapenade**; **sausage and mash**; **lamb chop with new potatoes**; **cold (or warm) roast beef**; and **meat and potato pie**. These wines are also good with **Provençal stuffed vegetables** and **roasted Mediterranean vegetables scattered with thyme, garlic and rosemary**.

M

Madeira

what it tastes like: Madeira is almost immortal; it lasts so long that, when talking about a bottle from a particular year, it is not enough to use the usual shorthand of '01 or '98, it is necessary to specify the century.

'If I refer to "old" Madeira, I'm really talking about something from the 1800s,' clarified Chris Blandy, CEO of Blandy's, as he showed me around the family bottle vault in Funchal, in which there were bottles going back as far as 1811.

Madeira is a fortified wine made on the small Portuguese island from which it takes its name and which lies about 700 kilometres off the African coast on more or less the same latitude as Casablanca. It's a wine that is pushed to extremes long before bottling, through exposure to oxygen and to heat (pipes of Madeira used to be carried as ballast in the holds of ships voyaging to the New World, so the wine passed through the tropics). As a consequence, Madeira is virtually indestructible, and the very best wines get better and better with age. A truly great Madeira doesn't fade, it becomes more itself with every decade that passes.

The best wines, and the ones made in the vintage style for keeping, are those made with named grapes. The four most common – from driest to richest and sweetest – are sercial, verdelho, bual and malmsey, all of them white grapes. Sercial tastes like roasted almonds and the white and green peelings of sweet-and-sour eating and cooking apples; verdelho often has a gently tropical dried-peach flavour; bual is more raisined, with hints of caramel, parkin and allspice; malmsey is all about the mellow, rich flavour of roasted nuts, raisins and dried figs and bonfire toffee. You might also encounter wines made from the rare terrantez (they're usually particularly nutty) or bastardo, which fall in the middle of the dry–sweet spectrum. The common threads in all Madeira are dried fruit and nuts, a gentle crème brûlée, and an almost blinding acidity, which cuts through the sugar and tastes like crystallized lemon and grapefruit peel exploding in your mouth and after you swallow ('You feel it here,' as Humberto Jardim, president of Henriques & Henriques, said to me, drawing two fingers down his neck).

Cheaper styles – the majority of Madeira – are usually made with the red grape tinta negra and are likely to taste warmly of molasses, fruit cake, parkin, and raisins. The flavours are simpler than those of vintage wines made from a declared grape, but they still taste like Christmas in a glass.

what to eat: I've heard some enthusiasts say they enjoy Madeira with curry, as if it were a chutney. For me, Madeira is a wine less for the table and more for the armchair: a drink for mid-morning, late afternoon or after dinner (those time slots are more hypothetical than realistic, at least in my life, but I live in hope).

You may want food to nibble with it. A glass of Madeira makes a good snack with a handful of **almonds** or a piece of **hard cheese**. Try dry, fierce sercial with Cheddar or Wensleydale, or the richer, fuller bual with blue cheese – salty Roquefort or Stichelton. The chef Fergus Henderson is known for his highly civilized habit of taking a glass of 100-year-old Madeira and a slice of **seed cake** for elevenses. (His restaurant St John in Farringdon, London, sells fine old Madeiras by the glass – these wines last for years once the bottle is opened, which makes them excellent restaurant wines as well as excellent anniversary wines – you can splash out on a bottle and enjoy occasional celebratory glasses over a year or more.) I'm right with Fergus on the cake: dry cake goes superbly well with Madeira. By dry cake, which doesn't sound very appetizing, I mean either traditional seed cake or the dense sponge cake with the crusted sugar top that in the UK is called Madeira cake (in Madeira they have no idea what we mean by this) and which is usually made using butter and a higher proportion of flour than you would put in a Victoria sponge and baked in a loaf tin.

Madeira also tastes good with dried-fruit-packed **panforte** and with **mince pies**.

M

The less expensive, sweeter styles (either made from a blend of bual and malmsey or from tinta negra mole) can work well with **chocolate**. I also like these simpler, highly Christmassy, wines with **bolo de mel da Madeira** – which translates as Madeira honey cake, although none of the recipes I've seen contain any actual honey. I first ate this after completing a tasting at Blandy's, where my tasting notes, particularly for the wines made with bual, contained words such as 'ginger', 'cloves', 'allspice', 'parkin' and 'almonds.' At the end of the tasting I was given a small, dense piece of cake made with precisely those ingredients. Perfection. It's traditionally eaten on Madeira at Christmas.

malbec
also known as cot

what it tastes like: There are two very different styles of malbec: one grown in Argentina and one in France. Malbec in Argentina is such a huge success that, for the moment at least, it has eclipsed the wines it makes in its French homeland. I would like to celebrate both.

The malbec of Cahors – the so-called 'black wines' – in the Lot department of south-west France has traditionally been a very dense and tannic wine. Deep-coloured, intense and hard when young, Cahors defines the word tannin. The wines are stern and can take decades to come around; when they do they are a true delight. I remember tasting my first thirty-year-old Cahors, without knowing what it was, and thinking it seemed to be an old bordeaux, but not quite. There is a pleasure in old wine quite unlike the pleasure you get from young wine and with Cahors, which ages incredibly well, you can have that for a fraction of the cost of a claret.

The malbec of Argentina, by contrast, is still intense and still deeply coloured but much more exuberant and bouncy. It has a piercing, fruity quality. It smells of violets, blueberries, mulberries and earth, and tastes of liquorice, chocolate and an abundance of black, juicy berries. As the tannins have a supple quality, it is readily drunk young. Argentina's biggest and best malbec-growing area is the province of Mendoza, which is itself divided into many regions and subregions, each with its own taste profile. Altitude plays a big part in the eventual flavour of the wine. Malbec is also produced high up in Salta, to the north, where it makes impressively refined wines, as well as in Patagonia in the south and in the hot province of La Rioja.

Malbec has become such a huge export for Latin America that its style has also begun to influence France: it is now possible to find malbec in Cahors that is vinified not in the old-fashioned, gritty, grippy style but to be fresher and more approachable when it is young – more forward, more fruity.

what to eat: In Argentina it is almost impossible to avoid **steak**, and surely only a vegetarian would want to. A juicy sirloin from a cow that has grazed on the pampas is about as good as it gets, though you might want to hold the chimichurri (parsley, oregano, garlic and chilli) sauce, which isn't perfect with the wine. In Mendoza, steak is served with **humita** – a steamed corn husk filled with corn ground with milk – and perhaps a salad of palm hearts. Wherever you go in the country, **beef** is on the menu – and this is where tannic but ripe malbec really shines, its lushness enhancing the plushness of the meat while the protein in the meat feels to soften the wine.

One of the most luxurious beef recipes I've eaten with malbec was called Lomo Tata, a family recipe from the Catena family, who make wine in Argentina, that was written up by the food and drink expert Fiona Beckett in *Decanter* magazine back in 2001. It uses beef fillet, prunes, pancetta and redcurrant jelly – I've sometimes added bay leaves too – and is glorious with the sweet, deep fruit of Argentine malbec. Delicious – and the recipe is online in the *Decanter* archives.

The Gaucho Grill in London has a magnificent selection of wines from Argentina but I don't think I've ever been there without ordering a steak. I asked Phil Crozier, the restaurant's Head of Wine, who spends a lot of time in Argentina tasting and eating if there was anything he liked to drink with malbec that didn't involve rump, fillet or sirloin. He said he likes to drink malbec from Luján de Cuyo with **spaghetti bolognaise**, a match that reminded me of ragù with soft barbera. 'There's a silkiness to wine from Luján that you don't get with the Uco Valley, where the wines are more nervous, more tense. I'd be more likely to have an Uco malbec with a rib roast. Getting away from beef, I make a kind of smoked pork and lentil soup and that's good with malbec. Also just plain **pork chops** are very nice, or tomato sauce with pork and Uco Valley malbec.'

Along the same lines, the thump and gloss of malbec from a sunnier climate, or made in a more modern way in France, works well with all kinds of **spicy pork dishes**, such as **pulled pork with a sweetly spicy sauce**.

Old-school styles of Cahors are also excellent with steak, although in a different way. These wines go very well with the heavy local food – **cassoulet** and **spicy Toulouse sausages** and **magret de canard** – and they are exceptionally good as they age, becoming less heavy and more scented and open, with a library smell. I remember drinking one in the company of a man called Anthony Gladstone-Thompson, a Francophile who was kindly helping me with some bookshelves. Anthony was quite particular about his Cahors and I don't think mine came up to scratch, but his suggestion that I pop to the butcher and fry up a pile of merguez sausages to have with it was spot on.

what the winemakers eat

Gaston Williams, Achaval Ferrer, Argentina: 'Of course the first place would be for a barbecue. As for the rest, locro is maybe our most traditional dish for winter time: a dense stew based on corn and sweet potato with meat, potato, beans, vegetables and red sausage. And since we also had a lot of Italian immigration a good fettuccine alla puttanesca would marry perfectly with our malbec.'

Tatiana Sielecki, Revancha, Argentina: 'As true Argentines, we love our malbec with a good "asado" (barbecue). We tend to have it with medium-rare T-bone or rib eye. The only sauce we put on our steak is chimichurri but just salt also works! The secret is in the experience of the "asado-man". In terms of sides, we usually do grilled potatoes and some mixed green salads.'

marsanne

This white grape makes aromatic wines that are reminiscent of marzipan and almond blossom, with flashes of rich lemon. It's known as a grape of the Rhône, where, as in California, it is blended with roussanne (and other varieties), but the largest marsanne holding in the world is actually in the wine and wetlands area of Nagambie Lakes, Victoria, in Australia. Here, Tahbilk make a marsanne that is distinctively Australian in style, faintly reminiscent of dried grass, marmalade, dried orange rind and honeysuckle. I've enjoyed drinking this wine in Vietnamese restaurants in London; Tahbilk themselves suggest having it with **asparagus, Parmesan and mushroom spaghetti** (the recipe is on their website); **belly of pork rubbed with Asian spices** is also a good choice.

See also Rhône – white blends.

mencía

what it tastes like: An earthy-tasting red grape grown in the regions of Bierzo and Ribeira Sacra in north-west Spain as well as in the Dão in Portugal, mencía has recently become very fashionable. It is brilliant with dinner because it has a savoury quality that gets along well with flavours that can rub more sweetly fruity wines up the wrong way. It is relatively low in acidity, usually medium-bodied, and can taste quite rustic – with a scent of roasted and fresh berries, a smoky-savoury nuance and a gentle florality.

what to eat: If you chill it slightly, mencía can be light enough to go with fish – say, **cod with green lentils**. It is superb with **slow-roast shoulder of pork**, perhaps served with smoky mashed potatoes. It would go well with most red-meated Spanish dishes. More usefully, its combination of savour and non-heaviness means that it works with all sorts of tricky dinners. As Willie Lebus of Bibendum Wine pointed out to me, Bierzo is the ideal wine to open with Diana Henry's '**Roast Jerusalem artichokes and chicken with anchovy, walnut and parsley relish**' (the recipe is in her *A Bird in the Hand*, a treasure of a book). This would be a curveball of a dinner for most wines, the bitterness of the walnuts, the leafy parsley, salty anchovy and awkward artichokes, wrong-footing any sweetly ripe red, while most whites just don't feel savoury or substantial enough. Mencía solves the problem beautifully, and is a great card to play whenever you encounter similar ingredients.

Mencía is also good with the **stuffed breads** you find in Galicia – so substantial they need a red wine.

M

M

merlot

what it tastes like: Merlot is a tough grape to recognize because it can have all kinds of different flavours, though stewed damsons are very often in there. Its most salient feature is a silky, smooth texture. At its lightest, merlot can be lively, fresh and gently leafy. In a warm climate, if it is allowed to get very ripe, and the wine is over-extracted and oaked, it becomes a thickly solid builder's tea of a wine: high in alcohol, dense, tasting of plums, drinking chocolate powder, blackberries, red and black liquorice, spices and coffee.

Merlot is soft and easy, not spiky with acidity or tannin. This innocuousness has given it a mass-market appeal, and seen the grape widely planted on an international scale, from California to Chile to Australia to South Africa. It has also been derided as the blandest of red grapes and, to be fair, there is a lot of cheap, dull merlot swilling around that is little more than slightly sweet, grape-based, fruity alcohol. The better stuff – usually found in cooler areas, such as Sonoma, Washington State or Margaret River – has a velvet texture and fine tannins.

Merlot is (almost always) at its best in blends. It is like Polyfilla; it creeps in there, filling holes and smoothing gaps. It also has a tremendous capacity to take on the personality of other grapes. Bottle merlot with 10 per cent carmenère (a low enough amount that it does not need to be declared on the front label, which can still simply say 'Merlot') and, hey presto, you get a much more interesting wine. Merlot is found in very good blends in Bergerac, Margaret River and the Supertuscans of central Italy. It is famously at its finest in Bordeaux, where it is not just the most widely planted grape but also an essential part of the bordeaux blend, bringing suppleness and succulence to cabernet sauvignon's awkward corners. Because merlot is approachable young, producers add more of it to wines intended for early drinking. For instance, most of the inexpensive wine bottled as bordeaux or bordeaux superieur. On the more cabernet-dominated left-bank first wines will often have a higher proportion of cabernet sauvignon, while the second wine of the same château majors on merlot. It's on the right bank of Bordeaux – in St Emilion, Pomerol and the satellite appellations of Lalande-de-Pomerol, Castillon Côtes de Bordeaux and Montagne-, Lussac-, Puisseguin- and St-Georges St-Emilion – that merlot really shines, taking primary place in the blend. In St Emilion especially, merlot often has the densely spicy taste of fruitcake and the capacity to age for many years. It's unusual to find bordeaux that is made entirely from merlot, but among the exceptions are two of the grandest wine names in the world: Petrus and Le Pin.

what to eat: So often straight merlot is less a wine for which you think, 'Oh, that's a lovely combination,' than one that just slips down, in a generic red-vinous-fuel-drunk-on-the-sofa-watching-*House-of-Cards*-box-sets kind of way. That said, inexpensive merlot, especially the roasted-plums-and-cocoa-nibs versions from Chile, is such an easy, comforting wine that it is a great mood (and to some extent taste) match with full-flavoured comfort food. Its glossy solidity is perfect with **cottage or shepherd's pie**; the refried beans, cheese and soured cream of **enchiladas**; **burgers**; **chilli con carne** ramped up with a square of bitter chocolate; **barbecue sauce**; and **heavy meat marinades**.

Juicy merlot and plump merlot-cabernet blends from Australia and the US are also good with **sweet roast gammon**, **steak with a sesame-dressed salad** and lamb dinners that incorporate a fruity element – for example, **lamb and redcurrant burgers** or lamb with a redcurrant reduction.

More savoury merlot blends, which would typically but not exclusively be from Bergerac, Bordeaux or Tuscany, go well with **rich pâtés** and **terrines**; **duck** (magret de canard, roast duck); **roast beef**; and **meat casseroles**.

The heft of even the finest merlot-based wine is not always a natural with food, particularly when it's young. Jane Anson, a wine

M

expert and writer based in Bordeaux, points out that, when it comes to St Emilion, 'Some of the supercharged wines of recent years can be overpowering with what's on the plate.' She says she loves to find 'older vintages that remind me of what a perfect combination the merlot grape grown on a clay and limestone soil can be. Last Christmas, to eat with our turkey brined for twenty-four hours so that it's lovely and juicy, we opened a magnum of Chateau Beauséjour-Duffau-Lagarosse 1985 (nowadays just called Beauséjour) that had softened to an irresistible blend of Black Mission figs, truffles, leather and ever so gentle liquorice. It made the whole lunch better. I remember we also had very **slow-roasted carrots**, so they were slightly caramelized. Those flavours, particularly, would be too subtle with a fruit-bombed young St Emilion.'

A maturing St Emilion or other merlot-based bordeaux would be excellent with the earthy taste of a **roast rib of beef**, or with **venison**. Older St Emilion, which is less juicy and chocolatey, and tastes more autumnal, leathery and measured, works very well with **veal chop with dauphinoise potatoes** or a simple **boeuf bourguignon**. **Roasted root vegetables – butternut squash, parsnips, turnips, carrots – with sage or thyme** (or both) work well too. The traditional match is **lampreys cooked in red wine**. My favourite St Emilion dinners are brasserie food; visit the excellent L'Envers du Décor in the narrow streets of St Emilion itself for inspiration. Last time I was there I ate a kind of **shepherd's pie, but one that was made with duck and topped with sweet potato**. It was rich and unctuous and beyond gorgeous with a bottle of Château La Tour Figeac.

what the winemakers eat
Stéphanie de Boüard-Rivoal, Chateau Angélus, St Emilion, France: 'One thing I love is black truffle risotto. I'd say to pick a wine that's in the right period for that, and 2000 would be ideal for me but of course if I had a 1990 I wouldn't say no . . . I also love to have a nice piece of veal with some mushroom. And some fish, in particular turbot, can be very good with our wines. That might sound surprising but if you have a wine that's not too young, and one from a vintage that's not a blockbuster, for example 1998 or 2001, it's very good.'

Château Troplong Mondot, St Emilion, France. This château has a restaurant whose menu is designed to showcase the wines and includes dishes such as breast of pigeon roasted with herbs, and breast of partridge stuffed with cabbage and lard d'Arnad, with roasted parsnip tips, slow-cooked thighs and game stock with Cognac.

See also Pomerol.

mourvèdre

also known as mataro, monastrell

what it tastes like: There is an element of the romantic hero to this grape. Its high tannin content can make it tough and unapproachable, yet in the right conditions these are transformed into an attractive gruffness with no shortage of character and integrity.

It's called mataro in Australia and California, and known as monastrell in Spain, and along France's Mediterranean coast it flourishes as mourvèdre.

Mourvèdre is dark, feral and slightly rough. High in alcohol, with a rasp of dried Mediterranean herbs and a hint of violets, old leather and farmyards, it adds a gamey spice to Châteauneuf-du-Pape blends, but (like many of us) it loves heat and reaches its pinnacle further south still, in the blistering amphitheatre of Bandol, where it has a kind of wild elegance that forms the mainstay of a blend that may also include grenache, cinsault, syrah and carignan.

As monastrell and as mataro this grape makes less wild and more solidly textured wines – inky and opaque, with a scent of brambles and a touch of sweet violets. In Spain, monastrell is often sweetly dense, redolent of spicy blueberries.

what to eat: Bandol loves **thyme** and **garlic**. It's the perfect wine to pour on a sunny summer's night with grilled or **griddled red peppers, aubergines and courgettes doused in olive oil and sprinkled with thyme** (add pommes dauphinoise and green salad to make up a meal). Its heady aromatics also suit **ratatouille; stuffed Provençal vegetables** filled with herbs and rice and **black olives** and tomatoes; **ragout of wild mushrooms with thyme; peppers** drizzled with a garlic and anchovy pesto dressing; and in the same way the garlic burn and warm spice of **merguez sausages**.

It sounds thoughtlessly back-of-supermarket-label to suggest

M

putting wine with **grilled meat**, but it's a seriously good combination here. The animal scent of Bandol is great with the blackened char you get from a hot grill or burning coals, whether the meat in question is decent butcher's chicken, guinea fowl or lamb.

Lamb is Bandol's favourite meat. It already smells of rosemary, even when it's raw, and unbasted, and there is a real resonance with the dried-herb scent of French mourvèdre. Any kind of **slow-cooked lamb casserole** flavoured with **Mediterranean herbs** (bay leaves, rosemary, thyme, garlic) is good here.

The more juicy styles of the grape in Spain and Australia (labelled as monastrell or mataro) bring out the fruitiness of a rich **morcilla** and can also work as a foil to the rasp of cumin and coriander seeds when they are combined with rich meat. Perhaps try it with a **spinach, morcilla and chorizo salad** or a **lamb and prune tagine**, or Moroccan-spiced slow-cooked lamb with date and almond couscous.

Mourvèdre in all its forms also has the depth that's required to stand up to **venison** and other game (**pheasant**, **roast duck**, **rabbit**, **grouse**). Choose the gamey scent of an older French wine to pick up on the feral scent of well-hung meat. Younger Bandol will cut, say, a **venison and juniper casserole** or **fricassee of rabbit with thyme and cheesy noodles** with its herbal riff and tannic punctuation.

The solid, fruity versions from California, Australia and Spain act more as stomach-warmers and boot-warmers – if you have a venison stew and you're serving it with polenta, then the wine will be just as heavy and closely textured as the food. I like the bluffness of Australian mataro with **rare venison and sesame noodles**, and the dark juiciness of a Spanish monastrell with **redcurrant and venison burgers topped with melted Roquefort**.

This grape is also good with **glossy beef casseroles**. Go for a French or Australian version if black olives, thyme, mushrooms or anchovies are involved.

what the winemakers eat
The legendary recipes of **Lulu Peyraud of Domaine Tempier, Bandol, France,** are collected in Richard Olney's wonderful and influential book *Lulu's Provençal Table*. They include potato and sorrel gratin, sardines grilles, gigot à la ficelle,

See also rosé.

bream with fennel and her famous recipe for bouillabaisse, which she liked to serve with a glass of young, chilled red Bandol. Guests of the chatelaine of Domaine Tempier also speak of being served small toasts with tapenade and a bowl of radishes with a cool aperitif glass of Tempier rosé (which contains about 50% mourvèdre).

Afshin Moulavi, Manousakis Winery, Crete: 'Free-range goat. Slowly roasted in a cast iron pot, the Greek way, with potatoes and some rosemary, and the sweetness of garlic.'

Muscadet

Muscadet is the daddy of fish wines. This dry white wine is made from melon de bourgogne grown on the Atlantic coast of France, around the mouth of the River Nantes. It is relatively neutral, sometimes now jokingly referred to as 'the picpoul of the north', and has a gently saline, stony flavour that might be enhanced by ageing on its lees (sur lie), giving it more body, and a slightly yeasty taste. Unpretentious and plain, a carafe of Muscadet happily sluices down most **white fish** – say, haddock with boiled potatoes and parsley sauce – or **fish pie**, or **fish and bay leaf brochettes**, as well as seafood – say, **spaghetti vongole**. It is superb with **moules marinière.**

muscat (moscato, muscatel, zibibbo)

Muscat is a catch-all term for a number of different grapes, not all of them related, though they do share the distinction of being the only grapes whose wine actually smells and tastes – of grapes. Muscat is used to make three distinct styles of wine: a dry white, which tastes of eau de cologne and orange-blossom water; a sweet but not *very* sweet sparkling or frizzante wine usually referred to as moscato, although the word is simply a synonym for muscat; and properly sticky sweet wines.

dry muscat This is not a hugely popular wine, though good examples can be found in Sicily (where it's known as zibibbo) and also Spain. It can taste good with **sea urchin pasta** and with **tandoori chicken**.

moscato This is a delightful lightly sparkling white wine that's low in alcohol and smells like fleshy white grapes do when you bite into them and a floral fragrance streams out. It's also reminiscent of melon, ripe nectarines and neroli. Moscato is sweet but it's a kind of isotonic sweetness – one that's easy to approach rather than one that weighs you down. The most attractive and delicate moscato comes from northern Italy – Moscato d'Asti is the best known. The style is now huge in the US, as well as in Australia, with American and Aussie versions often tasting less dancingly floral and more fruity – all nectarines, pineapple and starfruit. Moscato is a drink for sunny evenings and weekend afternoons, with a large bowl of **strawberries, nectarine** or **mango tart with crème pâtissière, apricots,** or **baked peaches with rose water**. Alternatively, Michela Marenco of Contero recommends her Moscato d'Asti di Strevi with 'fresh cheese: **Stracchino** or **fresh Gorgonzola**'.

sweet wines Muscat blanc à petit grains is the particular variety largely responsible for the vins doux naturels (fortified sweet wines) of Muscat de Beaumes de Venise and Muscat de St Jean de Minervois, which have grape-like freshness and an orange-blossom lift, as well as being sweet enough to drink with pudding. These wines go with **madeleines; nectarine or mango tart**; they freshen up **chocolate cake** and work well with **orange-scented bread and butter pudding**. The same grape makes superb Liqueur Muscat in Australia (look for Rutherglen Muscat) – a very sweet, dark fortified wine as rich as demerara sugar and caramel with hints of coffee and molasses. Rutherglen Muscat is gorgeous with **ice cream (plain or with pralines), pecan tart** and **crème caramel**. In Pantelleria, the island off Sicily, zibibbo (muscat of Alexandria) is used to make another sweet wine, Passito di Pantelleria, that tastes of dried apricots and peaches injected with light caramel. It's glorious with Christmas **mince pies**.

N

nebbiolo

also known as chiavenasca, spanna

what it tastes like: Roses and tar are the classic tasting notes for the tannic but also haunting and regal grape that makes Barolo and Barbaresco.

The first time I visited Piemonte, Chiara Boschis, maker of sublimely fragrant Barolo, broke into a – loud, possibly quite startling to other diners, – burst of Handel's 'Hallelujah Chorus' as the food and wine arrived at our restaurant table. The second time, standing on the steps of his family estate, Proprietà Sperino, in the foothills of the Alps, another winemaker, Luca De Marchi, got almost as spiritual when he tried to explain his feelings for nebbiolo:

'It's my personal opinion that nebbiolo is far better than pinot noir. I consider it so good that I don't consider it a grape. Nebbiolo is the only variety for which the description is "ethereal" – because nebbiolo is a state of mind.'

I know what he means. There are days when I hope I'll die and go to Piemonte. This north-western part of Italy, where November mists swirl into the valleys like an incoming tide (*nebbia* means fog in Italian), is virtually the only place in the world where nebbiolo is found.

Of the two most famous nebbiolo wines, Barolo is the aristocrat and expresses itself with finesse – look for the intense cherry-kirsch taste of wines from the village of Barolo itself – while Barbaresco tends to be more yielding earlier. Barbaresco is also, arguably, more populist: easier drinking, more open and loose. It often has more of a flavour of red fruit and rose hips, and a warm waft of sandalwood and suede.

Both are built for ageing – nebbiolo has masses of tannin and vibrant acidity – and can taste uncomfortably narrow and astringent when young. Fruity is not an adjective often applied to this grape. Its flavours are autumnal and they are savoury. It smells of roses and violets pressed in the pages of an old book. The more it ages, the more the scent of leather and dust, dried sour cherries, tar, liquorice root, incense and truffle unfold. Nebbiolo is awkward. It can't help itself, it's intellectual.

Winemakers in Piemonte say things like, 'Life has become too rushed,' but despite this resistance to the speed of the twenty-first century there is a resurgence of an earlier-drinking style of nebbiolo, which spends less time, and sometimes no time, in oak and is more approachable when young. These wines are usually made under the Langhe Nebbiolo banner, and although it's a more lowly label, one of these wines from a top producer usually offers more pleasure than a cheap version of Barolo.

Almost nowhere beyond Piemonte (and Lombardy, which neighbours it) has succeeded in growing nebbiolo that is capable of making good wine, but the exceptions are, unexpectedly, Australian. The antipodean style is smoother and less wild than its Italian counterpart but still unmistakably, wonderfully nebbiolo.

what to eat: The savoury gravity and bite of nebbiolo provide a beautiful counterpoint to **creamy soufflés and sauces**, **eggs** and **cheese**. A classic dish is fonduta, an incredibly rich fondue using Fontina cheese (from the Valle d'Aosta), butter and egg yolks that goes very well with the vigour of a young wine. Nebbiolo is also good with a gooey slice of thick **onion tart**. Because of its tannic punctuation, nebbiolo is very at home with a side salad of **bitter leaves** – rocket, crimson radicchio or white endive. This makes onion tart or a rich cheese soufflé with a winter salad a pretty perfect supper with a glass of nebbiolo. At home I often **stuff onions** with a fried mixture of their own chopped up innards, rosemary, cheese (Parmesan or Toma) and cream, wrap them in prosciutto and bake them in the oven. They make a great supper with a side of chicory, tomato and radicchio salad and also work as a side themselves, with tagliata and rocket.

Nebbiolo's autumnal flavours suit **autumnal food**. It loves **pumpkins**, **squashes**, and **mushrooms**, so try stuffed pumpkin; **pumpkin and sage risotto**; **roasted squash with roast pork and** fennel seeds; raw and cooked **mushroom salads** or any of these flavours in stuffed pasta with ricotta.

Despite its might, nebbiolo also has a certain delicacy and lighter young versions (say, a fragrant, unoaked Langhe Nebbiolo, or a Barolo in a silkier style) are strangely good with the tuna and veal dish that is **vitello tonnato**, or with **osso buco**, **veal chop** and **braised fennel**, or veal **saltimbocca**.

The younger the wine, the more fat it can take. You might put an older, fully mature nebbiolo with lean bresaola and use a young one to cut through the fattiness of **duck** or **goose**. There is no nebbiolo, young or old, princely or humble (actually, I should say relatively humble, as I am not sure that any nebbiolo is truly humble), that is not superb with beef. A few suggestions: an unctuous, slow-cooked **beef casserole** (with mushrooms, maybe) served with **grainy polenta**; griddled steaks and **bone marrow** with a salt and olive oil parsley salad; **carne cruda** – the Italian version of steak tartare, which is very simply dressed with just olive oil, salt and pepper and lemon juice.

They don't just know how to make wines in Piemonte, they know how to eat as well. I once sat in on an excruciating (for me) conversation in a small bar in Serralunga in which one local was describing the eating habits of the English to another as if detailing the feeding habits of an alien species of ants: 'They go to the supermarket and they buy a plastic carton with something in it like spaghetti and ragù and they take it home and they put it in the microwave. *Fa schiffo* [It's revolting].'

Likewise nebbiolo has very little respect for that sort of fast food. It is very happy with the other sort of fast food: good ingredients, simply cooked – for example, **tagliolini with butter and good cheese**. Because it is such a distinctive grape and because food and drink in Piemonte are so intertwined, the best eating ideas come from the same place as the wine.

Besides the cream and butter typical of anywhere north of the olive oil belt, the Piemontese eat wild mushrooms and game (**pheasants, quail, hare**); **stinco di vitello** (braised veal shank); and a range of home-made **pork salamis and spicy sausages** (such as salsiccia di bra). Nebbiolo is at home with all of these. It also goes with simple **risotto milanese** and **chicken liver crostini**.

Rosemary, **thyme** and **sage** are good nebbiolo herbs. Try making **roast quail and sage** from the *River Café Easy Cook Book* – quails, slicked in olive oil, rolled in large amounts of chopped sage and sea salt and roasted until crispy. In autumn I love to buy **pumpkin ravioli** from Lina Stores in Soho, and serve it with melted butter spiked with fragrant fried sage leaves.

The grape's earthy quality and its often grainy texture mean it's also comfortable with **polenta** and **chickpeas**.

I haven't even mentioned **truffles** yet. Piemonte is home to the exquisite delicacy that is the white truffle – tartufo bianco – celebrated by the Alba truffle fair, which runs from mid-October to mid-November. The best ways to enjoy fragrant, musky truffles are the simplest – shaved on to the local, hand-made tajarin pasta (tagliolini), on a fried egg and in fonduta. Or in a soufflé.

During truffle season, everyone becomes a truffle hunter. I remember a winemaker telling me his rubbish had not been collected for two weeks because the bin men had all gone looking for truffles. It was generally accepted that this was a reasonable priority. I can see why. Nebbiolo and white truffles is as good as the eating and drinking experience gets.

what the winemakers eat

Luke Lambert, Yarra Valley, Australia: 'One of my favourite dishes to cook and feed visitors is three-cheese, black-truffle-topped, braised-wild-deer-ragù lasagne. It's a mouthful to say and a handful to eat, but a perfect match to our nebbiolo.

'The wild deer in the Yarra are particularly tasty in a slow-cooked tomato-and-herb-rich ragù, sandwiched between some home-made pasta sheets that my daughter rolls out. (She's only six but knows it's got to be egg yolks only, so the pasta is a radioactive-yellow colour to be extra tasty.) Then unhealthy amounts of Tomme de Chèvre, Comté and Parmigiano Reggiano on top. The key ingredient is freshly shaved black truffle over the top. One of my grape suppliers, Greg Kerr of Tibooburra Vineyard in the Upper Yarra, established a truffière ten years ago and every July gets a small but steady supply of excellent black truffles. When they're in season it's the perfect way to tie the deer lasagne with the nebbiolo.'

Mario Fontana, Cascina Fontana, Barolo, Italy: 'Langhe Nebbiolo I like in summer, a little bit chilled, with a tomato salad with red onion in it. Barolo? There are two different times to drink Barolo. I like it most of all when it's young with brasato [a typical Piemontese dish of a joint of beef cooked in Barolo and served with the reduced cooking liquid]. Then there's the second part of Barolo, later, when you open an older bottle more than twenty years old *after* a family lunch. I remember all the lunches when I was small and all the adults stayed two or three hours just talking, calmly, over a bottle of old Barolo and I didn't understand. Now I understand. And always when I have a bottle of old Barolo, I remember that.'

Finally, I am told the late **Aldo Conterno**, on being asked what he drank his Barolo with, used to reply: 'With television.'

nerello mascalese

This Sicilian grape makes exciting pale red wines on the volcanic soil of the slopes of Mount Etna. Its light body and ability to express a sense of place mean it is often compared to pinot noir, though its taste is usually more savage and herbal: this is a wine reminiscent of rust, black tea, smoke, minerals and spice, as well as silk and wild red berries. I would want to drink this with food that also had a wild side. If you were making a pasta sauce, you'd need to use **proper pancetta** with a slightly dirty, feral taste and not clean bacon. It goes with the earthy taste of **panelle** (Sicilian chickpea fritters), with **barbecued sardines**, with **rustic sausages** and **salamis** and **'nduja gnocchi**, and **Sicilian fish stew**. Most of all, with simple southern Italian food that has not been too cleaned-up.

nero d'avola

Nero d'avola thrives in Sicily where it makes red wines that taste of plums, mulberries, dried red cherries and cranberries, and sun-baked earth. It can be medium-bodied, sappy and refreshing or, when aged in oak, deep and spicily rich, with hints of tobacco, but it usually has a softness to its texture. Those lighter versions (and also those when nero d'avola is blended with frappato as in Cerasuolo di Vittoria) can be very good with **fish**, in particular oily fish like sardines or tuna but also with **white fish cooked in a tomato sauce**. Nero d'avola has the perfect balance of savouriness and ripe fruit for that tricky Sicilian dish, **pasta con sarde** (pasta with pine nuts, sardines, fennel tops, raisins, onion and chilli). The grape is actually superb with meaty sweet-sour dishes such as **coniglio in agrodolce** (sweet and sour rabbit) or **caponata**. Speaking of caponata, **aubergines** in almost all guises are wonderful with silky nero d'avola: try **pasta alla norma; griddled aubergines with courgettes, olive oil and herbs; aubergine rolls filled with ricotta or with feta and basil; aubergine tagine; salad of aubergine with peppers and pomegranate seeds; baked aubergine with tomato and pesto; roasted aubergine with anchovies**. You get the idea. Nero d'avola has a fruitiness that suits the gleam of **pomegranate seeds**, perhaps in a chicken or squeaky halloumi salad. The meatier oaked wines are good with – well, meat. Try a fatty **pork burger** or a **Vietnamese pork belly bun; oxtail stew; or slow-cooked shoulder of pork with spices and date and almond cous cous**.

N

orange wine

A pretty amber in colour, this is a niche but also increasingly fashionable style of wine made from white grapes that is traditional in Georgia but made all over the world. The fermenting grape juice (known as must) is left in contact with the grape skins for several days, weeks or even months, during which time it extracts both colour and tannin from the skin. The result is a wine marked by its texture, and grippy feel. Flavours of course depend on the particular grape varieties used but, while tannic, they tend to be more subtle and less likely to have wine tasters reaching for the 'gooseberry, kumquats, lemon' fruit bowl descriptors than white wines made in the ordinary way. The lack of strident flavours to create potential clashes makes orange wines exceptionally good food wines. The quietly assertive texture helps too. There is no need to think too hard about what you drink these with. Pretty much any lighter food will work. I particularly enjoy orange wines with **langoustine** or **crab pasta**. They are also good at standing their ground with potentially tricky food, such as **Middle Eastern meze** with all its garlic and competing flavours, as well as **Ottolenghi salads** , whose herbs, spices and sweet-and-sour mixture can undermine ordinary wines.

P

picpoul

Saline and refreshing, picpoul used to be introduced as the Muscadet of the south. Now it's so fashionable, you're more likely to hear people try to persuade you to drink Muscadet by calling it the picpoul of the north. The word picpoul is said to mean lip-stinger in the old Oc language and it's sometimes a surprise that a white wine as light and invigorating as picpoul de Pinet is made in the hot, dry Mediterranean climate of the Languedoc. Many of the vineyards of picpoul de Pinet overlook the Bassin de Thau, a huge saltwater lagoon. Locally, picpoul is what you'd drink with the **oysters** freshly plucked from the oyster beds here. It's a great wine for **seafood**, from **moules marinière** to **prawn cocktail**, and simply cooked **white fish generally**. I really like it with **fish burritos** – fish marinated with a paste of blitzed cumin, coriander, fresh coriander, chilli and olive oil and wrapped into a soft tortilla with lime mayonnaise, halves of cherry tomato and chunks of cucumber. Mostly it's a fantastic salty, tangy aperitif that you can't help but carry on drinking whatever happens to be next for dinner.

pinot blanc
also known as pinot bianco, weissburgunder

what it tastes like: In northern Italy, pinot bianco is orange-tinged and crisp. It fits together with a mosaic-like precision and is as focused as cold vodka. In Alsace, pinot blanc makes sparkling as well as still wines, which tend to be rounder and more viscous, almost smoky and musky, with a bit of a roil. In Austria, as weissburgunder, it's taken more seriously and sometimes aged in oak. In Oregon, as pinot blanc, it's refreshing and bright.

what to eat: Pinot bianco is a hugely underrated aperitif, a deliciously fresh wine that picks its way across the palate. The crisper incarnations are good with **Vietnamese rolls** filled with prawns and kumquats, or **orange and fennel salad** with a simple chicken kebab. Most versions also work well with **sushi rolls**, **dim sum**, **shellfish** and **prawn cocktail**. While the musky, viscous wines from Alsace are also delicious with **quiche**, **sloppy onion tart**, **white asparagus tart**, **soft white cheese** and **sauerkraut**.

what the winemakers eat
Aurelia Gouges-Haynes, whose family makes a deliciously pert, unexpected **pinot blanc in Burgundy, France**: 'Lunch-time in Burgundy, jambon persillée. In London, seafood starter.'

pinot grigio
also known as pinot gris and grauburgunder

what it tastes like: The convention with this grape is that when you see the words 'pinot grigio' you can expect a crisp, dry, neutral wine, perhaps with a hint of citrus, and a suggestion of stone. 'Pinot gris', conversely, is likely to be off-dry, and aromatic – floral, perhaps scented like rose petals, and fuller and heavier in the mouth.

At its lowest common denominator, pinot grigio is so invisible you can hardly tell it is there. This has made it hugely popular and also hugely unpopular: people sneer at its vapidity. I have never felt comfortable with pinot-grigio-bashing – a simple, cold, vestigially lemony wine makes a perfect afternoon or early evening thirst-slaker. Italy is a big producer of this style of pinot grigio; it makes so much I sometimes imagine lakes filled with it. Other European countries, notably Hungary, have cashed in on this success, sometimes labelling innocuous pinot grigio in a suspiciously italiano way for more cachet.

Italy also makes spectacularly good pinot grigio. In the mountains of the Alto Adige in the north and in Friuli-Venezia-Giulia in the north-east (in Collio, Colli Orientali and Isonzo), you can find wines that are chiselled and precise, with a clarity that makes them a pleasure to drink.

Winemakers opting to make richer and more aromatic versions of this wine usually helpfully opt to label it pinot gris.

P

In Alsace, pinot gris is particularly distinctive: spicy, roiling with flavour, with notes of honeysuckle, neroli, ginger and musk and a touch of smoke. Alsatian pinot gris might also be dry, off-dry, medium-dry or an intensely sweet dessert wine, made from individually selected berries. In New Zealand, pinot gris still smells prettily floral but is usually simpler and clearer, and off-dry wines (say, up to about 7g of sugar per litre) are currently hugely popular. In the US, Oregon is a pinot gris challenger too, though its wines are often fermented to dryness, with a fruity, melon-like taste.

Pinot grigio is known for its white wine, but the grape actually has a pink, speckled skin, so it can also make wines that are faintly pink – what the French call gris – or, if the fermenting grape juice is left longer in contact with the colour-holding skins, with a surprising depth of colour.

what to eat: Pinot grigio delle Tre Venezie is one of the first wines I remember ordering, as a treat, in my university student days. Back then, crisply citric pinot grigio marked a serious step-up from the gut-rot that was the college bar red and we used to order it on rare meals out at a café chain called the Dôme. I still love to have pinot grigio with **Dôme salad** – it's made with curly endive or cos lettuce, chunks of avocado, fried lardons and grated Gruyère. You arrange the leaves, fried lardons and avocado in a dish, sprinkle the Gruyère over the top, heat the vinaigrette in the lardons pan, making sure to scrape up all the crisp fatty bits, and when the vinaigrette is warm pour it over the salad so that the cheese slightly melts. Serve with crusty white country bread and a crisp glass of pinot grigio.

With a cool glass of pinot grigio from Collio, as gently precise as a snow crystal, I like to put out a wooden board of **Stracchino** (a fresh, young, creamy cow's cheese found in the Veneto, Lombardy and Piemonte), **juicy slices of pear** with the skin still on for texture and **grissini** or bread.

Dry pinot grigio is also good with the sweet, delicate taste of **carpaccio of white fish** – scallops or sea bass; **spaghetti with prawns and a raw tomato sauce**; **white fish cooked en papillote**; **fish with parsley sauce**; **ocean pie** – in fact, with any delicate or creamy seafood or white fish dish, because the wine acts as a cleanser between mouthfuls.

You could also drink clean-cut pinot grigio with **pasta with pesto** (though I usually prefer a wine with a bit more sharpness and elbow); **mozzarella, pine nut and aubergine salad**; creamy pasta dishes such as **spaghetti carbonara**; **asparagus, pea** or **seafood risotto**; or with crunchy **Vietnamese rolls**.

The texture and weight of richer off-dry pinot gris, particularly those smoky wines from Alsace, are good with smoky and/or cheesy foods, such as **smoked ham** or **smoked cheese** in a **creamy pasta sauce**. Try them with **macaroni cheese**, **Tomme de Savoie**, or with **flammekueche**, the Alsatian speciality that consists of a parchment-thin pizza base, crispy and almost burnt round the edges, topped with cheese and bacon.

Off- or medium-dry pinot gris works really well with **spicy food**. The lift of aromatics and the gentle sweetness mingle beautifully with the fragrant sweetness of **coconut milk curries** such as **Thai green curry**. Pinot gris is also great with Peter Gordon's **nam phrik num dressing**, which is made by liquidizing mango, ginger, chillies, coriander, nam pla and mint. Nam phrik num is energizing with roast, fried or poached **salmon fillets** (you could also serve it with chicken) and an off-dry pinot gris is the perfect match.

Other spicy food that works well with off-dry pinot gris includes **quails rubbed with rose harissa** and **roasted pork or roasted pork belly marinated in five-spice, garlic and soy sauce**. I also like pinot gris with **roast duck with a soy and hoisin sauce**, or with roast **duck à l'orange** – the succulence of the white wine is perfect with the meltingly soft meat and the citrus is better with white wine than with red.

what the winemakers eat
Clive Jones, General Manager, Nautilus, Marlborough, New Zealand: 'One of the best matches we've had with our off-dry pinot gris is abalone with garlic and ginger, stir-fried up. The wine has texture and doesn't just sit in the background waiting for the other flavours to come through.'

pinot noir

also known as spätburgunder, blauburgunder

what it tastes like: Pinot is hard to grow but magical when it's right. In the words of Aubert de Villaine, proprietor of Domaine de la Romanée Conti, 'Pinot noir does not exist. It's a ghost.' The very best is exactly that: sublimely effortless, treading so lightly you experience it as a seamlessly fluent, graceful song of a wine. I have seen grown men tearing up over pinot noir, and that's on the first sip (and usually either DRC or Domaine des Lambrays Clos des Lambrays is the culprit).

Good cheap versions are a different wine altogether, but they can provide huge pleasure too, particularly when drunk in their first flush of youth. Young pinot might be so softly rounded as to seem almost sweet, or filled with sappy verve and crunchy with red berries. Pinot is always a light (in taste as well as appearance) grape, but it is also deeply marked by the place in which it's grown.

Burgundy is where pinot noir reaches its finest and most dream-like expression, though the best wines command steep prices and are made in such small quantities that securing an allocation demands planning and persistence, and often also big spending. This is also a complex and highly fragmented region. Vineyards here are not measured in hectares like they are everywhere else, but in ares (as the word suggests, an are is a hundredth of a hectare). The intricate patchwork of growers and crus means that Burgundy's wines take a lifetime to get to know. They range from the light, transparent, cherryish pinot noirs of Mercurey in the Côte Chalonnaise to the plush, crushed crimson velvets of Pommard to the firmer, iron-framed, sinewy black fruit of Nuits-St-Georges to the pretty wild strawberries and cherry blossom of Morey-St-Denis. The most humble wines are labelled Bourgogne Rouge and are like pencil drawings, precise and sleek and fine. The great ones are loved because as they age the corporeal qualities of the grape fall away, leaving autumn leaves and gentle decay. The imprint of the land seems to rise out of the glass.

Around the rest of the world, relative newcomer New Zealand is the most exciting country for pinot noir, offering superb value as well as wines that soar and stand on the edge of greatness. The wines have a brighter, more piercing quality – more fruit, less earth. In Central Otago, you find richness and intensity, raspberries, the deep flavours of roasted fruits, tinges of black tea, coffee and dried herbs. Marlborough pinot seems slippy, lithe and light, a soprano of a pinot noir, hitting you high on the nose with its perfume; the classic Martinborough style is somewhere between the two.

In Australia, excellent pinot noir can be found in Tasmania (it's very finely delineated here, and high and bright), as well as in the Victorian regions of Geelong, Gippsland, Yarra and also the Mornington Peninsula, where pinot unfurls gently, like the petals of a giant peony, lush and elegant at once. Back in Europe, Germany is also taking pinot noir seriously – plantings of the grape more than tripled between 1980 and 2012 – with impressive and increasingly fêted results. German pinot noir is often savoury and stern, with clear lines and an earthy undertow, while Austrian pinot noir is seamless and a little more yielding.

In the Americas, Canada, Oregon and parts of California, such as Russian River, Sonoma (ripe and effortless and lacking tartness), Carneros (plump, but marked by a pleasing acidic sheen) and Monterey (loose and juicy with a confectionery flavour), have also forged a reputation as makers of good pinot noir. Further south, Chile is determined to prove that its cooler regions, such as Bío-Bío and Malleco, can do it too and I often find this a good hunting ground for the cheaper crunchy, red-fruit styles. South African pinot noir tends to be bigger-boned and firmer, often with a smoky/liquorice/umami flavour.

Pinot noir is also of course the most widely planted grape in Champagne.

what to eat: Silky pinot noir at any level is superb with **roast beef**, be it rib, fillet or a simple topside. Its light touch means it is delicious with the halfway houses of **pork** (it can even take on fennel-rubbed pork crackling, but hold the apple sauce) and **veal** (chop or sweetbreads). It is also the ultimate wine for **duck** – nothing goes with duck quite like pinot noir. Just think of the fatty, melting flesh of a roasted whole duck cut through with a slightly chilled pinot noir. Or fat pink magrets with crispy skin eaten with the silky whisper of a pinot reminiscent of summer berries. Or **smoked duck** with peas cooked in lettuce and pancetta with a young, spring-like pinot from just about anywhere. This grape also works well with chicken, though my preference would be for the meatier, firmer flesh of a **Label Anglais** or similar bird, perhaps served with roasted **new potatoes with thyme** or as **chicken fricassee**: pinot noir will emphasize the more sinewy side of the chicken. And it is often the first choice to go with **game** – just remember that the more hung the game, the older the pinot needs to be, as both wine and animal game up in the same way.

Pinot noir can also be a terrific accompaniment to fish: **tender pink salmon fillets** that have been fried or chargrilled (think Sonoma pinot noir with fire-roasted sockeye salmon); **seared tuna**; **red mullet** (maybe red mullet poached in veal stock); **meaty cod wrapped in prosciutto**. It also works well with terrines – for instance, **pork, pistachio and duck terrine** – and with **thyme**.

Pinot noir might be versatile, drinking as beautifully with its classic match, **boeuf bourguignon**, as it does with **sushi** or with **rib of beef marinated in Asian spices**, but let the bottle steer you towards the accent flavours on the plate.

I love the frisky leap of a young pinot noir from Burgundy with **griddled lamb chop and spring vegetables**. More earthy, savoury and/or older pinots have a particular affinity with **mushrooms, truffles, horseradish** and **peppercorns**. So try a red burgundy or a more complex New Zealand pinot with **mushroom risotto**, classically cooked **rib of beef** or **macaroni cheese luxuriously interlaced with truffle or porcini**.

Brighter, richer wines (I'm especially looking to some of those from New Zealand, Australia, California and Chile here) and/or young wines (pick one that veers towards the juicy berry rather than the lean-savour end of the taste spectrum) are good with fruits – **figs, blackberries, raspberries, cranberries** and **dried cherries** – for instance, with roast duck and cherries. The sweet ripeness of these wines also suits the richness of **balsamic vinegar** as well as **roast butternut squash, sweet potato** and other **roasted root vegetables**. A classic match here would be a young Central Otago pinot with **duck roasted with red onions, beetroot, carrots and parsnips**, or a **pork burger in a bun**. The berry taste of southern hemisphere or young Californian pinot noir is great with **Thanksgiving dinner** – it has a brightness that appeals to the tang of **cranberry sauce**. It's also good with roast **chicken** or **slow-cooked shoulder of pork with roasted sweet potatoes doused in chilli and ginger** on the side. These more emphatic, plusher pinots, particularly those from Central Otago or Chile, are the ones I'd choose to drink with **barbecued pork marinated in a sticky sauce** of balsamic vinegar, ketchup, orange, garlic and smoked paprika; **sweetly spiced red cabbage**; **hog roast**; or with a **confit of duck** if it came with a **pancetta and hazelnut slaw, poached pear and crispy potatoes** (that's a dish from the menu of the excellent restaurant at Carrick in Central Otago). The robust yet bright flavours of Chilean pinot noir, in particular, work well with **sweet-and-sour pork**, or **duck with hoisin sauce**.

The lithe, high notes of young Marlborough pinot noir are particularly good with **rare-cooked beef in salads with herbs, shoots and Asian dressings**. For example, it's great with Thai beef salad sprinkled with gritty rice powder, dressed with a mixture of lime juice and nam pla and covered with fresh mint leaves and sliced shallots.

More savoury, herbaceous incarnations (for example, a Bourgogne Rouge or a Givry or a minerallic German or Austrian pinot) are good with **calves' liver and bacon** and with **calves' sweetbreads**. They can also take on **mint, fennel, chervil, tarragon** and **hot pickled red cabbage** (not all at once). A simple dinner I sometimes cook at home is **fresh tagliatelle with ricotta, mint and figs** – maybe followed, if friends are over, with slow-roast pork covered in garlic and fennel seeds. I ate this once with a pinot from Germany – Schneider Weiler Schlipf Spätburgunder CS – and the cool, mineral lines of the German wine were gorgeous with both courses.

Again looking at herbs and spices, a firm pinot noir from, say, Nuits-St-Georges or Central Otago would go well with the rich, earthy aromatics of **juniper** – say, **pork with a stuffing of juniper and thyme and coriander seed and finely grated lemon rind**.

Pinot noir has good acidity, so it can cut right through the creamy sauces of classical French cuisine – and stand up to contemporary Asian-influenced dishes containing **teriyaki, sesame, chilli** or **soy**. The younger and more vibrant the wine, the more chilli, soy, salt or cream you can afford in the food. Think of it as a balance.

If you were to have just one higher-end emergency red – let's say a £15–25er – on the rack, pinot noir would be my number one choice. It is the ultimate food wine. It goes with everything – well, almost everything – which I particularly like when you are looking for a wine to take you all the way through dinner, with no fuss.

A mature burgundy or other fine wine is probably best enjoyed either on its own or with the simplest possible food. If you are eating, then with the mushroomy accents of an older fine wine, a bird that is faintly gamey, but not so much that it overpowers the delicacy of the wine, is a good match: for instance, **partridge**, **quail**, **roast pheasant**, **goose**. Or **veal** or a good **firm-meated chicken, plainly cooked.**

what the winemakers eat

Olive Hamilton Russell, Hamilton Russell Vineyards, Hemel-en-Aarde, South Africa, is author of the book *Entertaining: A Year on a Cape Wine Estate*: 'A lot of friends pre-email before coming to stay to say, "Please, mushroom risotto." We enjoy foraging on the property, where we can find five different kinds of boletus mushrooms. The ones that have slightly slimy caps so are not as pleasant to eat fresh we slice, oven-dry and then powder in the coffee grinder. We use this mushroom powder to flavour the risotto stock so it's very deep and meaty. We also put a bit of Marmite in there. If we really want to show off and we've got the time, I do biltong ravioli. Or sometimes five ravioli filled with five different kinds of venison. To make beef biltong ravioli, the biltong needs to be really dry and you blend it in a coffee grinder and fry it up with finely chopped mushroom, sometimes also some Marmite or Bovril again, then a bit of olive oil. That's the filling. Then I do a sauce that sometimes has fresh porcini in it, sometimes a little hint of chilli, because with young pinot noir a little tiny hint of heat works with the younger, more aggressive tannins. We also find with young wine that saltiness can just help fill out the mid-palate a bit and highlight more of its red fruit. And finish with fried sage leaves.'

Thierry Brouin, Domaine des Lambrays, Burgundy, France: 'In our wines we are looking for finesse, elegance and complexity, so nothing too complex in the food. Chicken from Bresse or veal with mushrooms.'

Ruud Maasdam of Staete Landt, Marlborough, New Zealand: 'Venison. Lightly toasted on the outside, pink inside. The spice in our pinot (something between nutmeg and cinnamon) gets enhanced by the meat. I do this (not often enough) on my own barbecue.'

Nigel Greening, Felton Road, Central Otago, New Zealand: 'With pinot, people always turn to meat, or maybe robust fish. There are some interesting other directions: potatoes. I once had a memorable evening at Domaine de l'Arlot with [then] winemaker Jean-Pierre de Smet, where we sat in the kitchen garden drinking old bottles and eating ratte potatoes (grown in the Clos de l'Arlot, so 1er cru potatoes!) roasted with thyme, with our fingers. For our own pinot, one of the best matches I have ever seen for our Block 5 was Japanese noodles (udon) baked with cream and black truffle. I have also made savoury pork tart tatin, using shallots, quince and parsnips in place of the apple (leave the butter in but not the sugar). Then, having turned the tatin over, carefully insert chunks of slow-roasted, crisp pork into the tatin. This is, of course, an invitation to challenge the abilities of statins to keep one alive.'

Jasmine Hirsch, Hirsch Vineyards, Sonoma Coast, US: 'Some years ago my father wrote about his favourite pairings for our wines. This is more about the emotional and historical connection between the wine and food of a particular place than about food pairings per se:

> The Hirsch Vineyard is in view of the Pacific Ocean less than three miles away at Ft. Ross in Sonoma County. This was a sheep ranch when we came here in 1978. There are mushrooms, wild salad greens,

oysters and mussels in the coves and bays. Wild turkey, deer, feral pigs, quail, pigeon and game birds inhabit the land. Some of the most succulent salmon (mostly used to) swim in the waters and spawn in the streams. The Hirsch Vineyard typically produces wines of great balance and site specificity that have the acidic structure to pair with raw fish and steak; fish stew or dishes made from the wild pigs that roam the ranch; or with the lambs that our neighbors still raise.

'My own favourite pairing for our pinot noirs, especially after they've had a few years in the cellar, would be a simple roast chicken. It's one of my favourite foods, and it's a simple and elegant canvas against which to let the complexities of older pinot noir shine.'

Michael Seresin, Seresin Estate, Marlborough, New Zealand: 'Kahawai is an oily fish – like a big mackerel – that you find in New Zealand and is beautiful when cooked very quickly in the wood-burning stove on a huge iron skillet. I love that with our pinot noir. I'm not a meat-eater and one of my other favourite dishes with our pinot is vegetarian. Get all the root vegetables you can think of – carrots, sweet potatoes, normal potatoes, turnips, parsnips, swede – slice them up, put them on the big iron skillet with thyme and rosemary and olive oil, then put them in the wood-burning oven and throw branches of the herbs on to the fire as well. I love the smokiness with the pinot. Also, the next morning you smell of the woodsmoke, your skin, your hair, everything.'

Adolfo Hurtado, Cono Sur, Chile: 'Tuna fish, rare and hopefully with a bit of cranberry sauce on top. I would eat that with our Pinot Noir Reserva Especial.'

pinotage

This red grape found in South Africa polarizes opinions like no other. It can taste and smell of smoke, burning rubber and roasted coffee beans. Detractors say: Best drunk with roadkill. Fans say: You just haven't had the right pinotage yet. It's huge and chocolatey and brilliant with strong barbecue sauces and meat.

Pomerol

This small appellation, about thirty kilometres from Bordeaux, on the right bank of the river, has risen and risen over the past few decades. Its signature grape is merlot, but merlot (with a splash of cabernet franc) here creates wines that taste quite unlike any other merlot-cabernet franc blend. Pomerol is unique and so sought after that it deserves its own entry.

what it tastes like: Pomerol wines are notable for their quite exceptional drinkability. Like fine pinot noir, they just slip down, combining a kind of pom-pom-like velvet and rounded luxuriance with restraint and gentle refreshment. Pomerol is almost always a blend of grapes (the famous exceptions being Le Pin and Petrus); the vineyard in Pomerol is planted with around 80 per cent merlot, 15 per cent cabernet franc and a bit of cabernet sauvignon and malbec. As an aside, I also privately classify Cheval Blanc as a Pomerol. Anyone who has read Neal Martin's classic reference book *Pomerol* will know that he feels much the same way; there is a 'secret chapter' on Cheval Blanc which, being a St Emilion, has absolutely no place there. But then, Cheval Blanc is an anomaly in St Emilion. Its vineyards sit right next to Pomerol (beside L'Evangile and La Conseillante to be precise) and the wine tastes like Pomerol, perhaps because so many of the vines are planted on clay, and the wine is very marked by its cabernet franc content.

It's cabernet franc that brings a redcurrant-leaf fragrance and freshness to Pomerol. These are wines made for long ageing, their robust yet silky texture resolving gently over the years, initially smelling floral, and of soft red fruits and oak spice, then later maturing to smell of mushrooms, wet clay and truffles.

If Pomerol is out of budget, check out the wines of nearby Côtes de Bordeaux Castillon, which also rely on cabernet franc and merlot and share a certain voluptuous ease.

P

what to eat: Beef is often eaten with wines from every part of Bordeaux, but when it comes to Pomerol there is one cut that is particularly superb. **Fillet of beef** (I am imagining a moo-ingly blue fillet) has a tender juiciness that is glorious in combination with Pomerol's velvet texture. The melting softness of the beef fillet meets the velvet of the wine like a cuddle. Pomerol is a wine that, old or young, suits the juicy fibres of pink more than well-cooked meat. **Duck** is another classic match. As Pomerol is plump and rich, it responds well to plumply rich food: the intensity of a much-reduced **meaty jus**; **slow-cooked meat dishes**; **oxtail**; **beef cheeks**; **pommes dauphinoise**.

Mushrooms go nicely too as they underscore the scent of ceps and bosky undergrowth found more and more in the wine as it ages. Some mushroom menu ideas are: **guinea fowl and mushroom casserole**; **beef Wellington**; **beef and cep stew**; **fricassee of mushrooms**; **veal chop with mushrooms**; **tagliatelle with girolles, cream and parsley**.

The older it gets, the more Pomerol moves in this quite magical fungal direction, towards **truffles**, which are superb with Pomerol, particularly when it's mature and it becomes hard to tell exactly where the truffle smell is coming from – wine or food. With mature wines, keep it simple: maybe serve a very plain risotto made with meaty stock and covered with slivers of truffle. With younger wines, it works to mix in more vibrant ingredients. For instance, a youngish Pomerol is gorgeous with **fillet of beef with a salad of warm new potatoes tossed with asparagus, green beans, parsley, basil leaf and truffle oil dressing** (don't make the dressing too acidic). With pretty much any Pomerol it's hard not to love an unctuously rich **Wagyu beef burger topped with truffle shavings**.

At Château La Pointe they have an extremely good cook who doesn't get bogged down with the heavy, traditional French cuisine that undoubtedly works with bordeaux wine but doesn't always appeal to contemporary palates. At La Pointe we ate **Wagyu cured beef and carpaccio of tuna dressed with a drizzle of sesame and olive oil and dotted with dried tomatoes and balsamic vinegar** that detonated intense little explosions of umami. We drank a young Pomerol (the 2010) with a lot of energy packed into it. The generous brightness of the wine was beautiful with the Asian-Italian flavours in the food.

'I like food pairings that are different and unusual,' said director Eric Monneret. 'There's a new generation of drinkers who, of course, like duck and like beef, but prefer to eat different food. They are interested in having fresher food, even fish, perhaps in a red wine reduction. For me it's not a crime to drink a Pomerol that's made for ageing when it's only three or four years old. It goes with different kinds of food.'

This is a good point. Younger wines can handle more intensity and bright acidity in the food. Older wines require gentler handling, though, thanks to their plushness, can still take a bit of gentle spice on the meat.

Ingredients that can be deployed to make a contemporary plate of food that goes with young Pomerol include **mojama** (sun-dried tuna), **cured beef**, **mellow balsamic vinegar**, **truffle oil**, **fresh truffles**, **slow-oven-dried or sun-dried tomatoes** or **coriander seeds**. Steer clear of sharper wine vinegars and lemon juice as the acidity slices aggressively into the lushness of the wine, interrupting its smooth flow.

I asked author Neal Martin what he liked to eat with Pomerol and he handed me the menu to his book launch, which was held at The Square in London. 'I asked them to cook the simplest food they had ever cooked. Starting with **mushrooms on toast**.' The menu for the launch of *Pomerol* on 25 January 2013:

Mushrooms on Toast
with 1986, 1990 and 2001 Certan de May

Roast Pyrenean Lamb with a Gratin Dauphinoise
with 1989 VCC, 1989 and 1990 La Conseillante

Rib of Aged Beef with Oxtail Spring Rolls and Bone Marrow
with 1966 Gombarde Guillot, 1971 La Fleur-Pétrus, 1955 VCC, 1964 L'Evangile

Truffled Brie de Meaux
with 1995 Clinet, 1995 Lafleur, 1996 L'Eglise Clinet

port

Each time I pour a glass of port I regret not drinking it more often. This is a fortified wine that feels fortifying. It is generous, intense and luxuriously deep. It has a cosseting sweetness, but in the better ports there is also a hint of the wildness of the Douro Valley in Portugal, where the grapes are grown. I think we forget about port because it is old-fashioned. Vintage port, in particular, takes so long to mature that it seems to go hand in hand with an ancestral cellar and the kind of generous grand- or godparents to which few wine drinkers have access. It's a mistake not to take more pleasure from port, though. It is a hugely satisfying drink. There are many earlier-drinking styles and all are relatively good value, considering how much flavour is packed into them.

white port White in colour, it tastes a little nutty and is best drunk in Oporto, on a hot day, mixed with tonic and with a plate of **salted almonds** or **cashews** close to hand.

ruby Inexpensive and uncomplicated, this is the port you will buy to make Cumberland sauce or leave out for Santa on Christmas Eve. Named for its bright jewel colour, it is made from a blend of ports from different years, and is bottled young. It usually tastes like squished red and black berries. Poor versions smell uncomfortably stewed. Good ones are comforting and sweetly easy. I would pour a sneaky glass of this on a Sunday, or at lunchtime in the no-man's-land between Christmas and New Year, and drink it with a **bread roll filled with juicy, home-roasted gammon**. It can be used to **poach pears** and is good drunk with **chocolate** or with lighter chocolate desserts, such as a **milk and plain chocolate mousse** or **mousse cake**.

late bottled vintage (LBV) As the name suggests, this is port from a single vintage that ages in wood and is bottled relatively late, between four and six years after the harvest. It's a marked step up from ruby. I think of more serious versions as being like baby vintage ports. You can expect an LBV to be more structured than a ruby port: they smell of spice, dried fruit, tobacco, damsons, and forest berries. You might be tempted by LBV if you are a fan

P

of high-quality **Cumberland sauce** and want something a bit more luxurious than ruby – especially considering that it is the duty of every weekend cook to pour themselves a small glass during the cooking, for quality-control purposes. Having more power and vigour than ruby, LBV excels with **rich chocolate desserts** and those with **chocolate with nuts, raisins and dried figs**. It has a firmness that keeps the sweetness in check. So, good things to eat with LBV include **plain chocolate mousse, chocolate nemesis, chocolate tart, crunchy chocolate biscuit cake, chocolate covered figs, chocolate mousse with Armagnac-soaked prunes, gooey chocolate puddings** and so on. LBV is also a classic match with **Stilton**, though I'm not convinced they actually work from a taste point of view – blue cheese makes port taste slightly odd and vice versa. But everyone loves the festivity and occasion of getting stuck in to the decanter and the truckle of Stilton and that's more important. I do love having both those strong flavours on the table, but prefer the taste of LBV with aged, hard cheese such as **Comté**. **Mince pies** are good with LBV too.

tawny and colheita Named for its colour, true tawny is aged for a long time in oak so that it mellows and fades before being bottled, first to garnet and, if it continues to age in cask, eventually to a honeyed amber. Tawny port may be blended from different years. Colheita, on the other hand, is a tawny from a single vintage and is increasingly labelled as 'single harvest tawny' to make that distinction clear. Also, because only Portuguese-speakers can pronounce colheita (it's col-ye-ta).

Tawny – and especially colheita, of which I am a huge fan – is the great, undervalued port style and it's no coincidence that these are also the wines that all the port shippers drink most often. Best enjoyed slightly chilled, they have a silky, luscious texture and taste of caramel, brazil nuts and dried fruit, with hints of roasted coffee and orange peel.

Tawny is the best port of all to match with **hard cheese**. It is superb with **mature Gouda** and **Manchego**; each picks up the creamy, caramel, nutty flavours in the other. It is also good with Portuguese **Queijo da Serra** (also known as Queijo Serra da Estrela), which is made with sheep's milk amidst the crags and gorges of Portugal's highest mountain range, as well as with **Gorgonzola** and other **blue cheeses**.

Salted roast almonds or **air-dried hams** make a good snack with luscious tawny.

As far as desserts go, tawny suits chocolate puddings and also has an affinity with roasted nuts and dried fruit, or a combination of these. Think along the lines of **nutty chocolate truffles**, a **sweet walnut tart, fig tart** or the **spice of mince pies, panforte** and **panettone**. It brings a caramel warmth to desserts that might be slightly dry – for instance, **almond tart** or **Madeira cake**. Tawny's butterscotch notes and soft texture slip in beautifully with dairy, too: think of **eggy, milky desserts** such as **rice pudding, crème brûlée, crème caramel** and **pastel de nata** – the Portuguese custard tarts. Tawny often has orange-rind accents and it's lovely with **caramelized oranges** as well as with **bread and butter pudding**, bringing the citrus, dried fruit and custard all together in one dish.

vintage The grandest and longest-lived port of all, vintage is made only in the very best years, when a port house 'declares' the quality of grapes in their vineyard is good enough. It is very dense and tannic when young but mellows in the bottle over decades, slowly unfurling, becoming paler in colour, filled with flavours of dried fruit and nuts. Vintage port is such a spectacular wine I don't see why anyone would want to be distracting themselves by eating with it. Maybe just the odd paring of **hard cheese**, or a piece of **bitter chocolate**, or a puff of **cigar smoke**.

what the winemakers eat

Gilly Robertson, Taylor's: 'We are mad about our Chip Dry white port in virtually all soups. It gives a lovely nutty flavour and improves even the most boring of vegetable soups. The other luxurious suggestion with chilled tawny port is pan-fried foie gras.' Indeed: both the tawny port and the foie gras have a luscious texture.

Sophia Bergquist, Quinta de la Rosa: 'With our ten-year-old tawny, I love the chocolate orange tart that they make at Moro restaurant in London.'

Paul Symington, Symington Family Estates: 'There is no finer way to end a great lunch or dinner than with a chilled tawny port. Since electricity was first introduced at our Quinta do Bomfim in the Douro in the 1940s, we discovered that lightly chilling our cask-aged tawny ports significantly increased our own and our guests' consumption and pleasure. A well-chilled Graham's 20-year-old tawny also guarantees a wonderfully prolonged lunch time and comprehensively improves the conversation well into the afternoon.

'I would serve Graham's 20 with a crème queimado (in English, crème caramel) that Ermelinda, our cook at Quinta do Bomfim, produces using the traditional method of burning the sugar onto the top of the crème queimado with an old-fashioned hot iron. The aromas that emanate from the kitchen while she is doing this are irresistible.'

Priorat

The renaissance of the small region of Priorat, south-west of Barcelona in Spain, is very recent, but its plush red wines have already won a keen following and soaring reputation that command prices to match. Based on garnacha and cariñena (mazuelo/carignan) grown on the rugged Mediterranean hillsides, the wines are bold and high in alcohol, and taste of roasted plums, wet stone and rich berry liqueur. They work with **rich, slow-cooked meat** dishes.

what the winemakers eat

Alvaro Palacios, Priorat, Spain: 'Something I really love to pair with the wines of Priorat is the seafood by the coast close to Priorat, which is about twenty kilometres away. At the harbour of the village of Cambrils there are several exquisite restaurants that prepare the best seafood of these waters. A bottle of an elegant and refreshing L'Ermita – for example, 2006 or 2012 – is good with small baby octopus sautéed in olive oil and a tiny hint of garlic and parsley. I also enjoy this lively garnacha with the best sea bass and red sea bream roasted or baked by itself and with some "samfaina" by the side, which is our kind of Catalonian ratatouille, tomatoes, red and green peppers, onions, aubergine and potatoes.'

prosecco

Real prosecco tastes of pear skins and juicy ripe pear flesh and feels as light and clean on your tongue as a snowflake. I can still remember my first-ever glass. I sipped it at a bar beside the Spanish Steps in Rome (I know, it should really have been in Venice – prosecco is a Venetian drink, made from a grape that is now called glera) and ate grissini and grainy chunks of proper Parmigiano Reggiano and slices of prosciutto. Just thinking about the taste of that cold November evening still makes me happy. Prosecco is mostly about friends, chatter and unwinding, of course. It is a frivolous, upbeat swish of a drink. But with a good one, I do hanker for **grainy Parmesan**. Or maybe **Pecorino**. It's the pear thing. The Italians have a saying, '*Non dire al contadino com'è buona la pera con il pecorino*' (roughly translated: 'Don't tell the peasants how good pear is with Pecorino') and the match works even when the taste of pear is just in the wine. Failing proper pecorino, Parmesan or **prosciutto**, then any combination of **antipasti** makes merry alongside prosecco. Failing that, I'll take crisps.

P

R

Rhône – white blends

what it tastes like: Too often overlooked, these are wines whose taste is all the better for having a nebulous quality that is hard to describe; there may be hints of quince, almond paste, fennel tops, beeswax, sunflower seeds or white peaches, but the overall picture is far more than the sum of these pulled-out parts. But I'm generalizing: the Rhône blend is not universal – it varies according to which appellation you are in. Northern Rhône whites (Hermitage, Crozes-Hermitage, St Joseph, St Peray) are majestic creatures made from marsanne and roussanne, grapes that can be reminiscent of almond paste, aniseed and almond blossom but are also capable of creating grand wines with a nuttiness, a gentle spice and huge atmosphere that are built for long-term ageing. White Châteauneuf-du-Pape may also include white grenache, clairette (I love this grape – it tastes of waxy white blossom), bourboulenc and picpoul; it is more fragrant, subtle and limpid. White Côtes du Rhône, Gigondas, Luberon and Lirac may add to all these grapes the honeysuckle notes of viognier and also ugni blanc. Some white Rhônes might have a gleaming trace of vanilla-spiced oak; others may be oaked but in a more subtle way. The lesser wines may simply be unoaked blends of two or three of the permitted white grapes, but they are usually still beautifully understated, perhaps tasting fractionally of peach, ginger, pear, herbs and white blossom.

White Rhône blends – that is, white wines made from a combination of the above grapes – are also found elsewhere in the world, most notably in South Africa and in California, where they often have a sunnier warmth and a more overtly fruity taste.

what to eat: With the simpler Côtes du Rhône, Luberon or southern Rhône blends, I tend to go for **chicken** and **white fish** dishes. I know this sounds dull but bear with me. These are wines that will sweetly bring out the savoury flavour of **crispy, buttery fish skin**. They work well with the middle notes in food that are not so much brought to attention – the gentle richness where garlic meets the meatiness in chicken stock, the full riciness of rice, or the fleshy succulence of a fish that has been cooked with herbs. I love them with the classic one-pot **chicken with forty cloves of garlic**. While staying with a friend in the Dentelles on a working 'let's taste wine, write, cook, eat, go for walks and do yoga in the courtyard' holiday once, I made Rick Stein's recipe for **roasted sea bass with pastis and Camargue rice risotto** (it's in his *French Odyssey* book). We ate it with white wine made by Château St Cosme, which is based in Gigondas. I think we might have opened a bottle of white Lirac as well. Perfect combination. **Pan-fried fish** or **roasted trout with a tangle of leeks sweated in butter and almonds** would have been good with the wine too.

Those wines that are heavier in marsanne and/or roussanne (for example, those from the northern Rhône) have more nuttiness and warmth and go well with the stronger flavours of **skate** or the **bisquey taste of shellfish** – for instance, with **crab ravioli with a butter and shrimp sauce** or with fish served or cooked in a rich bisque. They can also take on spice mixes such as fire spice or **vadouvan** (try broccoli stalks or cauliflower vadouvan) and they are good with **roast pork**, too.

what the winemakers eat
Randall Grahm, Bonny Doon Vineyard, California, US: 'We make a wine called Le Cigare Blanc, which is a blend of roussanne and grenache blanc. It is an extremely savoury wine, often with a suggestion of quince, pears and anise (or fennel). I have found that it makes an absolutely wonderful pairing with seafood, especially lobster and scallops, or, if one has the great opportunity, uni (sea urchin). An uni risotto is about perfect. But any dish that can include seafood and perhaps fennel is a home run with this wine. I've also had it in a Japanese restaurant with a hand-roll (frankly, I've forgotten the fish that was used, but very likely hamachi). What really made the dish just infinitely resonate was the pairing of the

wine with the sweet rice and the freshly grated wasabi. Maybe there is something about real wasabi (much milder than what one typically finds) that makes it almost more akin to that fennel note in the wine, but this pairing was just cosmic.'

Emilie at Domaine du Père Caboche, Châteauneuf-du-Pape, Rhône, France: 'White Châteauneuf-du-Pape Domaine du Père Caboche is lovely with Saint Jacques poêlées – seared scallops – as a starter.'

riesling

what it tastes like: Riesling is a bracing white grape most easily recognized by its piercing acidity, plus its intense lime scent when it's young and the strangely petrol-like fragrance it can develop as it ages.

It is a paradox of a grape – admired and adored by wine lovers, but not popular with everyone else. Or, as American wine importer Terry Theise once put it, 'People are happy to say they drink dry riesling but the numbers don't support it. There's still a disconnect between what people say and what they pony up for.'

For a long time it has been fashionable to urge people to Drink More Riesling. I often fear I'll answer the front door to find a couple of riesling supporters handing out 'The Riesling Tower' pamphlets, determined to help me on to a path of righteous riesling-loving. I'm not going to be like that. I think riesling is great. If you don't agree, we can still be friends. For those who think they might be a convert if only it were easier to find the type of riesling you like, I hope this brief guide is helpful.

Young dry riesling tastes like a sharp blade of steel swishing through an airborne fresh lime. This is a grape that has a brain-rinsing acidity to match that of sauvignon blanc. Riesling is not always dry, of course. It is made in a range of sweetness levels from off-dry to very sweet and it's thanks to its raging acidity that the sweeter wines still taste perky and alert. Riesling unfurls as it ages, unleashing flavours from wild honey to lime blossom to toast to paraffin.

For an international tour of riesling styles, where better to start than in Eden. The Eden and the Clare Valleys, to the north

R

of Adelaide, are Australia's most fêted riesling areas, producing wine so dry yet so refreshing the effect is like a drink in the desert. There's often a delicate smell of lilac and the citrus here is sharp and pungent – think freshly squeezed lime juice mixed with lime rind and preserved limes, all pulped with ice to make a keenly exhilarating glass of wine. When these wines age, the fresh lime falls back and the preserved lime is foregrounded; also you don't just feel that riesling petrol-tremor brushing your nostrils, you almost hear the throat-clearing throttle of a motorcar with the top down. Superb dry riesling is also made in the south-west of Australia, in Great Southern, where the refreshing taste of lime is met with a tang of clementine and mandarin.

Riesling from New Zealand has a similar limpidity but tends to be less arid and more juicy. It is made in dry, off-dry or medium-dry styles.

Washington State riesling may be dry or off-dry and has a subtle juiciness – there's more ripe pear, and the lime is sweet lime cordial rather than a squeeze of raw lime juice.

European riesling is equally piercing but more finely delineated. Riesling from Alsace is usually dry and its steely acidity often has a delicately stony edge, with hints of raw citrus fruit (orange and lemon as well as lime). Alsatian wines are often textural too, roiling in your mouth, and, as they mature, that creamy texture takes on a smoky, toasty, petrol-like edge. Dry riesling is also made in Austria, where it tends to a sleek, underlying minerality – an austere, hidden force in the wine. The alcohol might be slightly higher, making it feel broader in the mouth. 'It's orchestral, like a blast from the orchestra pit – the first chord of *Don Giovanni*, with so much detail,' as wine expert Joe Wadsack memorably describes it.

Germany, of course, is riesling's most famous home. Here, too, it is possible to find perfectly dry riesling, sometimes with a seltzer-like taste. German riesling styles move from steely, with apple and cool citrus notes, to ample and luscious – wines with sweetness and the taste of atomized nectarines. Unlike Australian riesling, which is almost painfully direct, German riesling, especially when it is not perfectly dry, waltzes.

Each region has its own distinctive personality. Mosel riesling is grown on slate and tastes racy, apple-blossom fresh, girlishly light and nimble on its feet. Rheingau riesling is more earthly, sometimes with a putty-ish taste. Rheinhessen riesling is leaner. Nahe riesling has a softness, like the brush of downy dove feathers.

And sweetness? The burst of juice when you bite into a green apple, or a ripe melon, is sweet, but the sensation is of refreshment and uplift, not of sugar. So it ought to be with a non-dry riesling.

A problem, and, I think, one of the reasons for riesling's unpopularity, is that it isn't easy to assess from the label exactly how sweet a German wine might be: can you expect a tangy, sharp sweetness like that of a green apple? Soft sweetness as in a peach or ripe melon? Or the luscious sweetness of apple strudel?

The German category of Prädikatswein (superior quality wine) is classified according to the density of the must (grape juice) at harvest, measured in Oechsle. As density increases according to the amount of sugar present, this is effectively a measure of sweetness. However, when it comes to interpreting these classifications there are a few catches. The first is that classification is by minimum Oechsle levels, rather than by bands with a fixed upper as well as lower limit. This means that a wine producer could choose to classify a wine made from must with a very high Oechsle level in one of the lower categories. The second catch is that the Oechsle level is a measure of the sweetness of the grape juice, not of the finished wine. Fermentation turns sugar into alcohol but fermentation may be stopped early, before all the sugar has been converted into alcohol. Therefore to work out the precise dryness of the finished wine, you would need to look at the alcoholic strength, and at the classification (and know the numbers associated with the classification) and do some mental arithmetic.

The classification system is therefore a triumph of technical detail over information that might actually be of use to the drinker. However, it does give a ballpark guide as to how dry (or sweet) you might expect a wine to be. In ascending order of sweetness of the must used to make the wine, the classifications are: kabinett, spätlese (late harvest) and auslese (selected harvest), beerenauslese (berry selected harvest) and eiswein and trockenbeerenauslese (dry berry selection – these wines are made from shrivelled berries that may have been affected by botrytis).

The best approach to drinking is to forget precision and embrace the idea that the interpretation of the style is philosophical rather than absolute.

As Peter Karsten, winemaker at Gut Hermannsberg, said to me, 'Kabinett is less a technical entity, more a wine style that for me is very, very fine and light in alcohol, made from grapes grown in vineyard sites that ripen not too early, not too late.' I love the kabinett style. These wines have a refreshing quality – the sweetness is carried on a wave of energy and glittering acidity. Spätlese styles, by contrast, are usually markedly heavier with sugar, tending to fall in the medium-sweet range, auslese is heavier still and anything beyond it firmly in the dessert (or light dessert) wine region. Riesling is also used to make deliciously upbeat and refreshing sparkling wine, sekt. The Germans keep too much of this to themselves.

Finally, a word about ice wine (Canada) or eiswein (Germany). This is made from grapes picked only after they have frozen on the vine. In the northern hemisphere, the necessary frost may not arrive until the end of December (picking on Christmas Day does happen). The risk of leaving berries on the vine for so long makes these delicacies very expensive, but the wines are wonderful: incredibly sweet, like sultanas dripping with apple juice, honey and lime marmalade, with the riesling acidity scything through so that they do not cloy.

what to eat: Whether it's the brain-rinsing cut and slice of a bone-dry wine from the Eden Valley, or the gentle tonic and dance of a sweeter Mosel, a cold glass of riesling makes a brilliant stand-alone aperitif.

Riesling is also an outstanding food wine. There is almost no end to the number of dishes it complements (and which return the favour) and riesling has the distinction of counting **Thai** and **Vietnamese** as well as traditional European food among its best dinner table companions.

Riesling has a luminosity that is perfectly met by the salty-sour-sweet flavours found in **South-East Asian** and **fusion food**. Its vibrant citrus soars beside the sear of **fresh lime**, the fire of **ginger** and the tang of **green mango and papaya**; its lively acidity is the perfect foil for the saltiness of **nam pla**; and its flighty energy is good with **fresh coriander** and **lemongrass**. However, it's worth considering sweetness levels.

With dry riesling, eat dishes that are either very mild or contain no chilli at all, because unless a wine is slightly sweet the heat of chilli strips it so that its fruit and flavour almost disappear, leaving only a scorch of acidity. The zesty alertness of young, dry Australian or almost-dry Martinborough riesling is great with **soba noodles with snow peas, julienned carrots, edamame and a ginger and sesame sauce**; or with **steamed white fish with ginger, torn coriander leaves and kaffir lime**.

Riesling (from anywhere) in which sweetness is more evident comes into its own when **chilli** heat is also involved, which means that the burn of Vietnamese, Thai and other spicy South-East Asian dishes (and their derivatives) go brilliantly. Think **som tam** (Thai papaya salad); **larp gai** (Laotian chicken salad); **crunchy Vietnamese noodle salads**; **stir-fried prawns with chilli and tomato**; **Thai green or red curry**; **banh mi** (Vietnamese pulled pork sandwich); or **chicken marinated in chopped lemongrass, shallots, chilli and lime juice, then eaten hot, with rice, wrapped into parcels with flat lettuce leaves**.

Off- and medium-dry rieslings are great with hot spice mixes from other parts of the world too. **Jerk seasoning** is perfect with fruity riesling, as is **ras-el-hanout**. I once spent a happy afternoon in the kitchen of extremely good cook and Master of Wine Natasha Hughes. We had a lot of bottles of riesling and a table heaving with food. One of the dishes Natasha made that day was a favourite of hers: **quails marinated in a mixture of ras-el-hanout and olive oil** and then roasted until the skin crisped and the flesh was cooked. They were delicious with Ernst Loosen's Erdener Treppchen.

The cool-yet-hot flavours of a **fresh tomato, spring (or red) onion and chilli salsa** are also great with the lime-burst of riesling. Try a dry-ish Australian, New Zealand, South African or Chilean riesling with **snapper or sea bream with a coriander, lime and tomato tortilla salsa and guacamole and tortilla chips.** Take away the rich corn flavour of the tortilla chip and guacamole and the clean focus of a Rheinhessen riesling would be delicious with the fresh slices of spring onions and the bright herbs and tomatoes.

The more sugar in the bottle, the hotter you can go with the

R

chilli while still being able to taste the wine, though wines that are only off-dry can sometimes be good with dishes that vary in heat factor. For example, I once enjoyed a riesling from Weingut Peter Lauer in Germany with **barbecued Thai chicken wings** that were hot on the outside and gentler once you got beyond the marinated skin and into the flesh. The Lauer wines are made with natural yeast and have a chiselled detail and breadth that met the punctuation of the spice perfectly.

Non-dry riesling is also good with dishes that are markedly sweet-sour, whether chilli heat is involved or not. For instance, off-dry riesling works well with **salads whose dressing is sweetened with honey, pomegranate molasses or maple syrup.** And a kabinett-level German riesling is good with **Vietnamese rice noodles with sticky prawns**, where the prawns are fried with honey and soy sauce; or with **chicken or fish marinated in teriyaki and hoisin, served with a sweet-sour peanut butter and lime Asian coleslaw**.

In a similar way, the gently sweet waltz of young off- or medium-dry rieslings (in particular those from Germany) also goes well with salads containing nectar-like fruit. I love these wines with **peach, lime, mozzarella and rocket salad**; Ottolenghi's recipe for **chicken in a boiled orange syrup with green herbs**; or **quince and Dolcelatte salad**.

Match the flavours of the wine to the mood of those on the plate. Food involving more tropical accents such as **kumquats, starfruit** or **peaches** invite you to the more luscious styles of Washington State, the antipodes, or Chile. German riesling leans towards orchard fruits. The piercing, arid lime of Australian riesling or the brightness of a riesling from Chile goes well with **papaya, watercress, feta and lime-dressed salad**.

Not-quite-dry and medium-dry rieslings are brilliant at bridging the gap between more traditional, European savoury meat and juicy fruit combinations, as well as meats with a sweet, fruity marinade. They are particularly good with fatty protein – **pork** and **goose** are real riesling stars – as their acidity is refreshing between mouthfuls.

Riesling that's even slightly sweeter than perfectly dry, so that its bony acidity is softened and the wine feels sour and sweet, like biting into a Discovery apple, is terrific with **pig and fruit**. Think slow-roast pork with apricots; barbecue ribs covered in a sweet sauce; **pork with fruit chutney**; sausagemeat and fruit mixtures of all kinds, from **pork and apple sausages** to **pork and apricot burgers**; **roast pork with a sweetly fruity stuffing**; morcilla with apple compote; spicy-marinated belly of or roast pork with all the crackling works, with an apple sauce.

With non-dry riesling try **roast goose with a fruity stuffing** (apricot, apple, orange zest and coriander; prune, apricot and apple; apples, prunes and pine nuts, and so on); **roast goose with slightly sweet red cabbage**; **smoked goose and orange salad**; or slices of **smoked goose served with apple slices caramelized in a frying pan** with butter and sugar.

Dry riesling goes well with the same meats when they are not being eaten with so much sweet fruit. I tend to prefer Alsatian, Austrian, Washington State, New Zealand and German rieslings to their more boisterous Australian counterparts here, but it's a matter of personal taste.

Smoked goose is delicious with a dry, mineral-charged riesling: try a young, dry Rheingau with **smoked goose on crispbread with a very sparing amount of crème fraîche. Roasted belly of pork and pommes boulangère and a more savoury red cabbage** mix also goes well with dry riesling.

Riesling (young or old) also brings out the pink succulence of a **gammon** joint – and it doesn't even need to be sweet to do so. At the family dinner for my grandmother's ninetieth birthday one December, we drank a steely dry Alsace riesling (from Hugel) with honey roast gammon, roast potatoes and leek gratin and it was perfect.

In Alsace, their richly dry rieslings, young and old, are often drunk with **coq au riesling** – a chicken casserole in a creamy sauce with grapes, sometimes served with buttery noodles on the side.

The flavours of dry European riesling that's beginning to mature are also very good with other creamy or rich Alsatian dishes, such as **onion tart**; **tartiflette**; **baeckeoffe** (pork slow-cooked in a white wine sauce); **sausages and choucroute** and **tart flambée** (bacon and onion tart).

The more herbal, aniseed and mineral characteristics of European rieslings can work with **dill** and cool-tasting herbs and pickled **capers** and **gherkins**. Delicate Austrian riesling, Alsace riesling or the more seltzery dry styles of German riesling are a good match for **white fish baked en papillote with branches of herbs**, perhaps with a fennel salad or **hot smoked salmon with dill** and a daub of crème fraîche. Some sommeliers suggest young, dry German rieslings with cured fish, though I almost always prefer it with fish that is cooked – I have a particular loathing for riesling with smoked salmon, but that's personal taste, and many disagree. What I do like are **cured herrings** – not rollmops but the good stuff from Denmark – with dry Rheingau or Rheinhessen.

Wines of Germany likes to promote similar 'Nordic Pairings' such as a dry to off-dry Nahe or Mosel riesling with **salted sea trout, sorrel purée and vinegar-marinated cucumbers**.

Dry Rheingau is also spectacular with **asparagus**, especially juicy white asparagus.

These cleaner styles of dry riesling, as well as those from Marlborough and Martinborough in New Zealand, also fit well with **salty tempura – of vegetables or of fish**.

Finally, a half-German friend introduced me to **riesling soup**, which is made with shallots, leeks, riesling, chicken stock (I guess you could substitute good vegetable stock) and cream. It's a way to drink and eat at the same time.

R

RIESLING SOUP
Serves 4

- 2 small onions, peeled and roughly chopped
- 2 leeks, trimmed and chopped
- 1 clove of garlic, roughly chopped
- 25g butter
- 1 tablespoon plain flour
- 250ml dry riesling
- 400ml light vegetable or chicken stock
- salt and white pepper
- a handful of flat-leaf parsley, finely chopped

for the croutons
- 2 thick slices of crusty white bread, crusts cut off
- butter

Gently cook the onions, leeks and garlic in the butter for about 10 minutes, until completely soft. Sprinkle over the flour and stir into the vegetables. Keep stirring over the heat for 3–4 minutes to cook out the raw taste of the flour. Add the wine, gradually stirring all the time until it is fully incorporated. Simmer for 10 minutes, then add the stock and simmer again for 15 minutes. Use a stick blender to whizz the soup smooth. Taste and season with salt and pepper. If you want to serve croutons, cut the bread into cubes and fry in butter until golden. Stir the parsley into the soup before serving. Add a few croutons to each bowl if you like.

sweet wines Riesling makes excellent dessert wines; it has such fierce acidity that the wine remains refreshing even when it is very sweet. Its appley flavours make it a natural with **tarte tatin**. Andrew Hedley, an Englishman who makes superb rieslings at seven different levels of sweetness, three of them properly sweet, at Framingham in Marlborough, New Zealand, says: 'These are cheese wines. I like dry, hard cheeses with these. **Old, salty, hard cheeses**.' Just the job.

what the winemakers eat
Jeff Grosset, Grosset Wines, Clare Valley, Australia: 'With our Polish Hill riesling, oysters are just a natural. I remember one winemaker having Polish Hill riesling at his wedding, with oysters, and standing outside the church at the top of a hill and thinking that was all pretty much ideal. Our wines are often put with delicate flavours, and that's fine, but they can go with bold flavours too, as long as the food's not too creamy and not too hot with chilli.'

Kaoru Hugel, Hugel & Fils, Alsace, France (Kaoru is the Japanese wife of the late Etienne Hugel): 'The Gentil Hugel is made from riesling along with gewürztraminer, pinot gris, muscat, pinot blanc and sylvaner and it goes very well with any food, especially Vietnamese, Chinese and Thai, you don't really have to think about it. The Jubilee riesling is more minerally,

R

so with that I choose Japanese fish with a sweet sauce, like a miso paste. In Japan we also have chawanmushi, a kind of egg pudding, but savoury, which is served as an appetizer and the Jubilee is very good with that.'

Jim Bowskill, viticulturalist at Framingham, Marlborough, New Zealand: 'My girlfriend does the cooking. The only time I cook is if I've got a wine I want to drink and I think, "What shall I eat with this?" And mostly it's riesling, so mostly it's pork. With our Old Vine Riesling I like to get a couple of pork chops and some apples and onions. You peel, core and slice the apples and chop the onions and make a bed of them in a Le Creuset-type pot. If you want to go crazy, you can add Asian spices like star anise. Last time I put apple juice in. Then you put the pork chops on top and bake it – at about 180°C, I suppose – until all the onion and apple mushes up and the pork is cooked.'

Ernie Loosen, Dr Loosen, Mosel, Germany, sent this recipe for Arctic char ceviche, adding: 'Our Dr Loosen Red Slate dry will complete the treat.'

ARCTIC CHAR CEVICHE WITH ICED FENNEL
Serves 4 as a starter

- ¼ fennel bulb
- 2 cloves of garlic, peeled
- 100ml vegetable oil
- 2– 4 fillets of Arctic char or any white Atlantic flatfish (without skin and bones)
- salt
- juice of 3 limes
- 1 tablespoon roasted sesame seeds
- a pinch of Piment d'Espelette (or cayenne)
- garlic oil
- 3 spring onions, cut into thin slices

Remove the stalk of the quartered fennel bulb and freeze the bulb. Cut the garlic into thin slices, pour vegetable oil over them and let them sit for at least 1 hour. Cut the fish into slices approximately 1cm thick, season with salt and pour freshly squeezed lime juice over the top. Mix well, then add the sesame seeds, Piment d'Espelette, a dash of garlic oil and if necessary some more salt. Mix the spring onions with the fish. Arrange on four plates and top with finely grated frozen fennel.

Stephanie Toole, Mount Horrocks, Clare Valley, Australia: 'Living in the country, I tend to cook as much local produce as possible. With our whites, the local seafood is always sensational. We have a delicate white fish in South Australia, the King George whiting,* which is unsurpassed in the world with riesling. I just quickly sear it on the grill plate with lemon, and have it with young Clare riesling, it's just so vibrant and fresh. On a trip to London recently I had dinner at Arbutus in Soho and their custard tart was gorgeous with our dessert riesling.'

* David Gleave of Liberty Wines, the UK importer of Mount Horrocks, suggests John Dory as a substitute.

About half a dozen Australian wine producers, among them Peter Gago of Penfolds and Jeff Grosset, and not all of them best known for their white wines, put King George whiting and riesling forward as their favourite home-food-and-wine combination. It's clearly fantastic.

Charles Smith, Charles Smith Wines, Washington State, US: 'I'll give a shout-out back to Germany and Austria and have my Kung Fu Girl riesling with schnitzel with fresh-squeezed lemon and beautiful salt and a side of cucumber salad. It's great in the winter and delicious in the summer.'

rosé

Whatever the question, rosé is often a good answer. A summer evening with **Gorgonzola, spinach and walnut salad,** followed by **grilled squid** and **barbecued butterflied leg of lamb** and a wild salsa verde? **Sardines** cooked with basil and tomatoes and onion under the grill? A very mild, savoury **tagine**? **Aubergine parmigiana** made in a lighter style with lemon thyme and crème fraîche? Rosé, rosé, rosé and rosé are all happy answers to what to put in your glass.

The trick for picking the right rosé is to think first about sweetness and secondly about power. With any savoury and non-spicy dinner and all of the above (with the possible exception of the tagine, depending on how hot it was), I would pick a dry rosé.

The very best dry rosés are those made in Provence (the appellations include Côtes de Provence and Bandol), using a blend of red grapes, usually based on grenache and cinsault, often also including mourvèdre and the local tibouren among others. Though very pale to look at and delicate to taste, these wines have an unexpected tenacity and hold. The more herbaceous and savoury they are when you drink them without food, the more power they seem to have when you drink them with dinner. And I do quite like to still be able to taste my wine at the table.

The one drawback of rosés from Provence is that they are relatively low in acid, which isn't always great when it comes to very acidic food, such as heavily dressed salads, or very fatty food, which they can't fight their way through. Provençal rosé does go very well with **bloomy-rind cheese** such as **Brie** or **Camembert**, but it falters when it comes to a gloopy dish like macaroni cheese. For this, or for the aubergine parmigiana, I'd pick a rosé with more bite: perhaps a sangiovese rosé from Italy, or one of the overlooked but very good savoury rosés from the Veneto (Ca' dei Frati make an excellent one). Or a rosé that is still dry and savoury but has more oomph, such as Adi Badenhorst's Secateurs rosé from South Africa, a Rioja Rosado or a rosé from Lebanon. Lebanon is almost secretly making superb rosé wine. The grapes used are the same as in Provence (for me, cinsault is often the secret to a good pink), but the wines have more colour and bolder flavours. Bolder wines are better for claggy cooked cheese or strong tomato sauces.

And by the way, a note on colour: pale rosé is a stylistic preference, not an indication of quality. There are other variables, such as the fact that some grapes contain more pigment than others. But as a general rule, a darker shade simply means the grape skins have spent longer in contact with the fermenting juice, so that more colour, tannin and flavour compounds have been extracted from them.

On to spicy and/or sweet food. The presence of spice and especially chilli can strip a wine of its flavour. Eat a hot and spicy tagine, take a sip of wine, and the wine will taste like water with some alcohol in it. This effect is easily counteracted by picking a wine that is not perfectly dry. Sweetness is a good thing when it comes to wine and spice. So rosés that are off- or even medium-dry are a gift for spicy Asian food. Non-dry rosé also works perfectly when there are sweet ingredients on the plate: for instance, ripe fruit, honey, maple-glazed vegetables or pomegranate molasses. **Blue cheese and pear salad**; **prune tagine** (which combines spice *and* fruit); contemporary **salads with hot-sweet-sour dressings** are all dinners for which I'd choose a slightly sweet rather than a dry pink wine.

what the winemakers eat

Jean-François Ott, Domaines Ott, Provence, France: The dish I eat very often and that goes so well with both the rosé and the blanc de blancs from our winery, is grilled fish. It can be dorade (sea bream), or even sea bass (wild). You just scale the fish, put olive oil inside and outside the fish, add garlic, a sliced onion, two tomatoes, a glass of white or rosé wine, salt and pepper and then you put them in a baking dish in a hot oven (around 180°C) for about 14 minutes. The fish should be easy to cut but almost uncooked near the bones. Then you can serve it as it is and you will have a good balance between all the tastes.'

Charlie Melton, Charles Melton Wines, Barossa, Australia: 'For our Rosé of Virginia, choose your dish for la dolce vita. A great buffalo mozzarella and roma tomato salad, or home-made charcuterie, along with, of course, the shaded pergola and a view of the closest body of water, shared with your significant other. Make sure your significant other is cool and your rosé chilled.'

R

S

Sancerre

One of the very best summer lunches is a glass of cold Sancerre with **Crottins de Chavignol** (the goat's cheese that has been produced in the tiny village of Chavignol in the Loire since the sixteenth century) cut in half, put on slices of toasted baguette, grilled until they melt, then served on simple, buttery green lettuce leaves (Batavia for choice) and dressed with white wine vinegar and mustard vinaigrette. It is a classic and traditional match for the flinty, grassy verve of Sancerre, but see *sauvignon blanc* for more on this appellation.

See sauvignon blanc.

sangiovese

Also known as brunello, morellino, nielluccio

what it tastes like: Like so many red Italian grapes, sangiovese has a tang of cherries and refreshing acidity. It is a bloody life force of a wine that can also have hints of dried herbs, tea and, as it ages, a scent of mushrooms, autumn leaves, church incense, leather, earth and dust. It makes medium- to full- (in the case of a heavily oaked Brunello) bodied wines that are essentially the anti-merlot. Where merlot is smooth, as if it's been filled in and grouted up, sangiovese has texture, like the crenellations of the battlements found all over Tuscany, the region that is sangiovese's main home.

Towards the Tuscan coast, in the Maremma, where it is known as morellino, sangiovese makes particularly bright, juicy wines, tending more towards stewed damsons, sour cherries and leather, with less of the dust found inland.

Chianti is sangiovese's best-known incarnation. It may be a basic wine that tastes of sour cherries and dusty tea leaves; have farmyardy notes and a rustic feel; or be powerful but still elegant – a wine capable of ageing for many years. Chianti Classico, which lies in the tangle of hills between Florence and Siena, is the heartland of the region, and makes some of the best-quality wines; but you can also find excellent wines from the subzone of Chianti Rufina (particularly poised, elegant and light) and Chianti Colli Senesi. All Chianti must be based on sangiovese (80 per cent is the minimum) but it's also permitted to add a proportion of other grapes to the blend and, naturally, this affects the taste. The local canaiolo brings a distinctive fragrance of cathedral incense, while cabernet sauvignon adds flesh and might to sangiovese's bony frame.

The grandest sangiovese, and one of Italy's great red wines, is Brunello di Montalcino (brunello is the local name for sangiovese), made in and around the hill-town of Montalcino, which was the last outpost of the Republic of Siena against the Medicis. These wines are darker in colour, richer and rounder to taste, heavier and deeper than any Chianti. They must be aged for four years before release and are wines built for the long haul. Rosso di Montalcino is the younger and more affordable sibling.

The wines from the town of Montepulciano – Vino Nobile di Montepulciano is the big one, Rosso di Montepulciano the baby – are also based on sangiovese. They are much chunkier than Chianti but not as magisterial as the wines from Montalcino.

Sangiovese also grows elsewhere in central Italy, as well as on Corsica, where it is known as nielluccio and makes fragrant, loose, scented wines. Beyond Europe, it is widely grown in Argentina, occasionally found in Australia, where the wines taste more compact and less crenellated, and a little in California.

One final point: the type of oak used for sangiovese has a big impact on style and flavour, with large, traditional, Slavonian botte bringing more sangiovese clarity and smaller French oak barriques slightly filling in its natural texture to give a smoother structure.

S

what to eat: Italian reds are fantastic food wines and sangiovese is no exception. It has good acidity, which makes it refreshing and ensures it can contend with the verve of **cooked tomato sauces** on pizzas and pasta – just about any type of **savoury tomato pizza** or **red pasta sauce**, from ragù alla bolognese to amatriciana to vermicelli with aubergines, peppers and tomatoes, works well with sangiovese.

It also meshes well with the rustic quality of many, many

traditional central Italian dishes: ask a producer what he likes to eat with his own wine and he will look confused – 'My wines are very good with food, but I am eating everything.' Everything in this context means, of course, everything Italian and local. In Tuscany one reason local food and wine go so well together is that each has angles and corners. The effect is not that they jostle, more that they complete each other.

The first time I really understood what sangiovese and food were all about was at the table of Giuseppe Mazzocolin at Felsina Berardenga. It was a hot summer's day and we had been walking around the vineyards on this former hunting reserve in the south of the Chianti Classico area. Giuseppe had pointed out the great mass of the inactive volcano of Monte Amiata, which guards the province of Siena – 'This is the same view as you would have seen one thousand years ago' –and given us his thoughts on sangiovese: 'It is a very Italian grape, as are teroldego, and aglianico. Tobacco, smoke, mushrooms, truffles, cassis, blueberries ... and dust. *Polvere.* These are the nuances you find in our wines.' Then we went into the cool interior of the stone house and sat down to lunch: shallow bowls of **zuppa di ceci (thick chickpea soup)** seasoned with olive oil made on the property, and a glass of Felsina sangiovese to wash it down.

The earthy, gritty, sandpaper feel of the roughly puréed chickpeas perfectly met the dustiness and texture of sangiovese. It was rustic food. But it was also a feast. We mopped our bowls with estate olive oil and bread and drank more sangiovese and could not have been more satisfied. Such a plate of food and glass of wine is all you need to eat and drink well.

Sangiovese would still fit, though perhaps not quite so snugly, if the chickpea soup were more contemporary: blitzed to a smoother purée and pepped up with red chilli, a squeeze of lemon and chopped coriander. It also goes well with **chickpea crostini, hummus,** and any meaty dinner in which earthy chickpeas are the main accompaniment. The grainy texture of **polenta** also works well with sangiovese, perhaps served with **mushrooms** and a rocket salad as a main meal, or as a side. In fact, mushrooms go beautifully with sangiovese which itself tastes more and more fungal the older it gets: think of a **fricassee of wild mushrooms, porcini-based pasta** or risotto, **mushrooms stuffed with pine nuts and parmesan**, or slow-cooked stews to which dried mushrooms add a savoury layer of intensity.

True sangiovese has a rasping tannic astringency that – hallelujah – would not exist if the wine had been invented in the twenty-first century and anyone from a marketing department or focus group had got involved. When that tannin encounters meat (protein) the perception of astringency is reduced, meaning you experience a softer wine than when you drink sangiovese with no food, but not one that goes completely floppy when faced with a steak or salami.

Chianti, of course, being lighter than wines from either Montepulciano or Montalcino, is the more refreshing with food. 'The acid cleanses the mouth, so it prepares the mouth for receiving the next bite and so gives emphasis to the food,' says Tommaso Marrochesi Marzi of Bibbiano. 'With Chianti Classico we are not producing heavy wines, so they remain enjoyable for the entire meal, even when you are digesting the food, you are not overwhelmed by the heaviness of the alcohol.'

One local (to Chianti) carnivorous speciality is **Chianina beef**. The Antica Macelleria Cecchini in the village of Panzano – or 'The Gastronomic Republic of Panzano', as Dario the butcher with a big personality calls it – is part of a mini carnivorous empire consisting of a butcher's and a couple of restaurants where you can buy and eat Chianina beef in great quantity while gazing out over the vineyards of Chianti Classico. Not to be missed if you are in the area.

Bistecca alla Fiorentina (chargrilled T-bone steak) is a classic with sangiovese too, as is **tagliata** – steak cooked on a griddle, sliced into pink strips and plated up with **rocket and a lemon juice and olive oil dressing**. Sangiovese goes well here not just because of the protein element but also because, being astringent, it is not wrong-footed by the bitterness of the leaves.

There are thought to be around 150,000 wild boar in Tuscany, rampaging in packs to keep the wolves at bay, guzzling grapes and damaging vines in any vineyard that has not been carefully and expensively fenced. For winemakers, eating **wild boar** is therefore a form of revenge served piping hot. Wild boar is excellent in a slow-cooked stew infused with bay leaves, juniper and thyme with wet **polenta** on the side. It also makes excellent salami, filled pasta and ragù.

Sangiovese has a dusty, outdoorsy taste. It is good with **porchetta** (slow-roast a shoulder of pork with fennel seeds to get an approximation of the street van classic) or with fat **herb and garlic sausages, perhaps cooked with little brown Umbrian lentils, onions, celery and pancetta. Hunter's kebabs** – made by skewering pork loin, lemon chunks, fat pieces of Italian sausage, bay leaves and rolled-up prosciutto, all sprinkled with salt and finely chopped sage – are a treat with the roughest bottle of sangiovese you can muster.

It also works very well with **game** from **rabbit** to **pheasant** to **grouse**, as well as with **offal**; think tripe, or home-made **chicken liver pâté full of capers and gherkins** (because sangiovese can take the acidity and bitterness in them) on toast made from unsalted Tuscan bread, or **calves' liver with bacon.**

What type of sangiovese you pick is largely a matter of taste and budget, but consider the weight of the wine and its fruit against that of the food. Corsican niellucio is less noticeably acidic than some sangiovese but particularly fragrant, almost florally herbaceous, and it's good with herbs and fragrant stews. With the richer fruitiness of wines from the Tuscan coast, warmer flavours can be good – say, **beef with balsamic vinegar** or pasta with a warm rather than coolly herbaceous tomato sauce, such as **pasta all'amatriciana**. You might want to think twice before opening a sturdy and heavily fruity young Vino Nobile di Montepulciano or a Brunello di Montalcino Riserva with a lighter dinner of, say, **chicken**, or **griddled veal chops with braised fennel**, or **stuffed Parmesan and rosemary onions** (though an *older* one, or a Rosso from either Montepulciano or Montalcino, would be perfect). If the veal is cooked in a slightly spicy sauce and served with **patate alla fattoressa** – waxy yellow potatoes cooked with tomatoes, sage, olive oil, dried red chilli and onions – then the meatiness of even a youthful Brunello is very appealing.

In terms of herbs, sangiovese loves **sage** and **rosemary**. It is also happy with **fennel**, or fennel seeds or frondy fennel tops, and bitter vegetables and leaves such as **chicory, sprouts, rocket** and **braised** or chargrilled radicchio. At an Italian trattoria in Manhattan I once ate a bowl of penne all'amatriciana with a side of sliced sprouts which had been fried, then topped with grated Pecorino. It's a dinner I've been repeating at home ever since, and I usually open a simple, Slavonian oak-aged Chianti to go with it.

Roast chicken with diced potatoes cooked in the oven with garlic, branches of rosemary and olive oil is good with a lighter Chianti Rufina or Chianti Colli Senesi.

At Selvapiana, a wine producer in Chianti Rufina, they still fondly remember a visit from the late Rose Gray, who established The River Café in London. She insisted on taking home with her a giant pumpkin, all wrapped up in towels, a great spectacle that made the owner, Francesco, exclaim with delight, 'I've finally met someone madder than me.' **Pumpkin** and **squash** do go well with sangiovese. Try **roast squash with olive oil and sage**; **thick soup made with butternut squash fried with pancetta, fennel, garlic, chilli and pancetta** and served over roasted sourdough; **pumpkin pasta with sage butter** with Rosso di Montalcino or Rosso di Montepulciano, or with Chianti for that matter.

Grouse is very fine with a rich, regal Brunello di Montalcino, but you might want to put a slice of toasted sourdough and olive oil drizzled with cooking juices with it too. Traditional British turkey Christmas dinner becomes sangiovese-friendly if the stuffing is **chestnutty** and savoury (use thyme and/or sage and/or parsley) and the sprouts are finely sliced and cooked in cream and Parmesan. Or cook **pheasant in red wine with pancetta and sage** and eat it with a good sangiovese of any description.

If eating lamb, I sometimes take the opposite approach and look for a wine rather than a food tweak. **Sangiovese and lamb** go well, but cabernet sauvignon and lamb together are so good that sangiovese with a splash of cabernet sauvignon in the blend is exceptional. Such blending is permitted in Chianti and of course also IGT (Indicazione geografica tipica) wines where anything goes, but not in Montalcino or Montepulciano. Just 5–10 per cent of cabernet sauvignon is enough.

One of my favourite ways to enjoy sangiovese (with or without the splash of cabernet) is with **antipasti** followed by a plate heaped with **cotolette d'agnello** (those little, lollipop-like lamb chops) cooked quickly on a barbecue or in a griddle pan, with lemon halves on standby for squeezing, and green salad as a third, refreshing, course. I also like **butterflied shoulder of lamb rubbed with rosemary, garlic and anchovies and served with warm cannellini beans mixed with chopped rosemary, crème fraîche and garlic**, which I've occasionally eaten with Fontodi's Vigna del Sorbo.

Sometimes all you need is something very simple to eat. I like toast with Rosso di Montalcino. Not cotton-wool toast but properly made **Italian bread toasted over a fire** or blackened on a hob griddle. On a visit to Conti Costanti, in the heart of Montalcino, our host Andrea Costanti cut some pieces of unsalted Tuscan bread, charred them on an open fire, and we drizzled them with olive oil and sprinkled them with salt. 'I like this with Rosso di Montalcino,' said Andrea. Then reminded us that the Tuscan unsalted bread is mentioned by Dante in Canto XVII of *Paradiso* in the context of exile: *'Tu proverai sì come sa di sale/lo pane altrui, e come è duro calle/lo scendere e 'l salir per l'altrui scale'* ('You will see how salty is the taste of other men's bread, and how hard is the way up and down other men's stairs'). So, simple in one way, but carrying centuries of history, literature and culture. In a single mouthful. Or two, if you count the wine.

As ever, with the finest wines, I go for the simplest foods: **bistecca alla fiorentina** or a plate of **sausages** is really all you need with, say, a maturing Brunello di Montalcino.

When drinking sangiovese, do say: 'By Jove, this is good stuff' (*sanguis Jovis* – the blood of Jove, Roman god of sky and thunder). Don't say: 'I ate his liver with fava beans and a nice Chianti.' (In *The Silence of the Lambs* – the book – Lecter actually says with a 'big Amarone'. For the film, this was altered to a wine considered to be more recognizable to cinema audiences.)

what the winemakers eat
Roberto Stucchi, Badia a Coltibuono, Chianti Classico, Italy: 'When I am having my own wine at home it's usually the Chianti Classico "annata". My youngest daughter (seventeen) is a strict vegetarian so we often have meatless dinners, and I find that my wine works well even on a simple risotto with

seasonal vegetables. One of my favourite pairings, though, is with a simple braised rabbit recipe made with garlic and herbs from the garden (sage, rosemary, thyme), and stewed with a little beer (red, preferably). This is usually served with rice (basmati or ribe) or with roasted potatoes.'

David Gleave, Greenstone Vineyard, Heathcote, Australia: Like so many other wine producers, David wanted to say butterflied leg of lamb with rosemary, but for the sake of variety I made him pick again. He settled on: 'Wagyu beef, if that doesn't sound too, you know ... But really good, grass-fed beef is what they have in Chianti and it just tastes really good with sangiovese. In Australia? Kangaroo, marinated with lemon juice and white wine to tenderize it a bit – it tastes gamey, medium-game I'd say, with more texture than venison.'

Tommaso Marrocchesi Marzi, Bibbiano, Chianti Classico, Italy: 'I like tripe. Trippa alla fiorentina, which is cooked in a tomato sauce, also trippa alla senese with tomato and sausage. I drink our Montornello wine with it. It has the right consistency to face the tripe.'

Monty Waldin, a biodynamic wine consultant who lives in Brunello di Montalcino, Italy: 'My five pennies concern crostini in Montalcino – usually made with chicken liver, but that made from chicken spleen (Francesco Cinzano told me) is said to be more traditional. Most will say you should drink Brunello with crostini, but as they are an entrée a Rosso would be more usual.'

Sauternes and other sweet sauvignon blanc and/or semillon wines

what it tastes like: Sauternes, the world's most celebrated sweet wine, is made amidst the rolling vineyards to the south of the Bordeaux region, where the confluence of the cold Ciron and the warmer waters of the Garonne helps to create damp autumnal mists that allow botrytis – noble rot – to flourish. Bunches of botrytized

S

sauvignon blanc or semillon grapes do not look pretty, with their shrivelled skins and grey, cobwebby rot, but they make intensely sweet, golden wine that smells and tastes of saffron, frangipani, crystallized pineapple, mandarins, caramelized orchard fruit, roasted mango and lime marmalade.

Other sweet wines made from sauvignon blanc, semillon, and in some cases also muscadelle, with varying degrees of noble rot, include Barsac, Sainte Croix du Mont, Cadillac and Loupiac, all of which come from the Sauternes environs. Similarly styled sweet wines can also be found in other parts of the world. They often have slightly less refreshing acidity and bolder flavours.

what to eat: **Foie gras** and Sauternes: ridiculously, embarrassingly decadent, but also one of the great clichés of food and wine matching, as the unctuousness of the goose or duck liver melds with the sweet saffron and crystallized fruit sumptuousness of the wine. For me it is too much, too rich, I don't like it, but the last place I expected to get backup for this view was at Château d'Yquem, home not just to the world's most famous Sauternes but to the world's most famous sweet wine full stop.

'Don't bother with foie gras,' said my guide. Then she shook her head violently. 'No. Not Sauternes with foie gras. We do not advise it.' The reason for this restraint was then delivered with gravity: 'You can't serve red wines after sweet wine. And you will want to go on, to a good bottle of red wine, maybe even white, afterwards. So it is very important not to have sweet wine first.' True – eating sugar in any form does wreck your ability to taste dry wine. But, amazingly enough, foie gras does not have to be a precursor to a giant and exhausting banquet. It's miles better and much more appreciated as a huge treat of an evening snack – though I'd open a bottle of sweet Jurançon – less marmaladey, more refreshing – in preference to Sauternes.

At Château d'Yquem they recommend this style of sweet wine made with nobly rotted semillon and sauvignon blanc with dishes such as **Peking duck**, or a plate of **blue cheese** – but not with dessert.

I almost agree. My instinct with pudding wine is that it's almost always best drunk *as* pudding. But Sauternes *can* work very well with desserts, provided they are not too heavy. Its crystallized orchard fruit and pineapple flavours are brilliant with **tarte tatin**, **baked peaches**, **Madeira cake**, or with a big bowl full of **roasted pineapple and fresh mango**. A friend, Miles Davis, who has a lovely way with food, once served it with **home-made coconut ice cream, physalis and roasted pineapple**, a genius dessert. I've also seen chefs pick up on the distinctive **saffron** notes in the wine, putting a **vanilla and saffron ice cream with fruit and home-made biscuits**. I would serve other wines made with nobly rotted sauvignon, semillon and muscadelle in the same way, bearing in mind that Sauternes satellites will taste lighter, less concentrated and more refreshing, while other wines, such as Australia's Noble One, made entirely from semillon, can taste thicker, and more caramelized.

But perhaps the ultimate way to drink this style of wine is with a plate of **lemon madeleines**, hot and straight out of the oven.

sauvignon blanc

what it tastes like: Sauvignon blanc has bite. Drunk icy cold, it can feel like the scented rush of cold air would if you were to abseil down mountain slopes with rocky streams, lemon groves, stripy gooseberries and elderflower trees below. Depending on where it comes from, sauvignon blanc can taste vividly green and grassy, or sweeter, like nectarines and passion fruit, but thanks to its ringing acidity it is always refreshing.

Some of sauvignon blanc's most elegant incarnations are found in the glittering Loire, which is home to the prestigious appellations of Sancerre and Pouilly-Fumé, as well as the satellite regions of Quincy, Reuilly and Menetou Salon. These wines have finesse and they taste sharp – reminiscent of nettles, hedgerows, elderflowers, yellow and green citrus and grass. There's often a mineral edge too – Sancerre and Pouilly-Fumé in particular often smell of gunflint. The better wines have depth and complexity – like broad rivers with swirling undercurrents – as well as tension and surface friskiness. The Loire also produces Sauvignon de Touraine: a simpler, grassy breeze of a sauvignon blanc full of the youthful energy of spring.

Further south, in Bordeaux, the most sought-after sauvignon

blanc is oaked and blended with semillon (see below) or sweet (see *Sauternes*), but the grape is also used to make dry wines that are calm, controlled and taste of lemon, nettles and green herbs. The Entre-Deux-Mers is a particularly good source of these zesty, straightforward bottles. Sauvignon blanc is also grown elsewhere in France, and throughout Europe, making notably precise wines in north-east Italy.

Sauvignon blanc from Marlborough, on New Zealand's South Island, has an extraordinary luminosity. The first commercial plantings of this grape were only made there in 1973, but the combination of light, soil and climate proved so perfect that within a generation it had become a modern classic. Marlborough sauvignon has an electric pungency and often tastes tropical, with hints of passion fruit as well as snow peas, gooseberries and that terrifying descriptor, cat's pee (Kiwis now refer to 'boxwood' instead, to make it sound nicer). Riper grapes may veer towards nectarine flavours, producing wines with the delicious taste of a peach daiquiri. Those from the cooler subregion of the Awatere Valley tend to be more linear and smell like the dark green stems of tomatoes do when you brush past them, and tend to have a more direct, less juicy, feel – all tense barbed wire and green leaves.

These descriptors are not just fanciful. The chemical compounds behind these green smells are methoxypyrazines. They can be detected by the human nose at tiny concentrations of just two parts per trillion. One in particular (3-isobutyl-2-methoxypyrazine) has also been found in raw vegetables, including green peas, bell peppers and tomatoes, which helps to explain why these foods go so well with the wine.

Many sauvignons from South Africa share an element of this rocky, smoky, green tomato scent – look for wines from Darling, Elgin, Cape Point and Constantia – but are gentler and more lemony than those from the Awatere.

In Australia, the most crisp and vital sauvignon blancs come from cooler climates; wines from the Adelaide Hills have a very tranquil, slightly rounded, clean lemon taste and Margaret River sauvignon (which is often blended with semillon, see sauvignon blanc-semillon blends) also has bright clarity.

Those from Chile often taste fleshier and sweeter, though this is illusory not actual sweetness, with a sherbet-lemon edge. There's typically a flavour of snow peas and green capsicum, too, while the best, from coastal areas such as Leyda, which are cooled by the breezes caused by the Humboldt Current dragging icy water up from Antarctica, are more taut and defined – and back to gooseberry fool again. In the US, sauvignon blanc is often known as fumé blanc. Sauvignon blanc from California tends to be made in a riper style, with a much broader frame and an almost chardonnay-like feel. It often has a ripe melon fleshiness, a touch of pink grapefruit and dill, and sometimes also a bit of oak.

In many of the places where sauvignon blanc is grown it's becoming fashionable to leave the wine on its lees for a few months, and/or to age a small portion (say 5–10 per cent) in oak to add to the texture, weight and complexity of the finished wine. These wines have less of a whoosh, gulp, stick-your-head-out-of-a-car-window briskness.

Sauvignon blanc fully aged in oak, on the other hand, often tastes like roasted grapefruit, fennel tops, barbecued lemons and dill. The green sinew and citrus of the grapes melds with the grain of the barrel and the texture of the wine becomes richer and beeswaxy, and vegetal flavours emerge. Beyond Bordeaux, sauvignon blanc is matured in barrel by ambitious winemakers in many regions from the Loire, where it retains its minerality and savour, to Marlborough in New Zealand, where it tends to taste more peachy, warm and tropical. Barrel ageing is an even more common practice where the sauvignon-semillon blend is concerned.

S

See Sauternes, sauvignon blanc-semillon blends.

what to eat: The crisp tang of sauvignon blanc fits beautifully against **tomatoes**, whose edgy acidity can sometimes unsettle white wine. I often put greener-tasting sauvignons with raw tomatoes. A makeshift lunch featuring a big plate of **sliced red tomatoes in olive oil and vinegar, scattered with coriander or chives** is delicious with the simplest bottle. **Panzanella** (the Italian bread and tomato salad) is excellent too, while the chalky grassiness of European sauvignon blanc is a good fit with the acidity of crumbly **feta**, making a big bowl of tomatoes, olives, feta, cucumber and onion – **Greek salad** – an ideal Touraine sauvignon lunch.

These greener-tasting sauvignons have the cool, hard edge to stand up to tomatoes mixed with raw onions, spring onions and/or raw garlic, as in **gazpacho** or **salbitxada**, the Catalan sauce. If you are thinking of salads, or chargrilled kebabs, they also work well with all those vegetables besides tomatoes that share the aromatic pyrazine characteristics – **pea shoots, mangetout, freshly podded peas, asparagus** and **crunchy green capsicum.**

A tomato-based **salsa cruda** (uncooked sauce) for pasta also goes with a cool-climate unoaked sauvignon blanc (from Europe or from the Awatere Valley in Marlborough) – especially if you're stirring oven-dried tomato, courgettes and gratings of lemon rind into it rather than the salty capers or olives that might tempt me towards a more astringent white such as verdicchio. Similarly, cool, clean sauvignon blancs work well with tomato-based fish stews.

Fattoush, with its warm sprinkling of sumac, is good with almost any sauvignon blanc, though especially with the more tropical tasting versions from Chile or New Zealand.

With luminous, fatter-tasting sauvignons, including many from Marlborough in New Zealand, I often veer towards tomato salads with more exotic accompaniments. For example, a tomato, avocado, coriander and lemon juice **guacamole** eaten with the warm corn flavour of tortilla chips; or **tomato salads served with spicy chicken**.

Other good tomato-accented options include light fish, such as **sea bass roasted with vine tomatoes** – beautiful with Sancerre or a linear Marlborough sauvignon blanc – or **warm tomato tart.**

The sharp, flickering lemon and grassy edge of sauvignon from the Loire or Entre-deux-Mers is delicious with fresh green spears of **asparagus** (not with too much butter) either steamed or chargrilled. Fatter white asparagus is more suited to sauvignon from Chile, the Pays d'Oc, California or Australia.

The classic match with Sancerre, the most famous sauvignon blanc of them all, is **Crottins de Chavignol**, but beware attempts to extend this pleasure beyond the Loire. Chef, wine lover and restaurateur (of The Harrow at Little Bedwyn) Roger Jones says, 'The one thing that doesn't go with goat's cheese is sauvignon blanc. Sancerre is different.' I think it depends on the goat's cheese and on the wine – I enjoy the pungency of the cheese with other Loire sauvignons – but it's true that it can be an awkward partnership with fuller, fruitier wines, and Jones understands food and wine in a way that is rare even among professionals. He has a talent for making flavours lift, and your heart sing, and can make food dove-tailed to a particular wine so that the combination is unusually satisfying.

The rest of us can settle for looking at accents rather than nuance. Those greener, grassier sauvignons unsurprisingly lean towards **fish**, **chicken** and **salads prepared with cool green herbs** – mint, parsley, chervil, watercress – and lemon. Simple unoaked white bordeaux is a good match for **sushi**.

Scallops, either fried so that the edges turn gold and sweetly caramelized, or neatly sliced into a carpaccio, also go very well with sauvignon blanc, but what will you pick? For **carpaccio of scallops with olive oil and asparagus or pea shoots**, the wine needs to be delicate and calm. With orange zest and pink grapefruit, a less controlled, more tropical-flavoured wine is a better option. A richer, riper sauvignon blanc will coo to the sweetness of fried scallops, but if there's pea purée on the side you might want to split the difference with a simple wine from Marlborough (say, Villa Maria or Montana), which will really pop against that taste of freshly podded pea, or go right back to green and pull up the more earthy, grassy flavours with a Loire wine.

Wines from Chile and South Africa as well as New Zealand play really well with sweetly succulent seafood, not just scallops, but also **crab**, **lobster** and **crayfish**. You can also put them with red meat, if the meat is served with a yoghurt sauce (think **spicy meatballs with lashings of tzatziki**), which would almost curdle in the mouth if it met red wine.

The piercing luminosity of sauvignon blanc from Marlborough would be beautiful with Thai food if it weren't for the chilli, which kills dry wine. I often pour it as an aperitif before the bird's-eyes kick in as it acts as a cue for the lemongrass, galangal and bright herbs that will follow.

S

The tingling pink grapefruit, nectarine, white currant, passion fruit and starfruit flavours you find alongside the green gooseberry in riper sauvignons from New Zealand and elsewhere bring a juicy succulence to **air-dried hams**, and go beautifully with **peach, lime and mozzarella salad**. Put them with dishes with more tropical or Asian accents and the savoury-sweet flavour-pops of fusion food. For instance, with **burrata with Cape gooseberries and asparagus** or with **tuna served with cool slices of watermelon** or **cold chicken and mango salad or noodles**. These warmer sauvignon blancs are particularly good with the intense, umami burst of flavour in slow-oven-dried or sun-dried tomatoes too.

Roger Jones makes an intense cured salmon with earthy beetroot purée and smoked tomato, to go with the melon and guava flavours of one particular Marlborough sauvignon blanc, called Dog Point. He has been generous enough to share the recipe. When I saw Roger making this it was with a great big piece of fish, and he wasn't using quantities, simply layering fish, slices of citrus and salt, which is a fine way to go about things if you are happy to freestyle it. This is a recipe adapted for smaller quantities and home-cooking.

ROGER JONES'S KALEIDOSCOPE CITRUS-CURED SALMON
Serves 4–6

You will need to start this the day before you want to eat as the fish has to be refrigerated overnight.

- 1 pink grapefruit
- 1 blood orange
- 1 lime
- 4 tablespoons rock salt
- 500g freedom salmon fillet, all in one piece

for the roasted beetroot purée
- 450g raw beetroots, scrubbed and trimmed but not peeled
- salt and pepper

for the slow-roast tomatoes
· 6 vine tomatoes, quartered

To cure the salmon, cut the top and bottom off each of the fruits, then use a sharp knife to cut away the peel and pith, keeping the shape of the fruit. Cut across into thin rounds. Put half the fruit slices in the base of a small ceramic dish. Sprinkle with half the salt, then lay the salmon on top. Sprinkle over the rest of the salt and then cover with the rest of the citrus slices. Do not press. Put in the fridge and leave overnight.

To make the purée, heat the oven to 200°C/400°F/gas mark 6. Wrap each beetroot individually in foil, seasoning as you do. Put the beetroots in a shallow roasting tin and roast for 1–1½ hours until they are really tender – the timing will depend on the size of your beetroots. When they are done you will be able to pierce them easily with a skewer or sharp knife, so just keep cooking until you get to this stage. Take them out of the oven and leave to cool in the foil, then use a sharp knife to slip off the skins. Chop the beetroots roughly and blend to a purée with some seasoning (add a splash of boiling water if needed to help it along).

To make the tomatoes, heat the oven to 140°C/275°F/gas mark 1. Line a baking tray with baking parchment. Sit the tomatoes flesh side up on the parchment, season lightly and roast for 2 hours.

The next day, take the salmon from the dish and rinse under cold water. Pat dry with kitchen paper. Use a sharp knife to thinly slice. Serve with the beetroot purée and tomatoes.

Some of the fuller, riper sauvignon blancs that have been made using wild yeast and perhaps also enriched by ageing the wine on its lees, and/or ageing a small proportion (say, 10–15 per cent) of the wine in oak so that you can't quite taste toasty wood but do notice that the wine feels rounder and more substantial, are particularly good at taking on the fuller, more exuberant flavours of fusion food, as well as fuller-flavoured **roast ham** or **pork**. For instance, wine from the cult Sancerre grower François Cotat is made with late-picked grapes fermented with natural yeast in old barrels. Way more complex and waxy than your average Sancerre, it's delicious with **roast gammon**. These richer, wild-fermented styles also go well with **black cardamom** – try a black cardamom and lobster laksa with a bottle of Greywacke or Dog Point.

oaked sauvignon blanc The rich mineral and flint of an oaked Loire or Bordeaux sauvignon has the weight for foods that are a little bit richer: for instance, it is a good match for **bitter leaf salad with bresaola and a tangy goat's curd dressing**. The aniseed and citrus flavour of Loire or Bordeaux sauvignon blanc with oak also goes very well with **tarragon**, or with **fish in a creamy sauce**.

The softer, warmer – starfruit, peach and bergamot – flavours of oaked sauvignon blanc from New Zealand, the US and Chile are good with **chicken shashlik**, **pork cooked with apricot stuffing**, or **belly of pork rubbed with Asian spices**. At an event organized by New Zealand Wine Growers, Roger Jones made gooily soft **slow-cooked pork cheeks with Chinese spices** to go with Dog Point Section 94 (a Marlborough sauvignon that is naturally fermented in oak and tastes of peach and gunflint and waxy citrus).

what the winemakers eat
Patricia Luneau, Domaine Jean Teiller, Menetou Salon, Loire, France: 'We love to have goat's cheese salad with our wine. My father is a former chef and also makes a beautiful casserole with veal marinated in Menetou Salon and cooked with shallots and mushrooms. This is another of his recipes, for zander, a freshwater fish caught locally in the Loire.'

FILET DE SANDRE AUX AGRUMES
(FILLET OF ZANDER WITH CITRUS)
Serves 4

- 1 knob of butter
- 2 grapefruits, peeled and the flesh diced, keeping the juice
- 2 oranges, peeled and the flesh diced, keeping the juice
- salt and pepper
- olive oil
- 4 zander fillets, skin on, seasoned with salt and pepper

Heat the butter in a pan. When it has melted, add the citrus fruit. Cook gently for a minute, then add the reserved juice, season with salt and pepper and cook for a minute more. In a frying pan, heat a small amount of olive oil and cook the fish, skin side down, for a couple of minutes, until the skin is golden, then turn it over to finish cooking. Just before serving, reheat the citrus sauce so that it is hot. Serve the fish with the citrus sauce and a glass of Menetou Salon.

Kevin Judd, Greywacke, Marlborough, New Zealand: 'I do think the Wild Ferment Greywacke sauvignon blanc, which is fermented using wild yeast in old oak barrels, really suits rich shellfish. A memorable thing from my days at Cloudy Bay was a crayfish-based bisque with oysters in it that used to be served with Te Koko, Cloudy's oak-fermented sauvignon.'

Emmanuelle Mellot, Domaine Alphonse Mellot, Sancerre, France: 'All the cheeses.'

Belinda Jackson, General Manager, Blind River, Awatere Valley, Marlborough, New Zealand and co-author of *Marlborough on the Menu*: 'With sauvignon blanc everybody always says, "Blah, blah, seafood, blah blah," but Marlborough sauvignon blanc is pungent, you have to

S

zhuzh the food up. Our wine loves scallops but maybe with tomatoes blanched, skinned, deseeded and chopped up, and also dill. I also love oysters because I like the iodine effect with the texture of our sauvignon blanc. Rather than give people fixed recipes, I like to steer them towards ingredients: as well as tomatoes and dill, look at pesto, capers, goat's cheese, and asparagus.'

Matt Sutherland, Dog Point, Marlborough, New Zealand: 'Fresh green-lip mussels, cooked on the barbecue with sauvignon blanc used like oil over them. We do a *lot* of sauvignon blanc and mussels.'

sauvignon blanc-semillon blends

what it tastes like: Young, unoaked sauvignon-semillon blends are refreshing, citrusy wines and the more semillon there is compared to sauvignon, the more litheness and zip they have.

Sauvignon-semillon is most famously made in Bordeaux – the combination is known as the white bordeaux blend – where floral muscadelle and nettly sauvignon gris are sometimes also added to the mix. Because these wines are not usually labelled in a way that tells the drinker what's inside the bottle, they often fly under the radar, but the inexpensive versions (often from the Entre-Deux-Mers) are great wines to take to the beach or drink in the garden on a hot day. Unoaked sauvignon-semillon blends are also a staple of Bergerac, as well as of Margaret River, on the wild western coast of Australia, where they taste very different – more luminous, and of cold-pressed gooseberries.

The reputation of this blend, however, rests on its richer, oaked wines. In Bordeaux, the most prestigious are made in Graves, and its subregion of Pessac-Léognan, which begins in the suburbs to the south of the city. These whites don't just smell of baked grapefruit and Meyer lemons and dried citrus peel, they also have salinity, like oysters, and a hit of fennel tops, smoke and pine (a reminder of the pine-fringed beaches of Cap Ferret and Arcachon to the west). I love to drink them very young, but they are really wines made for the long haul; with time the bright fruit will die away and they will begin to smell of woodsmoke, mushrooms and faded lemon. This richer style of white is becoming increasingly fashionable among other winemakers in Bordeaux too – some impressive whites are made in the Médoc by châteaux such as Cos d'Estournel, whose primary reputation is for reds.

Semillon-sauvignon from Australia – Margaret River is the leading region for this blend – is an entirely different prospect. As winemaker Vanya Cullen says, 'In Australia the land is so ancient and the wine gives the connection to it.' Here, the insistent dig of lemon and grapefruit is less pronounced and the taste is more one of cold-pressed gooseberries, white currants, salad cream, hay and white asparagus.

what to eat: The brisk nettles and citrus of an inexpensive, young, unoaked Bordeaux Blanc or Margaret River blend are lovely with the **parsley, lemon and tomatoes of tabbouleh**; with **asparagus**, either green or white; or with **broad beans and peas**.

Sauv-sem goes very well with the **coriander, lemongrass** and **galangal** flavours in **Thai food**, particularly when there's a high proportion of semillon in the blend – though beware chilli. It also suits **fish** and **seafood**, but the match gets a whole lot more interesting once you put some oak in the blend.

Semillon loves **tarragon** and oaked sauv-sem goes very well with this herb – think **chicken roasted with tarragon butter**; **chicken in a creamy tarragon sauce**; or **tarragon potato salad**. These wines have a pine-like scent that also falls in nicely with **dill, caraway** and **fennel**, making them a good match for **salmon on rye**; **hot new potatoes with hot-smoked salmon and cold crème fraîche**; and **fennel and potato gratin**. The same wines are also brilliant with fish in creamy sauces. I particularly love the crunch of a gratin with the oak spice, and the resonance of the pieces of **smoked fish in a fish pie** with the smoky-oak-roasted-citrus notes in the wine. **Samphire** makes a good accompaniment too. I tend to head to Bordeaux with this food, as these wines sing more with the savoury and herbal qualities of a dish; those from Margaret River or elsewhere in the New World tend to boost the sweet succulence of the fish.

Younger oaked bordeaux blanc has the edge to match **creamy**

S

cheeses such as **Brillat-Savarin**, and it's good with **white fish in a butter, caper and lemon sauce**. It's also delicious with **duxelles of mushrooms** spruced up with either lemon thyme or tarragon and served on toast, with endive salad and a lemon dressing.

With a Pessac-Léognan that is beginning to mature, so that it grows gently smoky and begins to smell earthy, like mushrooms, try **roasted monkfish with girolles**; **veal chop in a creamy sauce**; **truffled Brie**; **chicken roasted with truffle butter pressed under the skin**; **seared scallops** (with truffles or without) or **carpaccio of scallop** (with truffles or without).

The glacial softness of oaked Margaret River sem-sauv is also beautiful with the sweetness of scallops, either prepared as carpaccio or caramelized in a frying pan (I particularly like Fraser Gallop for this). The same wines go well with **smoked chicken, perhaps served in a noodle and coriander dish**, or in a salad with mango; and with **pumpkin caprese** (slices of roasted pumpkin interleaved with slices of mozzarella, scattered with toasted pumpkin seeds and basil).

Another good match for sauv-sem blends is **roast pork**. Pick a bordeaux if the pork is roasted with fennel seeds; an Australian wine if the accompaniments involve Asian spices or stone fruit.

what the winemakers eat

Vanya Cullen, Cullen Wines, Margaret River, Australia: 'I love going down to the coast on a low-swell day, and getting some abalone off the rocks. To be able to taste the sea with the wine is really special. The other one is picking biodynamic broad beans from the garden and eating them the day they're picked with a bit of olive oil and Parmesan and a glass of our semillon-sauvignon blanc.'

Laurent Lebrun, Château Olivier, Pessac-Léognan, France: 'I've enjoyed some memorable food matching with some Chinese food, which goes well with the minerality and tension of older Château Olivier. In Guangzhou, in south-central China, I once had a very fine dining experience with abalone in a light soup and also with some eel. Last night we made monkfish curry for friends and ate it with a young Château

Olivier Blanc, just a couple of years old. The wine was a very nice match, with its zesty aromas and tenderness/roundness and complexity going well with the spiciness and sweetness of the dish.'

MONKFISH IN RED CURRY
Serves 6

- 2 red onions, peeled and chopped
- 1 red pepper, deseeded and sliced
- sunflower oil, for frying
- 2 tablespoons red curry paste
- 1.5kg monkfish in sections
- 1 stick of lemongrass, finely chopped
- 2 limes, squeezed
- 100ml coconut milk
- 1 sweet potato, peeled and diced
- 3 tomatoes, finely chopped
- a small bunch coriander, roughly chopped
- 500g fresh green peas
- salt and pepper

In a large casserole dish, sauté the onions and red pepper in a little sunflower oil until soft. Add the curry paste and stir until fragrant. Add the sections of monkfish and cook, turning once, until seared on both sides. Add the lemongrass, lime juice, coconut milk, sweet potato and tomatoes. Stir and continue to cook on a slow heat for 30 minutes. About 5 minutes before serving, add the coriander and the peas (uncooked) and season to taste. Serve with plain rice.

Olivier Bernard, Domaine de Chevalier Pessac-Léognan, Bordeaux, France: Bernard says he enjoys drinking youngish bottles of white Domaine de Chevalier with the crab remoulade served at Parisian restaurant Taillevent. The dish is made by mixing finely diced carrot, celery and courgettes with chopped dill and a mayonnaise, cream and lemon sauce and topping it with finely sliced radish arranged in a spiral: 'The crab, the creaminess of the dish, and the dill, all go very well with wines like this.'

savagnin

Savagnin is the mountain grape of the Jura in France, white, intensely mineral, sometimes almost salty and hazelnutty, reminiscent of hay and white peach but also direct and focused as a blade. I was astonished to discover, in *Wine Grapes* by Jancis Robinson, Julia Harding and José Vouillamoz, that savagnin and gewürztraminer (which reeks of lychees and rose water) are clonal variations of the same grape variety. It is *the* wine to drink with **Vacherin Mont d'Or**, the creamy, pongy Swiss cheese that's usually eaten heated so that it goes very runny. Also great with **fondue**, **trout cooked with almonds and leeks** or **hazelnut and Parmesan-crusted chicken**.

semillon

what it tastes like: Young semillon is bright and crisp, all meadow grass, lemon and lime, but as it ages an unnerving transformation occurs. Notes of hay, lemon curd, wax and lanolin creep in and the wine begins to taste so toasty and spicy you would swear it had been aged in oak – even when it hasn't.

In the Hunter Valley to the north of Sydney in Australia, they make superb dry semillon – it's low in alcohol (typically around 10.5 or 11% abv), zippy, lithe, tastes of lemongrass, and is equally delicious whether drunk young or left to age in the bottle so that it acquires toasty complexity. Elsewhere in Australia, semillon tends to have more alcohol and more might. It may be aged in oak, and sometimes smells of salad cream, white asparagus and the inside of a brand-new leather handbag. That's a jarring image, I know.

There is also a lot of semillon in France, concentrated around Bordeaux and Bergerac, and some in the US in California and Washington State, but here, as in Margaret River, Australia, it is most often seen blended with sauvignon blanc (see *sauvignon blanc-semillon blends*). Semillon also makes highly prized dessert wines, both as a partner (again) of sauvignon blanc (see *Sauternes*) and also in its own right. Sweet semillon is unctuous and tastes of marzipan, marmalade and poached apricots.

what to eat: Hunter Valley semillon that is young and unoaked will go beautifully with any food with which you want a refreshing, dry wine with a chase of citrus; it acts as a cleanser that makes the next mouthful of food seem more intense.

Green or white asparagus and **stir-fried Asian greens** are good with young semillon, as are **salads that combine fruit, cheese and the peppery taste of radish sprouts**.

The lemongrass tang of young semillon is great with seafood – **juicy fat prawns, smoked salmon, prawn dumplings** or **sushi**. Its citrusy cut and thrust is lively with spicy prawns and coriander tomato salsa, too. But, young or old, I like this grape most of all with **crispy soft-shell crab** or with **hot smoked salmon** served with a smear of crème fraîche and horseradish on toast. Pick a young wine for zip, or a more mature one to enjoy the interplay of its smoky, toasty taste with the crunch of the soft-shell crab and the smokiness of the salmon. The texture of older semillon is also very good with the sweet-and-herbs taste of **gravadlax** with a potato and fennel salad. And the nuttiness of older semillon plays nicely with **macadamia-crusted yellow-tail, barramundi or snapper fillet**.

Dill and **tarragon** are both good semillon herbs.

Semillon also works well with the clean flavours of **Asian-influenced dishes that aren't chilli-hot**, such as **gingery pork noodles with bok choy**; **vegetable ramen**; or **fish or crab cakes made with lemongrass, coriander and galangal**. Again, pick a younger wine for freshness and an older one to emphasize the spice.

The lime and sand tang of a Barossa semillon is a huge treat with **lobster with lime butter**. These bigger, more toasty Barossa semillons, or those semillons with some age, are also a good foil to pork, in particular **pork stir fry** or **pork chop served with the lemon and almonds of Skordalia**.

what the winemakers eat
Iain Riggs, Brokenwood, Hunter Valley, Australia: 'The way we serve young semillon at the winery is to get a couple of dozen shucked oysters, fill the shells with cold semillon and serve it like a shot. At home? Well, the same. There's also a big fish co-op down in Newcastle so we get a kind of prawn we call

schoolies and – this is going to sound really bad – get a slice of fresh white bread, put a big layer of butter on it, then a layer of schoolies, then shitloads of salt and pepper, then another slice of bread and really get into it with the young semillon.'

Jeff Vejr, wine consultant and owner of Golden Cluster winery, Oregon, US: 'Recently, at Holdfast Dining in Portland, Oregon, chefs Joel Stocks and Will Preisch introduced me to chawanmushi. I put my 2013 Golden Cluster Coury semillon with this amazing traditional Japanese dish. Chawanmushi is an egg custard that usually contains soy sauce, mushrooms, dashi, gingko seeds, mirin, and shrimp. There is a porcini mushroom and mineral note to my 2013 semillon that was an amazing compliment to the texture and flavours of the truffle chawanmushi.'

See also Sauternes, sauvignon blanc-semillon blends.

sherry

what it tastes like: Sherry has a distinctive, nutty, yeasty smell and it comes in many styles, only a few of which are sweet. Dry sherry is not just one of the most undervalued wines in the world, it's also a consummate food wine. This Spanish fortified wine isn't as strong as many imagine either – manzanilla often has an abv of 15% and tastes crisp rather than nose-singeingly hot. Here is a brief guide to style, arranged to run from the lightest and driest to the richest and sweetest, followed by cream, a hybrid.

manzanilla The lightest and most delicate of all, manzanilla is made in the seaside town of Sanlúcar de Barrameda. Manzanilla is the fine bone china of sherry. Pale in colour, it smells of sea spray, chamomile, and iodine and is best served with the cold frisson of a bottle that has come straight from the fridge.

fino Fino is made in the old Moorish-Christian frontier town of Jerez, from which sherry takes its name. It is similar to manzanilla but bigger-boned and more robust, with a punchy tang of fresh-baked sourdough, roasted almonds and just-struck match. Like manzanilla, it's dry and best served chilled.

amontillado Deeper in colour, amontillado begins ageing under the thin white layer of yeast, flor, that protects fino and manzanilla from oxygenation throughout their lives in the solera (maturation system), but is then fortified so that the flor dies and the wine continues to mature without it. Amontillado tastes richer and more nutty.

palo cortado This is somewhat mysterious, in that it is possible to consult various books and sherry producers, and get different answers about what exactly palo cortado might be. I always imagined that palo cortado was an accident, formed on the rare occasions when the flor on a cask of sherry destined to become fino or possibly amontillado died away for natural reasons, leaving the wine exposed to the air. But I defer to Beltran Domecq, President of the Sherry Consejo, who told me, 'No, no, palo cortado is selected as one of the delicate wines in the bodega. It begins as a fino and is fortified to 15 per cent but then you later refortify it to 17 per cent. It is more delicate than an amontillado and it undergoes biological ageing for more years.'

oloroso The darkest and richest of the potentially dry sherries, oloroso is selected from the initial casks as the most robust and least delicate of the wines available in the winery, and fortified to a higher level of alcohol, so the flor never develops. It is a pale mahogany colour and tastes of dried figs, raisins and hazelnuts. Oloroso may be dry or sweetened.

PX Many producers claim it to be the world's sweetest wine, and it's certainly up there. PX sherry is made using the pedro ximénez grape. The colour of black treacle, it smells of molasses, tastes of drippingly sweet liquidized raisins, and contains something like 400–450g of sugar in every litre; I've heard tell of PX with as much as 620g, which would be extraordinarily viscous and sweet.

cream Cream sherries are simply blends of the other six styles, with PX providing the sweetness.

This range of classifications means that sherry often confuses, but in reality it is the simplest of wines. It is made in one place

(Andalusia in the south-west of Spain). It relies on one grape (palomino, which makes up about 95 per cent of the vineyard; two others, PX and moscatel, used largely for sweetening, make up the deficit). Also there are no pesky vintages to worry about – sherry is matured using a solera system of fractional blending, in which barrels that are partially empty because wine has been drawn from them for bottling are topped up from younger barrels, which in turn are topped up with wine from even younger barrels, and so on, so that the barrels are never emptied and may contain droplets of wine that are as old as the winery itself.

what to eat: **Salted marcona almonds**. Snug-skinned green **manzanilla olives**, which came originally from Seville. **Tortilla**. Tender, succulent **jamón ibérico de bellota** and all other **charcuterie**, ideally freshly sliced from a great leg of ham seconds before you eat it. It might be a cliché but it's a good cliché – sherry takes you straight to the tapas bar.

Manzanilla and fino have the delicacy and finesse to start you off on olives, **salty roasted nuts, crisps, toast and aioli, pan con tomate, tortilla, croquetas,** and **shellfish**. The crisp edge and salty crackle of manzanilla are the perfect seasoning for **fresh oysters**. A chilled glass of either is glorious with **razor clams** or **prawns dripping in garlicky butter or oil**. Both manzanilla and fino also cut pleasingly through the light batter of **fritto misto** and complement **boquerones** and **chargrilled squid**.

Spears of griddled or steamed **asparagus** are very good with manzanilla, or with fino if there is aioli or hollandaise on the side. I also like drinking these lighter styles with air-dried ham, but a sherry in a richer register – an amontillado or palo cortado – emphasizes the savoury, meaty flavours, rather than the salt, of, say, **chorizo** or **lomo** in a quite delicious way.

Fino is superb with **smoked salmon**, **smoked duck** and also the umami intensity of **mojama** – tuna cured in salt and dried in the Spanish sun. A colleague still, slightly alarmingly, likes to recall one of his favourite ever mojama plates of food, with the sense of wonder and moment others might reserve for an Olympic gold performance on track or field: 'The Copa Jerez [an international food and sherry matching competition], 2007, the US contestant was a bloke called Andy Nusser and he put mojama with duck egg, a take on an eggs and bacon breakfast, with a glass of fino sherry. Just brilliant.' Indeed it was.

Fino is perfect with **gazpacho** – a swig of one (all fresh tomatoes, cucumber, sweet peppers, raw onions and vinegar), a sip of the other, all summer long.

In fact sherry in general is almost the only wine I recommend to drink with **soup** of any kind. It acts as seasoning: a mouthful of fino with fish soup, or a sip of amontillado or palo cortado with Brown Windsor soup. It has a natural affinity with **tomatoes**, which is why a glass of fino is so good with toast scraped with garlic and topped with chopped tomatoes, and why amontillado (fino if you don't have it) is an essential addition to a jug full of **Bloody Mary.**

Sherry's vibrant earthiness and oxidative tones are lovely with **morcilla** (black pudding) and its savoury qualities intensify the flavours of **mushrooms**; try a glass (fino, palo cortado or amontillado for choice) with wild mushrooms on toast or with a mushroom tortilla.

It is good with **beef and mushroom stews**, too – pick a fino if you prefer the freshness or an amontillado or palo cortado for more oomph and to amplify the darker, meaty flavours in the pot. The Spanish are perfectly at ease with the idea of pouring a glass of sherry not just as an aperitif but also with a big plate of food. This practice deserves to become more widespread, not least because sherry is one of the most underappreciated wines in the world. You get so much for your money.

Imagine, on a cold winter's night, a plateful of **sweet roasted parsnips and a bowl of slow-cooked beef and thyme casserole to which you have added some porcini or shiitake mushrooms**, so that it is rich with umami. There is a splash of sherry in the cooking pot and a sneaky glass of amontillado at your elbow – that seems a pretty perfect scenario to me.

Likewise, oloroso is good with **slow-cooked beef cheeks**; palo cortado with **morcilla and garlic mash**; and a cold glass of fino with a piece of **cod, garlicky aioli and a gratin of Jerusalem artichokes**. You can also make a comforting dish of **potatoes with caramelized onions and artichoke hearts** that is so good all you need to make a dinner of it is a chicory salad. And a glass of fino. The recipe

S

below is based on a dish I ate one January in the bright sunshine of Jerez when visiting Harvey's bodega. The original recipe used fresh artichokes, and was sent to me without any quantities at all, but this works very well.

PATATAS CON ALCAUCILES
(POTATOES WITH ARTICHOKES)
Serves 4

- 3 medium (about 300g) potatoes, peeled and sliced ½ cm thick
- olive oil
- 1 large Spanish onion, halved and sliced
- 4 cloves of garlic, sliced
- 2 bay leaves
- a small bunch of flat-leaf parsley, chopped
- 2 × 180g cans or jars of artichoke hearts in olive oil, drained and thickly sliced
- 175ml fino
- salt and freshly ground black pepper
- 2 tablespoons breadcrumbs

Drop the potatoes into a pan of boiling salted water and simmer for 3–4 minutes until just tender. Heat the oven to 190°C/375°F/gas mark 5. Heat 3 tablespoons olive oil in a large, wide, ovenproof pan. Add the onions, garlic and bay leaves and cook until the onions are soft and golden, about 10 minutes. Add the parsley, artichoke hearts and the fino and season. Simmer for 5 minutes. Discard the bay leaves before adding the potatoes and turning them around in the pan. Spread everything out evenly, then sprinkle with breadcrumbs and a little more olive oil. Transfer the pan to the oven and bake for 30 minutes until golden.

Many sherry producers also like to drink sherry with **game**, though I usually prefer a glass of red. Sherry does go extremely well with a cheeseboard, though. Think of the vegetal nuttiness of a really **good Cheddar** with manzanilla pasada (an extra-aged manzanilla); **young Manchego** with fino or amontillado; palo cortado with a **dry, old Manchego**; or oloroso with strong blue cheese such as **Picos de Europa**. The nuts and dried fruit flavours of amontillado and oloroso, sweet or dry, act like the densely packed fig and almond wheels you have with cheese.

These are all European foods, but sherry's affinity with both umami and seafood suggests alternatives from cuisines beyond its homeland borders.

As Jesús Barquín of Equipo Navazos puts it, 'Of course an array of our wines are the best possible matches for a wide selection of the best Spanish food. But one tends to take that for granted. Those wines and food have grown together. In a wider approach, there is some kind of magic in the fact that the best and most authentic sherry wines outstandingly match **Asian food** in general, particularly **sushi** (fino, manzanilla) and also **spicy South-Eastern dishes** (amontillado, palo cortado, even oloroso).'

Quite so. I like **nigiri** with fino, or an en rama manzanilla (an en rama sherry is one that has been bottled without fining or filtration, so has the brightness of a wine drawn straight from the cask in the bodega). The intense burst of **salmon roe** is electrifying with a fino or an amontillado. And **soft-shell crab nam rolls** are glorious with the clean, seaside riff of a fine manzanilla. Japan repays the compliment too – some sake drinks very well with certain tapas.

On to sweet wines. Cream sherry has become *vinum non gratum*, despite the truly delicious artisan versions being made by some producers. All cream sherry, however, is spectacular with **fresh oranges**. In Jerez I was offered a huge bowl full of sliced oranges, drizzled with sugar syrup marinated with cloves and cinnamon; wonderful with Harvey's Bristol Cream.

The nuts and raisins flavours of sweet oloroso are good with **milky rice pudding**.

The best use of very sweet PX sherry, which tastes of molasses and molten raisins, is to pour it **over ice cream**.

what the winemakers eat

Tim Holt of Barbadillo, Spain: 'With Barbadillo Solear manzanilla I like mantis shrimp, known as galeras, simply steamed with sea salt. We have this frequently in the evening in winter, which is when they are in season. The local boats come in in the afternoon and they need to be done live. Tuna sashimi is excellent too: the tuna season is in spring and early summer and fished just off our coast in the traditional way using the *almadraba* [a labyrinthine system of nets that draw the fish into a central pool].

'You generally find that marinated fish works well with manzanilla. My brother-in-law does a ceviche from the bream and sea bass he catches just off Sanlúcar's coast. In this case the marinade is lime, although one of the best-ever matches with manzanilla is boquerones en vinagre. (vinaigrette anchovies). It's not something we do at home, though. Same goes for shrimp fritters , in theory easy to do at home, but it involves deep-frying shrimps in a batter, so it's best to have it in the bars so your house doesn't smell of deep-fried shrimp.

'My other favourite sherry at home is dry amontillado. I have this more frequently in the winter and I have to break open a bottle of the Principe amontillado (fifteen years old) from Barbadillo when I have the following tapas: salchichon, longaniza, salami or Iberian Serrano ham. The higher alcohol dissolves all the fatty content so you have an explosion on the palate of the cured and nutty flavours combined.

'Finally, and also good with oloroso or amontillado, is a very basic and traditional dish which we have in the cooler months called 'lentejas' (lentils), This is a hot pot dish with lentils, chorizo, bacon, carrot, onion, green peppers, celery, whole garlic and extra virgin olive oil, slow-cooked and consumed the next day or the following. This is a typical Andalusian home-cooked dish and rarely offered in bars.'

Jesús Barquín of Equipo Navazos, Spain: 'If I needed to pick only one specific match as deliciously harmonious, then our La Bota de Amontillado No. 59 or No. 61 with the best and freshest raw oysters you may find. More generally, mature fino or manzanilla pasada [aged manzanilla] with a whole kaiseki menu at the Restaurant Goto in Singapore, or bone-dry palo cortado with curry of beef cheeks at Restaurant Sudestada in Madrid, or with almost any kind of curry chez some friends of mine in Bayswater, and finally very old amontillado with sashimi with a touch of wasabi at Dos Palillos in Barcelona.'

Javier Hidalgo, Bodegas Hidalgo La Gitana: Javier's suggestions for when to drink and what to drink with sherry ran to several pages so I have narrowed them down to four.

1. 'Back in late June I was driving a herd of cattle from Extremadura to Castilla. We started early in the morning and made a stop by 10 a.m. While the cattle ate grass and drank, we had some food: cheese and charcuterie. Then I produced oloroso and amontillado (both totally dry). The first matched very well the cheese (Manchego), the chorizo and the black pudding. The second matched the ham and the lomo to perfection.'
2. 'I used to spend time in Seattle, as my US agents are based there. It rains in Seattle more than in Cornwall and when my colleagues were having tea in the afternoon I drank cream sherry. It is very well suited to cakes in a wet climate.'
3. 'Can you think of anything with fried egg? Dry oloroso.'
4. 'A good way to remove the hangover on the following morning: a glass of amontillado with sugar and the yolk of an egg.'

Supertuscan

what it tastes like: Supertuscan is the name originally given to insurgent wines made in Tuscany either using international varieties such as cabernet sauvignon, cabernet franc and merlot, or made entirely from sangiovese (extraordinarily, an all-sangiovese wine did not used to be permitted within the Chianti Classico discipline). The wines were so successful that the use of certain quantities of these grapes, as well as all-sangiovese bottlings, has now been variously legitimized within the Chianti Classico,

Bolgheri, Bolgheri-Sassicaia and Toscana appellations. However, the term Supertuscan remains a useful catch-all for a modern style of Tuscan red in which Bordeaux varieties dominate, and is particularly used to refer to the extravagant and extravagantly successful reds such as Sassicaia and Ornellaia from coastal Tuscany.

Supertuscans, even those based on cabernet sauvignon, tend to be plusher than most left-bank claret, veering more towards Pomerol and St Emilion in their generosity of texture. They are bold and usually also have a taste of sour cherries that marks them out as Italian.

what to eat: Supertuscans aren't quite such willing foods wines as those from elsewhere in Italy, though I do love a sangiovese and cabernet sauvignon blend with **lamb**, or with the char of **barbecued meat**. The more upmarket Supertuscans made entirely from international varieties suit simple food (or no food at all). **Red meat, veal, chunky sausages** and **game** go well, whether cooked in classic French style or served with more Italian accompaniments such as **polenta** or the creamy-gritty texture of white **beans**. Think **pot-roasted pheasant, grouse with pancetta** or a simple piece of grilled beef or a veal chop with a rich jus or a **cannellini or borlotti bean** salad on the side.

See also pigeon. Or, as Lodovico Antinori says on p. 139, Colombaccio sui crostini.

syrah
also known as shiraz
what it tastes like: Syrah is powerful and perfumed. It might smell of black peppercorns, violets, baked raspberries, blackberries, liquorice, tobacco and even eucalyptus. It can be intensely, richly fruity – a vinous cuddle of a wine, all mulberries and raspberry jelly, but it can also be blood-stirringly savage, with a feral, gamey edge.

This red grape has two linguistic identities, too: syrah and shiraz. It was once the case that Europeans talked about syrah, while the New World grew shiraz. Now it's more complicated. Some syrah/shiraz is labelled to reflect the style of wine in the bottle, or at least to reflect the winemaker's ambition for the wine he has put in the bottle. Winemakers whose sights are on refined perfume, stony minerality and perhaps also inscrutability tend to refer to their wine as syrah. Those (often working in warmer climates) who favour riper grapes, higher alcohols and a great unleashing of booming fruit call it shiraz.

Wherever it is grown, syrah is a swarthy grape. Its perfume may be like a song, but there is also a lot of tannin and a meaty, savoury bulk. Depending on the soil in which it's grown, there may also be minerality that makes tasting it feel like licking basalt or granite or smooth stones.

Its floral scent is more often found in cooler climates, such as the Rhône, syrah's fine-wine stronghold, but not everyone can smell it. The scent of violets depends on a molecule called beta-ionone, which, thanks to genetic variations in olfactory receptors, around 40 per cent of the population is unable to detect.

Another hallmark of Rhône syrah is the tickle of freshly cracked black peppercorns – fierce but also finessed, caught on the insides of your nostrils just under the bridge of your nose.

The different aromas in wine can create peculiar associations. For me, a sniff of a syrah from its historic home in the northern Rhône often brings to mind an image of a gnarled, blackened fence post. I think this is because, somewhere in the profile of all those fêted northern Rhône syrahs, there is a sense of woodland, dark undergrowth, wildness, and the undiscovered outdoors.

Each Rhône appellation has its own distinctive character: wines from St Joseph often have a fruity exuberance underlying their cool minerality; Hermitage is imposing; Cornas is rustic and black-booted; Côte-Rôtie is elegant and highly scented.

Liquorice – root rather than bootlaces – tobacco, earth and the smell of hot stones are also typical Rhône tasting notes and may also be found in other cooler-climate syrahs. These wines often smell of the oily sizzle of browning bacon fat as well as bonfire smoke.

The Australians call syrah, 'shiraz' and it was with the rise of Australian wine in the late twentieth century that we came to know shiraz as another creature. Shiraz still has that black, rich fruit and a soaring perfume but it is more luscious, with no hint of dank undergrowth. The smell of baked raspberries is often found in Aussie shiraz, along with that of juicy mulberries, red and black liquorice bootlaces, and dark chocolate.

S

Under the scorch of the Barossa sun shiraz can be huge: purply-violet, intense, high in alcohol (15% abv or over), rich in fruit, more like a blood transfusion than a wine. Plush shiraz from the McLaren Vale often smells of eucalyptus. In the cooler Hunter Valley, you pick up more earthiness (these wines are sometimes described as cabbagey). While in Heathcote, in Victoria, you find earthy shiraz/syrah that is powerful but also finely delineated – as if its base is carved from coal and stone.

In New Zealand, the region of Gimblett Gravels in Hawke's Bay is renowned for the bright quality of its syrah; in South Africa, shiraz can be thick and heavily smoky though a few producers, notably Mullineux in Swartland, are making truly impressive, streamlined syrah-labelled wines that rival, if not beat, those of a similar price from the northern Rhône.

Chile, too, shows promise that syrah is a grape that might be particularly successful in its soil. Matetic is the standard-bearer here, while the Italian Giorgio Flessati also makes a very inky syrah in the fierce ultraviolet light of the Elqui Valley on the fringe of the Atacama Desert, where all the star-gazers go for the clear skies. 'It's eight light minutes from here to the sun. Sirius is eight light years away,' he told me as we stood at an observatory in the mountains one night, looking at Jupiter's orange stripes and all the constellations wheeling across the sky. His syrah is smoky and tastes of bitumen, and needs to be drunk with food.

In North America syrah is most enthusiastically embraced in Washington State.

Of course, syrah is also a grape with fantastic ageing potential. Good oaked syrah can be aged for many decades and, as it does, its fruitiness recedes and a gamey savour comes increasingly to the fore, with the smell of the wine pluming out of the glass.

syrah blends In the Côte-Rôtie in France, syrah and viognier were historically co-planted and they are still, sometimes, blended, though only a tiny percentage of viognier ever makes its way into the bottle. The white grape adds more perfume and creates a levitating effect, appearing to lift and amplify syrah's heavier aromatics.

Allied with grenache, syrah also forms part of the Côtes du

Rhône blend and, again alongside grenache, it is used in the named villages in the southern Rhône – Gigondas, Vacqueyras, Cairanne and so on – as well as being one of the possible constituents of Châteauneuf-du-Pape. Throughout southern France it also adds backbone and dried-herb scent to blended reds such as St Chinian, Faugères and Corbières. In the US, syrah is one of the grapes used by the self-styled 'Rhône Rangers' to make red wines that pay homage to those from France, but which are often plusher and thicker.

In Australia syrah combines with cabernet sauvignon to form what wine expert Matthew Jukes calls the Great Australian Red – 'the blend that defines Australia'. I have a real weak spot for Australian syrah-cabernet. It is such a cosy wine, but it can also be grand – Penfolds' much-lauded Grange is a multi-district blend of cabernet and syrah.

what to eat: **Lamb** is the first meat that comes to mind when there's a bottle of syrah I want to drink, but syrah is such an aromatic grape that it's as much about the herbs, spices and other fragrant ingredients in the dish as it is about the protein.

Syrah loves **garlic, thyme and dried herbes de Provence**. **Rosemary** is a fantastic syrah herb too. Its woody-herbal scent plays into the dusty, dried-herb, garrigue-like smell of wines from the Rhône and the south of France, and also taps into the warm eucalyptus scent that comes with the heavy fruit of shiraz from McLaren Vale. This works especially well if you have Mediterranean vegetables such as **red peppers and tomatoes stuffed with garlic, rosemary, thyme and rice**, or in combination with lamb: butterflied leg of lamb covered with a paste of pulverized raw garlic, rosemary, anchovies and olive oil and cooked for about 15 minutes in a hot oven is an easy and much-loved syrah dinner.

The suggestion that syrah can smell of pepper is not fanciful. The most powerful aroma compound yet identified in black and white peppercorns is called rotundone. This has also been found to be present in some syrah wines, albeit in much lower concentrations by a factor of about 10,000. It's thanks partly to this peppery scent that syrah has the clout to stand up to **heavily seasoned meat** – for instance, ordinary **pork sausages packed with sea salt, black pepper and more of that aromatic rosemary** – and

S

it's why freshly cracked black peppercorns can be such a pleasing combination with this grape.

One of my favourite simple syrah dinners is steak with a freshly cracked black pepper crust.

STEAK WITH FRESHLY CRACKED BLACK PEPPERCORNS
Serves 4

Until I made this for the first time, I was a black peppercorn peasant who paid no attention to the type of pepper I was buying and certainly not to how long it had been languishing in the cupboard. Now I appreciate the crackling, floral, dizzying smell of freshly smashed peppercorns so much I pay as much attention to them as some do to their coffee. I eat this with a fiery salad of watercress or rocket and spinach. An inexpensive syrah from South Africa or France works beautifully.

- 2 beef stock cubes
- 3 teaspoons Dijon mustard
- 4 pieces of fillet steak, weighing about 175g each
- 4 tablespoons top-quality black peppercorns
- olive oil, for frying

Crumble or squash the stock cubes in a small dish and use the back of a teaspoon to mix in the mustard until you have a thick paste. Rub the paste into both sides of each steak. Smash the peppercorns using a mortar and pestle until they are lightly crushed but not powdered. Transfer the smashed peppercorns to a plate and dip both sides of each of the steaks in so that they are coated with pepper. When you are ready to eat, heat a little oil in a frying pan and cook the steaks to your preferred cuisson. If you want to make a sauce, once the steaks are removed to plates, use some of the drinking wine to deglaze the pan, bringing it to a brisk bubble and scraping the meaty, peppery gubbins off the bottom of the pan as you do so.

Syrah can also work well with **dry, mildly spiced Indian food**. For example, put an Australian shiraz with a **spice-crusted fillet of beef**, or a smoky, earthy syrah from South Africa with a green **lentil dhal** or **spicy veggie lentil burgers**.

Syrah is not for delicate ingredients, but the luscious bitter-sweetness of Australian shiraz can be a fine partner to Asian-style rubs, particularly those with a slight element of sticky sweetness. Try a hefty Barossa or McLaren Vale shiraz or an Aussie syrah-cabernet with **beef short ribs marinated in five-spice and hoisin sauce** or an Aussie shiraz from anywhere with a **roasted duck breast with plum sauce and sesame noodles**. Or why not marinate a big beef rib for a couple of hours in equal parts of teriyaki and soy sauce, a slice of finely chopped root ginger, a finely chopped red chilli, a finely chopped clove of garlic, a dash of sesame oil, a spoonful of olive oil and a small bunch of fresh chopped coriander, then barbecue or roast until done, and open a bottle of more restrained and red-fruited Adelaide Hills shiraz, or a cabernet-shiraz blend, to go with it? Southern hemisphere shiraz is also lovely with the richness of **pulled pork** and all its saucy accoutrements.

Other successful marriages between the Australian shiraz-cabernet blend and Asian spices that I've enjoyed – in restaurants, needless to say, not at home – include **quail with shichimi pepper and wilted spring onions**, as well as **aged sirloin with mooli ponzu sauce** and **sautéed wild mushrooms**.

Meat-wise, syrah also responds extremely well to full-flavoured meat such as **venison**, **wild boar** and **duck**. This is particularly true of more savoury versions, say, from the Rhone, Languedoc, Chile or South Africa. Think of the baked herbs of a Rhône syrah or the inky smoke of a South African syrah with a wintry venison casserole with polenta. Syrah grows more feral with age as it loses the puppy fat of its early fruit and begins to smell gamey and wild, so there is no problem putting older, finer wines with gamey food. The opposite, in fact, as John Livingstone-Learmonth suggests in his comments in *Wines of the Northern Rhône* on food to accompany red Hermitage:

> Jean-Louis Chave is another to distinguish by vintage style; for him a fruit-finesse vintage like 1985 goes well

with lamb, while the bigger vintages are more suited to venison. Past twelve years old, one moves more towards fuller, denser dishes. A daube or beef casserole, meat stew or jugged hare are ideal. So, too, is classic rich game like venison or wild boar.

One of Gérard Chave's [Jean-Louis's father's] main dishes is his young goat, or cabri; this has sweetness in its flavour, and is a wonderful companion for a Chave Hermitage rouge that is around twenty years old.

Continuing the theme of hearty meat dishes, a northern Rhône – say, a brighter, fruitier St Joseph – or a more savoury Heathcote syrah is good with a rich **black olive and beef stew**. A Crozes-Hermitage or vin de pays syrah works well **with smoky German sausage with spiced red cabbage** on the side. **Beef roasted with chestnuts and served with maple-syrup roast parsnips and crinkly winter greens** would go well with a syrah from anywhere – pick a riper shiraz to play to the sweetness of the chestnuts and maple syrup, or a cooler syrah to underscore the more savoury greens.

Syrah will also be very happy to accompany the leftovers of a roast lamb the next day. Just get some pitta or flatbread, pop the lamb bits in the oven with chilli sauce until they are piping hot and make your own **kebabs** with yoghurt and finely shredded iceburg lettuce. Serve with an inexpensive syrah or syrah blend.

what the winemakers eat

Gary Mills, Jamsheed Wines, Victoria, Australia: 'What I think goes best with the wines depends on the vintage, but I could generalize by saying that the four vineyards all have their favourite protein to match them. With the Beechworth Syrah I like pork; with the Seville (from the Yarra Valley) marbled beef – the acidity cuts well through the fat; with Garden Gully (Great Western) – saltbush lamb; and with Pyren (Pyrenees) – probably lamb again but with a heavier sauce or marinade.

'One thing we love to cook at home when we are trying our syrahs is a simple pasta dish: Heat a little olive oil and chopped fennel in a pan. Add a bit of continental sausage and hot cacciatore sausage that you have first skinned and minced, or finely chopped. Don't put too much meat in. Stir until browned, then throw in some chopped tomatoes and chopped garlic, simmer, then add fresh peas and a dash of syrah and serve with farfalle pasta.

'My syrahs always have an agave/mescal edge to the palate and therefore Mexican food lends itself well, too. For the release of one vintage of twelve syrahs we invited a group of somms up to the winery and cooked pulled pork tacos. The pork was a large shoulder boiled with bay leaves, then pulled apart and fried in a lot of olive oil, chipotle and garlic. Towards the end of the frying you add raisins and almond flakes and chipotle adobo sauce. The tacos were served with raw, shredded cabbage dressed with lime salt and pepper; barbecued chipotle-smeared corn salsa made from corn, finely diced red onion, coriander, salt, pepper and lime; guacamole; natural yoghurt in place of soured cream; and cheese. We barbecued some white corn tortilla and it seriously rocked the house.'

Olivier Clape, Domaine Clape, Cornas, France: 'So, food with Cornas . . . I'll say usually we cook civet de sanglier (wild boar) or chevreuil (deer) – with Cornas sauce of course. Sometimes those animals eat our grapes, so sometimes it's good to eat one of them and to know that they have eaten Cornas syrah. We used to eat hare à la royale and bécasse [woodcock] as well, but it is not so common any more. Very rare to find. The vegetables to go with both those dishes will be potatoes dauphinoise, carrots, cardoons.'

Ron Laughton, Jasper Hill, Heathcote, Australia: Besides making superb shiraz, Laughton is one of the very few winemakers outside Italy to make excellent nebbiolo. He sent me this recipe for what he calls 'my easy rabbit dish' along with a short note: 'We won't go into the crazy politics of the introduction of rabbits (and foxes) into Australia in early colonial times and the devastation they have caused since, but leave it as: the more rabbits we can eat, the better.' He uses a bottle of Jasper Hill in the casserole as well as a bottle to drink with it, which is more than a bit pricy for those of us who aren't

Ron. I would be tempted to cook with a cheaper shiraz and save the Jasper Hill for the glass.

'Section a rabbit into six pieces. In an ovenproof dish, marinate for 24–48 hours in a bottle of Jasper Hill Georgia's Paddock Shiraz to which you have added a small can of green peppercorns – the French ones with a green label. After marinating, dip each piece of rabbit in flour, then braise for a few minutes in a hot, oiled pan. Add some onion while braising if you wish. Return the rabbit pieces and pan juices to the marinade, cover and cook in a slow oven until you think it is done. Serve with buttery mashed potato, green veggies and another bottle of Georgia's Paddock Shiraz. Simple and yum!'

Jorge Matetic, Matetic Vineyards, Chile: 'With our EQ Syrah, lamb shank for sure. In the vineyard restaurant it's cooked in a wine reduction for a long time until the meat falls off the bone. Usually it comes with mashed potato. We also have a beef rib that goes in the oven for 4 hours with onions and carrots.'

Andrea Mullineux, Mullineux & Leeu Family Wines, South Africa: 'For our syrah, which is elegant and perfumed with what I refer to as fresh tannins (from the whole cluster fermentation), roasted rosemary and garlic lamb is a classic, beautiful pairing. However, on my travels I was introduced to a new combo that took me by surprise. In Norway they love fish with serious red wine and what I found worked incredibly well was firm (texture is important) white fish such as halibut, monkfish or kingklip pan-seared and roasted with our Mullineux Syrah.'

Yann Chave, Domaine Yann Chave, Crozes-Hermitage, France: 'A meal that I love with a Crozes-Hermitage Le Rouvre is civet de chevreuil mariné façon grand veneur – there's a recipe online at cuisineactuelle.fr.'

T

tannat

Tannat is found in Uruguay and is also the red grape that dominates the blend of Madiran in south-west France. It tastes of cacao nibs, tobacco and elderberries and, as its name suggests, is highly tannic, so suits protein or fat, which have a softening effect. Avoid lighter foods, which will be overpowered. **Moussaka** or **aubergine parmigiana** work well, as do **grilled red meats**, **spicy sausages, salami,** and **hearty meaty plates of food such as stews and braises**. Some hard cheeses work well with tannat too: **aged Comté** is good with a mature Madiran, as is **Esbareich**, a semi-hard cheese with a nutty flavour.

tempranillo

also known as tinta del país, tinto fino, tinta roriz

what it tastes like: Young tempranillo tastes of bright red fruit with a bit of a crunch and a lick of russet – redcurrants and strawberries with a suggestion of tomato and tobacco. Add in some oak and age and you get more savoury flavours – cedar wood, dried herbs, more tobacco, old saddles, nutmeg, cloves, spice, mulching leaves, coconut, vanilla and strawberries allowed to ripen so long they are almost rotten when you eat them.

This grape is the star of Spain's two best-known reds: Ribera del Duero and Rioja. In Ribera del Duero tinto fino, as the local strain of tempranillo is called, is usually bottled neat and only sometimes blended with a little cabernet or merlot. It makes wines that are particularly concentrated, dark-fruited and firm (admittedly sometimes because there's so much oak). Confusingly, Rioja may be made from 100 per cent tempranillo, but does not actually have to contain any tempranillo at all. In practice, tempranillo does form the base of most bottles of Rioja, either in pure form or as the anchor of a tempranillo-based blend also featuring one or more of garnacha tinta, graciano and mazuelo.

Tempranillo is also grown throughout the rest of Spain and in every location the impact of oak (or no oak) is keenly felt. American oak brings a sweet vanilla perfume and sometimes also a suggestion of coconut. French oak is more savoury. Going from not at all woody to very woody, the words joven, crianza, reserva and gran reserva give an indication of how much exposure to oak the wine has had.

In Rioja, a Joven spends no time in oak barrels, Crianza and Reserva at least one year, and a Gran Reserva at least two years. Some wines spend so long in brand-new toasty oak that the spicy wood is almost a greater influence than the grapes themselves – the gran reserva style of Rioja is as much about the oak as it is about the wine.

As tinta roriz, tempranillo is also used in Portugal, notably in the Douro Valley, where it forms part of the blend in table wines as well as port.

What is particularly attractive about tempranillo is its mellow smoothness. It is not angular with acidity or huge tannin, but rounded like a rubber ball.

It is a remarkably transportable grape, capable of making good wine beyond its homeland of the Iberian peninsula, but for some reason there hasn't been a huge rush to plant it. Good examples are found in Australia (where it is sometimes blended with 15 per cent shiraz, which doesn't have to be declared on the label and has the effect of Aussie-ing it up) and California as well as in Argentina.

what to eat: Tempranillo's mellow quality melds beautifully with meat that has been cooked so long and so slowly that it is almost melting off the bone. So it loves roast pork but it especially loves **overnight-roasted shoulder of pork**, perhaps served with a vegetable and potato gratin seasoned with nutmeg. Its strawberry brightness and tomato ketchup sweetness also go well with **pulled pork served on a toasted roll with barbecue sauce.**

A young and energetic tempranillo is superb with little **pink lamb cutlets**, but a Ribera or Rioja that has begun to mature so that it smells of autumn leaves goes with **slow-cooked lamb** like no other wine. A classic Spanish dish is **lecho al horno** – slow-roasted suckling lamb cooked in an open oven. In *Arabesque: A Taste of*

Morocco, Turkey and Lebanon, Claudia Roden has a beautiful recipe for 'Crispy-skinned shoulder of lamb stuffed with dates, cinnamon and almonds and served with couscous' that is lovely with a Ribera del Duero or Rioja that is past its first flush of youth.

Where sweeter flavours such as dates or a vanilla sauce are incorporated into a dish, you might prefer to pick a tempranillo made using American oak, whose own vanilla overtones will meld with those on the plate.

Gentle spices are a very good match for oaked tempranillo and the grape's rounded feel. Think cooked **garlic**, **nutmeg**, **cinnamon**, **cloves**, **cumin** and **mace** – but the spice that has tempranillo's name written all over it is **paprika**. Sweet smoked paprika, hot smoked paprika, plain paprika, it doesn't matter which; the addition of this russet spice to a dish always makes me consider opening a tempranillo of one sort or another.

Pick a Rioja reserva with **lamb chops rubbed with cumin, paprika, garlic and coriander seeds**. Choose the vigour and freshness of a young, unoaked tempranillo to go with **tender white octopus, thinly sliced, drizzled with olive oil and sprinkled with paprika**. Pour a Crianza with a **garlicky, paprika-spiked chickpea and tomato and spinach salsa**.

Chorizo is of course flavoured with paprika and it is quite hard to find a dish involving **chorizo** that does not taste great with tempranillo. A few examples: **squid and chorizo and red pepper stew**; **hake cooked with chorizo**; **meatballs with clams, chorizo and squid**; **chickpea and chorizo soup**; **leeks with a warm chorizo dressing**.

All kinds of Spanish **cured hams** are good with tempranillo – try local charcuterie with local wines. Also delicious are **Spanish rice dishes** that start by frying onions and peppers very slowly until they soften into a golden soffritto. The caramelized vegetables infuse the rice with a glistening sweetness that melts into tempranillo's open arms. This is the case for both meaty and non-meaty dishes, such as **aubergine and tomato rice**, or **paella with saffron and monkfish and giant prawns and artichokes**.

Heavier, more oaky tempranillo is good with heavier, more unctuous meat dishes, such as **oxtail stew**, **goat kid**, or **braised beef cheeks**.

T

The roundness of tempranillo also works well with the richness of **corn**. It seems to suit **nachos** (as long as the chilli isn't too strong) and **enchiladas** and I've enjoyed it with a light meal consisting of **polenta** cooked in a round dish, then sliced into thin galettes which are layered with crème fraîche, griddled red peppers and other salad ingredients.

In terms of vegetables, tempranillo's territory is more sweeter roots than spiky greens. It is lovely with **roasted beetroot, carrots, parsnips and turnip**, or with **griddled red and yellow peppers** or the unctuousness of **cooked aubergine**. Its sweet spiciness also works well with hard cheeses such as **Manchego**.

what the winemakers eat

Guillermo de Aranzabal, la Rioja Alta, Rioja, Spain: 'The general assumption is that red wines don't match fish. But I love a nice, grilled rodaballo (turbot) together with a "904". The La Rioja Alta Gran Reserva 904 is a very elegant, sophisticated and complex wine. Both the wine and the turbot are so delicate and deep that I think they perfectly complement each other. When I go to Elcano or Kaia, both excellent restaurants in Getaria, a coastal town in northern Spain, 904 and rodaballo are a no-brainer selection.'

José Manuel Ortega, a Spaniard who runs wineries in Argentina as well as O. Fournier in Ribera del Duero: 'With my tempranillo from Spain I would go for grilled swordfish, taking a more eclectic approach to food pairing. The scent from our Ribera del Duero Alfa Spiga Tempranillo can sure match the aromas from the fish.'

torrentes

So perfumed that you can smell its freesia-like scent in the vineyard, yards away from the plant, torrontes is a yellow-skinned grape that makes the signature white wine of Argentina. Its eau de cologne flavour is best enjoyed very well chilled, as an aperitif, and it makes a beautifully refreshing **granita**, too. Those who've visited Argentina love drinking it with **empanadas**. This is a mood match more than a taste match. It just makes you feel as if you're there.

touriga nacional

This high quality Portuguese grape makes deep, dark red wines with a touch of wildness that makes me think of Grendel knocking at the door. It's found in the Dão and the Douro (where it is used to make port as well as normal drinking wines). Young touriga nacional, bucking and kicking like an unbroken horse, is excellent with black pudding – there's a pleasing clash of ferocity and richness. Touriga and also touriga blends work very well with **rustic red meat casseroles, game (venison and rabbit, particularly if scented with juniper), guinea fowl, goat, roast pork and peppery sauces**.

See also Douro reds, port.

T

V

Valpolicella

Valpolicella is the Venetian red that tastes of amarena cherries and dust, and is made from a blend of local grapes that include corvina. It's light, sappy, and good served slightly chilled. Drink it with a simple **risotto**; with **chicken roasted with thyme**, or use it to wash down **pizza** or tomato-based pasta. Valpolicella has an edge and a refreshing acidity that make it a good summer red, like an Italian Beaujolais: try it with **rare tuna steaks**; **red mullet with tomatoes and black olives**; **spicy beef kebabs done on the barbecue**; **Parmesan**; or **swordfish steaks**.

Valpolicella Ripasso is a wine that has been passed over the shrivelled skins used to make Amarone; it is richer and more perfumed, sometimes with a whiff of furniture polish. As the winemaker at Monte dei Ragni puts it: 'Ripasso is very particular. It is only made in Valpolicella, so you get a bit of the taste of fresh grapes, a bit of the taste of the passito grapes, so it becomes more structured.'

Ripasso works with all the above and is good with heavier dishes too – for instance, with **aubergine parmigiana and rocket salad**, or if you want a red that's not too intense to drink with **braised beef with olives**.

verdejo

Verdejo is grown in Rueda in Spain, where it makes crisp wines that taste of citrus, almonds, bay leaves and nettles. It is often combined with sauvignon blanc; these wines tend to be lighter and more racy, but it can also have a little more weight and nutty roundness. Lighter versions make a good aperitif, and are refreshing with tapas and all forms of **fried fish**, from the Andalusian pescaito frito (pieces of fish dipped in flour and deep-fried) to fillets of white fish shallow-fried in oil or butter, served plain or perhaps with capers.

Fuller versions are refreshing with fresh seafood and excellent with nutty recipes, such as **trout with leeks and almonds**; **spaghetti with blue cheese and walnuts**; **Roquefort, blue cheese, walnut and endive salad**; or **pork with almond sauce**.

viognier

what it tastes like: Voluptuous, floral and redolent of white peaches, viognier is responsible for the heady, dusky, romantic Rhône wine, Condrieu. It is also grown across the Mediterranean coast of southern France where, as in the Rhône, it's sometimes blended with marsanne and roussanne (see *Rhône – white blends*). Australia produces some notably good examples of viognier, thanks largely to the work of Yalumba, who made the first commercial plantings (just 1.2 hectares) of this white grape back in 1980 and now sell its wines around the globe. Viognier has also been embraced in California and Virginia and is increasingly popular in South Africa, often as a blending component. When oaked it becomes heavy and blowsy and can be almost giddily fragrant, like honeysuckle and jasmine. Simpler viognier is never exactly crisp – this is a low-acid grape – but it may be clear and fresh, with French versions showing just a subtle lift of the scent of a garden in Provence in the early morning, while those from Australia or other warmer climates tend more towards the peach and apricot skin scent. It's essential to consider the temperature at which you drink viognier. The colder it gets, the more the texture disappears (some prefer this), and as it warms up it becomes more bountiful, sometimes getting really over the top.

See also Rhône – white blends.

what to eat: Viognier's gentle spice, white flower and apricot fragrance emphasizes the succulence of seafood, from **langoustine** to **crayfish**, **lobster** to **crab**. It's a hedonistic choice with big fat **prawns sizzling in butter** and the aromatics give a lift to **prawn and mango salad** or **firm white fish** such as halibut.

Sensual viognier also rejoices in **pork or chicken dishes with a fruity element**: for instance, **coronation chicken** or **curried chicken with peaches** or **a pork, peach and noodle salad with hoisin sauce, sesame oil and fresh mint and basil**. These richer dishes can work even with oaked viogniers, whose richness and subtle notes of star anise and melon mingle with the fruit and spice. Thai food is a good option provided the heat is low: say, **poached, torn chicken salad with shredded cabbage, coriander, bean shoots and sesame,** or **pad Thai,** or **barbecued prawns with dipping sauces.**

On a more savoury level, **eggy quiche** and **onion-based dishes** such as **caramelized onion tart** or **tartiflette** are also good. Jason Yapp, the wine merchant who imports Condrieu star Domaine Georges Vernay into the UK, has another match: 'For years my father, Robin, who set up Yapp Brothers, was going on and on about how much he loved to drink viognier with **quenelles de brochet.** They're little pike dumplings that basically take a team of people about two days to make one. So we went to Condrieu, got a table at Le Beau Rivage, where they were on the menu, €36 as a starter, quite good going, but we had them, and a Vernay viognier and the earth did move.'

what the winemakers eat

Louisa Rose, Yalumba, Australia: 'My perfect food match for viognier is tagine: fruit + meat + spices.'

Christine Vernay, Domaine Georges Vernay, Condrieu, France: 'I like the pairing of St Jacques with our wines. The tender and gourmet texture goes very well with viognier. A slightly (but not too) acidic sauce such as broth with ginger, lemongrass and coriander, allows the vine to express itself even better. The minerality of our wines, and this salty taste gives the dish a nice balance, which is the most important thing between dishes and wines.'

Z

zinfandel

Also known as primitivo

what it tastes like: Zinfandel is a red grape that is used to make wines in shades of red and pink and very pale blush – the so-called 'white zinfandel', a mass-market style that usually has a confectionery taste and edge of sweetness.

California is zinfandel's adopted home, producing reds that burst with fruitiness; are often high in alcohol; and have a mouth-saturating taste of ripe brambles, spicy berries and blueberry jam. As the wines slip down, a pleasing rasp reminiscent of cough mixture, a suggestion of smoke and sometimes also the heat of the alcohol make themselves known. American oak is often used with zinfandel, seasoning it with a woody, vanilla taste. DNA testing has proved that the grape known in southern Italy as primitivo is genetically identical to zinfandel. Italian versions are also smooth, luscious and juicy, often tasting strongly of brambles but perhaps also with a tang of black cherry too and sometimes less of a tang of cough mixture.

what to eat: The sensation of sweetness that comes partly from the high alcohol endears zinfandel to luscious **sweet vegetables**, as well as certain types of spice. **Chipotle paste, cloves, paprika, nutmeg, cayenne, coriander, ginger** and **cinnamon** are all good zinfandel seasonings. Try this grape with **onions and carrots roasted until the edges are caramelized; pumpkin pie; red peppers stuffed with Cajun-spiced rice; sweet potato mashed with cayenne and coriander; roasted butternut squash;** highly seasoned **burgers (veggie or meat);** or **buttermilk-soaked barbecued chicken served with a crunchy, chipotle-flavoured slaw.**

Zinfandel goes well with Mexican food, such as **spicy empanadas, refried beans** and **nachos**. And it's good with the spice and sweet meat of **barbecue sauces** (on burgers or with pulled pork), **jambalaya** and **boudin** – the Cajun sausage stuffed with pork, seasoning and rice.

Its explosive fruitiness helps zinfandel to work well with meat served with sweet or fruity sauces: for instance, **roast gammon cooked in Coca-Cola**; the blackened roast gammon served with citrus rum and raisin sauce from *Delia's Winter Collection*; or the spread of plain meats with sweet accompaniments served at Thanksgiving.

I particularly like the black cherries and damsons flavour of Italian versions with **red pepper and aubergine pasta sauces**; and with **pizza topped with hot salami and caramelized red onion**.

LISTS

Wines that go with everything (well, nearly everything)

rosé Pale dry rosé (from Provence or elsewhere) is a wine that flutters happily along with almost any food, including roast leg of lamb hot off the barbecue, sushi, salade niçoise and camembert. It's not great with chilli-heat but a sweeter rosé (from Anjou, Australia, or America, perhaps) can fill the gap here.

Italian reds Most Italian wines have good acidity, which gives them a mouth-watering food-friendliness.

riesling When I first encountered riesling, way back, I struggled to find food that would go with the off-dry styles of wine. That's because my diet was almost exclusively anglo or Italian – all savoury stodge, meat and potato, or pasta in simple sauces. Off-dry riesling is superb with food that incorporates sweet ingredients (such as pomegranate molasses, or sweet potato) and it's good with chilli-heat. This makes it a great choice for much tricky south-east Asian food, Ottolenghi-style salads, and fusion food. It's also brilliant with pork. And with fatty meat combined with sweet fruit, for example pork and apple or smoked goose and apple. How could we live without it?

orange wine Leave the fermenting juice of white grapes in contact with the skins for long enough and you end up with wine that glows amber and tastes slightly tannic. Orange wine is like a good conversationalist who can receive as well as transmit. It doesn't tend to get in the way of food, but it has presence too.

Southern Rhône reds and other GSM (grenache-syrah-mourvèdre blends)

If your dinners revolve around Elizabeth David-style food; sausages; roast meats with a Mediterranean slant; and long, slow-cooked casseroles then this style of red wine will be very at ease on your table.

pinot noir Light enough to go with meatier fish; good with washed rind cheeses; delicious with game birds; with pork, and with beef and with chicken. If you find the right sort of pinot noir for the particular dish this grape can also work with some of the trickier accent flavours such as fennel seeds, and Indian spices and it has a sappy quality that works with vegetable-based dishes from dauphinoise potatoes to roast pumpkin.

lower alcohol wines Lower alcohol wines tend to be a more congenial companion to most foods than their nostril-singeing high alcohol counterparts.

Food that goes with everything (well, nearly everything)

butterflied leg of lamb, roasted with rosemary, anchovies and garlic We're talking red here but it's hard to think of a bottle that wouldn't be delicious with this. Pick a wine you love from Barossa shiraz to Loire cabernet franc and you are in for a treat.

boeuf à la gardiane This slow-cooked beef and olive daube from the southern Rhône is particularly suited to the savoury flavours of European red wine from Portugal, France and Italy but it also rejoices in GSM blends, cabernet sauvignon, syrah, pinot noir and merlot from just about anywhere as well as grapes such as mencía (from Spain).

roast chicken Red, white, or pink, take your pick. The accompaniments might have something to say about what's in your glass but the chicken itself will be happy with anything.

charcuterie Salamis and hams are very good with wine – and not just red wine either. White can be superbly flattering to charcuterie, and vice versa, as can rosé.

mushrooms on toast I genuinely can't think of a red wine that would be upset by (or would upset) mushrooms. Perhaps it's all that umami. But white wine can also be incredibly delicious: chardonnay is gorgeous with mushrooms; sauvignon blanc goes well if you add a squeeze of lemon and some herbs to the mixture; and Rhône whites and Rioja are good too.

steak Quite simply, red wine heaven.

Favourite matches
Albariño and crab toasts

Fino sherry and jamón ibérica de bellota

Sancerre and grilled Crottins de Chavignol on toasted baguette with flat green lettuce

Chablis and gougères

Nebbiolo and truffles

Unexpected matches
Cabernet franc and strawberries

Aged blanc de blancs champagne and blue cheese

Fish finger and ketchup sandwiches with cheap red wine

ACKNOWLEDGEMENTS

owe thanks to all those friends and winemakers who have filled my glass and plate with delicious wines and food over the years.

In addition, I would like to thank:

Nick Rumsby, whose idea this was. All those who assisted with the buttonholing of winemakers. These include Julie Maitland, Claudia Brown, Andre Morgenthal, Doug Wregg, Ben Henshaw, John Franklin, Kate Sweet and Matt Walls, and I know there were many more.

Charlotte Hey for winkling the potato and artichoke recipe out of Spain (and translating it so I didn't mess it up). Janine Ratcliffe, who converted many mouthwatering but rambling descriptions of dishes into recipes that could actually be followed. The wonderful testers at Granta, who tightened and improved to an astonishingly professional degree those recipes that Janine had nothing to do with – Iain Chapple, Lamorna Elmer, Mercedes Forest, Luke Niema and Angela Rose.

Martin McElroy, who requested the hangover entry, and Sally Bishop, who suggested 'fridge raid'. Monty Waldin, for emailing calming pictures of Seresin horses as laptop frenzy increased as the (first) deadline drew nearer. And Jason Yapp, who writes brilliant tasting notes, has excellent ideas for food matches and sent over wonderful snippets from arcane books.

Eagle-eyed readers Nina Caplan, Andy Neather, Christine Austin, Jo Wehring, Derek Smedley, Anne Burchett, Hazel Macrae and Colin Patch. For exuberance, inspiration and being a brilliant sounding board, Joe Wadsack. For his thoughts on fine wine and food, Neal Martin. For never once calling me a misery guts when I spent yet another weekend in, writing – all my friends. For advice and inspiration on food, Anna Colquhoun. For cheery advice on all manner of things, Christian Seely, Helen McGinn, Dan Jago and Jane Fryer. For translation, Takaya Imamura.

Tasting and testing companions who also offered moral support by the bucketload, as well as those already mentioned, include Claire Allfree, Sasha Slater, Gavanndra Hodge, Mike Higgins, George Smart, Linda Moore, Jo Wehring, Verity Smith, Jenny Coad, Miles Davis, Claire Williamson, Tom Ashworth and Charles Lea.

And of course then there are those with a more direct involvement. Thank you, Lizzy Kremer, for being firm and beady as well as patient, inspiring and kind, and thank you, Harriet Moore, who, I suspect, could organize my chaotic administration in a morning given half a chance. Thank you, Laura Barber, a perfect, astonishingly efficient, witty and effective editor, and friend. Thanks to Iain Chapple, a great wine conspirator, and Christine Lo, for her extreme patience and care, as well as all at Granta, a dream team. And thanks to designer Michael Salu.

Additional thanks go to all those named in these pages who have been kind enough to share their thoughts, expertise and their recipes: namely Maria José Sevilla, Marc Kent, Tim Adams, Jonny Moore, Christine Parkinson, Bob Lindo, Sarah Jane Evans, Ferran Centelles, Eric Monneret, Martin Lam, Maria Carola de la Fuente, Ian Kellett, Annie Millton, James Lewisohn, Magandeep Singh, Sebastian Payne, Wojciech Bońkowski, Lodovico Antinori, Ole Udsen, Emily O'Hare, Randall Grahm, Joe Wadsack, Ben Henshaw, Luigi Tecce, Jean-Philippe Blot, Philippe Vatan, Christian Seely, Vanya Cullen, Véronique Sanders, Duncan Meyers, Derek Mossman Knapp, Didier Defaix, Benoît Gouez, Olivier Collard, Jérôme Philipon, Josh Bergström, Alex Moreau, Judy Finn, Rozy Gunn, Mike Aylward, Julien Barraud, Laurent Pillot, Claudia Brown, Adam Mason, Tessa Laroche, Andrea Mullineux, Brad Greatrix, Annie Lindo, Edouard Parinet, Álvaro Palacios, Norrel Robertson, Emilie Boisson, Stephen Pannell, Justin Howard-Sneyd, Jesus Madrazo, Martin and Anna Arndorfer, Phil Crozier, Alfredo Marqués, Michela Marenco, Luke Lambert, Mario Fontana, Aurelia Gouges-Haynes, Clive Jones, Olive Hamilton Russell, Thierry Brouin, Ruud Maasdam, Nigel Greening, Jasmine Hirsch, Michael Seresin, Adolfo Hurtado, Gilly Robertson, Sophia Bergquist, Natasha Hughes, Jeff Grosset, Kaoru Hugel, Jim Bowskill, Ernie Loosen, Stephanie Toole, Charles Smith, Giuseppe Mazzocolin, Roberto Stucchi, David Gleave, Tommaso Marrocchesi Marzi, Monty Waldin, Miles Davis, Roger Jones, Patricia Luneau, Emmanuelle Mellot, Belinda Jackson, Matt Sutherland, Laurent Lebrun, Olivier Bernard, Iain Riggs, Jeff Vejr, Jesús Barquín, Tim Holt, Javier Hidalgo, Gary Mills, Olivier Clape, Ron Laughton, Jorge Matetic, Yann Chave, Guillermo de Aranzabal, José Manuel Ortega , Jean-François Ott, Charlie Melton, Stéphanie de Boüard-Rivoal, Louisa Rose and Christine Vernay.

And finally thanks to little Francesca, who could have made the last 50,000 words impossible to write – but didn't.

INDEX OF RECIPES

&

INDEX

INDEX OF RECIPES

INDEX

Page numbers in **bold** denote the grape or wine's main entry, in which its flavour and what to eat with it is described. Page numbers in *italics* denote a food as a game-changer ingredient.

strawberries and claret

melon and moscato

white truffles and nebbiolo

bouillabaisse and fino

radicchio and barbera

Victoria Moore is the wine correspondent for the *Telegraph* and writes a monthly column for *BBC Good Food* . She has also written on wine, spirits and the psychology of smell for the *New Statesman*, the *Daily Mail*, the *Guardian* and *Psychologies*, and appeared frequently on radio and television. She has been named Fortnum & Mason Drink Writer of the Year (2013), Louis Roederer International Wine Columnist of the Year (2011 and 2015) and Online Communicator of the Year (2015), and *Class* magazine Drink Writer of the Year (2009).

Her first book was *How To Drink*, also published by Granta Books. She lives in London.

www.howtodrink.co.uk

preserved lemon and assyrtiko

salmon and white burgundy

asparagus and sauvignon blanc

paella and rioja rosado

crayfish mayo and chardonnay